Crude Existence

A banner hanging over the main road to Cabinda city bears the words of Agostinho Neto, Angola's first president: "The most important [concern] is to resolve the problems of the people."

Crude Existence

*Environment and the Politics of Oil
in Northern Angola*

KRISTIN REED

Global, Area, and International Archive
University of California Press

BERKELEY   LOS ANGELES   LONDON

The Global, Area, and International Archive (GAIA) is an initiative of International and Area Studies, University of California, Berkeley, in partnership with the University of California Press, the California Digital Library, and international research programs across the UC system. GAIA volumes, which are published in both print and open-access digital editions, represent the best traditions of regional studies, reconfigured through fresh global, transnational, and thematic perspectives.

University of California Press, one of the most distinguished university presses in the United States, enriches lives around the world by advancing scholarship in the humanities, social sciences, and natural sciences. Its activities are supported by the UC Press Foundation and by philanthropic contributions from individuals and institutions. For more information, visit www.ucpress.edu.

University of California Press
Berkeley and Los Angeles, California

University of California Press, Ltd.
London, England

Library of Congress Cataloging-in-Publication Data

Reed, Kristin, 1977–
    Crude existence : environment and the politics of oil in Northern Angola / Kristin Reed.
        p.   cm. (Global, area, and international archive ; 12)
    Includes bibliographical references (p.   ) and index.
    ISBN 978-0-520-25822-8 (pbk. : alk. paper)   1. Petroleum industry and trade—Angola.   2. Petroleum industry and trade—Government policy—Angola.   3. Petroleum industry and trade—Social aspects—Angola.   4. Petroleum industry and trade—Environmental aspects—Angola.   5. Political violence—Angola.   6. Angola—Politics and government—1975–   7. Angola—Economic conditions—1975–
8. Angola—Social conditions.   I. Title.

HD9577.A52R44   2009
967.304'2—dc22   2009023254

Manufactured in the United States of America

18   17   16   15   14   13   12   11   10   09
10   9   8   7   6   5   4   3   2   1

The paper used in this publication meets the minimum requirements of ANSI/NISO Z39.48 – 1992 (R 1997) (Permanence of Paper).

To Ginger, who inspired me with her daring struggle for a better existence

Contents

Illustrations and Tables

Acknowledgments

This book began with the idea of undertaking fieldwork in Angola's oil-rich northwest because I had found little information on the daily struggles of Angolans living near sites of extraction. The concept was simple, though the logistics seemed daunting. Still, my adviser, Nancy Peluso, never doubted the feasibility (or the saneness) of my research plan. I am wholeheartedly grateful to Nancy for her unflinching support and keen theoretical insights derived from innovative political ecology analyses of violent environments. I also owe thanks to Claudia Carr for expressing endless enthusiasm for my project and sharing her profound understanding of extractive systems from the ground level to the transnational scene. My gratitude also extends to Michael Watts for his wisdom, quick wit, and the astute critiques in his wealth of work on the particularities of petro-capitalism and petro-violence. I am truly appreciative for the generous intellectual backing from this remarkable team of scholars.

A generous National Science Foundation Graduate Research Fellowship (2002–5) and a supplementary Doctoral Dissertation Research Improvement Grant (2005) provided the financial backbone for this research. I am also grateful for the additional support provided by the UC Berkeley Human Rights Center (summer 2003) as well as the Andrew and Mary Thompson Rocca Pre-Dissertation (2003) and Dissertation (2004) Awards. A Clyde Sanfred Johnson Memorial Scholarship (2005) enabled me to present my early findings at the African Studies Association's annual meeting in November 2005. I am thankful to Bruce Wright of the Conservation Science Institute for providing me with a venue for collaboration and outreach. I also acknowledge the backing of Robert and Eleanor Frisby for enriching my life and this work.

My fantastic support network in the field made this research possible.

Given the repressive atmosphere in Angola, I refrain from naming most individuals here for fear of compromising their future work and welfare. I accept all responsibility for the statements made in this book; the ideas presented should not be regarded as a reflection of the beliefs of the institutions or individuals that have helped me. That said, I wish to thank friends at the Angola Instituto de Pesquisa, Open Society International, Pesnorte, Fundo Apoio Social, Mpalabanda, Grémio ABC, the offices of the Instituto de Pesca Artesanal in Soyo and Cabinda, the Direcção Provincial de Agricultura e Ambiente in Cabinda, the Universidade Católica de Angola, the Catholic parishes in Cabinda and Soyo, Save the Children, and all of the staff members who kindly provided support and logistical assistance.

I offer the deepest *obrigada* to my dear Cabindan family, my kindhearted Brazilian sister, the couple in Luanda who first opened their doors to me, and all of the friends who shared their homes and laughter. My appreciation also goes to the group of American scholars and humanitarian workers in Angola who offered me a place to stay and proposed a meaningful excursion or shared in a fun diversion. Likewise, I am entirely indebted to all of my informants who patiently shared their time and views with me—this work would not have been possible without them. And to those fearless campaigners for human rights without fear of being named, I express my utmost gratitude to Francisco Luemba, a dear friend and tireless advocate for justice, as well as Agostinho Chicaia, Rafael Marques, and José Marcos Mavungo.

I extend my gratitude to Publications Director Nathan MacBrien and the Editorial Board of the Global, Area, and International Archive at the University of California; Jean-Michel Mabeko-Tali; and my anonymous reviewers for precise, discerning critiques. The University of California, Berkeley presented a stimulating and inspiring environment for my intellectual and personal growth. My work benefited greatly from discussions hosted at UC Berkeley by the International Oil Working Group chaired by Claudia Carr with transcontinental input from Jeffrey Gritzner, transatlantic contributions from Irene Gerlach, and participation by Joshua Dimon, Anna Zalik, Logan Hennessey, Adam Gray and Kathy Sheetz. I am also grateful to Juliet Christian-Smith for her able organizational guidance on muddled early versions. Daniel Graham also provided constructive comments. Professors Isha Ray, Jeff Romm, Dara O'Rourke, Percy Hintzen, and Rachel Shigekane assisted with the methodological and conceptual formation of this research. Philippe Le Billon offered helpful comments during a visit to the Environmental Politics Colloquium. Jenn Boggs created the stunning set of maps included here from limited resources. Additionally, individual discussions with Irene Gerlach, Dorian Fougères, Logan Hennessey, Mara Decker, Robin Turner, Catherine Corson, Dan Fahey, Katherine Gifford, and Camille Pannu contributed to this work.

I am especially beholden to a few individuals for their extraordinary support in the pre-publication phase. Elizabeth Havice slogged through numerous drafts with positive determination and sharp feedback on a systemic scale. Jennifer Brass relied on her deep knowledge of African politics to contribute sound structural critiques. Mike Leonard marshaled his professional journalistic expertise to provide extensive editorial comments. Zoe Reed applied her poetic license to revitalize subheadings, and Beau Perry found time to patiently wade through pages of detail. A team of angel editors helped me in a difficult time: Renee Snyder, Carrie Sue Casey, Mara Decker, Oleg Nodelman, Rachel Brass, Brandy Faulkner, Amanda Neville, Jen Brass, and Phil Carter.

Finally, I owe an enormous debt of gratitude to my friends and family for their encouragement. My partner, Beau, has been supportive and encouraging at every turn on this tortuous journey. I also extend my heartfelt appreciation to T.J. and Ginger, Marty and Sue, Zoe and Tom, the extended Reed and Frisby families, the Perry and Smith clans, and support networks in San Francisco and Chicago, Skipperdee, and, ultimately, Nzambi.

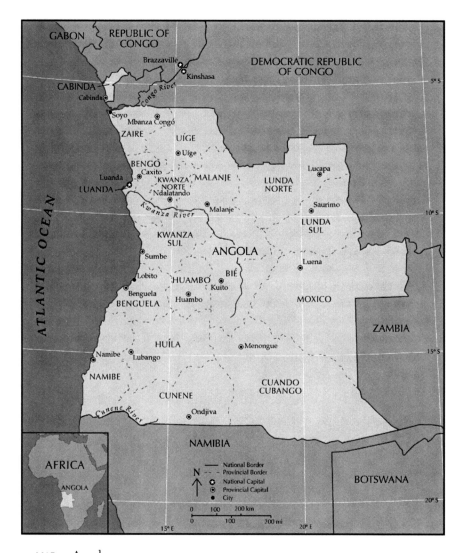

MAP 1. Angola

1. Washing Ashore

Waves rolled toward a wide beach where a group of fishermen hauled in a net, keeping pace with the crash and flow of the foam-white surf. Their calloused hands clutched at the worn rope, steadied against the ocean's tugging withdrawal. And then, poised for its return, the fishermen turned their backs to the sea, dug their toes into the sinking sand and heaved forward. Once they had dragged the net onto the beach, the men appraised its meager contents, negotiating with a fish trader. She rinsed handfuls of the silvery, long-whiskered fish in seawater and dropped them in her blue plastic tub. The water receded and advanced again, swirling around and between the wide, steady feet of the youngest fisherman of the group. "There are no longer fish here," he declared.

These waves washed ashore in Fútila, a community neighboring the Chevron oil base in Cabinda.[1] Although the territory is considered part of Angola, the Democratic Republic of Congo's run to the sea separates Cabinda from the mainland. Chevron operates two oil concessions offshore of Cabinda, pumping out one-third of Angola's production of nearly 2 million barrels of crude oil per day.[2]

Stained swathes of sand hint at the way oil has destroyed lives and livelihoods in Fútila; however, oil's distorting and degrading effects spread far beyond the extractive zones of northwestern Angola. Rather than contribute to peace and development, Angola's oil wealth has fueled petro-violence—conflicts bankrolled by oil revenues and struggles waged for control of oil reserves. A brutal war wracked the country from 1975 to 2002. Political deception and economic exclusion reinforced a movement for Cabindan independence from Angola. The government responded with militant repression. As oil spills degraded the marine environment, oil revenues corrupted the political environment. Officials used corporate compensation and patronage schemes to hush protests. Petro-capitalism—the paradoxical coupling of vast resource wealth and desperate poverty in countries dependent on oil revenues—deepened the conflicts as Angola's elevated military and security budgets eclipsed social spending.

This book examines how petro-capitalism and petro-violence shape the lives of people in Angola's northwestern extractive zones. Communities overlapping or adjacent to oil concessions bear the unequal burden of pollution and violence associated with extractive activities but receive little of the wealth generated. Dissident voices are silenced through threats or acts of violence, patronage networks, and corporate compensation. Moreover, the Angolan government and transnational oil corporations perpetuate the inequitable distribution of oil wealth through complementary, and sometimes collaborative, strategies to gain and maintain access to oil.[3] Their resource control strategies include concession contracts, terrorizing military campaigns, corporate compensation, and oil-backed development schemes. Each of these strategies emerged from particular convergences of violence, exclusion, and degradation. Together they provide the repressive means to preserve Angola's exclusionary system of governance.

Angola is the second-largest oil producer in Sub-Saharan Africa and ranks 17th in crude oil production globally (EIA 2008). Angola's oil-fueled violence and capitalist dynamics received scant attention until Human Rights Watch and Global Witness began investigating the diversion of oil revenues for arms and personal enrichment in the mid-1990s.[4] Influential works by Tony Hodges showed how the country's leaders used resource revenues to bolster their power, undermine their enemies, and disempower the masses.[5] A Catholic Relief Services report authored by Ian Gary and Terry Karl entitled *Bottom of the Barrel: Africa's Oil Boom and the Poor* clearly outlined the destructive implications of Angola's oil production on the poor. In his own subsequent work, a contributing writer to the CRS report, Ricardo Soares de Oliveira (2007), presented powerful critiques of the national oil company, Sonangol, and the manner in which its competence enabled Angola's survival as a "successful failed state." James Ferguson (2006) distinguished the ordered oil sector from the dysfunctional remainder of the Angolan economy and theorized the "Angolan model" of detached sectoral self-sufficiency facilitating extraction in the midst of disorder and violence.

These works present powerful accounts of petro-capitalism and petro-violence at Angola's highest levels, yet community-level studies of the destructive dynamics associated with oil extraction in the country are virtually non-existent. Some scholars downplay the significance of localized struggles around oil in the extractive zones of northern Angola. Hodges dismisses the "risk of disputes" between oil corporations and communities living near sites of extraction in Cabinda and Zaire provinces due to their small populations and the largely offshore location of extractive activities (2003:151). He also distrusts the motives of Cabindans seeking independence from Angola, arguing that the prospect of undivided oil wealth spurs their protests more than any common ethnic identity or sense of economic injustice (159). Rather than reject the claims expressed by inhabitants of Angola's extractive zones on the basis of their perceived motivations or structural improbabilities, this book seeks to present the lived reality of extraction through their narratives and experiences.

KEY THEMES

Oil production is a capital-intensive, location-specific activity capable of generating exorbitant profits. Angola's oil sector is often referred to as an "enclave," denoting the lack of linkages to the rest of the economy. Noting this model of production, Ferguson (2006) cites Angola as a model in the globalized economy in which capital, rather than flowing evenly across terrain, "hops" to "usable" spaces secured by private security contractors. He contends that geographic and economic enclaves of extraction have helped Angola's oil sector withstand decades of violence. His model aptly portrays the spatial mechanisms that facilitate the exclusion of the populace from sharing the resource wealth. Nonetheless, barbed-wire fences and offshore buffer zones around extractive sites have not diminished disputes over the costs and benefits of extraction. Whereas Ferguson's model emphasizes how extractive enclaves function in spite of surrounding chaos, I stress the role of the enclave *at the center of* disputes, inextricably bound up in local conflicts. Extractive enclaves are the loci of conflicts about exclusion (e.g., resentment over mismanagement of oil monies) and degradation (e.g., oil spills or gas leaks). Moreover, revenues generated within the enclave finance the tools of violence and repression.

The concept of the enclave also extends to the political and economic particularities of oil-dependent states. The relationship between the Angolan government and transnational oil corporations forms the basis of the enclave economy and the distorted patterns of governance associated with petro-capitalism. In contrast with ordinary capitalist systems, petro-capitalism is founded on the premise of "wealth without work" (Collier and Hoeffler 2002). The enclave sector allows a select few government officials to collect resource rents by virtue of their position rather than their labor.

Accordingly, petro-capitalism involves a circular logic whereby government officials distribute oil revenues to a select, powerful few through patronage systems to maintain their access to those same revenues. The strength of a patronage network is not only measured by who it includes but also how many it excludes: the more revenues government leaders pump into patronage, the fewer funds remain to invest in the wider populace. The diversion of oil revenues from social services and other regular state functions to patronage systems undermines state capacity and legitimacy, but the enclave sector facilitates the government's hold on power despite state collapse (Soares de Oliveira 2008).

Internal contests and external interventions do arise to challenge the government's absolute stake in the oil sector. These disputes, as well as the government's repressive reaction to them, are forms of *petro-violence*, a term that encompasses all violent struggles over access and control of oil revenues. As Ferguson rightly notes, the enclaved nature of the oil sector enables both the government and transnational oil corporations to withstand petro-violence. Oil bases, defended by armed guards and razor-wire fences, are the physical enclaves constructed to protect corporations operating in volatile environments. Likewise, a centralized government backed by military force represents an institutional enclave designed to insulate rulers from overthrow. So long as they maintain nominal control over the institutional remains of the collapsed state, Angola's leaders retain access to oil revenues.

This book argues that the enclave does not simply endure petro-capitalism and petro-violence; it contributes to these distorting dynamics. While oil appears to generate wealth out of thin air for rulers in the capital city of Luanda, inhabitants of Angola's extractive zones live amid poverty and pollution. The erosion of state functions associated with petro-capitalism undermines the government's regulatory capacity and its will to check the externalities of oil extraction. "As the 'natural' relation between wealth and hard work became more obscure, the pollution of the land and waterways became more apparent" (Apter 2005:153).[6]

To limit protest, Angola's ruling party uses oil revenues to co-opt or violently subdue adversaries. Transnational oil corporations collaborate with the government to implement carrot-and-stick governance strategies, especially in the zones of extraction where communities struggle to cope with the externalities of the oil industry. These strategies respond to local discontent with a variety of complementary tactics including corporate compensation, oil-backed development, and violent repression.

Petro-capitalism and petro-violence link the detached enclave to the lived experience of extraction in Angola's oil-rich northwest. This book investigates petro-capitalism and petro-violence in the Angolan context and explores the role of the enclave economy in perpetuating them as twin forces. This relationship might best be described with the metaphor of a cyclone. The enclave harboring the joint interests of the Angolan state and transnational oil corporations rests safely in the eye of the storm while the whirling forces of petro-capitalism and petro-violence wreak havoc on their surroundings. The intensity of these forces is measured in terms of the gradient between the conditions in the eye and the eyewall. In meteorological terms, the eyewall marks the interface between the eye and the surrounding storms; it is the most dangerous and destructive location in a cyclone. In metaphorical terms, the eyewall represents Angola's extractive zones, where artisanal fishing and subsistence farming communities struggle to maintain their livelihoods in direct geographic proximity to oil extraction. Much as a cyclone generates powerful winds and waves across vast distances, the enclave economy unleashes waves of violence, exclusion, and degradation that ravage communities in the extractive zones and produce a harmful ripple effect in the rest of the country.

Violence, exclusion, and degradation are the three fluid themes that flow through this book and characterize resource struggles in Angola. Although these themes and their associated arguments are presented here as separate entities for heuristic purposes, they are not discrete. They appear in associated or related ways, surfacing like the wave action on Fútila's shores. What washes ashore in one wave is a configuration of nearly the same elements that swept in with the last wave, albeit in a slightly altered arrangement. As one wave recedes, tugging back and churning up old sediments, another builds anew from the same constitutive forces and spills back on the sand. With each ebb and flow, narratives of exclusion and violence merge, muddle, and melt, emerging again in union with evidence of degradation, before dissolving, only to reemerge fused in a renewed tale of exclusion to disperse once more. The process is not linear but cyclical, wherein elements conjoin not in jagged angles but in smooth, seamless flows.

Waves of exclusion, degradation, and violence wash over Angola's extractive zones. Some waves slip ashore, others crash with ferocity. Shifting tides govern the influence of the waters; the difference between high tide and low changes entire horizons. With each wave, the ocean steals away with part of the native shore and brings in foreign objects from its far-reaching currents. The inhabitants of the extractive zones wrestle with these waves, like the fishermen of Fútila in their tug-of-war with the ocean. They make claims for greater resource control with each heave of their net against the powerful swell of corporate and government forces.

Exclusion

Corruption is rampant in Angola.[7] A significant portion of the fantastic rents, signing bonuses, and royalties from Angola's offshore oil flow are diverted into offshore bank accounts; over four billion dollars in oil revenues bypassed state coffers between 1998 and 2002 (Pearce 2002b; HRW 2004c). Without dismissing the problem of corruption, this book employs the term *exclusion* to emphasize the other side of the coin: the benefits of oil lost (e.g., social services) with the diversion of public funds into private accounts. Roughly 70 percent of Angola's estimated population of 16 million lives in poverty (CIA 2007). All subterranean mineral wealth belongs to the state rather than the landholders, making oil a national resource. Citizens expect to be included in the distribution of oil's benefits, but the exclusionary force of petro-capitalism keeps them on the periphery.

Sustained by opaque accounting practices and corrupt networks, Angolan petro-capitalism has entrenched and enriched an elite circle, with President José Eduardo dos Santos at its center. The exclusionary distributive patterns of Angola's oil wealth follow a divisive model wherein "the elites are showered with every economic, social and political benefit, while others are abandoned and deprived of sustenance to survive" (Ong 1999:65).[8] Nowhere is this more blatant than in the extractive zones, where those excluded from the benefits of local oil extraction also suffer the costs. The chasm between the oil-rich and the dirt-poor is more pronounced due to the close proximity of communities to extractive operations and the relative disparity in wealth. Even the high walls surrounding oil compounds cannot hide the electric glow of streetlamps from poor neighbors navigating the dark of night with lanterns.

Degradation

Concession boundaries and fences encircling oil bases may restrict entrance or the practice of certain activities within their limits, but they cannot stop environmental externalities from bleeding beyond the confines of their compounds. Extraction-related pollution has contributed to the degradation of local ecosystems. Degradation, according to Blaikie and Brookfield, is a "perceptual term" which implies a degree of deterioration from an original condition or use criteria, taking into consideration the sensitivity or resilience of the environment in question (1987:4). This book employs the term degradation to describe the deterioration of lands and waters near the site of extraction, recognizing local claims that oil spills and gas flares respectively diminished plankton abundance offshore and decreased soil fertility onshore.

Ecological resilience varies within the extractive zone. Although the sandy soils in farm plots along the coastline are not very resilient, the Congo River's flush of nutrients and the thick mangrove stands along its wandering banks render fishing grounds near the river mouth a bit more resilient than Cabinda's offshore areas.[9] Since Angola's artisanal fisheries are largely an open resource for citizens and authorized parties with no catch limits, degradation begets further degradation in less resilient areas. As the pollution associated with oil extraction undermines their production, fishermen become more desperate and may actually deepen the crisis by selling whatever they can catch—including juvenile fish—on the informal market. The degradation of socioeconomic and cultural systems tied to the traditional fishing economy accompanies environmental degradation. Oil spills threaten not only fishers' sustenance and economic livelihoods but also their long-standing traditions and way of life. Ultimately, pollution undermines the very dignity and empowerment of local communities (Wiwa 2005).

Violence

Violent struggles over oil-rich territory and resource revenues began once transnational corporations began extracting Angola's crude. Scholars anticipate violence as an outcome of oil dependency (Collier and Hoeffler 1998, 2004). Distinctions must be drawn among the various forms of violence associated with extraction and each analyzed in its sociohistorical context. Repression, internationalized civil war, and secession are all common to Angola, but violence is not merely a function of oil's presence. Rather, violence represents a method for maintaining the existing social relations of access—or a means to dispute the unequal distribution of oil extraction's costs and benefits.

Violence can take both pre-emptive and enduring forms. In Cabinda, government troops terrorize the populace and hunt down dissidents in pre-emptive attempts to eliminate threats to resource access while securing control of onshore oilfields for future extraction. South of the Congo River, residents of the oil-producing municipality of Soyo endure painful memories of wartime occupation and continuing repression. Unwilling to support the political party that once brutalized them and acutely aware of the government's capacity for violence, inhabitants of Soyo begrudgingly acquiesce. The climate of fear and resignation impedes their ability to claim a larger share of Angola's resource wealth. Ultimately, Cabindans may confront a similar future if they succumb to the government's violent agenda to extinguish their desire for independence.

METHODS

This book marks an attempt to understand how oil shapes people's lives in Angola's oil-producing zones. Their experiences demonstrate how extraction compromises livelihoods in fishing and farming communities, the government fails to invest oil revenues in health and education, territorial struggles over oil-rich regions expose citizens to violence, and repressive policing muffles voices of protest. Given the objective of producing a community-level study, this book highlights the perspective of Angolans most vulnerable to the ills of petro-capitalism and petro-violence—specifically subsistence farmers, artisanal fishers, and fish traders. These persons may be collectively referred to as resource-dependent people, in recognition of their reliance on local ecosystems for subsistence needs and livelihoods. They are the most likely to suffer displacement or contamination when transnational oil corporations exploit oilfields in or near traditional lands and fishing grounds.

Case Study Context

To document the lived experiences of oil extraction, this book examines cases from two sites in northwest Angola. The first is the municipality of Soyo in Zaire province—the setting for a case depicting the legacy of petro-violence and the compound effects of onshore and offshore extraction.[10] Cabinda provides the geographical backdrop for three further case studies on environmental degradation, state-sponsored violence and local resistance, and corporate territorialization through oil-backed development projects.[11] The cases feature narratives on local resource access and control to provide insight into the lived reality of extraction. Each case confronts seemingly contradictory issues, such as petro-violence far from the site of extraction, or community health posts sponsored by the same corporations releasing toxic wastes into the local environment.

The majority of Angola's oil is produced offshore, and so the initial case studies center on the experience of fishing communities in the northwestern provinces of Cabinda and Zaire. Angola's coastline runs 1,650 kilometers along the Atlantic Ocean. The marine environment is characterized by the intersection of two powerful currents: the cold Benguela current

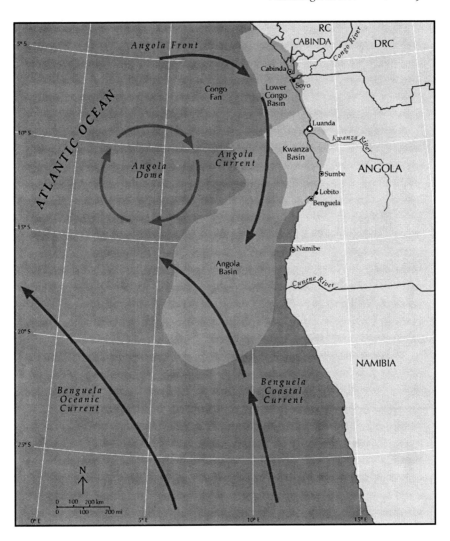

MAP 2. Ocean Currents

running northward and the tropical Angola current pushing southward. The junction of these two currents, known as the Angola-Benguela front, shifts seasonally between 15 and 19 degrees latitude and influences the local distribution of fish (Sardinha 2000). Offshore of Cabinda and Zaire provinces, where the Angola current predominates, the Congo River marks the greatest influence on the marine environment. The great river releases nearly 50 million metric tons of sediment annually, creating a submarine

fan stretching over 300,000 square kilometers in a watery world characterized by landslides and shifting currents (Morash 2003). This underwater
realm has yielded not only discoveries of gigantic oil fields but also troves
of previously unknown organisms. A survey conducted in Angola's offshore as part of the ongoing Census of Marine Life revealed that "eighty
percent of the species sampled were new to science" (Randerson 2003).

Angolan fisheries are divided into two categories: industrial and artisanal. During Angola's long war, violence and starvation drove many
impoverished Angolans to the sea, where they sought sustenance and peace
(FAO 2004). Artisanal fishers mainly target bottom-dwelling demersal
species such as grouper, croaker, snapper, sea bream, shark, catfish, and
spiny lobster for sale in local markets, while industrial operators—with
boats capable of sailing in high seas and sophisticated capturing devices—
pursue pelagic species from the open ocean like horse mackerel, sardines,
and tuna as well as shrimp and deep sea red crab for international seafood
markets. Industrial fishing activities are centered in the southern provinces of Benguela and Namibe, whereas most of Angola's 102 artisanal
fishing communities are in the northern region, often overlapping with
offshore oil production (Agostinho et al. 2005).

Three classes of artisanal fishermen ply the waters offshore of Cabinda
and Soyo: *armadores, pescadores de profissão,* and simple *pescadores.*
Armadores are the owners of the fishing nets and boats. They contract
pescadores de profissão—salaried professionals with experience and competence in repairing nets—and ordinary *pescadores* who earn wages proportional with the daily or weekly catch. Many of the latter, especially
those with *pirogas* or other nonmotorized boats, work independently of
armadores and fish mainly for subsistence but market a portion of their
catch to earn income. Only 20 percent of the boats employed in Angola's
artisanal fishing sector are motorized and fishers usually venture no farther than three nautical miles (roughly 5.5 kilometers) from shore (FAO
2004). Artisanal fishing outfits in northern Angola range from sleek fiberglass crafts to rough-hewn dugout canoes and vary in production levels
from small-market sales to simple subsistence. Fishermen use gillnets and
seine nets in deeper water, but in the littoral zone they sometimes employ
a fishing technique called *banda banda* in which fine-mesh beach seine
nets are launched from canoes in shallow water and pulled into shore.[12]

Nearly 35,000 artisanal fishers rely on the bounty of Angolan waters
and another 50,000 people participate in the artisanal fisheries sector, from
fish traders to net menders (FAO 2004). Within the artisanal sector, the
division of labor is split along gender lines; fishermen typically sell their

catch to female fish traders who process and resell the fish on the beach, at local markets, or by walking through the streets. Fish traders, locally referred to as *peixeiras*, are usually marginalized women of lower economic or social status.[13] Locally caught fish makes up 10 percent of total protein supply in Angola, and coastal communities especially rely on fish for their protein (WRI 2003). Fish traders in northwest Angola sell the catch fresh, dried, or smoked.[14] Local men praise the power of *caldo de peixe*, a fish broth, to cure a hangover. Women use dried or fresh fish to prepare *sacafolha* and *calulu*, regional specialties in Soyo and Cabinda, respectively featuring manioc leaves and a rich palm oil sauce.

In both Soyo and Cabinda, degradation on land and at sea exacerbates pressure on already-stressed communities where women work up to fifteen hours each day, taking care of domestic duties like cooking meals, finding firewood, and drawing water for daily use, as well as cultivating, harvesting, and marketing food crops (IFAD 2002a).[15] Local men spend more time searching for fish in the polluted seas. Women unable to coax crops out of degraded coastal soils walk several kilometers to farm plots farther from the extractive zones. The people of Soyo and Cabinda both relate the same characteristics of pollution associated with oil extraction in their narratives about environmental degradation.

Despite the similar way in which the inhabitants of Cabinda and Soyo mobilize spatialized identities, their narratives are founded on radically different worldviews. The people of Soyo consider themselves Angolans, requesting a fraction of the revenues extracted locally; whereas most inhabitants of Cabinda regard themselves as *not* Angolans but Cabindans, demand their independence from Angola, and seek *full* control over local oil extraction as well as the associated resource rents.

Ethnographic Perspective

As James Scott has shown (1985), even the weak and oppressed possess weapons of protest, including the use of narratives. In repressive environments, narratives are powerful tools for coping with violence and empowering subjects to articulate and come to terms with painful experiences (Jackson 2002). When embraced collectively, narratives present a powerful force for social change (Polletta 2006). Often revealing profound ethnographic insight, a narrative "achieves an amplitude that information lacks" when it is "passed on from mouth to mouth" (Benjamin 1968). Ethnographers commonly use narrative analysis to interpret metaphors, incorporate perceptions, or examine the role of memory and emotion in articulated experiences (Labov 1997). Additionally, an ethnographer must heed the context of narrative expression. The reason a story is told, the form of expression, and the setting in which it is relayed all contribute to its meaning (Polletta 2006).

An ethnographer must also position herself in the context of the research. This book focuses on interpreting the perceptions of my research subjects, but recognizing my own role as an ethnographer was not easy. In fact, it took a power outage. In a small village on the periphery of Cabinda, bats circled in the darkness of the living room beyond the faint spherical glow of a kerosene lamp. My interviewee took on a spectral tone in the pulsating lamplight. I alternated glances between him and my notebook, jotting down sentence fragments. Occasionally, I caught a glimpse of a wing in the darkened abyss or felt a slight rush of air from overhead. Mostly I could sense the bats but not make them out. An apt metaphor for fieldwork—while I collected material from the area illuminated before me, I felt as if I could not clearly discern what lay in the surrounding darkness. There were always limits to what I could perceive, experience, and understand. Gratefully, I have relied on the support of friends and colleagues to shed light on the cases discussed in this book, but I recognize my limited perspective and take full responsibility for the claims and conclusions herein.

The research presented in this book was drawn from three research trips. The first, a preliminary study, was from May to July 2003. The second was from May to August 2004, and the third from October 2004 to March 2005. With the exception of a weeklong visit to Gabela during November 2004 and a week's vacation in São Tomé over the holidays, I split my time between Luanda and Angola's two largest oil-producing areas—Soyo and Cabinda. While in Luanda, I interviewed officials at the Ministry of Fisheries, the Ministry of Urbanism and Environment, and the Ministry of Petroleum, as well as representatives of Total, Chevron, and other oil corporations operating in the country. Some corporate and government officials greeted me with suspicion, a few with openness, and many refused to grant me interviews. Some officials even seemed to be avoiding me. For instance, Total's representative for Corporate Social Responsibility was "away on duty" all six times I stopped by to make an appointment.

Most similar troubles led to insights. For example, the Ministry of Petroleum refused to share information on environmental standards with the Ministry of Urbanism and Environment, so I tried working with officials in the latter ministry's National Department of Environmental Quality to create a bilingual request for information on corporate environmental practices in Angola. After submitting the request to BPAmoco, Chevron,

Total, and ExxonMobil, the department received only a partial data set from ExxonMobil. The other corporations refused the appeal, citing policies of collaborating solely with the Ministry of Petroleum. The whole process took several months. Nevertheless, it revealed the highly centralized nature of the oil sector and the powerlessness of the Ministry of Urbanism and Environment.

Nor was the Ministry of Petroleum the only one to refuse my requests. The Ministry of Fisheries and the Ministry of Transport accepted my pleas for information with assurances that they would furnish data, kindly telling me to return week after week until I understood that the delays simply amounted to a refusal. Eventually a uniquely forthright government official told me that all statistics are considered politically charged. He divulged the government's fear that information on topics ranging from environmental emissions to basic population statistics by province could be used to criticize the ruling party.

In Soyo and Cabinda, I devised a survey to get a broader picture of extractive dynamics in resource-dependent communities.[16] I also conducted in-depth interviews with fishermen, fish traders, local government officials, and traditional authorities.[17] The traditional governance structure in Soyo complicated the process of setting up interviews and focus groups. I had to both pay homage to the proper authority before I could begin work in a village and politely stop in for a visit each time I passed through the neighborhood. The visits were enjoyable but time-consuming. And with Soyo's villagers, establishing trust also took time; initially they were shy and suspicious but revealed warm and welcoming personalities after a few visits. Before long, acquaintances called out greetings of *"Kolele!"* and teasingly inquired how my manioc crop was coming along. Geographic and language barriers also presented difficulties in Soyo. I am grateful to friends in Soyo who brokered my first contacts and provided a Kisolongo translator for interviews with locals who did not speak Portuguese, particularly elders. They also provided transportation support, facilitating journeys to the hard-to-reach villages across the Congo River like Tulombo and Bocolo.

I found two worlds in Cabinda. Travel was easy within the capital city and between the towns hugging the seashore. I walked around the city center almost daily and I could catch a taxi from the *praça* to almost anywhere along the Cabindan coast. Trips to the interior, however, were far more difficult. I regularly saw small groups of soldiers stationed in Cabinda's coastal towns, but the interior region swarmed with troops and many seemed eager to test their authority. I traveled only by private car and with a local companion for guidance and security. As in Soyo, I accessed Cabindan communities through trusted figures, such as Agostinho Chicaia—first during his tenure with the Provincial Directorate of Agriculture, Fisheries, and Environment and later as the leader of the civil society organization Mpalabanda.

Local authorities called *regedores* in Cabinda proved less reliable representatives of community interests than any *rei do povo* in Soyo, probably because the government had manipulated the structure and installed leaders less critical of the regime.[18] I quickly realized that Cabindan villagers and authority figures (or anyone with ties to the government) had vastly different outlooks on the political, economic, and military situation in the province. After completing a twenty-minute informal interview with the leader of a village in the Cabindan interior, a group of villagers led me around a corner. One of them looked about fearfully and discounted the leader's statements, saying, "He is lying because of his position." Another concurred, "He lives like a king." I adjusted my survey and interviews to deliberately seek opinions from leaders and villagers. I also used some local students in the survey process to test whether my appearance might influence respondents' answers—it did not seem to matter.[19] Interviews in coastal areas concentrated on experiences of degradation, while those in the interior region focused more on experiences of violence.[20] Cognizant of greater repression in the interior, I consciously omit the names of these villages in the text.

Simple experiences revealed the most about daily life in Cabinda. I spent Sunday mornings at the *Praia dos Pescadores* (Fishermen's Beach) on the edge of Cabinda city, enjoying the pleasures of ethnographic research. It was dirty and hot, but I relished the opportunity of sitting with the fish traders. At first, I found them to be wary and suspicious, but I learned after spending time with them that they were deeply caring women with a wonderfully raucous sense of humor. I discovered the value of rumors during these days. Even if they were exaggerated, rumors about the guerrilla forces fighting for Cabindan independence, the government planting poisonous manioc, and separatist sympathizers working for Chevron revealed the hopes, fears, and misgivings of the people. Kirsch (2002) recognizes how rumors can play a role in the expression and experience of state-sponsored terror. And Milton (2005) analyzes rumors as narratives meant to explain unclear situations or even create a pretext for action.

The most fundamental lesson I learned from my informants in Soyo and Cabinda was the value of suspicion and the indispensability of friendship. Given the sensitive nature of this research and the vulnerability of those who contributed to it, I have taken great care to protect the identities of my interviewees. While in the field, I transcribed coded notes of interviews into my computer, shredded the loose-leaf originals into tiny pieces and mixed the scraps into the fly-swarmed household wastebasket containing the daily fruit peels and fish guts. A dedicated friend helped me douse my survey sheets in kerosene and burn them until their charred remains floated off as ash in the wind. Naturally, I have also taken precautions to protect the identity of my informants in this book. Some of the characters described here are composites and none of the names are real—I have deliberately used common Angolan names.[21] The only names I have preserved as real, where appropriate, are those of corporate and public officials as quoted in newspaper and magazine articles.

The next two chapters review the literature on resource extraction, examine the historical background of extraction in Angola, and present the theoretical underpinnings of my analysis by exploring debates on the resource curse theory through the lens of political ecology. Chapter 2 outlines the exclusionary structure of petro-capitalism in Angola and the ways in which the state oil company Sonangol creates incentives to encourage investment in costly offshore extraction. Chapter 3 investigates Angola's history of petro-violence, emphasizing the role of oil in various forms of violence—including environmental degradation. These two chapters provide a framework for understanding the linkage between the enclave and lived experience of extraction by analyzing the twin forces of petro-capitalism and petro-violence in the Angolan context.

The four case study chapters that follow examine how the forces of petro-capitalism and petro-violence affect the lives of people in Angola's extractive zones. In each of these chapters, the themes of violence, degradation, and exclusion interact in distinctive ways. Chapter 4 turns to Soyo, a degraded municipality at the mouth of the Congo River, to examine how past violence and continuing repression constrain local protest and limit compensation measures and development programs. Chapter 5 jumps over the Congo River to the coastal villages of Cabinda to demonstrate how pollution associated with extraction disproportionately hurts the poorest fishermen, while Chevron's compensation efforts mostly offset the losses of the richest and most powerful. Chapters 4 and 5 also reveal how people in Soyo and Cabinda make claims to a portion of the revenues from local oil extraction by emphasizing their belonging to an oil-rich territory. Whereas claimants in Soyo express their entitlements as Angolans, Cabindans make claims based upon their separateness, reflecting their long struggle for independence. In fact, Cabindan narratives grounded in a seemingly viable political alternative—independence from Angola—served as useful tools for garnering corporate compensation and development until the government quashed the independence movement.

Chapters 6 and 7 explore the carrot-and-stick approach to territorializing Cabinda, a joint effort of the government and Chevron. Chapter 6 begins by examining the Angolan Armed Forces' military campaign to destroy the local movement for Cabindan independence and to gain physical control over the oil-rich territory. Interestingly, widespread human rights abuses perpetrated by the occupying forces provoked increased demands for Cabindan independence and the government pursued other tactics. In Chapter 7, the story continues with an examination of how the government, eager to win over Cabindans but facing budgetary constraints, used Chevron's interest in oil-backed development efforts to territorialize the unstable region—a classic counterinsurgency approach with a neoliberal twist. Corporate development schemes complemented the militant territorialization campaigns by luring the terrorized masses into government-controlled areas with promises of health care and education. Finally, the book closes with a prospective view of petro-capitalism and petro-violence as Angola nears peak oil production and a wider perspective on oil dependency.

2. Petro-Capitalism

Small ripples spread across the surface of the crescent-shaped Luanda Bay as a tanker truck pumped raw sewage into its stagnant waters. Snaked across the boardwalk, the sewage hose gurgled faintly. Joggers took wide strides over it, but none seemed to question its presence. It was as if their disregard signaled a begrudging concession of government diversions of oil revenues into patronage networks, illicit arms deals, and private accounts, which left little for investments in infrastructure or social services. The downtown streets of Luanda reek of urine and decay. The city's sanitary shortcomings reflect a lack of government investment in septic infrastructure. One-third of Luanda's four million inhabitants lack access to sanitation; the colonial era sewer system in place was built for a population of 750,000.[1]

Despite government accruals of oil revenues that totaled an estimated $16.8 billion in 2006 alone, most Angolans struggle to make ends meet (IMF 2007). The estimated per capita GDP was $6,500 in 2007, but 70 percent of the population survives on less than $1 per day and the poorest 26 percent scrape by with only 70 cents per day (CIA 2007; Fragoso 2003). The average life expectancy at birth is just under 41 years, and a third of Angolan children will not live to celebrate their fifth birthdays (UNDP 2003). Outbreaks of terrifying diseases like cholera and the Marburg virus, a hemorrhagic fever related to Ebola, challenge the inadequate health system. There are only 62 hospitals in the country and roughly 6 doctors and 110 nurses or technicians for every 100,000 Angolans (Colaço 2004; IRIN 2004d). Approximately 100,000 children under the age of 5 and 1,500 pregnant women die of malaria in Angola each year (WHO 2003). Educational statistics are equally dismal: 30 percent of Angolan children under the age of 11 have never been to school and 32 percent of the population over 15 years old cannot read (Rodrigues 2004; CIA 2007). Orphans of indigence or the war, 5,000 street children struggle to survive in the streets of Luanda, where they rummage through dumpsters for their next meal and huff petrol as a form of escape (Mason 2004).

THE CURSE OF OIL

Why are the citizens of a country swimming in oil wealth drowning in misery? OPEC founder Juan Pablo Perez Alfonzo blamed black gold's warped Midas-like "power to tarnish and turn everything into shit" for a similar scenario in Venezuela during the 1970s oil boom (Watts 1999:13). Likewise, some Angolan politicians say that oil—the very source of their wealth—brings a curse with its extraction. Seeking to explain the political and economic disparities and violence common to Angola and other oil-dependent countries, scholars theorize that crude wealth has constituted a curse rather than a blessing. Early proponents of this "resource curse" theory noted that states with greater natural resource wealth tended to grow more slowly than their resource-poor counterparts (Auty 1993, 1998, 2001; Sachs and Warner 1995, 2001). Lest observers judge Angola's spectacular growth rates averaging around 15 percent from 2004 to 2007 as indications of a healthy system, this chapter explores the wider political-economic repercussions of oil dependency, including economic distortions, internal conflict, and rent-seeking within the state.

Rafael Marques, an Angolan journalist and civil society activist, rejected the hypothesis that oil is responsible for his country's dysfunctional state. He declared, "It's fashionable to say that we are cursed by our mineral riches. That's not true. We are cursed by our leaders" (Salopek 2000).[2] In this chapter and the next, I set my analysis between the somewhat deterministic leanings of the resource curse model and the more voluntaristic disposition offered by Marques, viewing oil not as a trigger but as a constitutive force behind Angola's political economy. Oil reinforced the extractive political institutions established under Portuguese colonial rule and added fuel to the fiery contests for control of the Angolan state after independence. Though it may spark visions of grandeur and finance extensive arsenals, however, oil is not a conjurer of kleptocrats or warlords. Oil should not be seen as an excuse for poor governance or violent repression. Such deterministic thinking creates the temptation to attribute all ills to oil, obfuscating the agency of individuals and their ability to uphold or dismantle degrading, violent, and exclusionary processes and institutions. Following Watts (2004), I explicitly emphasize the role of centralized government and transnational oil corporations in perpetuating economic and institutional reliance on oil, while rejecting explanations that muddle commodity determinism with enclave politics.

The enclave is not only a geographic descriptor for walled-off oil bases, it is also the conceptual site of partnership between the government and oil corporations. Each partner relies on the other for legitimacy. Government and corporate officials operate in tandem to manage resource control through co-optation and violence. The enclave is the structuring force behind petro-capitalism and petro-violence.

Petro-capitalism denotes the interplay between politics and economy in oil-dependent states. As the basis for government access to foreign exchange and recognition in the international economy, the "structuring impact of oil" enables the Angolan state's survival—and success—despite government officials' failure to execute basic state functions (Soares de Oliveira 2008:15). Angola's oil sector relies heavily on transnational corporations and international capital but depends little on the local economy. The Angolan model examined by James Ferguson, which I discussed in the previous chapter, aptly portrays the enclave sector as a secure site for capital investment protected by private contractors. With a few exceptions, this enclave model enabled oil corporations to continue extracting oil throughout Angola's terrible war. I argue that even though the enclave sector appears to function *despite* the surrounding chaos, it actually *produces* distortions in the dysfunctional remainder of the political economic system. Using the lens of political ecology, I focus on three particular distortions: exclusion, violence, and degradation.

Political ecology provides useful tools for exploring the multidimensional struggles over access and control of natural resources—in this case, over the benefits and costs associated with oil extraction. Many of its foundational texts emphasize the dialectic of nature and society, linking environmental degradation to political-economic processes (Blaikie 1985; Blaikie and Brookfield 1987). Grounded in a Marxian understanding of political economy, they underscore the power dynamics under the dominant capitalist system. They recognize relationships of scale, drawing connections between local or regional patterns of degradation, and transnational processes of capital accumulation (Hecht and Cockburn 1989). Political ecology diverges from structuralist Marxian perspectives by acknowledging agency in nature and by noting how the physical characteristics of natural resources influence the relations of production and processes of capital accumulation (Watts 1994). For example, Watts recognizes the "slick" material properties of oil in his characterizations of corruption generated through the exclusionary distribution of oil rents (2001:189).

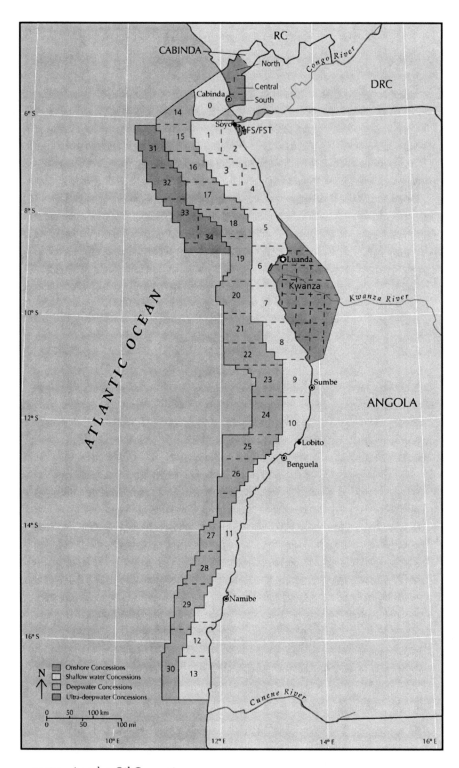

MAP 3. Angolan Oil Concessions

Oil is not the only extractive sector contributing to Angola's contorted political economy.[3] Angola is the world's third-largest exporter of uncut diamonds (Marques and de Campos 2004). Scholars contend that economic dependence on diamonds may also provoke similar outcomes as oil, especially civil war (Ross 2006, Lujala et al. 2005). Hodges (2001) and Le Billon (2001a) have drawn parallels between oil and diamonds—the country's second-most profitable sector. Transnational extractive corporations secure concessions in the diamond-rich Lunda provinces and new fields in Bié province through the government and operate alongside Angolan elites. President dos Santos' daughter, Isabel, is affiliated with Sodiam/LKI—a subset of Endiama, the Angolan national diamond company, which works in partnership with South African industry leader De Beers (Marques 2005a).[4] Despite nominal adherence to the Kimberley process—a system designed to restrict trade in "blood diamonds"—continuing violence in the Lunda provinces mars the brilliance of Angola's exported gems. National police and private security firms have perpetrated egregious human rights violations against individual fortune-seeking alluvial diamond diggers called *garimpeiros*, ranging from torture, beatings, and sexual assault to arbitrary detention, extrajudicial killings, and forced relocation of villages from diamond concessions (ibid.).

If the extraction of diamonds engenders a similar suite of violent, exclusionary, and degrading processes, why focus on oil? The political economy of oil differs from that of diamonds; it saturates every aspect of Angolan governance and yet its influence spreads far beyond national borders. I offer three reasons for oil's unique role in Angola. First, oil accounts for 90–95 percent of Angolan exports and 80 percent of Angola's tax revenues (IMF 2007; ANGOP 2008e). The oil sector generates more than 50 percent of Angolan GDP, whereas diamonds generate 5 percent (ANGOP 2008e; AfDB/OECD 2005). Second, oil is a strategic resource for industrialized and industrializing economies dependent on fossil fuel, whereas diamonds are largely a luxury item of constructed value. Oil-hungry countries like the United States and China are eager to secure their share of Angolan oil. Third, given that the vast majority of the country's oil is extracted from offshore fields beyond the sight of most Angolans, a powerful fetishism occludes the relations of its production and the processes through which it generates government revenues. Although oil dominates the "Economia" section of the daily *Jornal de Angola*, few Angolans speak of the oil fields offshore except to imply that whatever wealth they generate is diverted into offshore bank accounts by the president and his cronies. Fewer Angolans have first-hand knowledge of the sector; the skills required for entry-level posts in the industry are unattainable without a foreign scholarship or training from the exclusive National Petroleum Institute.

THE STRUCTURE OF THE ANGOLAN PETRO-STATE

The foundations of the Angolan petro-state reside in the laws and processes promoting partnerships between the state and transnational oil corporations (Sawyer 2004:14). For half a century, agreements between Angolan officials and oil corporations in the capital city of Luanda have given access rights to transnational corporations for oil extraction and capital accumulation. In some cases, the history of extraction even predates the Angolan government. The extractive rights assigned to Chevron and Total in Soyo were grounded in colonial-era joint ventures negotiated between Cabinda Gulf Oil, Petrofina, and Texaco and Portuguese administrators.

Following Angola's independence from Portugal, the government established Sonangol as the national oil company in 1976 and pronounced it the sole concessionaire for exploration and production two years later. During Angola's period of socialist rule between 1975 and 1990, the government declared that "all the minerals in Angola belong to the Angolan people" under the Mining Law of May 1979 (Bhagavan 1986:38). Once Angola transitioned to a capitalist system in 1991, the government extended the precept of eminent domain to offshore zones through Decree Law 23/92. This legislation declared that "all of the natural resources existing in the ground or underground, in interior waters, in territorial seas, on the continental shelf and in the exclusive economic zone are the property of the State, which determines the conditions of their exploitation and utilization" (Paiva 1998:15).

Although the Angolan state owns the country's oil, it entrusts transnational corporations with the task of extracting it from subterranean fields within a specific area, referred to as a concession. Five types of concessions are inscribed on the Angolan map: onshore, shallow water (up to 300 meters), deepwater (300 to 1,500 meters), ultra-deepwater (1,500 to 2,500 meters), and ultra-ultra deepwater (more than 2,500 meters).[5] Three blocks (North, Central, and South) in Cabinda, two blocks in Congo (Soyo's FS and FST), and twenty-three more recently delineated blocks (Tobias, Galinda, and KON_01 through KON_21) in the Kwanza Basin constitute Angola's onshore production area. Offshore, fifty concessions are demarcated within the limits of Angola's 550,000 km^2 exclusive economic zone. Shallow water Blocks 0 through 13 hug the Angolan coastline from Cabinda to the mouth of the Cunene River; Blocks 14 to 30 divide the deepwater zone; and Blocks

31 through 45 sit in the ultra-deep.[6] Ultra-ultra deepwater Blocks 46 through 50 mark the frontiers of exploration.

Sonangol facilitates investment in the Angolan oil sector in two ways.[7] First, it offers favorable financial incentives. Although many countries offer corporations the incentive of "uplift," wherein they may recalculate amortizable costs by increasing their initial value by a specific percentage, Angola's uplift of 50 percent is considered high (IMF 2005). Second, Sonangol negotiates production sharing agreements (PSAs) with transnational oil corporations. Whereas joint ventures, the system employed during the colonial period, required significant capital investments from both partners at the outset, the PSA model allows Sonangol to boost oil development without large capital outlays on its part.[8] Despite bearing the full burden of capital investment, oil corporations also prefer PSAs because they guarantee rights to the oil reserves, offer an opportunity to earn massive profits, and ensure predictable tax and regulation regimes (Muttitt 2005). To spread the costs and risk, the corporations organize themselves into consortia as they bid for exploration and production rights. Each corporation within a given consortium assumes a division of the shares of costs and profits proportional to its interest stake, and one corporation per consortium (usually the highest stakeholder) vies for the role of operator of the concession. Officials from Angola's national oil company even created Sonangol Pesquisa e Produção, an exploration and production firm, to join these consortia as a shareholder and/or operator.[9]

As concessionaire, Sonangol selects the most attractive bid for each concession block based upon the technological and experiential capacity of the proposed operator, the combined portfolio of the partners, and the heft of the signature bonus offered. These bonuses are substantial. In 2006, the Chinese oil firm Sinopec reportedly offered $1.1 billion in signature bonuses for each portion of the vaunted deepwater blocks 17 and 18 relinquished by other transnational oil corporations. The Office of the President officially receives 55 percent of all signature bonuses (Le Billon 2001a). Consortia also designate an additional *social* bonus, a fraction of the amount offered as the signature bonus, apportioned to socioeconomic development projects in the country. Fuzzy accounting impedes most efforts to track these funds.

Once Sonangol announces the consortium to which it will award a concession, the parties negotiate a PSA. These confidential contracts outline the power relations between the state and corporation at multiple levels, delineating "the conditions under which capital has access to the land [or offshore exclusive economic zone] for the purposes of production and accumulation" (Fine 1984 as quoted in Watts 2001). These conditions include, but are not limited to: a timetable for seismic testing and exploration, the schedule for payments and royalties accrued to the state, stipulations on sourcing of Angolan goods and employees, and the oil-backed development initiatives to be undertaken by the consortium under the terms of the social bonus. If the operator awarded the PSA discovers oil in commercial quantities, the consortium can either commit to extracting the oil within the fixed timeframe or relinquish the concession, or portions of it.[10] Should the consortium commit to production, a final joint authorization from Sonangol and the equity partners must precede any field development. If the consortium fails to discover or develop commercial finds in the allotted exploration and development phases, usually three years each, the partners lose all of the capital invested in the signing and social bonuses as well as all exploration expenditures. These losses can be quite substantial, especially in offshore areas.

Venturing Offshore

Petroleum geologists once theorized that "reservoirs decrease in number and deteriorate in quality with depth"; however, finds from 1985 to 2001 changed their outlook (Total 2003a). They identified prolific zones where the convergence of submarine sediment fans spreading from the mouths of large rivers and mature source rocks in deep water created the ideal conditions for reservoirs. The sedimentary basins into which the mighty Mississippi, Niger, and Congo Rivers flow have trapped hydrocarbons in lithified turbidite "fan" formations in the Gulf of Mexico, Nigeria's Niger Delta, and Angola's Lower Congo basin. The reservoir rocks along Angola's oil-rich northern coast are known locally as the Pinda carbonate.[11]

Cabinda's shallow-water Block 0 has produced more oil than any other concession in Angolan history; Cabinda Gulf Oil (now owned by Chevron) announced significant discoveries in the formation off the Cabindan coast in 1968 (Koning 2002). Finds in deepwater Block 15 and ultra-deepwater Block 31 due west of Soyo have shifted new development and corporate attention both southward and farther offshore. Following a remarkable rate of deepwater discoveries in Blocks 14, 15, 17, and 18, bidding for ultra-deepwater Blocks 31 to 34 reached a fever pitch in the late 1990s. Whereas oil corporations consider striking oil in four out of ten exploration wells a favorable rate of return, Renato Aguilar noted Angola's deepwater strike rate in the late 1990s was "almost ten out of ten," including "such huge discoveries as Dalia field in Block 17, which is believed to contain more than 1 billion barrels, the equivalent of one-fifth of Britain's entire known reserves" (2001:40).

Offshore production demands larger infusions of capital and more skilled labor to produce oil at greater depths. As such, deepwater petroleum deposits must be sufficiently large to justify the exponential costs of production.[12] Deepwater wells can cost up to ten times the amount of a well in shallow water. In 2000, Total's fields at 1,500 meters depth had to be "sufficiently large" (i.e., capable of yielding at least 500 million barrels of oil) to justify extraction costs of $4.70 per barrel (Sebastião and Londa 2009).[13]

The substantial expenditures required prior to producing the first barrel of oil create an incentive for expedited extraction to offset the costs (Navarre and Lheure 2003). To maintain their competitive edge, drilling contractors developed faster, more automated units (Manchon 2003). Roughnecks man the automated systems with sophisticated computer technology, trading their oily work gloves for joysticks. The new drillships operate in waters up to 3,000 meters deep, boring through an additional 6,000 meters of subsurface rock and sediment to reach oil deposits (Mouawad 2005). Many of the units also feature directional drilling, facilitating horizontal access to deposits. The Pride Angola, of Houston-based Pride International Inc., measures 205 meters long and 30 meters wide, stores up to 1,800 cubic meters of drilling mud, and features a derrick with 680 metric tons of lifting capacity (Manchon 2003:34). This deepwater drillship leased for a daily fee of $162,000 in 2005, but other ultra-deepwater drilling vessels cost up to $250,000 per day depending upon their capacity (Rach 2003; Gazaniol 2003:40).

Offshore extractive technologies are constantly evolving and improving. The 100-acre Summerland field near Santa Barbara, California, was one of the world's first offshore production sites, pumping out two barrels per day from derricks set on piers in 1896.[14] As offshore production expanded across the globe and into deeper waters, oil corporations began to employ fixed platforms in water depths of up to 500 meters. To extract oil at depths greater than 500 meters, corporations favor floating production storage and offloading systems (FPSOs). This means that most of the oil produced from Angola's deepwater and ultra-deepwater concessions never touches Angolan soil. The concept for FPSOs evolved from the use of obsolete tankers as storage facilities as far back as 1936, but the contemporary form with a custom-built hull emerged in the mid-1970s; current models carry a price tag of nearly $1 billion apiece (Berthelot and Tonda 2003:80; *World Oil* 1980b). By 2003, six FPSOs were active or scheduled for production in Angola's deepwater: ExxonMobil's Hungo (Kizomba A), Kissanje (Kizomba B), and Atlantic (Xicomba); Total's Dalia and Girassol; and BP's Greater Plutonio.[15] These FPSOs varied in their first production dates between 2001 and 2007, but all were slated to operate in offshore depths ranging between 1,147 meters (3,763 feet) and 1,350 meters (4,429 feet) (Total 2003b).

Producing oil from deepwater and ultra-deepwater wells at the rapid rates necessary to keep costs down requires capable and diligent staff. Workers on offshore platforms and FPSOs in deeper waters can work up to twelve hours a day for two to four weeks at a time before taking an equal proportion of time off. The difficult conditions and risky nature of offshore extraction translate into high salaries, but only well-trained candidates are considered. Expatriate oil workers once dominated the Angolan oil and gas sector, yet the government has sought to create opportunities for nationals by decree. Under the Angolanization statutes delineated in Decree 20/82 of April 17, 1982, transnational oil corporations operating in Angola are required to invest in a training fund administered jointly by the Ministries of Finance, Education, and Petroleum (UNDP-WB 1989:64). The fund finances efforts to prepare Angolans for positions in the oil and gas industry, such as the courses offered by National Petroleum Institute (INP).[16] The required contribution amounts to roughly 15 cents on every barrel of oil produced, however, the modest stature of the INP would suggest that the fund also finances other institutions (UNDP-WB 1989:viii). Angolan law also stipulates that all foreign entities operating in the country hire at least seven Angolans for every three expatriates and create a "rigorous plan for training and/or development of Angolan technical staff with a view to the gradual occupation" of all posts occupied by foreigners (WB 2002:64).[17] Similarly, local content standards provide incentives for procurement of inputs from local businesses, spurring the creation of joint-venture firms with Sonangol.[18]

Both the Angolanization and local content initiatives have achieved a high level of adherence among oil corporations, but the narrow reach of the enclave sector limits their impact on the widely unskilled and unemployed masses. For the millions of barrels of oil extracted from Angolan fields each day, the sector employs relatively few workers—even Sonangol's 95-percent Angolan workforce counts just over 8,240 employees (Santana 2005; ANGOP 2008e). Only a fraction of aspirants claim these positions.

Mineral and oil sectors are commonly characterized by unidirectional resource flows providing benefits only to "gate-keeping elites" (Cooper 2001). These gatekeepers carefully guard opportunities in the sector, ensure their friends and relatives receive lucrative jobs, direct associated development projects to their hometowns, and channel contracts to favored businesses. The National Petroleum Institute admits mostly elite offspring with connections to the ruling party and, according to rumor, a few recruits from families wealthy enough to tender a two-thousand-dollar bribe.[19] Oil corporations perpetuate the exclusionary system by trading favors with political elites. One official explained, "To go farther [up the corporate ladder] you have to be from the highest family. . . . [W]hen those companies come to Angola they are looking for certain support . . . [T]hen in return they want them to hire their sons. After ten and twenty years, the richest families will still be the richest."

SUBSIDIZING INEQUALITY

A lopsided system of subsidies, underwritten by oil wealth, enabled the government to maintain elite oases in the midst of wartime chaos and to ignore deteriorating infrastructure, education, and health systems. At the height of the war, the government allocated 35 percent of education funding to overseas scholarships and reserved $400 million in electricity, water, transportation, and housing subsidies (Le Billon 2001a: 65).[20] Even after peace negotiations in 2002, the subsidy system remained largely intact.

Although utilities subsidies benefit one in eleven Angolans, paradoxically they mostly serve wealthier Angolans who have electricity and running water in their homes (de Carvalho 2004). The impoverished masses in Luanda's slums struggle to pay 4 cents per liter for water trucked in from the contaminated Bengo River, a price 160 times higher than the subsidized water piped into the homes of wealthier urbanites (LaFraniere 2006).[21] State electricity subsidies likewise benefit households on the few functioning sections of the colonial grid in coastal cities spared by the war. An article in the independent newspaper *Semanário Angolense* reported that "[t]he majority of the [oil] money is allocated to scholarships for higher level study abroad and non-basic services when what is urgently needed are [investments in] primary schooling as well as basic health care" (Neto 2003).

Rather than redistributing oil wealth to eradicate poverty or investing in new infrastructure, President dos Santos funnels a large proportion of government oil revenues into subsidies for his most powerful supporters. This subsidy system exemplifies the essence of Angolan petro-capitalism: channeling oil's benefits to a powerful few while excluding the vast majority. Instead of distributing the rents evenly among the population, top government officials strategically invest petrodollars in patronage networks and security to ensure continued access to resource rents in the future. This is the logic of the *rentier* state, wherein resource rents, outweighing taxes or any other revenue stream, instill dependency on extraction and reinforce exclusion.

The *rentier* state might appear to possess an almost magical capacity to spur universal progress and cure all of society's ills. Even so, leaders selectively invest oil revenues to construct "enclaves of privilege" in the midst of "an increasingly impoverished social environment palpably marked by abandonment and neglect" (Coronil 1997:385). A representative from a prominent Angolan NGO criticized his leaders for "sleeping in the shade of a banana tree as if all were well with the country and its people." The vision he conjured was the very image used in ads for Angola's national lottery.[22] Each scratch-off ticket was imprinted with the cartoon image of a man reclining under a banana tree with a hat shading his face, a cigar protruding from his wide grin, and a bulging moneybag propped on his belly. The ticket reads: "Buy, Scratch, Win . . . and sleep in the shade of a banana tree." Indeed, Paul Collier and Anke Hoeffler have likened gaining ownership of a natural resource to winning a lottery (2002), and Michael Watts likewise demonstrates how oil rents appear to materialize "out of thin air" rather than as the outcome of any work, contributing to "a sort of money fetishism" (1994:413). Angola pays tribute to this fetishism by imprinting the fifty kwanza bill with the image of an oil platform. Worth less than one dollar, the fifty kwanza bill is the closest most Angolans get to seeing the nation's oil wealth.[23]

Producing Distortions

Apart from the well-connected few who receive jobs and contracts in the oil industry, Angolans see few benefits from their country's oil wealth though they suffer its distorting effects. The extraction and export of non-renewable resources can ultimately render oil-dependent economies poorer. Prescient structural theorists warned against development centered on resource exports for three reasons: (1) ever worsening terms of trade tend to exacerbate inequality between rich industrialized countries and poor primary commodity exporters; (2) international commodities markets are marked by drastic price fluctuations; and (3) the dominance of foreign multinationals in resource extraction impedes growth in the rest of the economy because these companies repatriate their profits rather than making local investments (Ross 1999).

Drawing on the influences of dependency theory, scholars have recognized how resource access and control are influenced by relations of production at a global scale, wherein natural resource–rich peripheries are increasingly underdeveloped by capital rich cores (Bunker 1985; Hecht 1985).[24] The "nature-exporting societies" become locked into extractive patterns of underdevelopment, reinforcing specialization in the exported commodity and dependence on foreign exchange (Coronil 1997). Worse yet, both the discovery of or sharp price increases in exportable resources can result in "Dutch Disease," an economic distortion that drives up the exchange rate, which increases the costs of exporting other locally produced goods to the point that they become uncompetitive on the world market. It also decreases the cost of imports, making these more attractive to consumers. Dutch Disease can be profoundly damaging to undiversified economies and is difficult to overturn without severe policy adjustments (Parvin and Dezhbakhsh 1988). Even the tantalizing prospect of subsidizing underdeveloped agricultural and manufacturing sectors with oil revenues may reinforce dependency and undermine competitiveness (Coronil 1997).[25]

The Angolan populace suffers the distorting effects of oil dependency. Angola spent $6.6 billion on imported goods and services in 2004 (Sogge 2006). The wartime collapse of Angola's rural agrarian system and resultant reliance on petrodollar-financed imports also negatively affects cash-strapped urbanites who cannot afford enough food; 75 percent of the urban population does not consume the recommended number of minimum daily calories (ibid). The oil boom has driven up the cost of living in Luanda, where renting a home with running water, a generator, and a phone line can cost $15,000 per month (*Financial Express of India* 2005). With the national minimum salary at $50 per month, few can afford accommodations at even one-tenth this price. Many families crowd into minimalist apartments with no utilities on the urban fringe for $100 per month.

More than half of all Angolans are unemployed or underemployed (CIA 2007). Most merchants eke out a living in the informal sector. By pooling resources and dividing bulk supplies of imported goods—ranging from cigarettes to disposable diapers—into smaller saleable portions, they are able to earn a slight premium on each sale. Ironically, their impoverished customers who live day-to-day are more readily able to afford these smaller portions, though in the long run they may pay up to double the bulk price for the same quantity of goods. The informal market accounts for more than two-thirds of the economic transactions in Angola. Still, street merchants—including fish traders—live in fear of the harassment and extortion exacted by the fiscal police, a brutal sect of law enforcement officials charged with discouraging informal trade (*Semanário Angolense* 2003b).

A POLITICAL ECONOMY OF EXCLUSION

Resource rents fuel Angola's political system. If the government were to distribute an equal share of Angola's oil revenues to every citizen, each would receive a check for around $1,000—not much for the wealthy few navigating Luanda's potholed streets in Porsche Cayenne SUVs , but a sizeable sum to those earning $1,200 per year on the official minimum wage.[26] Instead of granting the broader populace an equal stake in the country's natural resource wealth, President dos Santos and the ruling party channel oil revenues into patronage networks. In power since Angola's independence in 1975, the MPLA (Movimento Popular de Libertação de Angola) uses oil monies to subvert the political opposition. Oil wealth finances the generous promotions or endowments opposition members receive after abandoning an antagonistic stance (Marques 2005c). Petrodollars underwrite artificial parties sponsored by the ruling party "to divide the opposition while creating an impression of pluralist diversity" (Hodges 2003:61).

Petrodollar Patronage

When José Eduardo dos Santos became Angola's second president in 1979, he discovered the utility of petrodollar patronage as an "instrument to build a political and economic order within a context of relative disorder" (Le Billon 2003:424). Unable or unwilling to shed some authoritarian vestiges of the old regime during Angola's transformation from socialism to democracy a decade later, dos Santos and his closest advisers fashioned a pacted democracy. Characteristically exclusionary, pacted democracies reinforce the distorted form of the petro-state through "clientelistic distribution, patronage and political rent seeking, in part by creating standard operating procedures based on excessive compromise and on conflict avoidance through the distribution of petrodollars" (Karl 1997:93). In Angola's pacted democracy "virtually all members of the political establishment" are rewarded with loyalty bonuses (Le Billon 2001a; Hodges 2003). This ruling strategy based on "containment through preemptive inclusion" discourages the opposition from effectively challenging the president (Karl 1997:93). By distributing annual bonuses of $30,000 cash or baskets of imported food to senior civil servants earning a pittance and brand new Audi A6 automobiles worth $70,000 apiece to Ministers of Parliament unable to afford the maintenance costs, President dos Santos has contrived a patronage network for his devotees as well as his opponents (Hodges 2003:61; Le Billon 2001a).

Angola's system of petrodollar patronage is abetted and enhanced by the centralized structure of government. The president has considerable authority to delineate the leadership of the executive and legislative branches. He retains the power to appoint the prime minister and the remaining members of the Council of Ministers in the executive branch, attorney general, deputy attorney general, and the judges of the High Council of the Judicial Bench. The president also appoints the governor for each of Angola's 18 provinces and the administrators of the 164 municipalities and 578 communes into which the provinces are divided.

The presidentialist structure of governance facilitates the channeling of oil revenues through patterns of fiscal centralization that undermine democratic accountability and equitable development.[27] It deepens the influence of the party in power, as the president appoints mostly members of his own party and a few opposition loyalists to occupy each post, and promotes allegiance to personalized and party politics rather than policy platforms.[28] President dos Santos has used his post and access to oil monies to exert his influence down to the most local administrative authorities, called *sobas*. Angolan civil society advocate Rafael Marques terms this system "jungle capitalism," recalling how Portuguese colonial rulers created the post of *soba* to increase their administrative and political control over remote areas (Marques 2005b). Following in the footsteps of these erstwhile overlords, the ruling party has used *sobas* to extend its control down to the community level. The party no longer uses *sobas* as official informants, as during the socialist period, but still relies on the functionaries to gather information and disseminate the party line. In 2004, the government paid each *soba* a paltry wage of 68 kwanzas (less than $1) per month, while the MPLA showered a select few loyalists with gifts of bicycles and radios.[29] Like other civil servants on starvation wages, most *sobas* remain devoted to the MPLA—both in the persistent hope that their loyalty might yield a return and for lack of an alternative. For, as Christine Messiant has written, "It is the very arbitrariness of the system that ensures compliance, not its legitimate authority" (2008:120).

Executives and ministers in the upper echelons of Angolan society also earn favors for their loyalty to the president and his party. Members of President dos Santos' inner circle have obtained profitable privileges in the fisheries, telecommunications, and diamond sectors. For most of Angola's post-colonial history, the vast sums of capital necessary to invest in the oil sector precluded the possibility of distributing preferential concession stakes to local investors.[30] In July 2003, Sonangol overturned this trend by awarding preferential exploration and service provision contracts to domestic firms in a closed bidding session for fields expected to produce

5,000 barrels per day (Santana 2005).[31] Some of the wealthiest, most influential Angolans earned stakes in the oil industry, including Secretary to the Council of Ministers António Van Dúnem, Angolan Ambassador to the UN Alfonso Van Dúnem Mbinda, Angolan Ambassador to Tanzania Brito Sozinho, and the President's eldest sister, Marta dos Santos (ibid).[32] This trend is expected to increase, since legislative changes enacted in 2004 created incentives for smaller firms to enter the Angolan oil sector (Hodges 2008:190).

Corrupting Expectations

Senior Adviser to the World Bank Charles McPherson declared oil wealth a "lightning rod for corruption" in Africa (Grundy 2004). Although the intentional diversion of public funds for private interests is punishable under Article 17 of Angola's Law on Crimes against the Economy, top MPLA officials have redirected a portion of state oil revenues into personal accounts.[33] A 2004 Human Rights Watch report cited a leaked internal study by the International Monetary Fund concluding that $4.2 billion in oil revenues had "disappeared" from state coffers between 1998 and 2002. The missing sum exceeded the government's total spending on social services during the same period by $800,000 (HRW 2004c). As news of the lost funds hit the press, European courts traced multi-million-dollar wire transfers from Angolan government accounts to private accounts in Luxembourg, the Cayman Islands, and Switzerland (Silverstein 2004). Watchdog groups claimed that President dos Santos and other officials transferred oil revenues to private accounts through intermediaries, which had supplied weapons to the MPLA during the war.[34]

Sonangol Chairman Manuel Vicente rejected the allegations of corruption as "all lies," and Minister of Finance José Pedro de Morais contested the reports, conceding just $673.5 million in discrepancies between public accounts and attributing the error to accounting "insufficiencies" (McMillan 2005; *O Apostolado* 2004h). Other reports blamed high inflation, shifting exchange rates, and government buybacks of Angolan currency (Salvador 2004; Kyle 2005). The scandal shook the public's already frail confidence in the government and its postwar reform process. Public suspicion resurged at the end of 2004 when Minister of Petroleum Desidério Costa erroneously announced the government's receipt of $8 billion in oil revenues for the year and President dos Santos later amended the figure to $3 billion (Van-Dunem 2005).[35]

Oil corporations extracting the crude from Angola's concessions play a vital role in supporting exclusionary policies. "Because of their key role as intermediaries between resources and markets, oil companies often come to support (willingly or unwillingly) autocratic regimes" (Le Billon 2001a). Despite corporate policies designed to avoid sustaining corruption, oil corporations are induced to submit to "the operational logic" of working in Angola (GW 2004). For example, President dos Santos asked corporations to contribute to the Fundação Eduardo dos Santos (FESA), his personal charity.[36] Chevron donated $50,000 annually to FESA and also contributed $50,000 to First Lady Ana Paula dos Santos' Lwini Fund for Social Solidarity (Eviatar 2004). These vanity charities primarily function as patronage mechanisms for the president rather than serving any social good (Messiant 1999).

The government exerts pressure on the hiring and procurement practices of transnational oil corporations operating in Angola. Sonangol encourages oil firms to hire well-connected job applicants.[37] Oil corporations are required to contract Teleservice, a private security company intimately tied to the Angolan military, to protect their installations. A revolving door guides elite Angolans between posts in the oil industry and government.[38] The rotation of officials between public and private offices ensures their likeminded interest in supporting the extractive aims of both the government and transnational corporations.

Contact with the excesses of the industry and its culture of consumption encourages greater rent seeking among government officials (Le Billon 2001a).[39] As guests of oil executives enjoying elaborate dinners held in spacious apartments rented at a cost of $20,000 per month, poorly paid civil servants who feel they deserve similarly lavish lifestyles may use their positions to garner extra income. Deputy Prime Minister Aguinaldo Jaime reportedly exercised his authority as head of the Angolan National Bank in 2002 to attempt a transfer of $50 million in state oil revenues to a personal account at a San Diego branch of the Bank of America before withdrawing the transaction under scrutiny (Silverstein 2004).

Angola's culture of corruption is not limited to its upper echelons. Even low-level accountants have colluded in schemes to enter the names of "phantom workers" on the payroll, and then collect and divide the salaries of these phony colleagues.[40] Angola's police notoriously solicit bribes labeled *gasosas*—the Angolan colloquial term for a soda pop—in place of issuing traffic violations. Similar petty forms of corruption also exist in African countries without oil, but the corruption attending oil wealth is attributed, in part, to the slippery material characteristics of oil as a natural resource and a commodity that can grease many palms (Watts 1994, 2001).

The greasy fingers of oil-backed patronage reach deep into the mechanics of the Angolan state; corruption is *expected* of government officials. When the diligent Vice Minister of Foreign Relations Pedro Romão jumped to his death from the rooftop balcony of Luanda's Hotel Presidente in August 2004, his boss eulogized him as a man of honesty and integrity. Once sources revealed that financial difficulties had driven Romão to suicide, people on the street speculated that perhaps the Vice Minister had been a little too honest. Some suggested that the monthly base salaries of the president ($2,700), prime minister ($2,000), ministers or governors ($1,800), and vice ministers or vice governors ($1,600) were tantamount to an "invitation to corruption" (*A Capital* 2004).

FORMATION OF THE ANGOLAN PETRO-STATE

"Petro-states are built on what already exists" (Karl 1997:74). The foundations of Angola's extractive, exclusionary patterns of governance reach back to colonial policies of enslavement, land expropriation, and forced labor. After independence, oil dependency deepened pre-existing divisions and intensified disparities. Dissecting the Angolan state to discover the pathology of exclusion reveals how the "petrolization of the policy environment" creates "unusually strong impediments to development on the domestic level" (Karl 1997:16). Once a government becomes dependent on oil rents, the seemingly inevitable process of petrolization reinforces state-centered, personalized, and exclusionary patterns of power, which weaken state institutions, impede government accountability, and limit economic diversification within extractive states. Angolan patronage networks are starkly delineated by decades of war and exclusion. This section examines the role of oil in shaping the Angolan petro-state, drawing attention to key historical details and conjunctures.

Dividing a Nation

Angola is a diverse and deeply divided nation. Nine major ethnolinguistic groups dominate Angola, but 75 percent of the population hails from one of the three largest—the Ovimbundu (37 percent), Mbundu (25 percent), and Bakongo (13 percent). Economic need and violent displacement forced much of the population to adopt Portuguese as a lingua franca. Whereas some no longer speak the traditional languages associated with their ethnic group, they often still associate with their geographic and linguistic traditions. The Ovimbundu are linked to west-central Angola's *Planalto* region and the Umbundu language; the Mbundu belonged to the old Ndongo kingdom

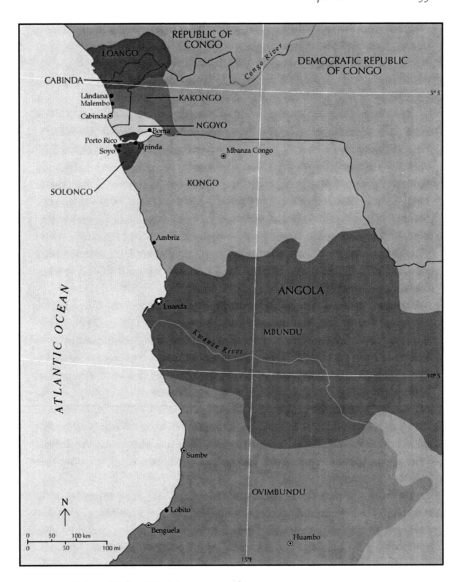

MAP 4. Selected Ethnic Divisions in Angola

and are connected with the territory stretching from Luanda inland and the Kimbundu language; and the Bakongo's Kongo ancestry ties them to the northern portion of the country and the Kikongo language.

During the struggle against Portuguese colonialism, Angola's three largest liberation groups drew strength from ethnic ties. The FNLA (Frente

Nacional de Libertação de Angola) generally comprised Bakongo, UNITA (União Nacional para a Independência Total de Angola) was made up primarily of Ovimbundu, and the MPLA was originally composed mostly of Mbundu and persons of mixed race (*mestiços*). FLEC (Frente para a Libertação do Enclave de Cabinda) joined Cabindans seeking independence separate from Angola.[41] Apart from ethnic affiliations, the liberation factions also split along religious lines. Methodists supported the MPLA, Baptists favored the FNLA, and Congregationalists backed UNITA, while Catholics became important to the separate struggle for independence in Cabinda.[42] Race, class, geography, and education also defined the movements. The MPLA drew support from the diverse coastal cities of Luanda, Benguela, and Lobito, counting urban blacks, *mestiço* bureaucrats, descendants of the Old Creole slavers, and leftist whites among its ranks, while UNITA claimed rural black peasants as its base.[43] Many FNLA leaders were educated in Leopoldville (current-day Kinshasa), whereas MPLA leaders had received instruction in Lisbon.[44]

Portugal granted Angola independence on November 11, 1975. Battles for leadership of the country continued between the FNLA, MPLA, and UNITA. The MPLA seized control of Luanda amidst the fighting in 1975 and installed a socialist model of government under President Agostinho Neto.[45] The MPLA defeated the FNLA in 1976, but the war between the MPLA and UNITA raged on. Oil revenues flowed into Luanda and the MPLA declared oil the property of all Angolans, though few saw improvements in their standard of living or witnessed much development financed by oil extraction.[46] They began to resent MPLA leaders for living comfortably as the colonial rulers had before them, ignoring the populace (Malaquias 2007:127).

On May 27, 1977, Nito Alves and José van Dunem attempted a coup d'état against President Agostinho Neto. The plotters promoted a populist platform urging a more radical revolutionary ideology and condemned the domination of top party positions by upper-class *mestiços* (Mabeko-Tali 2001a).[47] The coup attempt afforded the MPLA the chance to dispatch party "members who—whether sympathetic to the coup plotters or not—defended a people-centred approach to post-colonial politics" (Malaquias 2007:127). The ruling party unleashed a wave of violence in Luanda that killed 30,000 people, abandoned the ethos of *poder popular*, and centralized the government around the president and Central Committee (Mabeko-Tali 2001a).

The MPLA had transformed from a mass movement founded on romantic revolutionary ideals into "a small, closely-knit 'vanguard' party composed of (and seemingly existing for) a selected few" (Mabeko-Tali 2001a; Kaure 1999:24–5, parentheses original).[48] The MPLA essentially "discarded" the bulk of the population: "first in the rural areas, which were afflicted by war and had become irrelevant ever since the oil rent made it possible to buy food abroad; then in the cities, where poverty grew over time and political support dwindled" (Messiant 2008:96). Ultimately, "the ruling elites became progressively more 'comfortable' with neglecting the general population" (Vidal 2008b:211).

The MPLA's response to the coup reinforced Angola's designation as a *rentier* state: surviving on rents rather than the fruits of Angolan labor. Ironically, the MPLA renamed itself the MPLA Worker's Party (MPLA-PT) in December 1977. The party organized patronage networks through structured and monitored party organs such as the National Union of Angolan Workers (UNTA) and the Organization of Angolan Women (OMA), but distrustful leaders denied membership to some applicants on the basis of unknown or suspect revolutionary credentials (Kaure 1999:25). By the time Agostinho Neto passed away in September 1979, the party's membership had fallen to 16,500 from independence-era levels of 60,000 in 1975 (CR 2004). Neto's successor, President José Eduardo dos Santos, redoubled the country's reliance on oil revenues and Soviet support.[49] Oil revenues filled state coffers and Cuban soldiers equipped with Soviet Kalashnikovs protected government interests; the MPLA no longer needed the once-cherished *poder popular*.

Exclusion and oil dependency reinforced one another and increasingly defined Angola's postcolonial political economy along the contours of extraction. A drop in world oil prices, coupled with a decrease in oil production, diminished Angolan export revenues by 20 percent in 1981; the MPLA government responded by cutting imported goods and services (Bhagavan 1986:32).[50] Regrettably, the war continued to raze agricultural lands and terrorize farmers while extensive minefields undercut their productive capacity; only 2–3 percent of arable land was cultivated in the mid-1980s (Gunn 1987). Thus, shortages plagued official government shops, and though the illicit trade networks known as *candonga* offered a wider range of goods including fruits, vegetables, clothing, and charcoal, prices were exorbitant.[51] High-level government officials exacerbated the situation by promulgating economic policies that overvalued local currency. Such policies constricted the purchasing power of the vulnerable Angolan population but enabled powerful leaders to accumulate "large sums in convertible currency abroad through 'shady' import deals, granting of supply contracts to foreign companies, and the smuggling of diamonds" (Bhagavan 1986:41).[52]

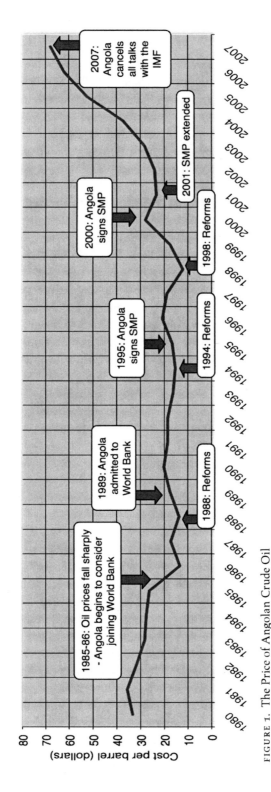

FIGURE 1. The Price of Angolan Crude Oil

NOTE: Based on "Free on Board" costs of Angolan crude sold to the United States as reported in the Environmental Information Agency's Petroleum Marketing monthly data, viewed online on June 23, 2008. For an example worksheet, go to: http://www.eia.doe.gov/pub/oil_gas/ petroleum/data_publications/petroleum_marketing_monthly/current/pdf/pmmtab24.pdf. Free on Board (FOB) is a term used in recognition that after the seller (in this case Angola) has loaded crude onto the tanker in port the buyer (the U.S.) assumes all costs and risks of loss or damage thereafter.

Angola's economic contortions instigated a "brain drain" wherein some 5,000 to 10,000 skilled elites—some of whom had held government posts—emigrated because they were disgruntled with their deteriorating quality of life (Bhagavan 1986:31). Still, the MPLA did little to diversify the economy or its leadership. President dos Santos developed an economic crisis plan aimed at increasing investment in the oil sector from $558 million in 1982 to $650 million by 1985 (Bhagavan 1986:85).[53] In December 1985, dos Santos convened the Second MPLA Congress. He reorganized the party, dismissing pro-Soviet and foundational *mestiço* figures, and replaced them with Old Creole leaders distinguished by their colonial-era military ties (Marcum 1986:29).[54]

Fluctuating Resolve

As Soviet disbursements declined and oil prices dropped sharply in 1985 and 1986, returning only $10 for every barrel of Angolan oil, President dos Santos hinted at joining the World Bank (Gunn 1987:56).[55] Citibank eased some of the country's financial stress with a new line of credit for the oil sector, but by 1987 the Angolan economy was desperate. The drastic drop in oil prices and further agricultural failures left the country with half the GDP it had earned in 1974 (Gunn 1987:64; Aguilar 2003). Angola implemented an economic and financial restructuring program in 1987 as part of its effort to meet International Monetary Fund (IMF) and World Bank requirements for loans (Kaure 1999:49). Party elites stalled some of the key reforms, so the World Bank granted Angola membership in 1989 but did not approve loans (Aguilar 2003; Kaure 1999:49). Loans were contingent upon the usual conditions of structural adjustment: privatization of national industries, currency devaluation, reduction of state expenditures, economic liberalization to encourage foreign direct investment, and mechanisms for fiscal transparency.[56]

Angola was disinclined to accept World Bank and IMF funding because of the "high non-financial costs of loans, both in terms of conditionality and the cumbersome administrative procedures leading to delays of disbursements" (Buira 2005:31). Fluctuating oil prices, however, threatened to force Angola into compliance. Angola's crude is generally light and sweet, with premium grades like Palanca selling at slightly higher prices.[57] As oil prices rose and fell in accordance with variations in the world market, the IMF and World Bank began to see a pattern: the government's fluctuating resolve to comply with their prescriptions corresponded to shifts in the price of crude.[58] As oil prices rose slightly in 1990, Angolan leaders seemed less interested in World Bank and IMF loans. For the next decade, Angola vacillated between accepting and resisting calls for neoliberal reform. Each time the price of Angolan crude slumped, the government became more amenable to reform. On several occasions, Angola even signed a Staff Monitored Program (SMP) with the IMF—a twelve-month observation period serving as a precursor to lending contingent upon implementation of prerequisite conditions.[59]

DEMOCRACY WITHOUT ACCOUNTABILITY

In 1990, the MPLA Congress announced Angola's transition to a social democracy founded on free-market principles intended to stimulate and diversify the economy (CR 2004). The following year, the MPLA ended one-party rule, declared opposition parties and civil society organizations legal, and promised to hold elections. Angolans regarded the MPLA's declaration of democracy with wary pragmatism; voters developed party allegiances more often to seek protection, to avoid starvation, or for fear of the enemy, than for interest in their policy platforms (Messiant 2008; Vidal 2008).

United Nations monitors declared Angola's September 1992 elections "free and fair" and reported that José Eduardo dos Santos of the MPLA had won the presidency with 49.5 percent of the votes. Opposition candidates Jonas Malheiro Savimbi and Holden Roberto earned 40 and 2.1 percent of the vote, respectively. The National Assembly election manifested a proportionally similar split, with the MPLA capturing 129 seats, UNITA winning 70, the FNLA earning 5, and the remaining 16 seats garnered by an assortment of small parties.[60] Angolans hoped their newly elected leaders could unite the country and end the war. Nonetheless, fighting between government forces and UNITA resumed after the elections.

As the price of crude dipped in 1994, the government acceded to IMF demands for privatization. President dos Santos simply distributed state-owned enterprises to favored party members, government officials, and military officers (Aguilar 2003). Oil prices remained low in 1995; Angola signed a Staff Monitored Programme (SMP) with the IMF as a measure of good faith. In an effort to comply with IMF conditionalities, the government devalued the currency by introducing a readjusted kwanza at the rate of 1 to 1,000 kwanzas and designed two laws on foreign investment to qualify.[61] Yet an economist remarked that Angola's laws still "reflect[ed] the mentality of a planned economy" as well as "the patrimonialism of Portuguese colonial rule, in which administration was essentially negotiation, bargaining and contracting about privileges rather than a comprehensible rational legal order" (Rosenn 1997:5). The price of oil stabilized after the signature of the 1995 SMP, and Angola abandoned planned reforms.

A sharp decline in crude prices drove the government back to the IMF in 1998. The war with UNITA had reached a crucial stage and funding shortfalls were complicating the government's military purchases. The IMF considered Luanda's few reforms insufficient for negotiation of an SMP. Ultimately, the government used oil to bail itself out. Sonangol auctioned off the country's ultra-deepwater concessions in 1999, which raised more than $900 million from signature bonuses.

International oil prices rose substantially in 1999 and 2000.[62] Still, the government calculated that rising crude prices would not cover interest payments on existing oil-backed loans or continued war efforts before revenues from new deepwater production reached state coffers in late 2007.[63] Officials in Luanda signed another SMP in April 2000, vowing to cut more state subsidies, submit to an audit of the oil sector, and make public accounts more transparent. The government negotiated an extension of the SMP in 2001 with a promise to implement the transparency policies requisite for loans (Neto 2003). In January 2002, the IMF recognized the government's failure to implement adequate transparency mechanisms and invalidated the SMP.

In April 2002, Angola's war officially ended. Government and UNITA leaders signed a memorandum of understanding at Luena, a town in Moxico province. Deputy Minister of Finance Eduardo Severim de Morais expressed hope that the IMF would ease its lending requirements in recognition of Angola's newfound peace. "We believe that thirty years of war were too high a price to pay by the people and that shock measures will add to the misery and poverty of Angolans," said Morais (*Angola Peace Monitor* 2004). The IMF did not back down on its requirements for transparency. Instead, the institution redefined the SMP as a means to encourage accountability in Angola.[64]

Pressing for Transparency

The IMF representative in Angola, Carlos Leite, recognized a window of opportunity to promote transparency *before* 2007, when new deepwater oil revenues would flow into government coffers (Melby 2003). International donors joined the IMF in demanding transparency reform. The timing was perfect. Angola planned to hold an international donor conference to raise the monies needed for postwar reconstruction efforts in 2003.[65] International donors felt frustrated with the government's lack of transparency and consistent failure to invest oil revenues in social services. Now that the war had ended, the donors considered it appropriate that the government stop relying on humanitarian agencies to provide for the populace. UK Representative Jeremy Greenstock announced to the Security Council that the UN Consolidated Inter-Agency Appeal's funding needs of $233 million could be fulfilled with three weeks' worth of oil revenues (UN 2002). After Global Witness released a report revealing that $1.7 billion had disappeared from the Angolan treasury each year between 1997 and 2001, donors resented the government's unwillingness to contribute to emergency feeding programs serving one million undernourished Angolans.

The donors made the postwar fundraising conference contingent upon the Angolan government's visible commitment to transparency. When the country's foreign reserves dropped from over $1 billion in July 2002 to $100-$200 million in February 2003, the government made some concessions (ICG 2003). Arvind Ganesan of Human Rights Watch, a leader in the movement for Angolan transparency, acknowledged that "Angola has made some positive steps," but he cautioned that while the government has reformed systems "to account for incoming money, [officials] have done less to account for how they spend the money, or where it goes" (IRIN 2004b).[66] Ultimately, more immediate problems in tsunami-affected areas of Indonesia and Sri Lanka turned donors' attention away from Angola before substantial gains in transparency could be made.

Rising oil prices also alleviated pressure on the Angolan government. In 2004, windfall profits generated $600 million in unexpected oil revenues (IRIN 2005c). The government received a record $10 billion in oil revenues in 2005. Although leaders did not reveal how much, they used a substantial portion of these funds as collateral for oil-backed loans to finance the country's external debt (IRIN 2004b).

Private and bilateral oil-backed loans also helped the government skirt calls for transparency. A group of European banks headed by BNP Paribas guaranteed the Angolan government $1 billion on oil collateral, while Sonangol negotiated a $2.5 billion oil-backed loan from Standard Chartered Bank the following year (Financial Times 2004a, 2004b). China's Eximbank also granted Angola a $2 billion oil-backed loan in 2004 and offered a separate $1 billion oil-backed loan in 2005.[67] According to the UN, "foreign credit and high oil prices allowed Angola to double its budget spending in 2006 to over $23 billion, compared with just $13 billion in 2005" (IRIN 2006b). Awash in windfall oil revenues and borrowed cash, the Angolan government cancelled all negotiations with the IMF in 2007.[68]

A VISCOUS COMMODITY

Petro-capitalism denotes an oil-dependent, exclusionary system of wealth creation and distribution. It is expressed through patterns of governance predicated on serving and preserving the interests of a powerful ruling class. Angolan subsidies—which essentially underwrite elites' education abroad rather than improve local schools—evidence this system.

The viscous quality of crude oil provides metaphoric insight into how the commodity seeps into institutions through petrodollar patronage networks designed to solidify the regime's continued access to oil revenues. Nevertheless, oil is not an intrinsically accursed resource that conceived the Angolan political economy in its slick image. Rather, a suite of political, structural, and geopolitical factors molded the Angolan variety of petro-capitalism. The structure of the sector itself, particularly the intricacies of the confidential concession contracts and the massive investments required for offshore extraction, contributes to an enclave model of production. The enclave enables the exclusionary distribution of oil revenues and heightens struggles over resource control.

For decades, Angolan leaders used war as a pretext for further state centralization and rule without accountability. The World Bank, IMF, and international donors focused on transparency as the means to improve governance, seeking to induce commitments during periods in which oil prices had fallen, but rising oil prices and oil-backed loans enabled the government to skirt calls for transparency. Still, transparency does not address the foundational assumption of the World Bank's neoliberal model for investment: that wealth will trickle down. Without addressing the central concern of redistribution of wealth, Angolan petro-capitalism will remain unchanged and the ruling party will retain its grip on power at any cost.

3. Petro-Violence

Waves charged toward the Cabo Ledo shoreline, breaking with violent explosions of sea foam. The thunderous roar of the waves drowned out the sounds on the promontory above, where Special Forces divisions of the Angolan army conducted training exercises from a former Portuguese military base. Portugal abandoned its military bases in Angola when the colonial power granted independence to its overseas territories in 1975. As Portuguese soldiers withdrew, new waves of violence swept across Angola propelled by petro-capitalism's insidious cousin: petro-violence.

Petro-violence describes the conflicts funded by oil revenues and struggles over control of oil reserves, but it also encompasses the biophysical violence wrought on ecosystems at the site of extraction (Watts 1994). Oil revenues backed the Angolan government's war effort to the tune of $500 million each year between 1993 and 2000 (Aguilar 2001). Still, "how a war is paid for is not equivalent to what caused a war" (Cramer 2002). Regional differences, foreign intervention, and ideological divides shaped the myriad forms of violence in Angola just as much as oil.

This chapter continues the discussion of the resource curse in the last chapter by examining the relationship of oil to particular forms of violence in Angola. The first section explores how internal schemes and international interventions to gain control of Angola's oilfields sustained and intensified violence. It reflects Soares de Oliveira's assertions about violence in Angola, namely that "the power of the state to kill has not been undermined by its lack of power or willingness to do just about everything else" and that "this power is more or less consistently deployed to protect and maximize resource extraction" (2007:112). The second section illustrates the ways in which pollution associated with extraction begets environmental violence, undermining resource-based livelihoods in extractive zones. Consideration of the biophysical form of petro-violence may seem contentious, but community-level studies have articulated pollution associated with extraction as a form of environmental violence (Watts 2001; Peluso and Watts 2001:23).[1]

RESOURCE OF VIOLENCE

Violence in oil-dependent states is often characterized as evidence of another facet of the resource curse.[2] States possessing valuable natural resources are more likely to suffer from civil wars and secessionist conflicts than their resource-poor counterparts (Collier and Hoeffler 1998, 2002, 2004; Collier 2000; Ross 1999). They also tend to be more repressive and less democratic (Ross 2001). Peluso and Watts (2001) dispute theories that view natural resources as a trigger for violence, while acknowledging tendencies toward conflict in geographical areas containing strategic and valuable resources. They caution that environmental violence must be analyzed within the context of constitutive power structures and political-economic processes. Watts further stresses how "oil's contribution to war or authoritarianism builds upon pre-existing (pre-oil) political dynamics" (Watts 2004:26). In this spirit, the following subsections avoid generalizations correlating oil's existence with particular forms of violence. Rather, they explore specific forms of petro-violence in Angola, examining the relationships between the disputants and their violent environments in three types of conflict: secession, civil war, and repression.

Defining Autonomy

Resource theorists ascribe both Cabindan appeals for independence and the Angolan government's refusal to relinquish Cabinda as a function of the territory's resource endowments. One scholar, citing 2001 production rates, noted that Cabinda's "strategic importance as the source of about two-thirds of Angola's oil production is almost certainly the main motive for separatism and also an iron clad reason why the government, whether controlled by the MPLA, UNITA or any other non-Cabindan party or ruler, would never consider letting the province secede" (Hodges 2003:159).[3] Another theorist contends that capital-intensive extraction of a "point resource" in a region distant from the "center of control" is predisposed to secessionist struggles (Le Billon 2001b). He postulates that calls for secession intensify when people in the extractive zones perceive the distant government as colluding with extractive interests without distributing resource wealth to local populations or offsetting ecological costs associated with extraction (ibid.:570).

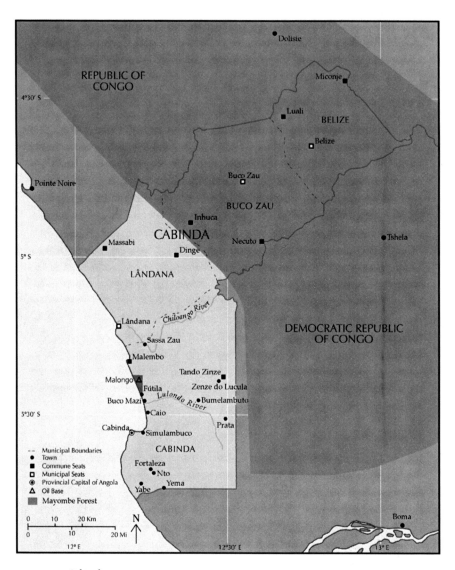

MAP 5. Cabinda

Whether termed secession or independence, Frente para a Libertação do Enclave de Cabinda (FLEC) is the entity striving for Cabinda's sovereignty. Proponents of the resource curse attribute Cabindans' allegiance to FLEC as evidence of a romantic, idealized belief that local leaders would better respect local entitlements and distribute revenues more evenly than the central government (Collier and Hoeffler 2002). It is difficult to know how FLEC would manage the oil revenues, but most Cabindans believe it could do no worse than the Angolan government. More than romantic ideals, Cabindan sympathies for FLEC are a real form of resistance, a challenge to the MPLA's exclusionary form of rule. Since oil fuels exclusion, Cabindans and FLEC have come to *identify* their struggle as about oil.[4] Still, they base their fundamental claims on more than oilfields. While many Cabindans employ oil imagery to add luster to their arguments, they articulate the foundation of their struggle for independence on a history of separate rule.

Whereas contiguous Angola south of the Congo River was a colony of Portugal, the 1885 Treaty of Simulambuco defined Cabinda as a protectorate.[5] After prolonged bargaining, Cabindan rulers accepted the Portuguese as their protectors and negotiated with them as equals (Luemba 2005a).[6] Portugal disregarded the distinction and subsumed Cabinda under the administration of Angola in 1956.[7] Four years later, the struggle for Cabindan independence formally began with the formation of the Movimento de Libertação do Enclave de Cabinda (MLEC).[8] Largely representing the coastal region, MLEC joined forces with Cabindans in the forested interior to create FLEC in 1963.[9] FLEC declared Cabinda a singular entity from the coast to the interior and maintained that Cabindans possessed political, social, and cultural institutions distinct from those of Angola. FLEC emphasized that Portugal's disparate treatment of Cabinda affirmed this difference.[10] In 1964, the Organization of African Unity recognized Cabinda as an autonomous entity, separate from Angola.[11]

FLEC issued reports to the international community stating that "Angolan and Portuguese imperialists were murdering, terrorizing and arresting people" in Cabinda (Marcum 1978:125). In response, one FLEC faction renounced the movement's founding principle of nonviolence to form the Junta Militar de Cabinda and confront the Portuguese, MPLA, and FNLA with arms (Luemba 2008.)[12] MPLA forces had begun anti-colonial military incursions against the Portuguese in Cabinda because competing FNLA forces had decimated their squadrons in the Dembos region to the northeast of Luanda and because Cabinda's strategic location offered opportunities for training new recruits.[13] MPLA leaders established a military base across the border at Dolisie in Congo-Brazzaville from which they planned raids on Portuguese posts in Cabinda.[14] The MPLA sent many inexperienced soldiers to the Second Military Front in Cabinda—President dos Santos even served there in his youth. Botched operations and poor reception instilled a lingering sense of resentment toward Cabindans in some of the young MPLA fighters stationed in Cabinda.[15]

Gulf Oil's announcement of major offshore oil discoveries in 1966 drew hopeful Cabindan refugees back in search of jobs and increased the visibility of FLEC.[16] Accessing Cabinda's oil wealth was not FLEC's primary intent for pursuing independence, but the movement did leverage the interests of collaborators—such as the French oil firm Elf and Zairean President Mobutu Sese Seko—in the territory's resources.[17] The discovery of oil in Cabinda emboldened both FLEC's suitors and adversaries. Following Gulf Oil's announcement, the MPLA abandoned its original conception of Cabinda as an autonomous state in a federalist Angolan system in favor of a unitary Angolan state with Cabinda fully subsumed under the centralized party leadership. Historians presume that Gulf Oil encouraged the MPLA leadership to consider the latter approach because the corporation feared that the FNLA's associates at Elf might challenge its holdings in Cabinda (Mabeko-Tali 2001b).

Once production began, revenues from Gulf Oil deepened Portugal's pockets and its resolve to hold on to Cabinda and Angola. Colonial rulers in Portugal watched the Angolan treasury's oil revenues jump from $11 million in 1969 to $61 million in 1972 (Harsch and Thomas 1976:19; Marcum 1978:423).[18] When the Arab-Israeli Yom Kippur war sent oil prices soaring in 1973, returns from Cabindan oil reached $400 million (Marcum 1978:237). Revenues from Cabinda's oilfields provided up to 60 percent of the funding for Portugal's repressive counter-insurgency campaigns in the early 1970s (Laidi 1990).[19] In April 1974, the prospects for independence appeared grim. The Portuguese army had 60,000 troops in the region, including 24,000 African soldiers, and a fleet of sophisticated American aircraft. Nevertheless, on April 25, 1974, a military coup led by soldiers with red carnations in the barrels of their rifles toppled the Caetano regime in Lisbon, brought General António Spínola to power, and promised freedom to all of the Portuguese overseas territories.

Nationalist sentiment and expectations of autonomy swelled in Cabinda (Marcum 1978:205).[20] Meanwhile, Spínola colluded with Zaire's President Mobutu and FNLA leader Holden Roberto on plans for a Zaire-Angola-Cabinda federation. Under this model, Mobutu and Roberto would jointly rule Angola and FLEC would control Cabinda, on the condition that all FLEC leaders take orders from Spínola and Mobutu (Ignatyev 1977:105, MacQueen 1997:167).[21]

Admiral Rosa Coutinho replaced Spínola on September 30, 1974. Coutinho favored Agostinho Neto's MPLA and planned a new course of decolonization envisioning Cabinda as part of a unitary Angolan state.[22] Under Coutinho's direction, colonial administrators banned FLEC. Hundreds of

MPLA troops occupied Cabinda on November 2, 1974; Portuguese soldiers either idly stood by or joined MPLA Commander Pédalé's forces (Tati 2002; Marcum 1978:254). The Portuguese army arrested Cabinda's governor, FLEC sympathizer Brigadier Themudo Barata, and replaced him with MPLA booster Colonel Lopes Alves. The French-Lebanese mercenary Jean-Kay and Alexandre Taty—of the previously formed Junta Militar faction—convinced mainstream FLEC leaders to create a formal military wing (Marcum 1978:254). Still, FLEC militants failed to stop the MPLA advance and retreated to Zaire.[23]

At the start of 1975, the MPLA publicly proclaimed its intention to annex Cabinda to the Angolan territory (Luemba 2008). On January 15, 1975, MPLA, FNLA, and UNITA representatives collectively signed the Alvor Accord on independence from Portugal and agreed to a transitional government devised in advance with Portuguese authorities.[24] With neither Cabindan consent nor representation, the group ratified the independence agreement, which recognized Cabinda as "an integral and indivisible part of Angola."[25]

FLEC denounced the accords and pleaded for support at the Organization of African Unity.[26] Premier Henri Lopez of Congo affirmed Cabinda's right to self-determination and one week later Mobutu, expressing similar sentiments, called for a referendum in Cabinda (Marcum 1978:437). To counter protests, the MPLA began a witch hunt of FLEC and its supporters in Cabinda, committing numerous human rights abuses including arbitrary detentions, summary executions, public shootings, and forced removal to labor camps in Bentiaba and Kibala (Tati 2002).

MPLA soldiers also targeted all remaining FNLA and UNITA soldiers in Cabinda, assuming complete military control over the oil-rich territory by mid-June 1975.[27] Fidel Castro sent Angola a squadron of 9 MiG-17Fs in December 1975, which President Neto routed directly to General Ramon Espinoza Martin's operation in Cabinda (Klaus 2003). Cuban soldiers guarded the perimeter of Cabinda's major oil base at Malongo. The MPLA recognized the importance of securing and protecting Cabindan oilfields. Although the country's crude oil production averaged only 157,770 barrels per day in 1975, Cabinda contributed 84.8 percent of the total (Biro 1976:1814).

Cabindans rejected the MPLA's occupation. They reasserted that their territory was not part of Angola and reiterated their right to self-determination, but the international community stood silent. Three decades later, many Cabindans still refuse to relinquish their desires for independence. Some say that FLEC guerrillas deep within Cabinda's forested interior continue to fight for their liberation.

Bleeding a Nation

Angola's twenty-seven-year post-independence conflict is best described as an internationalized civil war because both international and internal interests played a role in continuing the conflict.[28] Scholars often divide the war into two distinct periods divided by the fall of the Soviet Bloc. The first period began in 1975 as a fight between the three former liberation fronts: the MPLA, the FNLA, and UNITA. Cold War rivals propped up the opposing forces. The United States backed the FNLA until its demise and then joined with South Africa to support UNITA, while the USSR and Cuba supported the MPLA.[29]

UNITA recognized the strategic value of Cabindan oil revenues to the MPLA-led government in Luanda during the 1980s. The forces of UNITA leader Jonas Savimbi bombed an oil pipeline near the Cabindan town of Chimbolo on the night of July 14, 1984, killing nine persons—including two pregnant women—sleeping in a nearby house (MIPT 2005).[30] Savimbi's men struck again on July 21, 1985, shooting down a Chevron helicopter and killing its occupants. They sabotaged a Cabindan oil pipeline the following year (MIPT 2005; Gunn 1987:60). UNITA's South African allies also organized an attack on the oil storage tanks at Chevron's Malongo base. On May 19, 1985, Captain Wynand du Toit led a South African commando unit of 9 men equipped with 135 kilograms of TNT contact mines, 2 larger mines, and several plastic explosives to the base (Castro 1985). The commandos also carried propaganda, intending to leave UNITA pamphlets amidst the tanks' ruins, but MPLA forces captured the team before any damage was done and exposed the South African role in the sabotage plot (Gunn 1987:60).[31]

The U.S. government's support of UNITA put Chevron in an awkward and dangerous position. President Ronald Reagan criticized Chevron's friendly business relations with the "Marxist" MPLA government and the protection afforded to the Malongo installation by Cuban soldiers as contravening his support for UNITA.[32] He pressured Chevron to sell 20 percent of its interests in the Cabindan oilfields to the Italian firm Agip in 1986. Nonetheless, Chevron Overseas Petroleum's president professed an eagerness to expand operations in Angola.[33]

Cold War alliances intensified the battle for control of Angola until the fall of the Soviet Union in 1989. The number of Cuban soldiers in Angola peaked at 55,000 in 1987 during the battle of Cuito Cuanavale. A 1988 ceasefire and the ensuing New York Accords initiated the withdrawal of Cuban and South African troops. After losing Soviet sponsorship and

Cuban military support, the MPLA led Angola's transition from a socialist model of governance to a capitalist liberal democratic system.[34] In 1992, a temporary peace under the Bicesse Accords enabled multiparty elections. President dos Santos received a democratic mandate but Savimbi rejected his electoral defeat, and Angola returned to war.[35] This time, "there was no question of the Angolan war being about ideology or about anybody's freedom. It was about money" (Pearce 2005:155). MPLA leaders, army generals, and their partners in war enriched themselves through provisions contracts, land grabs, and illicit arms deals.[36] The terminology of conflict had also changed; it was no longer the MPLA's army fighting against UNITA but the government's Forças Armadas Angolanas (FAA) against the UNITA rebels. The new labels international observers applied reflected their altered perspective on the war more than any dramatic change on the battlefield (Messiant 2003). These interpretive shifts underscore the fact that history is also a narrative.[37]

The means by which both parties to the conflict financed their military operations had also changed. Angola's internationalized civil war had become a resource war. Without funds from their former allies, Savimbi and President dos Santos turned to their respective resources—UNITA's alluvial diamonds and the MPLA-led government's oil—to fuel the fight. Each sought to sever his opponent's access to resource wealth. In January 1993, UNITA destroyed storage tanks holding 400,000 barrels of crude worth an estimated $12 million dollars at Soyo's Quinfuquena oil terminal, which processed some 90,000 barrels of oil per day from onshore fields and offshore Blocks 1 and 2 (EIA 1995). Savimbi's forces were unable to reach most offshore platforms for lack of naval capacity. UNITA spared Elf's Block 3, which produced 160,000 barrels of oil per day, yet succeeded in shelling Texaco's shallow-water platform in Block 2 from shore in May 1993 (ibid.).[38] Texaco resumed activities in Block 2 after rerouting loading activities from Quinfuquena to Lombo East. Nevertheless, reports cited "proximity to UNITA rebels engaged in the ongoing civil war" as justification for the postponement of drilling activities in these blocks from 1993 to 1994 (*World Oil* 1993:104; *World Oil* 1995:112).

The government fought back, using oil revenues to pay between $2,000 and $8,000 in monthly salaries to private military contractors—many of whom hailed from the South African forces once allied with UNITA (Maier 1996:156, 159).[39] Private military contractors including MPRI, AirScan, Ango-Segu, Defence Systems Limited (DSL), and Executive Outcomes defended strategic sites, retook Soyo, and seized the alluvial diamond fields from UNITA.[40] Meanwhile, government officials successfully lobbied the

UN to institute a ban on diamond trading with UNITA, arguing that the trade fueled conflict. This ban led to the Kimberley process, which restricts trade in blood diamonds through mechanisms designed to track the stones from origin to destination.[41]

As UNITA searched for new sources of income in the late 1990s, increases in oil revenues and signature bonuses of $935 million on new ultra-deepwater concessions gave the government the upper hand (Hodges 2003). These funds enabled the government to increase security expenditures in 1998 by earmarking one-quarter of the budget for "defense and home affairs services" while continuing to ignore appeals for health and education (UPASC 1997b). Reverend Daniel Ntoni-Nzinga, an esteemed Baptist minister and a vital actor in Angola's growing peace movement, pointed out the disparate treatment of the oil and diamond sectors. Like diamonds, Angola's oil contributed to war and misery, but the UN did not create a process to track crude from its origin to the gas tank. The Reverend commented, "You talk about blood diamonds, this was blood oil" (Melby 2003:25).

Government forces ultimately won military control of Angola by implementing a scorched-earth tactic called *limpeza*—a clean-up strategy based on "systematically evacuating the areas of the countryside where UNITA was in control" leaving "no one to farm the land [so] there would be no food for UNITA's soldiers" (Pearce 2005:54). The Angolan Armed Forces razed crops, destroyed villages, and cut off supply of basic goods like salt and medicines, ultimately forcing UNITA supporters to abandon their allegiances and seek survival in government-controlled refugee camps (ibid:66). In 2002, surveillance planes tracking Savimbi tipped off FAA troops in Moxico province. The government soldiers ambushed the UNITA leader on February 22, riddling his body with fifteen bullets. On April 4, 2002, representatives of UNITA and the government signed the Luena Memorandum of Understanding, officially ending Angola's twenty-seven-year civil war.

After decades of conflict, Angolan leaders are arguably more experienced in violence than governance. The war left as deep and damaging a mark on Angola's political institutions as the landscape. Four thousand landmine fields pepper the provinces of Huambo, Bié, Cuando Cubango, and Malanje, and anti-vehicle mines deter passage on 70 percent of Angolan roads (ANGOP 2004i; *Los Angeles Times* 2004). International teams work determinedly to free the countryside of unexploded mines. Five to ten million small arms and light weapons remain in the hands of one-third of the Angolan population; these are often employed in violent acts of "survival through crime and banditry" (IRIN 2004j; Mvemba 2003).[42] The government implemented a disarmament campaign to encourage former soldiers and citizens to relinquish illegally owned guns and ammunition.

While NGOs de-mine the landscape and the government disarms the population, oil-hungry allies like the United States and China supply the Angolan Armed Forces with additional military training and weapons. As oil becomes scarcer, Michael Klare argues that access to and control over foreign oilfields will increasingly dominate the military objectives of industrialized economies dependent upon fossil fuels, especially the United States (Klare 2001).[43] The September 11, 2001, attacks on New York and Washington spurred American interest in utilizing and protecting oil sources located outside the Middle East.[44] The United States turned to Africa: a region accounting for 12 percent of the world's oil production in 2008 and expected to supply 25 percent by 2025 (EABW 2008; Klare 2004). Three months after the 9/11 terrorist attacks, the U.S. Coast Guard transferred the first of seven ships to the Nigerian navy to contribute to a patrolling and protection program aimed at securing oil resources in the Gulf of Guinea (*Semanário Angolense* 2003e). The Gulf of Guinea flanks some of Africa's largest oil-producing countries such as Nigeria, Angola, Equatorial Guinea, and Gabon.[45]

Angola ranks sixth on the list of oil suppliers to the United States at rates of 496,000 barrels per day (EIA 2007). The United States is keen to claim a larger proportion of Angola's oil, but the American earmark seems to be shrinking. Angola shipped 40 to 50 percent of its oil to the United States in 2004, whereas, in the previous decade the U.S. market received 71 percent (IRIN 2005b; WB 2005:52; Caley 1996). Strong bilateral ties are crucial to ensuring that Angola directs its oil to the United States, especially given that China imports 25 to 30 percent of Angola's oil production and has no qualms about lending billions to Angolan leaders despite transparency concerns (Eisenman 2006; IRIN 2005b).[46]

Military cooperation not only secures the source of U.S. oil imports, but also strengthens relations between the two countries. Between 2002 and 2004, Nigeria and Angola received nearly $300 million in American security aid, including surplus arms distributed through the Pentagon's Excess Defense Articles program (Klare 2004).[47] In May 2004, President dos Santos visited Washington to discuss assistance to Angola with U.S. President George W. Bush, Secretary of State Colin Powell, and members of Congress.[48] Nine days after dos Santos' meeting with Bush, Deputy Assistant Secretary of Defense for African Affairs Theresa Whelan arrived in Luanda to meet with Angolan Armed Forces Chief of Staff General Agostinho

Nelumba "Sanjar" and the Ministry of Defense. The Voice of America radio program quoted Whelan expressing her country's interest in "improving the military relationships and common interests between the two nations" (VoA 2004b). Oil is undeniably one of those common interests.

Repressing Rights

War-weariness and fear of state-sponsored repression prevent Angolans from challenging government misrule. Repression is the mainstay of Angolan governance. As in many petro-states, oil-enriched budgets facilitate vast expenditures to maintain internal security, what scholars term the "repression effect" (Ross 2001). Despite the war's end, Angola's "Defense and Order" line item actually increased from 12.5 percent of the state budget in 2004 to 17.9 percent in 2005 (GoA 2004).[49] Although budgetary allocations reflect spending priorities, numbers cannot adequately illustrate how the government employs Defense and Order spending to perpetuate a climate of fear. Freedom of expression has improved since the socialist period, but many Angolans allude to vestiges of the MPLA's old repressive security and information apparatus. They take care in how and with whom they share their thoughts.[50]

President dos Santos uses the national police, presidential guard, rapid intervention police, and national army to threaten critics and silence adversaries. From car washers to political candidates, Angolans critical of the dos Santos regime have suffered violent deaths. Members of the elite presidential guard tortured and killed car washer Arsénio Sebastião—a.k.a. rapper MCK—in retribution for his popular song "Technique, Causes, and Consequences" featuring the lyrics "we export oil and import suffering" and "the cause of Angolan suffering is born out of the philosophy of dehumanization" (Marques 2004e; Marques 2003a). They dragged the twenty-seven-year-old to the beach where they stabbed him, tied his hands with bootlaces, and left him to drown while threatening to shoot any bystanders who dared intervene.[51] Eight guardsmen stood trial on charges of illegal detention, torture, and execution, but the court acquitted them all (BDHRL 2004).

Under more mysterious circumstances, a politician died on July 2, 2004: the same day he publicly criticized dos Santos for delaying elections. Nfulumpinga Landu Victor was an outspoken civil society advocate, opposition parliamentarian, and presidential candidate with the Democratic Party for Progress—Angolan National Alliance (PDP-ANA). On the very evening Landu Victor vociferously challenged President dos Santos, three unidentified men assassinated him (Marques 2004a). The government claimed it was a carjacking. Noting previous acts of persecution, however, PDP-ANA's secretary general commented, "We believe without a doubt this act was ordered by the ruling MPLA" (IRIN 2004c).

Interpreting fact from fiction is difficult because state-sponsored repression has also undermined Angola's free press. The substance of news reports varies according to the source. The government newspaper refers to President José Eduardo dos Santos as JES, as if he were the first half of the second coming, whereas independent papers offer more critical perspectives. Angolan journalists are regularly paid to write pro-government stories and are harassed, beaten, detained, kept under surveillance, or actively investigated when they do not (BDHRL 2005). During the war, police questioned reporters who had criticized "draft evasion by those whose families could afford to send them abroad to study" and pressed their editors for the stories' sources (AI 1999).

The judiciary also keeps unruly reporters in check. Angolan courts charged journalist Rafael Marques with libel and violations of state security for criticizing President dos Santos in an article entitled "The Lipstick of Dictatorship."[52] Judge Joaquim de Abreu Cangato, an ex-Angolan secret police agent with no legal training, slapped Marques with a heavy fine and sentenced him to prison for six months.[53] The court also awarded $1,200 to Minister of Defense Kundy Paihama, one of five government and MPLA officials who brought defamation charges against *Semanário Angolense* editor Felisberto de Graça Campos for an article listing the fifty-nine richest Angolans.[54] The *Semanário Angolense* article insinuated that General Paihama and other millionaires on the list had engaged in corruption— whether by using their positions to earn favors or by siphoning off public funds to augment low government salaries.[55]

Access to information in Angola is restricted by geography and income. Angola's press law restricts private radio from broadcasting nationally. Therefore, the reach of critical media, such as the Catholic Church's *Rádio Ecclesia,* is confined to Luanda. Rural communities get information through the state-run *Rádio Nacional de Angola* and the daily *Jornal de Angola.* As governor of Huíla, General Kundy Paihama prohibited the local sale of independent newspapers such as *Agora, Folha 8,* and *Comércio Actualidade* because they featured unfavorable reviews of government policy (HRW 1998). Poorer households unable to afford a satellite and $720 in annual reception fees receive only government programming on *Televisão Pública de Angola.*[56]

A strong national military functions as an arm of the repressive state, inspiring fear and keeping protest in check. Angola has the second-largest standing army in Southern Africa and its soldiers are considered a powerful component of the African Union's peacekeeping force.[57] The FAA boasts 117,500 to 150,000 troops; 100,000 armed soldiers in thirty regiments constitute the army and 6,500 combatants form the Air Force (Davidson 2003). The troops are experienced fighters from long years of internal conflict and international battles in neighboring states. Angola's Air Force is also regarded as one of the best in sub-Saharan Africa, boasting a fleet of MiG-21s and MiG-24s from the days of Soviet support, as well as more recent acquisitions of Sukoi SU-27 and SU-24 planes (ibid).

The Angolan model, as James Ferguson has theorized, credits private security companies with securing extractive enclaves. Nonetheless, the Angolan army—together with allied forces like the Cuban military—has also played a strategic role in securing and protecting the extractive zones. In 2002, President dos Santos sent FAA troops to Cabinda as part of an effort to secure the onshore territory for extractive purposes. Personal and professional relationships link the FAA to private security companies. General Fernando Garcia Miala (a former FAA general and one-time head of Angolan national security and foreign intelligence) partnered with Santana André Pitra "Petroff" (the ex-minister of interior and general commander of the Angolan national police) to found Teleservice, the ubiquitous private security firm contracted to protect most of Angola's oil installations (Guardiola 2005). Most Teleservice guards are recruited from the Angolan national police and armed forces (WIN 2001).

The Angola model emphasizes the role of the enclave in helping transnational oil corporations withstand petro-violence. From within the protected confines of the enclave, corporations often contribute to petro-violence in the extractive zones. They can have a catalytic effect by creating opportunities for confrontation with military forces and, as in Nigeria and Colombia, even a direct effect by purchasing weapons for security forces (Pegg 2003). Local conflict benefits oil corporations when it drives up world oil prices or improves profit margins associated with risk.[58] Gulf Oil allegedly leveraged violence in Cabinda "as a means of extracting better advantage from contract negotiations" in 1977 (Marcum 1978:446).

DEGRADED ECOSYSTEMS, DEGRADED LIVELIHOODS

The degradation of ecosystems at the site of oil extraction—whether from accidental oil spills or intentional releases of toxic chemicals—represents a form of petro-violence equally dangerous to military and paramilitary violence. The costs and benefits of Angola's oil are distributed unevenly between a wealthy, seemingly impervious minority and the destitute, vulnerable majority. Fishing and farming communities suffer the additional costs of degradation in the extractive zones. In these contested spaces, disputes over extraction set the traditional subsistence rights of resource users in competition with the rights of the nation to benefit from the extraction of their natural resource heritage (Watts 1999).[59] To fishers and farmers, environmental struggles are commensurate with struggles over livelihoods (Peet and Watts 1996; Blaikie 1999; Bryant 1999).

Given the fluidity of the marine environment, fishers in Soyo and Cabinda are often unable to demonstrate the damage from offshore oil production on their activities. Unlike pollution from onshore oil production, environmental pollution from offshore spills, pipeline leaks, and processed water disposal may be dispersed by wave action and tides or absorbed by organisms before a community can visually detect harm or claim compensation for damages.[60] A single slick can spread quickly across the ocean surface and devastate multiple fishing communities. The nomadic nature of fish also exacerbates the effects of offshore pollution. Pelagic species frequenting contaminated platforms far from shore may be caught during forays into shallower water. Moreover, predatory fish may accumulate toxic levels of pollutants because the effects of contamination are magnified as they proceed up the food chain.

The effects of pollution associated with offshore oil reach deep into fishing communities. Contamination decreases the abundance and health of local fish; fishers and fish traders grapple with unsustainable livelihoods. In their desperation, they compete to catch and sell whatever fish remain—including juveniles and slow-reproducing species, like sharks. Their destructive anxiety reflects the degradation of fishing cultures in polluted, impoverished environments.

The environment and cultural practices are inextricably linked in resource-dependent communities. Kids grow up pushing the boats to shore, but with dwindling stocks their fishing futures are questionable. Even meals are uncertain for families who depend upon fish for sustenance. With so much insecurity, alcoholism and drug use rise, exacerbating internal conflicts. Traumatic stress syndromes, substance abuse, depression, and discord between friends and family are all common in resource-dependent communities struggling to cope with oil spills (Ott 2005). Monetary compensation distributed by the corporations responsible for pollution is an important first step toward recompense; however, money alone cannot begin to offset these damages, it only encourages dependency on oil corporations rather than supporting independent livelihoods.

Darkening Clouds

Environmental degradation is a form of petro-violence linked to oil extraction both on land and at sea. Nevertheless, key differences between onshore and offshore degradation govern their effects on local communities. Like the noxious fumes associated with gas flaring, a practice common to both production modalities, offshore oil spills are not easily contained. Half a liter of oil spilled in water can cover 4,047 m² of surface area.[61] As such, offshore spills have the capacity to degrade a wider area and affect a greater number of people. Whom they affect depends upon the spill's location. Artisanal fishermen are hurt most by spills close to shore, while accidents farther from shore are likely to damage the catch of semi-industrial and industrial fishermen as well as international fleets. A fishing community's ability to claim compensation for damages generally decreases in proportion to a spill's distance from shore. Nonetheless, even if an oil spill occurs far from shore, slicks can spread quickly with wind and wave action.

Studies of the marine environment in northern Angola indicate "the bulk of contamination is caused by oil activities" (Neto 1997). Oxygen deficiencies in the Congo Basin, which may be attributed to pollution associated with oil extraction, have resulted in high mortality of fish eggs, reduced recruitment rates, and diminishing numbers of fish stocks in Cabinda and Zaire provinces (GoA 2001:108). More studies are needed to elucidate the causal linkages. Regardless, the effects of oil exploration, development, production, and transport are known to seriously damage the health of local ecosystems and communities. The following analysis relies on the environmental advocate Dwight Holing's comprehensive review of environmental externalities associated with the offshore oil industry to highlight the dangers associated with each phase.

Exploration and development. During the exploration phase, operators emit a series of high-intensity and low-frequency sounds into the marine environment in order to develop graphic representations of subterranean oil reservoirs. Some 15 to 45 air guns used in the process fire shots every 10 to 25 seconds for weeks at a time, representing "the most severe acoustic insult to the marine environment . . . short of naval warfare," said Dr. Chris Clarke, director of the Bioacoustics Research Program at Cornell University (OFC 2006b). Seismic testing and noise pollution associated with oil exploration and production can disturb whale and turtle migrations, damage the auditory capacity of certain fish species, harm shellfish, fish eggs and fry, and drive fish away (Holing 1990:30). One study showed a decline of over

52 percent in total catch after seismic surveying, presumably related to dispersal (Holing 1990:34).

Once seismic surveys are complete, the operator decides where to drill for oil. One oil platform may drill between 70 and 100 wells, discharging more than 90,000 metric tons of drilling waste offshore over the course of operations (OFC 2006a). From a single shallow-water offshore well, operators can generate 1,800 metric tons of waste (Holing 1990:24).[62] The waste falls into two categories: cuttings and fluids. Cuttings are the bits of rock ground up by the drill bit and fluids are the liquids "designed to lubricate and cool the working drill bit and drill pipe, remove cuttings from the bottom of the well, control and regulate pressure, stabilize and seal the sides of the well and prevent accidental blowouts" (OFC 2006c). As the fluids, also referred to as drilling mud, are often recycled throughout the drilling process, cuttings make up a greater proportion of the wastes discharged during the early phases of drilling and more fluids are released in the later stages.[63] The coarser cuttings released during the drilling of a single well can travel up to 1,000 meters from the discharge point and often contain traces of arsenic, cadmium, chromium, copper, mercury, lead, and zinc liberated from the formation. According to Holing, "Drilling wastes disposed on the seafloor suffocate benthic organisms in a pancake of death" and "strip the surrounding water of oxygen" (1990:25).

The composition of drilling fluids influences their environmental impact. Since operators largely phased out oil-based muds during the mid-1990s, water-based and synthetic varieties are favored. Synthetic-based muds are less soluble in the offshore environment and more expensive, so water-based barite ($BaSO_4$) versions are commonly used.[64] To drill one offshore well requires 1,000 to 5,000 cubic meters of water-based drilling mud and, once discharged, the finely ground particles of barite from the fluid can travel up to 8,000 meters from a well (OFC 2006a).

U.S. government data indicate that the disposal of water-based drilling muds containing barite from offshore oil platforms generates islands of contaminated sediments at 100 times natural mercury concentrations and 12 times the mercury safety threshold set by the EPA (Raines and Finch 2002; Raines 2003). U.S. Mineral Management Service statistics show that the oil and gas industry discharges more than 450 million kilograms of mercury-contaminated drilling muds and lubricating fluids into the Gulf annually (GRN 2002).[65] Once the mercury is discharged into the marine environment, microorganisms transform the heavy metal into a more lethal compound called methylmercury. Fish using platforms as "artificial reefs" may become contaminated before they are captured and sold on the market. As mercury moves up the food chain, from microorganisms to snails to shrimp and crabs to small fish up to top predator species and on to people, methylmercury dangerously accumulates.

High concentrations of methylmercury can contribute to fetal birth defects; developmental disabilities and high blood pressure in children; and fatigue, memory loss, neurological damage, and increased risk of heart attack in adults. Methylmercury levels in amberjack, lingcod and, redfish were so high in U.S. Gulf coast states that they could not legally be sold in American supermarkets; up to 40 percent of the Gulf redfish between 16 and 26 inches tested revealed methylmercury concentrations of 1.5 parts per million (Raines 2002).[66] Tuna, king mackerel, swordfish, shark, and tilefish are also known to bioaccumulate dangerously high amounts of methylmercury. Several of the preferred species for consumption in northern Angola's coastal towns—including shark, corvina and grouper—are high enough on the food chain to present a methylmercury risk.

Safer synthetic drilling muds are widely available but more expensive, so operators continue to use water-based drilling fluids containing barite. In 1993, the Environmental Protection Agency limited mercury levels in water-based drilling fluids used in the United States to 1 milligram per kilogram of barite. Still, in areas where law does not prohibit the use of muds with elevated mercury concentrations, operators may not seek low-mercury alternatives. The United Nations Environmental Programme's Global Mercury Assessment cited no legislation relevant to limiting mercury discharges in Angola (UNEP 2002). Regardless of current standards, Angola's offshore environment may already be saturated with mercury from drilling muds used since the 1960s. In recent years, the Angolan oil industry sourced over 100 metric tons of barite annually at a cost of nearly $24 million from the United States, China, Morocco, India, and Mexico.[67]

Production. Flaring, the practice of burning of gases released at the wellhead, damages soil fertility by increasing acidity, decreasing phosphate and nitrate content, and leaving soils scorched and devoid of microbial activity (Denney 2005).[68] The carcinogenic pollutants released by flares can also seriously compromise the health of local communities. More than 250 toxins are released in flares including benzopyrene, benzene, carbon disulphide (CS_2), carbonyl sulphide (COS), and toluene; metals like mercury, arsenic and chromium; sour gas with hydrogen sulfide (H_2S) and sulfur dioxide (SO_2); as well as asthma-causing nitrogen oxides (NOx) and acid rain–producing sulfur oxides (SOx) (CPHA 2000; Holing 1990). A 1986 study in the *Southwestern Alberta Medical Diagnostic Review* detailed the effects of these pollutants associated with flaring on human health, listing symptoms such as "chills, fever, myalgia, respiratory irritation, nausea, vomiting and headaches"; systemic conditions like central nervous system damage, kidney and cardiovascular failure, and neurological disabilities; as well as contributions toward lung cancer, emphysema, and chronic bronchitis, endocrine disruption, immune dysfunction, and reproductive problems (CPHA 2000). Nigeria's Environmental Rights Action documented that flaring in the Bayelsa State in the Niger Delta presumably causes 4,960 cases of respiratory illness in local children, 120,000 asthma attacks, and 8 instances of cancer annually (Kirkland 2005). Pollutants from flares offshore can still affect onshore communities, as these pollutants can travel up to 300 kilometers from the flare site (OFC 2006a).

Oil corporations operating in Africa flare "gas equivalent to twelve times the energy that the continent uses" (EIA 2003). The World Bank reported that Angola accounted for 30 percent of the gas flared in Africa (Sonangol 2004c:20). As Angola's rate of oil production has increased, so has flaring. Estimates suggest that flaring increased from roughly 4 billion cubic meters in 1998 to almost 6.5 billion cubic meters in 2000 (ESMAP 2001:15). Chevron's Block o alone flared approximately 8.5 million cubic meters of associated gases per day in 1999, including up to 1.7 million cubic meters of hydrogen sulfide gas (H_2S) in Area A nearest the Cabindan coast (GPC 1999:22).[69]

The global oil industry is a dirty business. Flares from Chevron's operations spewed 13.4 million metric tons of CO_2-equivalent emissions into the atmosphere in 2005, accounting for one-quarter of the corporation's total greenhouse gas emissions (Chevron 2006a).[70] Flares from sub-Saharan Africa's oil industry emit more greenhouse gas components like carbon dioxide (CO_2) and methane (CH_4) into the environment than any other source on the continent (ERA 2005). Additionally, diesel equipment can generate more than 3,000 kg of NOx per day during well-testing activities alone (Holing 1990:25).

Oil seeps, leaks, and spills release polycyclic aromatic hydrocarbons (PAHs) into the marine environment in high concentrations. Natural oil seeps provided the first hints of Angolan oil reserves to 18th century explorers and they are still occasionally seen in satellite imagery.[71] Nonetheless, leaks and spills of oil associated with production are more common to the Angolan public. Citizens understand the danger of oil spills because these incidents attract attention, but few recognize the cumulative effects of spills or the insidious impact of chronic pipeline leaks.[72] PAHs are some of the more persistent and toxic components in crude oil; exposure to PAHs can cause genetic mutations, damage to the central nervous system, reproductive harm, and cancers in humans and wildlife.[73] Additionally, these hydrocarbons inflict long-term damage on fisheries. Exposure to PAHs not only provokes carcinogenic liver disease in fish but also interferes with their reproductive capacity (Johnston et al. 1998). Fish eggs and fry are extremely vulnerable to PAHs, meaning that an oil spill will not only damage current fish populations but future stocks as well (Holing 1990:29).

Apart from spills and pipeline leaks, PAHs enter the marine environment through the disposal of produced water routinely dumped from offshore platforms. As operators begin to extract oil from the reservoir, they also pump produced water out of the formation. Mercury, zinc, cadmium, lead, and PAHs are often dissolved in the wastewater, as well as radioactive isotopes like radium-226 and radium-228 (Holing 1990:24). Older reservoirs yield more produced water as the oil is depleted (Patin 1999). Operators run the produced water through separators to strip particulate and dispersed oil from the water before releasing it into the ocean, but concentrations of dissolved hydrocarbons ranging from 20 to 50 milligrams per liter discharged in produced water add up to an intentional release of thousands of metric tons of oil per year (ibid.).

The cumulative impact of PAHs discharged in produced water should not be dismissed. Norwegian scientists believe that produced water could be inflicting serious harm on cod in the North Sea and Alaskan scientists fear that produced water—with oil concentrations of 30 to 40 parts per million—dumped into the Cook Inlet is damaging one of the last great fisheries in the United States (Holing 1990). Concentrations in PAHs of naphthalene and aromatic compounds such as phenol, benzene, toluene, and xylene occurring in produced water can delay fish breeding patterns as well as harm fish eggs (Holing 1990:24). PAHs are toxic to fish eggs at the parts-per-billion level, and the U.S. EPA has discovered evidence of naphthalene concentrations in produced water released from oil platforms in American waters 100 times above limits set by the U.S. Fish and Wildlife Service (Holing 1990:29,24).

Oil pollution also presents a threat to fish nurseries, such as mangrove forests. The Angolan coast hosts seven mangrove species; their interwoven root systems provide shelter for crabs, prawns, and juvenile fish (WRI 2003). Mangroves are vulnerable to oil spills; affected trees need upward of twenty years to resuscitate root systems clogged with oil (Holing 1990:29). When scientists deployed dispersants—chemical agents sprayed over oil slicks to induce dispersion and dilution—on oiled mangrove test plots, most of the crustaceans in both the dispersant-oil and oil-only study plots died and dispersant application increased mortality of mangroves (Duke et al. 1998).

Dispersants contain surfactants, solvents, and additives hazardous to human health and the environment. After the Exxon Valdez tanker spilled over 40 million liters of crude oil into Alaska's Prince William Sound, cleanup crews employed Simple Green, Inipol EAP 22, and Corexit 9527. These surfactants and dispersants contain high concentrations of 2-butoxyethanol, a compound known to cause reproductive and fetal damage as well as harm to the liver, kidneys, and blood in humans (Ott 2005).[74] Inipol's next generation product IP-90 is currently used to disperse spills offshore of Angola, provoking concern from scientists.[75]

If dispersants may be lethally toxic and induce higher absorption of PAHs in aquatic organisms, why do oil corporations use them? Visible oil slicks generate public outcry and media frenzies that draw attention to the harmful environmental externalities associated with oil extraction. Once the oil is dispersed into the water column, however, only laboratory tests can prove the continued presence of contaminants. Few citizens or journalists possess either the capacity or long-term interest required for monitoring efforts. Therefore, to avoid public and media attention, oil corporations can apply dispersants immediately following a spill. Scientists suggest that such quick action actually could be more detrimental to marine ecosystems. An experiment in Norway found that the application of dispersants within a few hours of an oil spill increased lethal effects on aquatic organisms by denying acutely toxic monocyclic and polycyclic aromatic hydrocarbons the opportunity to evaporate from the slick's surface before drawing oil into the water column (French-McCay 2001). At the same time, scientists in Alaska showed that dispersants like Corexit 9500 are most effective at dispersing oil within the water column when sprayed on fresh crude and applied in high dispersant-to-oil ratios (White et al. 1999). Thus, it follows that the most efficient use of dispersants through immediate application and high doses may divert media and public attention, but could also be more detrimental to aquatic organisms than allowing the spill to mix naturally into the water column.

Hydraulic fracturing and waterflooding operations performed to stimulate oil production employ 2-butoxyethanol, benzene, toluene, naphthalene, trimethylnapthalene, ethylbenzene, and xylene (Nijhuis 2006:36). Halliburton, the corporation engaged in fracturing operations in northern Angola's offshore, earns 20 percent of its revenues (approximately $1.5 billion in 2005) through this technology, which essentially injects water and chemicals into wells at high pressure to fracture subsurface rocks and push oil and gas to the surface.[76] Fracturing and waterflooding operations challenge the structural stability of aquifers and can provoke saltwater intrusion. Worse still, Halliburton uses 2-butoxyethanol (marketed as Butyl Cellosolve® by Union Carbide), a chemical both odorless and tasteless at low concentrations, in fracturing activities. Through this process, Halliburton endangers domestic water wells near fracturing sites and puts locals at risk of ingesting, inhaling, or absorbing the chemical through the skin, and of developing adrenal tumors (Nijhuis 2006:36).

Transport. Goliath tankers exporting Angola's crude and smaller ships bringing refined fuels from Luanda to the major coastal cities also pose a threat to the marine environment (Sardinha 2000). On May 28, 1991, an explosion rocked the Liberian-registered supertanker ABT Summer, 1,120 kilometers off the Angolan coastline.[77] The ABT Summer's 260,000 metric-ton spill created a slick 17 nautical miles long and 3 nautical miles wide; it was the largest spill in Angolan waters and one of the worst tanker accidents in shipping history (McQuilling 2006).[78] The environmental effects of this colossal oil discharge remain unknown.

A TAINTED POLICY ENVIRONMENT

Sonangol's *Universo* Magazine clarified that the ABT Summer spill "was unconnected with Angola's offshore oil industry, and fortunately no oil washed onto the country's hundreds of miles of superb beaches," yet the incident "served to raise global awareness of the dangers of oil pollution" (Sonangol 2005). The massive spill failed to raise awareness in Angola; the government did not impose substantive anti-pollution laws on operators for another decade. The lack of regulation could not be attributed to ignorance, as President dos Santos' received a degree in Petroleum Engineering from Azerbaijan's Baku Oil Academy (Azerbaijan International 1996). He should have been familiar with oil's toxic legacy in the Caspian Sea, where "pollution control was almost nil, with leaking abandonments [and] debris in many places" (*World Oil* 1980a: 215).

Angola's minimalist regulatory environment appears deliberate — to make the country more attractive to oil corporations. The cost of developing a deepwater well in Angola, at about $15 to $25 million, is significantly less than the $50 million operators usually invest to develop a comparable well in the Gulf of Mexico (Ganaziol 2003:42). Angolan leaders intentionally constructed a circumscribed regulatory environment. One official claimed, "We must figure out how to attract companies; with the high costs of [offshore] production we cannot enforce so many regulations because it might affect competition . . . each regulation has an economic impact and may affect activity."

Of Angola's few environmental standards, most have been imposed after more than twenty years of extraction. For decades, there were no environmental laws. In 1998, Angolan leaders endorsed the Environmental Framework Act. Although this law defines a strict liability notion applicable to polluters in Articles 4 and 28, it does not delineate the particular forms of pollution outlawed and makes only general statements guaranteeing citizens the "right to live in a healthy and unpolluted environment" (WB 2002:52). Likewise, the Constitution nebulously states that the government of Angola "shall take the requisite measures to protect the environment," and the laws on foreign investment and economic activities vaguely call on investors to respect environmental norms as they conduct business (WB 2002:50; GoA 2001:18).

A World Bank report describing Angola's regulatory system and assessing the compliance of transnational oil corporations operating in the country noted that few regulations actually govern corporate activities. In the absence of regulations, corporations operating in Angola tout their voluntary practices under the banner of corporate social responsibility (CSR). The report stated, "In general terms, one may say that CSR codes of conduct correspond to the spirit of the international and national legislation" (WB 2002:12).

Appallingly, the World Bank describes reduction of greenhouse gases as "needless" given Angola's lack of regulation on emissions (WB 2002:50). Chevron and Total both pledged to cut greenhouse gas emissions from their operations drastically—but only after natural gas prices increased to the point that flaring became impractical. Some oil corporations initiate positive environmental programs, but they prefer to do so on a purely voluntary basis. For example, Chevron invests in an Energy and Biodiversity Initiative and promises to limit seismic activities during humpback whale migrations, while Total contributes to marine biodiversity and ecosystem protection efforts through its corporate foundation (WB 2002:48).

The trouble with trusting corporations to undertake voluntary environmental responsibility standards rather than setting clear regulatory guidelines is that corporations often only invest in voluntary efforts to their cost-effective ends. Once responsibility becomes too expensive, corporations are free to abandon their commitments. For example, Chevron transports contaminated drill cuttings from its shallow water operations but disposes of equivalent wastes from deepwater wells offshore.

Government officials eager to showcase Angola at the 2002 World Summit on Sustainable Development in Johannesburg announced the Decree on Environmental Protection in Petroleum Activities and drafted a National Oil Spill Contingency Plan. In 2005, the government finally released long-awaited decrees regulating oil industry waste management, operational discharges, and oil spill notification procedures.[79] The Ministry of Petroleum collaborated with industry experts on Angola's Decree on Environmental Protection in Petroleum Activities.[80] Under the decree, operators may dispose of water-based barite muds and synthetic drilling fluids at sea, but oil discharges on cuttings are limited to 1 percent of the total amount disposed and toxicity testing of select species is required to determine biodegradation and bioaccumulation of PAHs from these discharges. Civil servants possessing only a cursory knowledge of the hazards posed by oil extraction relied on expert opinion—from corporate oil representatives—to inform the regulations process.[81]

An industry insider argued that global coordination constrained Angola's regulatory structure. He explained, "You cannot get too detailed because you must take into consideration [the] harmonization of corporate practices." Transnational oil corporations often declare compliance with global industry standards, but there is no mandatory set of worldwide regulations and attempts at harmonization provoke a figurative race to the bottom. Even the relatively stringent U.S. paradigm is flawed, for it "lacks general biological process studies; does not pay enough attention to inshore, onshore and estuarine areas; has too narrow a focus on oil spills and not enough on the other potential impacts associated with development and production; overestimates potential recovery rates of ecosystems after damage in its environmental impact statements; and has largely ignored sub-lethal and chronic effects of oil and gas activities" (Holing 1990:30).

Undermining Enforcement

Decreased government regulation is an essential part of the neoliberal model, in which global markets supplant national oversight. Countries maintain regulatory systems to enforce harmonized regulations, yet the shift toward neoliberalism has "decapacitated" the state (Ferguson 2005). Environmental standards for oil corporations in Angola are set not by regulation but by negotiation. Communities in Soyo and Cabinda recognize how Angola's centralized presidentialist system of rule coupled with a decapacitated regulatory system contributes to local environmental degradation. An elder in Cabinda explained the consequences of this combination: "If Chevron does not like something it is simply a matter of calling José Eduardo dos Santos. Angolan laws are written in pencil; if they do not like one, he erases it." The elder called Angola not a democracy but a 'Santocracia'—a political system defined by the whims of the president.

The structural and social relations of oil dependency privilege opaque negotiations over transparent regulations. Oil corporations use their influence to weaken enforcement mechanisms, thus exacerbating the ecological impact of petro-violence. For example, the Ministry of Petroleum is expected to pay regular salaries for the three inspectors tasked to monitor Angola's offshore for oil spills, but oil corporations are expected to contribute to the travel, hotel, and incidental expenses incurred in the course of the inspectors' activities.[82] Moreover, the Ministry of Petroleum regularly grants exceptions to oil corporations on activities like flaring in the context of the confidential agreements negotiated between Sonangol and each consortium of oil corporations. The chairman of Sonangol, Manuel Vicente, testified, "Nowadays, the environment is an important consideration. . . . Our production sharing agreements include very specific clauses on the environment" (Vicente 2001). If these contracts delineate environmental protections or exceptions, however, they are not publicly disclosed.

This structural form of petro-violence diminishes the regulatory potential of bureaucrats. Some officials view jobs with transnational oil firms as their only route to escape the constraints of the petrodollar patronage system. A mid-level bureaucrat at the Ministry of Environment—in a department tasked with regulating extractive corporations—openly professed a deep desire to work for Chevron. He spoke of the firm's commitment to Angolan fisheries development. Discussing an "artificial reef" program proposed by Chevron, he opined, "Artificial reefs will help the artisanal fishermen to get out of poverty and lead a better life—this is the fundamental objective of the development of artificial reefs." Without artificial reefs, he argued, "the sea will be just water and there will be no habitat for fish." The bureaucrat neglected to explain how fish survived prior to the invention of "artificial reefs" and launched headlong into an animated description of a "sub-aquatic tourism" plan. As fish congregated around the abandoned oil installations, he expected tourists would snorkel near these "artificial reefs." Their interest in snorkeling there would drive demand for local tour guides and even a booming photo development and framing business as the tourists snapped away with their underwater cameras. His assumption that tourists might travel to Angola on photo safaris featuring contaminated old platforms seemed misguided. Moreover, the preliminary "artificial reef" studies had failed. The bureaucratic official admitted that the four containers Chevron dumped offshore in March 2001 had filled with sediment and no fish had been seen nearby. Still, he flashed a buoyant grin and added, "I was congratulated on my help [with the project] by Chevron and I have so many friends over there." This bureaucrat appeared more interested in creating justifications for extraction than regulating it; he was gunning for a job at Chevron.

Other government officials—especially those at the provincial level in Cabinda who witnessed the damage oil extraction had wrought on the local environment—were more skeptical of Chevron's environmental virtue. An official serving Cabinda's Provincial Directorate of Agriculture, Fisheries, and Environment worried that successive oil spills had severely damaged local plankton levels. He had submitted a proposal to the Ministry of Environment to study phytoplankton in Cabinda's littoral zone but was still awaiting a response five years later.

The Ministry of Petroleum often denies such research requests. An international team affiliated with the Benguela Current Large Marine Ecosystem (BCLME) program attempted to conduct research on the environmental impact of oil production in Angola's northwestern extractive zones. The Ministry of Petroleum thwarted the team's plans by denying access to critical records. The Ministry of Fisheries and National Institute of Fisheries Research (INIP) refused to play a facilitating role in obtaining requisite data from the Ministry of Petroleum and the local BCLME manager had no influence on their decision. The oil industry was equally uncooperative, referring researchers to a flawed industry-wide environmental monitoring program that fails to incorporate historical data. The Ministry of Petroleum did permit the R.V. Fridtjof Nansen research vessel to sample for hydrocarbons, heavy metals, and biota around production platforms in Block 2 just after Sonangol assumed the operator role from Chevron (by way of local subsidiary Texaco) in 2006. Allowing the study at this critical juncture presumably afforded Sonangol with a baseline from which it could deny responsibility for all pre-existing environmental damages. Still, it is unlikely that the results of this study will be made public or shared with the fishermen in Soyo whose fishing grounds overlap Block 2.

A RIGHT TO KNOW

In the past two chapters, the resource curse model has provided a lens to focus on the dynamics of exclusion, violence, and degradation in Angola. Rejecting determinism, they examine oil dependency as both a cause for these dynamics as well as a result of their influence on Angolan political economy. Such circular relationships and feedback loops have entrenched patterns of petro-capitalism and petro-violence in Angola.

Turning specifically to the influence of petro-violence, this chapter has highlighted the role of oil in various expressions of conflict and environmental damage. State dependence on oil revenues, contested entitlements, and structural violence shapes battles from Luanda to the extractive zones. Oil dependency privileges negotiation over regulation, undermining mechanisms for the enforcement of environmental standards. Negotiation exemplifies the exclusionary tactics fundamental to the Angolan petro-state by subjectively concentrating power in leaders rather than laws. Regulation, by contrast, relies on objective frameworks for determining accountability.

Petro-capitalism and petro-violence depend upon opacity. Deficient transparency in government accounting enables leaders to divert oil revenues for illegal arms deals and violent military campaigns. A lack of regulatory transparency permits corporations to withhold data on contamination from the communities bearing the toxic burden of oil pollution. Ironically, these communities bear the burden of proof when demanding accountability from oil corporations and their government. Environmental right-to-know legislation mandating transparent disclosure of the dangers to ecological and human health associated with oil extraction would shift the burden of proof to polluters.[83]

Angolan transparency activists have not yet embraced environmental right-to-know principles. A civil society advocate in Luanda expressed concern over environmental injustices, but she asserted that "the environment is a real luxury for people to be preoccupied with: most are concerned with work . . . poverty . . . the environment will come later." On the contrary, work, poverty, and the environment are inextricably connected in Angola's extractive zones. Artisanal fishers in Soyo and Cabinda constantly monitor the health of the local marine environment and seek to learn all that they can about the dangers of offshore oil production because they recognize fish are not only their supper but also the source of their livelihoods.

4. Shallow Graves

Waves tumbled toward the shore, breaking on a rusted tank half-interred in the sand. The tank and abandoned Soviet missiles in the bluffs above recalled battles between the government and UNITA. Like the tank, the painful memories of war remain only partially buried in Soyo.

Soyo sits in Angola's northwestern corner, where the Congo River slips along circuitous paths to the sea.[1] The municipality of 109,500 contains 35 percent of the population of Zaire province, with 19.6 inhabitants per square kilometer (GoA 2003a). Soyo town functions as the municipal seat; it has a population of 45,000—just 5,000 fewer inhabitants than Mbanza Kongo, the capital of Zaire province (WB 2005:138).[2] The main street hosts several banks, one hotel, two restaurants, a church, a clothing store, a police station, and several government offices. At the center of this seemingly sleepy town, a crumbling building marked by graffiti and bullet holes recalls its violent past.

Just north of town lies Kwanda Base, a logistical hub for Sonangol, ExxonMobil, BP, Total, and Chevron, as well as for maintenance and service contractors such as Petromar, Halliburton, and Schlumberger and supply chain management and shipping companies like Panalpina and DHL. The 160-hectare facility features a $16 million wharf to accommodate the monthly average of 130 ships that offload oilfield materials and deliver supply shipments to facilitate operations in Cabinda's Blocks 0 and 14, as well as Blocks 1, 2, 3, 14, 15, 31, and 32 offshore of Zaire province (*Jornal de Angola* 2005b). The thick, paved line drawn between Kwanda and Total's petroleum outpost at Quinfuquena strikes a bold contrast with the vast, sketched network of sandy roads across the municipality. To many in Soyo, the cracked pavement represents oil's broken promises. Oil promised wealth but degraded the natural resource base and undermined

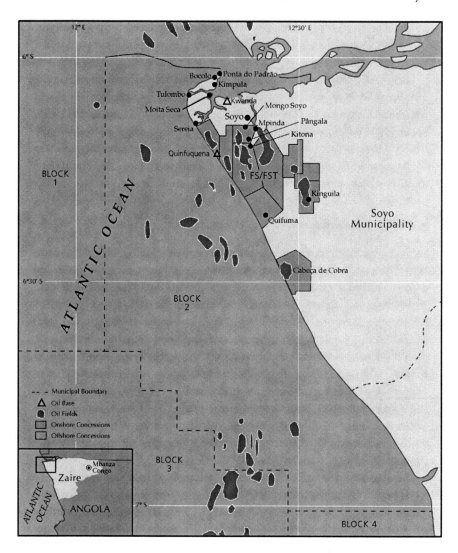

MAP 6. Oil Extraction in Soyo

social mores; it offered a few jobs but discriminated against undereducated locals and underscored differentiation within communities.

This chapter introduces the politics of oil in northern Angola and the enduring effects of petro-violence through the case of Soyo. Drawing on local narratives concerning Soyo's underdevelopment and environmental degradation, it examines how lingering effects of UNITA's occupation and continuing state-sponsored repression limit people's protest in the municipality. The brutality of the UNITA occupation scarred Soyo's residents. They are hesitant to criticize the MPLA-led government for fear of reprisal, yet they do not see UNITA as a promising alternative.

Effectively unable to protest degradation and underdevelopment, Soyo's inhabitants fail in battles for compensation and oil-backed development projects. Despite massive investments in a new liquefied natural gas plant, local people remain unlikely to benefit from the oil and gas sector. Despite the fact that they express resentment toward Cabindans for their success in this regard, Soyo's protesters vow never to use violence to pursue their aims. Perhaps, say some, this is one of the reasons for their failure.

A VIOLENT HISTORY OF EXPLOITATION

In the 1950s, few investors expressed interest in developing oilfields in infrastructure-poor regions like northwestern Angola, but one corporation defied convention and purchased its own rig to begin drilling in Soyo.[3] The Belgian firm Petrofina, Compagnie Financière Belge des Pétroles, first began prospecting in the region in 1953.[4] Petrofina gained exploration rights to Soyo in 1956 through holdings in the Petroleum Company of Angola (Petrangol), a joint venture between Belgian and Portuguese interests.[5] Over the next decade, Petrangol surveyed the Congo Basin extensively, conducting more than 7,500 kilometers of airborne magnetic surveys in 1958 and completing 1,500 kilometers of offshore seismic studies by 1966 (Hedberg et al. 1959:1640; Saint et al. 1967:151–153). Petrangol achieved first oil in 1966 from a well not far from the site of Soyo's historic Mpinda port, which once dispatched slaves across the Atlantic.[6]

Residents muffled their protests as Petrangol seized traditional lands, understanding that a threat of force backed all concessions and trumped traditional land claims. After independence, the Angolan government honored production agreements negotiated between Portuguese colonial authorities and Fina (formerly Petrofina) but altered them to include state interests. Fina developed most of Soyo's oilfields between 1972 and 1977. Neither the war for independence nor the first half of Angola's internationalized civil war had much impact on oil production in Soyo. During its post-elections offensive, however, UNITA captured most of Angola's territory outside the major cities—including Soyo.

Under the leadership of Jonas Savimbi, UNITA attacked Angola's extractive zones. The rebel forces choked flows of onshore oil revenues from Soyo to the government and bolstered their own income by mining and trading alluvial diamonds from Angola's remote Lunda region. UNITA severed the flow of one-third of Angola's oil revenues from reaching the Luanda government by destroying the Soyo oil base in 1993 and extracted up to $1 million in diamonds daily from the Lunda provinces by 1996 (Brittain 1998). Historians disagree on whether Savimbi captured Soyo with the intention of destroying oil infrastructure; yet scholars agree that Soyo's onshore installations on the sandy coastal plain proved easier targets than the hulking platforms offshore. UNITA may have first attacked Soyo with the intention of capturing a coastal town from the government and carving a menacing silhouette by kidnapping foreigners. Noting the government's reaction of concern for Soyo's onshore production facilities, oil storage tanks and strategic supply base for offshore extraction, UNITA then turned to sabotage in later operations.

Elf and Texaco respectively operated the approximately 4,000-km² concessions of Block 3 and Block 2 in the Congo basin offshore concession zone, while Fina operated two onshore concession areas—one in association with Sonangol and Texaco (FST), and the other with Sonangol alone (FS) (*World Oil* 1980a). On January 21, 1993, UNITA forces attacked Fina's onshore oil camp, fatally wounding a Frenchman and kidnapping seventeen foreigners, including three Britons, two Indonesians, and a German (MIPT 2005). A survivor of the kidnapping haltingly recounted the incident to me:

> They came from Cabeça de Cobra [in the south] when they captured Soyo. So, when they got here, the first zone they found was Acampamento 8 [the Fina camp], where we lived, ate and slept. At this time there were about 60 workers in the camp. . . . There were government soldiers in the area. But when UNITA came, they entered with great force and many fighters. No one expected that a group so large would come. They entered the camp at six in the morning, very early. . . . A helicopter succeeded in bringing a part of the staff to the platforms in the ocean, but the rest stayed behind . . . seventeen foreigners: Portuguese, Italians, Argentines and Britons—UNITA soldiers only took the foreigners to Uíge with them. . . . We were held captive for 21 days. We traveled to Uíge in the cars they stole from Fina. At times they gave us little food, but they too did not have food. . . . I do not know what their reason was for only taking the foreigners, maybe to upset the government, or possibly to halt oil production. In any case, oil production was stopped for nearly three years.

On March 5, 1993, helicopters landed in Soyo deploying a team of FAA commandos at Quinfuquena beach to protect the Texaco and Petrofina oil storage tanks. The commandos struggled to stave off a contingent of 500 UNITA fighters before seaborne reinforcements arrived six hours late due to a communications failure. Government troops encircled the valuable storage units with Russian tanks and anti-aircraft guns. Nearby Pângala station, pumping 27,000 barrels per day from onshore fields, recorded only minor damage from a government mortar or cannon shell (Powell 1993). An estimated 1,000 to 1,500 UNITA combatants inflicted heavy damage on the town of Soyo, looted Fina offices for computers to be sold on Kinshasa's black market, and drove local inhabitants into the bush. They left oil production facilities and the offshore supply base at Kwanda intact, blowing up only a small petrol storage tank at the port, but later that month UNITA raided another oil installation, killing two foreign oil workers—one Briton and one South African (MIPT 2005). Government forces maintained control of the area until May, when UNITA recaptured Soyo, inflicting heavy damage on oil infrastructure and disrupting operations.

Chevron, Texaco, Fina, and Elf allegedly pressured Sonangol to hire the private military firm Executive Outcomes to defend Soyo's remaining oil infrastructure (Soares de Oliveira 2007:116).[7] UNITA occupied 80 percent of Angola in 1993; but a series of government operations aided by private military contractors—including Executive Outcomes—successfully cut UNITA's control of the country to 40 percent by November 1994 (HRW 1996a, 1997a). In collaboration with Executive Outcomes, FAA soldiers retook a number of villages in Soyo's southern region (HRW 1996b).[8] As government forces and their private military partners pressed UNITA fighters into strategic withdrawal from Soyo in 1995, Savimbi's men vented their frustrations by murdering civilians and looting their homes (HRW 1996a). Soyo's inhabitants observed UNITA's retreat with painful memories and fearful anxiety that remain to this day.

Occupying Memories

Conducting my research in Soyo a decade after UNITA's occupation, I found it difficult to persuade informants to talk about the period. Many people escaped across the Congo River to Zaire or fled into the bush, but those trapped in Soyo suffered unspeakable cruelty. Survivors searched for words, some articulating their experiences in jagged fragments and others attempting to attach cogent descriptions to actions that defied rationality. An elder with watery eyes recalled lucidly how "everyone was full of fear" trying to hold onto their means of survival as UNITA proceeded to "steal everything." Only my friend Ana gave me more than a sentence on her experience of the UNITA occupation. She slumped against the wall, recalling with uncharacteristic brusqueness:

> There was no soap, no petrol, nothing. [My sister and I] survived by planting in the lowlands. We planted corn and peanuts. People became

merchants, selling and trading their own crops. UNITA would come silently after the evening meal when people had just hoped to relax. They would kidnap people and march them out for days on end. If they ever came back they would be emaciated and walking like sticks.

Interviewees who had escaped Soyo during the occupation spoke a bit more freely, drawing on the experiences of those who remained. They related how UNITA forces eliminated enemies by abduction and extrajudicial execution, terrorizing the remainder into submission. Young men lived dreading forced conscription into Savimbi's ranks. They dared not give voice to their fears or complaints. "It was comply first, complain later—and if you say no, that's it," said one man. He explained how UNITA punished suspected detractors by imprisoning them in half-buried salvaged shipping containers. Prisoners received only rations of canned tomato paste "and if you were lucky, you could catch a big cockroach and eat that."

The brutality of Savimbi's men incurred hostility in Soyo, which would later cost UNITA any hope of political support from the municipality. A resident explained:

> UNITA was also a little stupid when they came to a place and destroyed the things that were for the people . . . what did that mean? They made enemies with the people. They were trying to win the presidency, [but such a strategy] doesn't make sense. Better to put something there that people are lacking. Leave the bridge as it is, let the house remain.

UNITA never sought to earn the people of Soyo's respect or votes, only to dominate them with brute force. Residents rallied behind the MPLA-led government and the troops as they fought for control of the municipality. After the FAA won back part of Soyo, UNITA found cruel ways to discourage defection to the government-controlled zone. Amnesty International documented UNITA's public caning of João André Lina in 1995. Fifty blows to the back crippled Lina in retribution for his relatives' flight from the UNITA-controlled zone of Soyo to the government-held area (AI 1996a, 1997a).

Although many victims of war fled to the government-controlled zones seeking safety from UNITA's brutal tactics, FAA soldiers could also be cruel. The singular aim of the FAA's offensive to retake Soyo was to protect local oil installations. FAA General Teixeira de Brito stated, "We are not interested in taking prisoners in this war. There is no room for them"— and he quickly added, "We did capture a couple who were wounded, but they died" (Powell 1993). Human Rights Watch denounced both UNITA and FAA troops for "committing widespread abuses against the civilian population" during the war, including "physical and sexual assaults, rape, mutilations, forced conscription, abduction of women and girls, looting, and extrajudicial executions" (HRW 2003b).

Soyo's inhabitants spoke, albeit with hesitation, of abuses by UNITA soldiers, and a few apprehensively hinted at injustices by the FAA troops. One survivor alluded to difficulties in distinguishing between FAA and UNITA dress—uniform supplies dwindled after the loss of Cold War patrons—admitting that victims were often unable to identify soldiers perpetrating abuses.

Most families never recovered the bodies of their loved ones, and they struggled to bury painful memories of the conflict. On July 12, 1996, a chilling discovery reopened Soyo's wounds: a demining team unearthed a mass grave near the Kwanda oil base with at least sixty human skeletons, including those of women and children (HRW 1997a). The holes in the buried skulls revealed the deliberate, and likely arbitrary, nature of the massacre (AI 1996c). Neither UNITA nor FAA troops accepted responsibility for the atrocity. Government officials ignored human rights organizations' consistent appeals for both a "forensic or judicial inquiry into the circumstances in which the killings were carried out" and an investigation "to identify the victims and perpetrators" (AI 1997b; HRW 1997a). Amnesty International reported, "Local residents and journalists believe that the area contains other burial sites" (AI 1996c). Nevertheless, apart from a Saturday visit from a few parliamentarians, officials conducted no further investigations.

The oil industry recovered from the war and did not look back. A report released one month after the mass grave's discovery depicted Petrofina's readiness to reclaim their onshore holdings in Soyo; UNITA's destruction had diminished output to 500 barrels per day—produced from just 11 of the area's 86 wells (*World Oil* 1996:100). In August 1997, Petrofina announced a $50 million reconstruction effort to increase artificial lift, install new pumps and lines, and replace damaged units at Pângala and Quinfuquena. This effort boosted production from Soyo's fields to 22,000 or 23,000 barrels daily by year's end, surpassing the production rate of 20,000 barrels per day prior to UNITA's occupation (ibid.).

ONSHORE EXTRACTION

Petrofina's two onshore concessions operated by Fina Petroleum of Angola—Fina-Sonangol (FS) and Fina-Sonangol-Texaco (FST)—remain inscribed on Soyo's sandy lands.[9] Despite conducting business in Angola under local subsidiary names, stakeholders Fina and Texaco were respectively subsumed by supermajors Total and Chevron.[10] Many of Soyo's residents, unaware of global mergers and acquisitions or allegiant to local subsidiary names, continued to refer to these corporations as Fina and Texaco. Nevertheless, this chapter will henceforth identify the operator of Soyo's onshore fields as Total. (Total has since sold its 55.6 percent interest in Fina Petroleum of Angola to Sonangol, rendering Sonangol P&P with a 100 percent stake in FS and an 83.6 percent stake in FST. Chevron retains a 16.4 percent interest stake.)

The imaginative names of the oilfields in the FS and FST concessions evoke the silhouettes of features in the landscape (*Cabeça de Cobra*—head of the snake), mythological creatures (*Sereia*—mermaid), and even local professions (*Kinguila*—moneychanger). Nevertheless, the sites of extraction are mostly simple squares of sand cleared of vegetation surrounding rusted infrastructure. By 2004, the rigs yielded only 15,000 barrels each day: 39 of Total's 77 active onshore wells were closed.[11] At depths of 1,400 to 2,000 meters the wells are not considered very deep, but they are aging, and those depleted of natural gas require beam pumps to draw oil to the surface. In other wells, gas lift and hydraulic pump technologies facilitate extraction. New wells in the Cabeça de Cobra and Kinguila fields added 3,000 barrels daily in 2005, but production rates still fall far short of historical highs of 60,000 barrels per day (Mavinga 2004).

Although onshore concessions account for only a fraction of Angola's aggregate oil production, the onshore mode of extraction is unique in its effect on the people of Soyo municipality. Wells are scattered throughout the backyards and agricultural fields of Soyo's residents. Why would an oil corporation site wells in people's backyards? Two factors contribute to this phenomenon. First, oil is a spatially fixed resource; oil corporations can only extract oil where it is found.[12] Corporations conduct cost-benefit analyses and risk assessments, but they usually decide to proceed with extraction despite close proximity to populations or political volatility. Second, it is probable that Soyo was depopulated at the time that Total installed many of the oil wells. Government documents estimate that up to 60 percent of the municipal population fled Soyo between 1960 and 2001 to escape violence (GoA 2003a). Many sought refuge in the small islands carved out by the winding Congo River or traversed the fluid border into Mobutu's Zaire—later Kabila's Democratic Republic of Congo. As peace returned to Soyo, the refugees found their way home. In 2001, 19,102 persons displaced by the war returned to Soyo municipality from the Democratic Republic of Congo (WB 2005:138). Some returnees settled in the city; others sought to resurrect the homes they built and reseed the farms they nurtured before the war.[13]

An expatriate employee of Total said that when the oil corporation arrived in Soyo the town held "just a thousand folks and no roads, just sand tracks." He said Total's installation of a paved road and the promise of oil wealth lured new settlers to Soyo. Although the stretch of tarmac may have facilitated the return of displaced people, local narratives assert that, apart from a few thousand recent immigrants from the Democratic Republic of Congo, most of those who settled in Soyo after Total's arrival were returnees.[14] Elders from Pângala, Mongo Soyo, and Kitona assert traditional claims to the land through their Basolongo heritage and trace their specific land claims back to a colonial resettlement scheme in the early 1930s.[15] Many left one or more times to evade colonial forced labor policies, escape violence, or seek employment across the Congo River.[16] Even so, they always maintained parcels of land in the municipality.

Many of Soyo's elders said that Total arrived in their absence, paved roads, and ran transects through the municipality, appropriating lands presumed to be unused or unoccupied. One elderly resident clearly remembered, "My family moved here in 1932 when the colonial influx began. Oil came later. I had land for four sons, but the government gave it to Fina for the area of the well." His continuing narrative, infused with frustration and resignation, highlighted the context of repression and fear marking early oil development. The elder recalled, "When they came to our land, everyone was afraid—we could not say anything against the government." He noted that the oil corporation failed to seek permission from local traditional authorities and community members to develop the land. The first oil exploration activities he remembered were seismic tests, which made the earth tremble. Then, representatives of the oil corporation expropriated a portion of his land without compensation. A few neighbors received compensation, but just the equivalent of 200 to 500 kwanzas—or, at most, 1,000 kwanzas ($12). "Money cannot compensate for the loss of the land," he said between coughs.

After appropriating the tracts of land it desired, Total drilled wells. A smell began to issue from the wells. It grew stronger in the stillness of night. Staring at his feet, the elder told me that his crops began to "dry out" and he contracted a respiratory disease. He admitted that he had not initially linked the failure of his trees to bear fruit or his own deteriorating health to the oilwells.[17] He suddenly glanced to his right and wheezed his way over to a palm tree ten meters away. Grasping a large, nearly weightless coconut in his oversized hand, the exhausted elder reported that his coconuts no longer held milk nor meat and compared his shrunken oranges to lemons. With a grave sense of finality, he pronounced, "There has been no compensation for the loss of productivity." The elder pointed to the field behind his house, where two hissing oil wells sat amidst a wide, barren patch in bold contrast with the green of the densely planted surroundings. Black shadows stained the sandy soil at the base of the wells.

Oil spills are an ordinary part of onshore extraction in Soyo, for decrepit oil infrastructure regularly begets accidents. Soyo's degraded pipelines—some of which date back to the 1950s—present a threat to communities in the concessions. Roughly 500 kilometers of pipeline in various diameters and states of rusty decay connect across the municipality.[18] Total recently replaced sections of pipeline near the municipal water supply, but older portions continue to leak. Total recorded sizeable leaks on the CA-NZ-PG pipeline running from Cabeça de Cobra through N'Zombo to Pângala.[19] Oil workers admit that Soyo's pipelines "are rusty and they leak . . . everyday" to the point that they have taken to calling them "clamplines" because so many sections of pipeline are clamped to prevent leaks. One oilman acknowledged that as the local operator, Total appeared most responsible for pollution, but suggested that Sonangol—the majority shareholder in both FS and FST blocks—should also share the blame. He said, "Sonangol sometimes negates proposed upgrades because they do not have the money to put into the project—their partner share—so this can account for some environmental problems."

More disturbing than the profusion of spills from these leaky pipelines was Total's response to them. After a twenty-four-hour pipeline leak in September 1997 reportedly spilled crude over a 500-square-meter area, nearby residents reported negative health effects to corporate officials but they received neither acknowledgement nor compensation. A witness to the spill recalled that Total refused to remove the oil and merely covered up the affected area with a thin layer of soil. He attributed the shoddy remediation to the wartime mentality. Nevertheless, Total responded similarly to a postwar burst at well CA-12, covering the oil with 40 centimeters of earth as a remediation technique.

Pools of oil near production sites are not always associated with infrastructure malfunctions—they are sometimes intentional. In the process of extraction, Total often created pits for the collection of waste oil and associated chemicals. A resident oilman expressed concern about this practice, asserting that the pits posed a danger to Soyo's groundwater. He insisted, "This waste oil—it has all the kinds of chemicals that can destroy people's lives. They need to have a good management plan for this waste oil." Instead, Total mostly buried the waste pits or burned the contents, generating plumes of noxious gas. Total's records cited remediation activities at a couple of waste oil pits, but the concerned oilman questioned whether these efforts entailed little more than the usual "cover up" strategy.[20]

OFFSHORE EXTRACTION

Whereas onshore extraction threatens customary land claims, offshore operations jeopardize traditional fishing grounds. In addition to the land, the dominion of traditional leaders also extended over Soyo's shallow waters. Visitors once paid homage of food and drink in exchange for the right to fish these abundant waters. Nevertheless, just as concessions onshore disregard indigenous land claims, offshore blocks ignore local holdings in the sea. Fishermen argue that bureaucrats and oil executives direct the extraction of Soyo's riches from Luanda, excluding locals from decision-making processes. Local consultations, they contend, are charades: merely a rubber stamp for decisions made in secretive discussions in Luanda.

The centripetal character of negotiations between the Ministry of Petroleum and oil executives reinforces an optic by which oil outposts become defined by their relation to Luanda. Confidential production contracts negotiated between oil corporations and government officials in Luanda refer to platforms, fields, and wells in terms of their distance from the Angolan capital. For example, the Xicomba field in deepwater Block 15 operated by ExxonMobil (a.k.a. Esso Exploration Angola Ltd.) is cited as "approximately 230 miles northwest of Luanda," while BP's Palas-1 well sits "325 kilometers northwest" of the capital city.[21] Blocks 15 and 31 are located due west of Soyo in deep and ultra-deep waters, respectively, yet officials in Luanda decide the details of their development. The same holds true for the shallow waters where Blocks 1 and 2, operated by Eni and Chevron, overlap with artisanal fishing activities.[22] (Since the time of research, Sonangol has assumed the role of Block 2 operator from Chevron, and Tullow Oil has won the operator stake of relinquished Block 1/06. Eni continues as operator of the Safueiro field in Block 1.) Each day, artisanal fishers along the coasts of Zaire province study the ebb and flow of tides, heave their boats across the unyielding beach sands, and battle the crashing shore break as they set out to fish. Approximately 1,146 artisanal fishermen from 56 communities are scattered down the coast of Zaire province (Kilongo 2004:2). The fishers set out each morning in *canoas* or *pirogas* (dugout canoes powered by motor or manpower), *chatas* (open boats made of fiberglass or wood, sometimes with outboard motors), and *catrongas* (open or covered boats powered by internal motors). Of the 421 fishing boats in the province, 368 are canoes (37 with outboard motors and 331 without), 49 are *chatas* (15 with motors and 34 without) and four are *catrongas* with built-in motors (ibid.). Since nearly 87 percent of the artisanal fishing fleet in Zaire province relies on non-motorized vessels, most fishermen venture no farther than 200 meters from shore. Those with motors regularly travel up to 500 meters from shore, but rarely stray beyond a kilometer.

Given the limited mobility of artisanal fishers, their catch mostly comprises demersals (71 percent) and, to a lesser extent, pelagics (27 percent); the most commonly caught fish, in descending order, are croaker *(sciaenidae)*, sea catfish *(ariidae)*, dogfish sharks *(squalidae)*, sole *(soleidae)*, West African ilisha *(clupeidae)*, grunts *(pomadasyidae)*, rays *(rajidae)*, lesser African threadfin *(polynemidae)*, large-eye dentex *(sparidae)*, West African Spanish mackerel *(scombridae)*, and jacks *(carangidae)* (Kilongo 2004). The proceeds of collective catches—the fish caught through group effort setting and hauling nets on a *chata* or *catronga*—are distributed according to each fisher's rank, and a cut is reserved for the owner of the boat and nets. Occasionally, once the nets are set, individual fishermen drop a line in the water. All catches from line fishing are considered property of the individual.[23]

Missing Regulators

I spoke with both fishermen and local employees of the oil industry to learn more about the environmental impacts of offshore oil extraction in Soyo. Although fishermen cited difficulties in determining the origin of the spills, many witnessed multiple spills in Block 2.[24] Frustrated, many of the fishermen told me that the government failed to enforce environmental regulations to limit damage from the oil industry. One fisherman exclaimed, "Enforcement? It is non-existent!" Others acknowledged "a lack of capacity" within local agencies, noting that the municipality's sole enforcement boat had been drydocked for more than a year. Yet another claimed enforcement seemed near impossible because "the companies always evade the authorities."

The regulatory environment in Angola is weak and flexible. Regulations outlaw flaring of associated gases and discourage the use of non-aqueous drilling fluids, but the Ministry of Petroleum routinely grants exceptions. In some cases, the high costs of compliance coupled with a low level of enforcement encourage violations. "Implementation is the weakness of this country—what is on the books does not mean much," remarked a civil society advocate in Luanda.

Employees of the oil industry also expressed skepticism regarding the enforcement of national environmental regulations and the willingness of corporations to adhere to these standards. In reference to Angola's Decree on Environmental Protection in Petroleum Activities, a local oilman politely speculated, "Maybe it exists but it does not function—or maybe it does not exist. The problem is [that oil executives] are businessmen: profit is most important." His counterpart—a foul-mouthed expatriate—agreed. The roughneck bluntly derided the notion of oil corporations' concern for local ecosystems and the people dependent on them, suggesting that corporate actors both openly exerted undue influence over the formation of Angola's environmental regime and covertly flouted the regulations. He sneered, "They're both prostitutes and rapists. If they don't get you from the front, they'll get you from behind. They don't give a fuck. There's no one watching and the regulations don't mean shit."

In an environment characterized by poor enforcement and local desperation, degradation begets degradation. A report on artisanal fisheries in Zaire province noted that "the weak implementation of enforcement" has contributed to an environment "characterized by the constant violations of nurseries and spawning grounds" and resulted in the decrease of croaker, grunts, and black seabreams (Kilongo 2003). Fishermen unable to catch enough in degraded waters exploit juvenile fish and further undermine the resource base.

Pesnorte, a government-sponsored program tasked with developing artisanal fisheries, formed in recognition of the challenges to the artisanal fisheries sector in Zaire province. The fisheries development program began in 2002 with an initial loan of $7 million from the International Fund for Agricultural Development, a $1 million grant from the Belgian Survival Fund, and $620,000 from the Government of Angola (IFAD 2002b). Serving 50,000 beneficiaries, the program has expanded into every facet of the artisanal fisheries sector, assisting not only fishermen and fish traders but also auxiliary service providers such as boatmakers, net purveyors, and mechanics (ANGOP 2006b). In an effort to increase local artisanal production and improve marketing, Pesnorte negotiates fishermen's access to micro-credit and organizes fishing associations to promote competitive pricing. The program has facilitated fishers' purchases of nets and buoys and increased fish traders' access to salt and freezers.

Slashing Subsidies

One of the most common requests Pesnorte receives from fishers is for assistance in purchasing outboard motors and fuel to enable fishing expeditions farther from the coast. Noting the increasing trend of local artisanal fishers buying motors for their boats in the past decade, a provincial fisheries official remarked, "It is necessary because now their fish are far-ther away." Fishermen agreed. "Now, you have to go so far to find the fish. If you see oil in the water you know there will be no fish there; they have gone far from the oil," regretted a fisher waiting for fuel at the Soyo docks.

Fuel was in short supply. The Luanda refinery produced 37,000 barrels of gasoline and diesel fuel per day in 2004—8,000 fewer barrels than its top capacity—and the new facility in Lobito was not yet functioning (Cafussa 2004b). Shortages spurred long queues at fueling stations and prices in the informal sector soared to over eight times their official value (*Jornal de Angola* 2004n).[25] During the first four months of 2004, Angola spent over $100 million to import 217,000 metric tons of fuel to compensate for shortages (ibid.). Workers at the Luanda refinery insisted that Sonangol had artificially constructed the shortages: production rates were sufficient to satisfy demand and the imports were unnecessary. One employee sus-pected "a lot of dishonesty" behind the import strategy and called upon authorities to investigate the shortages "illicitly benefiting" Sonangol offi-cials diverting Angolan fuel into more lucrative markets (*Agora* 2004b).

The government slashed fuel subsidies as part of its vacillating com-pliance with IMF conditionalities in May 2004, and the price of gasoline nearly doubled.[26] Unlike housing and utilities subsidies, which primarily benefited rich elites, low gasoline prices moderated the cost of other market goods and services.[27] Informal market prices soared, especially in remote areas. In Luanda, taxi drivers and operators of the death-defying minivans called *candongueiros* flouted the government's attempts to limit fare hikes from the previous rate of 25 kwanzas by just 5 kwanzas and charged pas-sengers fees of 40 to 100 kwanzas (da Costa 2004; *Jornal de Angola* 2004f).

Government reporters reassured the angry populace that the new prices were considered low by international standards; however, criticism of the subsidy cuts was mounting throughout the country. Waiting for an electric-ity outage to pass, I sat on the Soyo docks with a friend as he surveyed the newspaper headlines. "This will be the MPLA's banana peel," predicted my friend, an optimistic critic of the dos Santos regime. Members of the UNITA opposition party expressed their concern that rising fuel costs would "pro-voke a greater erosion of workers' salaries" (*O Apostolado* 2004g). Secretary-General Manuel Viage of UNTA, the National Union of Angolan Workers, likewise critiqued the government's decision to cut fuel subsidies, citing the high cost of living in contrast with the paltry earnings afforded by the 2004 official minimum salary of $50 per month (*Jornal de Angola* 2004g). A schoolteacher struggling to survive on 8,000 kwanzas per month, nearly twice the minimum wage, told reporters that she once bought five bread rolls for 50 kwanzas—one for each of her children to eat for breakfast—but after the subsidy cuts, the price of bread doubled and her children had to suffice with dividing three rolls among them (*Agora* 2004c).

Shortages persisted and merchants in the informal market continued to increase their prices accordingly: a 20-kilogram tank of cooking gas officially valued at 1,200 kwanzas sold for up to 4,000 kwanzas on the informal market (Cavumbo 2004; Tunga 2005). Although Sonangol officials regularly printed ads in the national newspaper discouraging consumers from purchasing fuel products from unauthorized vendors for safety reasons, the national oil company could not satisfy demand. A doctor from Soyo's hospital professed to have witnessed a number of gruesome accidents provoked by exploding lamps, presumably filled with black market kerosene.

In the span of 10 months, subsidy cuts brought gasoline up to 40 kwanzas per liter from 12 and diesel to 29 kwanzas from 8. Kerosene reached a new high of 26 kwanzas per liter. Urban families struggled to buy cooking gas, while rural households with no electricity needed kerosene for lighting. Children of families too poor to purchase overpriced kerosene gave up their nighttime reading.[28] Women unable to afford cooking fuel advanced deforestation by resorting to charcoal and firewood.

The government assured artisanal fishermen in Soyo that it would continue to subsidize gasoline and diesel for their operations (Cafussa 2004b).[29] Sonangol promised two shipments of specially subsidized fuel each month to Soyo's Instituto de Pesca Artesanal (IPA). On days when the shipments arrived, fishermen hauled off drums containing 200 liters of gasoline at a cost of 4,400 kwanzas each; at a price of almost 25 cents per liter, they received a price break of 45 percent.[30] Irregular shipments provoked scuffles among fishermen displeased with one-drum limits: many considered five drums more reasonable given the uncertainty of supply. When Sonangol failed to deliver the promised fuel altogether, outraged artisanal fishermen accused corrupt bureaucrats of profit seeking through the diversion of fuel intended for the fisheries sector to the Democratic Republic of Congo.

Diverting Fuel

Subsidized or not, fuel proved difficult to obtain in Soyo because a large portion of Sonangol's shipments bled across the riverine border. During daytrips on the Congo River in November 2004 and January 2005, I noticed large skiffs overloaded with drums of fuel leaving Soyo's Kimbumba dock for the Democratic Republic of Congo. Locals told me that during the previous year one such boat heading to Muanda loaded with 40 drums sank at the mouth of the river, killing three people. An estimated 8,000 liters of fuel continued to leak from the rusting drums, contaminating the river and killing fish and their offspring.[31]

The illicit trade caught the attention of National Director of Customs Sílvio Burity. Condemning the trafficking, he criticized Sonangol employees who diverted gasoline, diesel, and kerosene from the depository withdrawn under the pretext of supplying local vendors (Cristóvão 2004). Burity threatened the traders with legal action, noting that their activities were in contravention of Law 6/99 regarding economic infractions (*Jornal de Angola* 2004a). In the first half of 2004, the Angolan government lost an estimated $2,786,253 as illegal traders rerouted nearly 22,362 metric tons of refined fuels, primarily gasoline, to the Democratic Republic of Congo (Cristóvão 2004).[32] Despite government threats and condemnation, locals told me that traffic in refined fuels from Kimbumba continued unabated a year later.

Intrigued by the illegal trade in fuel, I arranged a daytrip to Boma in the Democratic Republic of Congo in March 2005. Traveling upriver, my companions and I noted several makeshift barges ferrying drums from Kimbumba. Unfortunately, several kilometers outside of Boma we hit a sandbank and the propellers of our two outboard motors collided. As we slipped slowly along the river on a single impaired propeller, I noted the faint rainbow sheen of fuel floating on the water's surface. We faced a fierce interrogation by Congolese immigration and customs officials upon arrival in Boma and spent most of the day seeking out and negotiating a replacement propeller. After securing a used propeller from a shifty merchant in exchange for $100, a fish lunch, and a couple of beers, our captain eagerly fit the piece and prepared for our escape. Still, I could not leave without an answer to one question. Stopping in at a small kiosk, I asked what the going rate for gasoline was in Boma. It was 81 cents per liter—roughly $3.07 a gallon.[33]

We skipped down to the boat and shoved off just as a skiff bearing drums of fuel docked. As our fearless captain fought the rushing water, I ran through calculations in my head. The going price for a drum of gasoline at Kimbumba was 7,000 kwanzas—that was 35 kwanzas, about 40 cents, per liter for 200 liters. The 41-cent differential between the Kimbumba purchase price and the standard market price of gasoline in Boma allowed for a hefty profit margin. Officials with access to Sonangol's fuel stores could earn up to $80 per drum by diverting Soyo's gasoline to the Democratic Republic of Congo.[34] The night grew dark. We braced ourselves against the wind as the boat slapped down wildly on the turbulent river. My head swirling with numbers and my knuckles tightly gripping the bench, I glimpsed a glowing light on the horizon. The flares from offshore oil platforms welcomed us back to Soyo.

AN UNDERDEVELOPED MUNICIPALITY

For all the resource wealth—refined and crude—exported from Soyo, the municipality remains desperately underdeveloped. The few utilities installed in Soyo during the colonial period, when it was known as Santo António, were destroyed by war or neglect. Electricity and plumbing have not been restored to Pângala and other outlying communities but are mostly functional in Soyo town.[35] Other sectors, like communications, leapfrogged into the future. With only 133 of the 150 fixed telephone lines functioning, Soyo's residents have come to rely on the Unitel cellular network—a positive circumstance for Isabel dos Santos, who is both a primary stakeholder and the president's daughter (GoA 2003a). Soyo's water system is limited and shortages in town became more pronounced after October 2002 when oil companies and their counterparts at the Kwanda base began to consume municipal water for industrial use (Mavinga 2003a). In the rural reaches of Soyo municipality, only 45 percent of residents have access to potable water in their communities and many must walk two kilometers to bring water to their homes (GoA 2003a).

Zaire province covers 40,130 square kilometers and features 250 kilometers of breathtaking coastline flanked with billions of dollars' worth of oil infrastructure, but its inhabitants are impoverished and undereducated. A government report estimated that 74 percent of the total population of Zaire province and 29 percent of its school-aged children are illiterate (GoA 2003a). Only 39 percent of school-aged children in the province are enrolled in classes and just 25 percent of students meet the criteria established by the school board (ibid.). Local students have few scholastic targets to which they might aspire. Although a moderate number of schools offer primary education for six- to fourteen-year-olds, secondary schools, technical schools and pre-university courses are scarcer, and Zaire province offers no higher education—students must relocate to another province to attend university.[36] A handful of locals wealthy or intrepid enough to pursue schooling outside Soyo prove the exception to the rule, but oil corporations consider most local job seekers undereducated. They are, in the words of one executive, "only fit to cut grass."[37] The vast numbers of unemployed or underemployed vie for a limited number of unskilled casual positions. Disillusioned youths fear they have no future to work for and drop out of school, hastening the reality of a self-fulfilling prophecy.

On the whole, jobs are scarce in Zaire province. Only 5,000 families receive support from a salaried employee of the formal sector, whether public or private. Another 23,340 families cite small-scale farming and 1,298 families report artisanal fishing as the source of their sustenance and rely on trade in the informal sector to earn income (GoA 2003a). The lack of a deepwater port slows the flow of goods from Luanda to formal sector shops in Soyo, but a bustling business between informal merchants in Soyo and traders from the neighboring Democratic Republic of Congo supplies many of the goods for sale at the sprawling marketplace on the edge of Soyo town.[38] In the *praça, kinguilas* wave stacks of Angolan kwanzas, American dollars, and Congolese francs. Sacks of concrete slouch heavily near a wheelbarrow with signs advertising free delivery to customers. Women in colorful head wraps measure cupfuls of rice, salt, and flour from heaped mounds. Men cater to the growing population of alcoholics with boxes of red wine and shots of whiskey in plastic that resemble oversized condiment packets.

Merchants in the *praça* sell medications for every ailment or predicament without a prescription—from chloroquine, antibiotics, and contraceptives to painkillers, IVs, and immunizations—although their authenticity is questionable. The alternative, visiting the Soyo hospital, proves less convenient. With 71 beds and five doctors on contract from Cuba and Portugal, it is the largest and best-equipped medical facility in the province; but with only one doctor for every 1,500 patients, the sick are forced to wait (GoA 2003a). When I visited Soyo hospital in 2004, queues of listless mothers and their children sprawled on the benches and concrete patio outside the consultation room. Inside, a nurse handled open vials of blood and called forth patients for their blood tests, each time reaching for a clean needle without changing her latex gloves. Another nurse noted symptoms and made preliminary diagnoses for the usual diseases: malaria, diarrhea, typhoid fever, trypanosomiasis, measles, and tuberculosis. Many of these illnesses are linked to poor sanitary conditions: just 40 percent of Soyo's residents use latrines, and municipal waste collection systems are grossly insufficient (ibid.).

Although malaria represents the most common health threat in Soyo, AIDS is on the rise. Zaire province registered sixty-two cases of AIDS in the first four months of 2004; 42 of these cases corresponded to Soyo (*O Apostolado* 2004f). In 1991, health officials acknowledged the province's first AIDS patient in Soyo. A report released a decade later revealed 421 HIV-infected individuals living in the municipality (ANGOP 2001). Many residents attributed Soyo's rising rates of HIV/AIDS to illegal immigrants slipping across the fluid border of the Congo River. A traditional authority remarked, "We have a problem with AIDS because of the neighboring Congo—the women come here to engage in prostitution." His assessment seemed misleading. The sex workers were not all Congolese and the real problem was not the supply of prostitutes but the demand for them. A nightclub at the edge of town revealed one source of local demand for prostitution: oil workers spending some of their disposable income between shifts.[39]

Wishing Well

Soyo's residents once believed that oil might lift their municipality from poverty. Instead, it has not only undermined resource-based livelihoods but also created new internal divisions. During my interviews with fishers and farmers, I developed a picture of the uneven distribution of the costs and benefits of oil. To better understand the rift between the few locals working in the oil industry and the vast numbers excluded, I spoke with oil workers stationed at Kwanda Base. One of them admitted, "As you know, there are only bad feelings between someone who has something and someone who has nothing. Generally there is a bad feeling from the one who is not working. It happens in each society."

Almost everyone in Soyo dreams of working for an oil corporation—the salary and prestige are unrivaled. The positions in this labor-scarce industry are few, however, and the high-paying positions are filled in Luanda. With fewer connections, and often less education, Soyo's residents are at a disadvantage in their own territory and are usually relegated to unskilled "casual" positions as painters, landscapers, drivers, and the like for indeterminate periods. Apart from secretarial positions, almost all of the posts are occupied by men: oil corporations prefer not to hire women for technical jobs requiring long absences because of their familial obligations.[40]

Internal divisions within the industry also exist between Angolan workers and expatriates. Some of the foreign workers resented Angolanization statutes aimed at replacing them with nationals.[41] A few from the expat old guard considered the offshore platforms their turf and used racial epithets in reference to Angolan workers. One Angolan oil worker reluctantly recalled an incident in which his foreign supervisor referred to him as "boy," and another claimed that an expatriate once passed him a spanner on his foot rather than offering the tool by hand. Workers in Soyo are hesitant to protest poor treatment, however, because their employers often view participation in a strike as grounds for dismissal.[42]

Some Angolan workers considered the gap between national and expatriate salaries as contributing to the air of superiority adopted by foreigners. "Life is very difficult, it is very expensive. But someone who is living outside of his country, although he is assuming the same responsibilities as I do, he can earn more money due to the risk he takes in leaving his country to come here," explained an experienced worker at the Kwanda Base. On Soyo's Block 2, he said, "you see an American getting $12,000 in 28 days and a national employee gets $1,500" for an identical position or a "national is doing the same job as an engineer from France who gets $4,500 base monthly salary and an Angolan national can get $1,000." Angolan law prohibits salary discrimination between Angolans and expatriates, but oil corporations "exaggerate" risk premiums to attract skilled foreign laborers.[43] The oilman also expressed concern that low-level national employees, who generally undertake the most hazardous tasks, are more likely to risk exposure to "gases out there that could make one sterile," even though their salaries did not compensate for such risks. Breathing a long sigh, he confessed that despite the hazards nearly everyone in Soyo aspired to a job in the oil industry. "Even still," he said, "people from the government are leaving their posts to go work on the Base."

Angolanization of expatriate posts and local content standards represent part of a government effort to broaden economic opportunities in the national oil industry. The oil sector may not require more than several thousand laborers, but increasing local content can create jobs in auxiliary sectors. Angola may never produce large-scale technical infrastructure like the thirty-ton tension leg platform transported from South Korea for ExxonMobil's Kizomba B field, but nearly $2 billion worth of associated facilities and equipment could be manufactured in Angola (*Jornal de Angola* 2005a; Reuters 2003). The fruits, vegetables, fish, meat, and bottled water consumed in oil base cafeterias could also be sourced locally.

The opportunities for developing local staff and content in Soyo are significant. Still, the government sited training facilities and drew investment far outside of the oil-producing region. The National Petroleum Institute, Angola's academy grooming graduates for positions in the oil sector, is located 13 kilometers inland of Sumbe. Soyo's residents expressed frustration and confusion with this decision. "In Sumbe there is no oil," said one. Another expressed consternation over oil companies hiring and training employees from provinces that do not produce oil. He contended that oil was part of the environment and life experience of people in Soyo, so "it makes no sense to find someone from landlocked Cuando Cubango to work on an offshore platform. He has never been to the ocean, never seen petroleum, never seen oil industry activity." A Total executive agreed that a training academy in Soyo to train locals would be better because his employees—who came from well-connected families in Luanda and had the requisite technical training from their studies in Sumbe—complained too much about Soyo's intermittent electricity, poor nightlife, and inadequate housing. Nonetheless, Total donated $800,000 to expand the National Petroleum Institute (ANGOP 2008g).

Government decisions to site oil industry activities far outside the extractive zone reflect a desire to reward powerful interests. Lobito, a city boasting Angola's second-largest port and a strong merchant class, will host a $3.5 billion refinery expected to process 240,000 barrels per day.[44] The government also chose Lobito as the site for a new oil logistics and supply base, including a Sonamet submarine and survey machinery plant expected to employ some 800 Angolans. Clearly flummoxed, a resident of Soyo remarked, "They are building a base in Lobito—like the Kwanda base. They have oil in the South [but] not really a large amount like here in the North between Luanda, Soyo, and Cabinda." Despite his resentment that Lobito had been chosen over Soyo, he acknowledged Lobito's winning attribute: its decent port. I followed his gaze as he motioned toward the Kwanda port, where a large Halliburton ship dubbed the "War Admiral" dwarfed the docks as the crew prepared for offshore fracturing operations.

Turning Gas into Gold

The operators of Soyo's offshore blocks had money to burn; at least they flared the natural gas associated with the oil they extracted. Angola flares 70 percent of all associated gases from oil production. As the price of natural gas increased, however, operators questioned the economic rationality of flaring natural gas. Sonangol and Chevron discussed the possibility of constructing and jointly managing a liquefied natural gas (LNG) plant to process and export natural gas from offshore blocks in the Congo Basin. Estimates of Angola's natural gas reserves range between 283 and 566 billion cubic meters, with around 250 billion cubic meters in the basin south of the Congo River alone (Aguilar 2001:53).

As the potential profitability of the LNG project became increasingly evident, BP, ExxonMobil, and Total enlisted in the consortium.[45] After prolonged discussions over tax holidays and the site of the facility, the Angolan Council of Ministers approved plans to build the LNG terminal and liquefaction unit near Soyo in March 2005. The $10 billion project will produce 5 million metric tons of LNG annually (BP 2007a). Chevron will operate the plant, drawing the initial supply from Blocks 0, 14, 15, 17, and 18.[46] Other sources, including development of Blocks 1 and 2, are also under consideration. The project entered an initial engineering phase upon approval, and Soyo expects to make its first LNG deliveries in 2012 (De Sousa 2008).

Just months after Hurricanes Katrina, Rita, and Wilma diminished the natural gas supply to the southeastern United States, Chevron CEO Dave O'Reilly presented the Angola LNG project at a Joint Hearing of the Senate Energy and Natural Resource Committee and the Senate Commerce, Science and Transportation Committee. He remarked, "So, what actions are we taking now to supply natural gas to this market? We are co-leading a project to produce and liquefy natural gas in Angola, ship it across the Atlantic Ocean to a regasification facility in the U.S. Gulf Coast, and transport it via pipeline to the market" (O'Reilly 2005).

Despite high market demand in the United States, critics of intercontinental LNG projects such as Soyo's cite three concerns. First, the tankers transporting up to 125 million liters of extremely flammable LNG will require protection from the U.S. Coast Guard, as they could be used as a terrorist target capable of creating a fireball a half-kilometer wide (Helvarg 2006).[47] Second, it is anticipated that regasification plants in the United States, which will be sited by the environmentally unfriendly Federal Energy Regulatory Commission, will kill fish eggs, larvae, and fry, as well as zooplankton through open loop seawater heating systems (ibid.). Third, transnational oil corporations advertise natural gas as a cleaner-burning fuel, yet the liquefaction, transport, and re-gasification processes involved in marketing LNG internationally consume 18 to 40 percent more natural gas depending upon the efficiency standards of the LNG infrastructure (Coequyt and Albrecht 2004:9).

On the opposite side of the Atlantic, Manuel António, Soyo's Municipal Administrator, told international reporters, "This province is anxiously waiting for its own development either with the LNG project or with the increase in oil production and the growth of the sector" (Iley and Eisenstein 2004). The town buzzed with the news of the LNG terminal and liquefaction facility. But, as with oil, it seemed likely that the rosy image of development locals envisioned for the gas sector would prove too optimistic.

The discovery of a few locally held misconceptions darkened my outlook on the project. First, the municipal administrator touted the LNG project's capacity to employ 8,000 to 9,000 workers during the start-up phase in clearing brush from the site and assisting construction activities, yet corporate representatives of Angola LNG cautioned that qualified candidates for the 350 long-term positions will likely be sought from outside Soyo (Iley and Eisenstein 2004; BP 2007a). An industry insider claimed that, more than lacking qualifications, a dearth of connections will hinder locals from securing jobs in the LNG sector. "They will come to organize a test for face value—to say 'yes, we have been to Soyo but we could not hire anybody'—[but ultimately] they are going to hire people from Luanda and send them [to Soyo]," he predicted.

Second, the corporations invested in Soyo's LNG effort boasted their contribution to protecting the local environment by diminishing Angola's 85 percent natural gas flare rate.[48] Nevertheless, as with Russia's Sakhalin, Peru's Camisea, and Indonesia's Tangguh LNG projects, environmental advocates express concern that laying pipelines and directing tankers through the biologically diverse area around Soyo could prove detrimental to the sensitive ecosystem.

Third, many of Soyo's residents believe the LNG plant will finally solve their energy problems. A man in Mongo Soyo excitedly related, "We have heard that there is a company coming to bottle, distribute and sell gas to everyone—the LNG company, but they are still not here." He pronounced the letters *L-N-G* with precision, entrusting his hopes for a steady supply of electricity and cooking gas to the new entity. The LNG consortium, of course, planned to compress natural gas for more profitable Atlantic markets rather than domestic ones. Only Luanda, with 39.6 percent of its residents using gas stoves for cooking, presented a viable domestic market for LNG, but the government expressed little enthusiasm for creating the necessary infrastructure for LNG's distribution in Luanda or elsewhere in the country. To garner the highest profits from LNG produced in Soyo, the consortium will ship the majority to North America, Europe, and possibly South America, leaving a fraction of the incoming gas (at most 2.1 million cubic meters daily) for less-profitable domestic industrial uses such as a proposed ammonia and urea plant (Aguilar 2001:55).[49]

One final issue piqued my concern as the consortium finalized plans for the LNG plant in Soyo. I heard that its representatives had held a meeting to discuss the project with locals and to gather their input on site options for the facility. Faced with the choices of locating the LNG plant inside Kwanda, where its impact on local populations and the environment might be mitigated, or at the more ecologically sensitive fishing beach bordered by mangroves called Sereia, Soyo's people chose the latter.

Sereia, the Portuguese word for mermaid, was so named for sightings of these mythical creatures in nearby bends of the Congo River and its estuarine reaches. Fishermen in Soyo regaled me with stories of adventurous seafarers who made love to shallow-water sirens, but every tale invariably ended in lamentation of their dwindling numbers with the advent of oil extraction. Suspecting that the rare West African manatee (*Trichechus senegalensis*) inspired these romantic accounts, I found historical clues to their presence in the Congo estuary in accounts of a law in the Kongo kingdom, punishable by death, that fishermen hand over any captured "pig-fish" to the crown (Martins 1958:42). A few of Soyo's fishers confirmed that one of the species in decline was the *Ngulu a Maza*, a Kisolongo term literally meaning "pig of the water"—clearly a reference to the disappearing manatee.

Manatees and mermaids alike have all but abandoned these waters, leaving only a faint mystical memory in the minds of the eldest fishermen. Standing at the future site of the LNG plant in Sereia, I wondered why community members preferred this location. An attendee of the meeting with the LNG consortium explained their logic: if the consortium were to build the facility behind the gates of Kwanda, community members would more likely be excluded from the operations. They reasoned that if the consortium built the liquefaction plant in the midst of the poor fishing camp at Sereia, locals might be able to supervise the operations more closely and benefit from their proximity as neighbors.

The rationale for choosing Sereia implied the community's lack of trust in the oil sector as well as its desperation. For what returns had they prepared to brave the health and environmental risks of locating the LNG facility at Sereia? Did they hope to receive electricity or jobs? I recalled the words of a Total employee who claimed that people had moved close to new well sites in hopes of collecting compensation payments from the corporation.[50] Upon hearing his story I had dismissed the contention, assuming that migrants had settled there because Total had cleared the area of landmines. Looking out on the newly dredged canal at Sereia, however, I began to question my judgment.

THE CORPORATE CONTRIBUTION

Agip (now Eni) named the Safueiro well in honor of the African plum tree just as it gave the abandoned test wells in Block 1 names paying homage to Soyo's native coconut, avocado, papaya, and lime trees. The offshore orchard has borne few fruits for the residents of Soyo. Early corporate development efforts in Soyo were largely limited to the infrastructure necessary to extract oil and provide for expatriate workers. During the colonial period, Fina built the tarmac road linking Soyo town with operational hubs in Pângala, Quinfuquena, and Acampamento 8, with a network of unpaved roads providing access to wells. The oil company also constructed Bairro Fina, a neighborhood featuring 96 houses equipped with electricity and running water, a school, and a playground. This company town was less an investment in Soyo than an enticement for workers who relocated to the region. UNITA forces destroyed key portions of Soyo's oil infrastructure, but the road and Bairro Fina remain—albeit in degrees of disrepair.[51]

The few locals working in the oil sector questioned why Total and Chevron, multibillion dollar transationals raking in windfall profits, did not contribute more to Soyo. "The companies are not doing anything," alleged a local oilman. The excuses of the past would no longer suffice. "A good number of companies used to say 'because of the war, because of the war,' but now the war is finished. We are trying to see their strategies and see what they are doing for the communities now that we are not going to have more war," he told me.

I asked Soyo's municipal administrator whether he had seen a change in oil corporations' stance toward local communities since the war's end in 2002. He replied, "Lately we have noticed a bit . . . a small preoccupation with the poverty, illiteracy, and sickness . . . oil companies building schools and clinics, but I do not see this as sufficient. It is a drop of water in the ocean." I laughed knowingly when he related how Luandans and expatriates contracted to work at the Soyo oil base found Soyo's tiny airport lacking: it did not fit their vision of an oil-producing area. "So the place where the petroleum is cannot be like this, it has to be developed," he explained. "Coming into the airport they say, 'No, we're not getting out.' And we say, 'Soyo is here.' And they say 'No, I'm going to Soyo.' Why? What he saw did not indicate a production area. The petroleum zone is a developed zone."

The municipal administrator quoted an Angolan aphorism: "If you want to enhance your economic life a bit, make friends with a rich person."[52] But, he clarified, "It makes little sense for me to be poor alongside a rich person without getting anything from him—we cannot have a good relationship." Likewise, he reasoned that the corporations had a moral responsibility to raise the standard of living in Soyo.

Leveraging Development

Transnational oil corporations rarely engage in development efforts out of moral responsibility. Their development investments are designed to enhance relationships with the government and local communities as well as to improve their brand image. Oil corporations undertake projects alone or through block associations, wherein each corporation contributes a percentage of the project cost proportional to their interest stake in the concession. In many cases, the corporations or association will pay the fixed costs and will rely on the government to supply the staff and variable costs. Seeking to provide concrete evidence of their good works to shareholders, they often choose construction projects: for example, building schools or health posts. The government considers all projects contributing to "permanent development" tax deductible. Anyone, from community members to high-level government officials, can propose ideas to the oil corporations, but the individual corporation or block association determines which projects they want to support.

By law, the Angolan government must allocate 10 percent of the revenues derived from taxation of profits from oil produced in Zaire province to provincial development activities. Oil corporations pay the central government, which distributes the funds accordingly. Some of Soyo's residents privately accused corrupt leaders of swallowing most of the monies. Many preferred that corporations undertake development directly, rather than remit development funds to the government. One murmured, "They should stop paying the money to the government and should use it directly for development to build roads and schools themselves. The government is not going to develop this country with that money—it would be better to have the companies developing it."

Social projects could not begin to surmount Soyo's shortcomings, yet in the absence of government initiatives local people had begun to direct their developmental claims to the oil corporations. A Total official in Soyo claimed to spend at least one-third of his workday "dealing with the community" and their requests for schools, churches, cement, roofing materials, electricity, running water, and cooking gas.[53] Based upon his reports, executives at the corporate headquarters in Luanda mapped out construction of schools and health posts. Low-level employees from Soyo are all but excluded from the process. Apart from informal discussions at barbeques, local oil workers told me they had little input.

As in Cabinda, oil corporations' few efforts at community development in Soyo have mainly targeted the education and health sectors. As operator of offshore Block 2 and partner in the FST onshore concession through its Texaco subsidiary, Chevron presented a health post to the community of Pângala in 1998, provided assistance to Soyo's Kikudu and Pinda Catholic mission schools, and announced plans for agricultural assistance in Zaire province in 2004. ExxonMobil, the operator of deepwater Block 15 and a shareholder in ultra-deepwater Block 31, offered support to local anti-malaria programs and built a science lab with three new classrooms for 400 new students (ANGOP 2004f). The corporation also donated library books to Soyo's Daniel Vemba

High School. As a stakeholder in Block 15, but not yet producing as operator of ultra-deepwater Block 31, BP joined ExxonMobil's efforts. As operator of Soyo's onshore blocks and a holder of interest stakes in offshore Blocks 1, 2, and 31, Total allied with Pesnorte to build a school in Pângala. Sonangol, the national concessionaire and interest holder in both Soyo's onshore and Blocks 2 and 31 offshore of the municipality, refurbished a school dating back to the colonial era in Kitona. In conjunction with Chevron and ExxonMobil, Sonangol also helped construct and continues to financially assist a teacher training college run by ADPP, a Danish NGO closely aligned with President dos Santos.[54] Still, the number of oil-backed development projects in Soyo remains relatively small in comparison to Cabinda.

Milking Compensation

ExxonMobil, Total, Chevron, BP and Sonangol—the operators of concessions in Soyo—also have community development projects in Luanda. Nevertheless, when oil corporations unveil schools or health posts in Soyo, residents see these projects as more than just exercises in corporate responsibility—they construe them as compensation for all the failed promises of oil development. Despite inflicting damage to human and ecological health, the responsible companies rarely offer the affected communities in Soyo the usual form of compensation: monetary remuneration.

Total willingly contributes to social projects under the terms of its concession contract, yet the corporation has a reputation in Soyo for ignoring accidents and failing to pay compensation. When toxic gas leaked from one of Soyo's onshore wells in 1998, local people heard about this danger not from Total but from the Voice of America radio program. Another onshore well—Well 41 drilled in 1991—leaked poisonous gas on the night of February 6, 2004, intoxicating seventeen Pângala inhabitants and reportedly killing four goats. Again, Total failed to warn the community. Locals claimed the gas smelled of rotten eggs and those familiar with the odor presumed it to be highly toxic hydrogen sulfide (H_2S).

A few months after the incident, I sought out victims of the leak to learn more about their experience. One testified:

> When we started to feel bad around 4 P.M., we thought to contact Total, who could we call? We had no number or address for anyone. So, we were feeling bad and around 8 P.M. or 9 P.M. we were really sick and I began to vomit. I dropped my friend off at his house and went to look for my sisters at home and I found my niece vomiting and my sister was on the floor.

He remembered that the gas not only harmed people but also nearby plants and a group of goats, which ended up dying. Another victim recalled:

> The gas polluted the whole area and all of the people around were affected, including me. Three children fell ill . . . one my family brought to the hospital, but the others remained sick in the house where we heard the government announcement about gas of an unknown origin on the radio—and we knew the origin of that gas.

An oil worker familiar with Total's onshore operations contended that the leak "happened due to negligence" and criticized the corporation for refusing to accept responsibility. One of Total's employees noted with disdain that the corporation regularly subjected him to long safety meetings but willfully failed to inform local inhabitants of the risks associated with extraction. A representative of the Ministry of Environment in Luanda, Francisco Cristo João, reprimanded Total for not posting warning placards and commented that people should not be permitted to live so close to the onshore wells (Figueiredo 2004). Government officials in Soyo ignored the victims' pleas for information and intervention. One victim observed the car belonging to Soyo's municipal administrator "pass by with windows up, so as to not hear anyone."

Total also closed its ears to the victims of the incident. Superintendent Justin Combo suggested that locals had feigned their symptoms in an attempt to extort funds from the corporation, and onshore operations director José Dias Nogueira discounted the possibility of hydrogen sulfide gas in the area (Figueiredo 2004). Despite the fact that the corporation transported the most acutely intoxicated victims to a local clinic that evening, executives refused to pay compensation or to reimburse victims for medical expenses incurred by continuing symptoms like blurred vision, chest pains, dry cough, and terrible stomach pains. The supermajor's only contribution was an offering of five cartons of milk for a twenty-two-year-old victim (Marques 2004b).

During interviews on the incident, local inhabitants appeared unfazed by Total's reaction. They told me such incidents occurred with frequency, citing leaks that intoxicated soldiers stationed at Ngene 4 and other wells during the war as well as another episode in which villagers near the Quinfuquena installations fell ill when workers forgot to close a valve after maintenance activities. One of the victims of the February 2004 incident admitted he never expected to receive compensation. Citing other cases in which locals had demanded compensation, he sighed, "The government says that the communities should be compensated, but the corporations say, 'We are not to blame. Your government is to blame, we already paid them.'"[55] The victims could hold neither Total nor their government officials accountable for damages.

Fishermen suffering the effects of offshore pollution also lobbied concession operators and government leaders for compensation without success. As I spoke with Soyo's artisanal fishermen, they highlighted unfair differences in compensation between Soyo and Cabinda. They knew that Chevron granted fishers in Cabinda compensation for offshore spills.[56] Nonetheless, it seemed that fishermen in Soyo had received exaggerated reports on Chevron's compensation policy.

Spreading his net on the sand, a fisherman squinted at me in the glaring daylight. "In Cabinda, there was a spill and the fishermen could not fish for six months. They were compensated with enough money to buy cars, motors for their boats, and to construct houses. There have been times when we had so much oil in the water, but we never received compensation," he told me. A similar tale from another fisherman focused on how shortages in Soyo undermined his trade and revealed his assumptions about the developmental advantages of fishers to the north: "We cry for our children. We cannot freeze our catch because we have no ice. In Cabinda, they have ice and gasoline, so they do not suffer as much." He waved in the direction of a defunct generator presumably once employed to make ice and reiterated, "Diesel and water are difficult to obtain."

THE POLITICS OF INTIMIDATION

The strongest division in northern Angola exists between the two largest oil-producing provinces: Zaire and Cabinda. Whereas coastal communities in both provinces suffer the degrading effects of the oil industry—and the inhabitants of Soyo endure additional pollution from onshore installations—corporate development schemes and compensation measures are more common in Cabinda.

Some of Soyo's residents questioned whether differences in operatorship account for the disparity. They contrasted Chevron's domination of Cabinda's offshore Blocks 0 and 14 to the various operators of concessions offshore of Soyo: BP in ultra-deepwater Block 31, ExxonMobil in deepwater Block 15, and Eni and Chevron in shallow Blocks 1 and 2. Several of Soyo's fishermen postulated that the presence of multiple operators offshore confounded attempts to determine the origin of spills, whereas in Cabinda there was no confusion because Chevron operated both the shallow and deepwater blocks.

Moreover, they contended that as an American firm Chevron "has a different policy [emphasizing] greater community action" and a corporate "culture" featuring a stronger commitment to local training and development.

Differing corporate cultures and unclear accountability mechanisms accounted for some—but not all—of the differences in compensation and development. Like Cabindans, Soyo's residents subscribe to the squeaky wheel theory of development—translated locally as "the mouth that talks eats." Nevertheless, in contrast to Cabindans highlighting their differences from Angola, people in Soyo commonly emphasized their identity within the Angolan context to make claims to government goods and services as well as additional benefits associated with oil extraction in their municipality. Some even expressed disdain for Cabindans' desire for independence and their articulation of a unique identity. One man said, "In Soyo we have not been regionalists or tribalists. . . . It is different here—we are Angolans. Cabindans say that they are special, so the government has given them gifts, unlike us. Those of us who are not intellectuals, we hammer our heads to understand this." His companion joined the conversation claiming, "It is said that Cabinda must enjoy something special. . . . They say from Cabinda to Cunene, but when they arrive in Cabinda, it is different." He questioned why the government conceded more autonomy to this prodigal province.

The lack of a political alternative may explain why corporations and government officials can safely ignore Soyo. Cabinda's independence struggle inspires narratives on difference, represents a political alternative to the government's exclusionary ruling patterns, and provides an outlet for resistance. No such movement exists in Soyo. Opposition parties seem unable to secure a foothold in the municipality. Holden Roberto's FNLA once carried much of the former Kongo kingdom, but the party lost favor due to mercenary scandals and civilian abuses. If not for its brutality, UNITA might have had a chance to win over the people of Soyo, who never had been as keen on Roberto's faction as the rest of Zaire province. After government forces chased UNITA from Soyo, residents felt they owed their survival to the MPLA. With a firm grip on the municipality, however, the ruling party appears to feel it owes nothing to Soyo.

Unavailing Protest

In mid-2004, I convened a focus group of rising civil society advocates in Soyo to talk about local protests. António, Pedro, and a few friends from the communities of Kitona and Pângala had recently joined forces to protest the government's unfulfilled promises of electricity. They spoke first of a large protest for electricity in 2003. The demonstration drew everyone into the streets: women neglected their daily cultivation routines, elders postponed their backyard conversations, fishermen left their nets on dry land, and children abandoned their games in the sand. Young and old alike, hundreds of demonstrators blockaded the main tarmac road, marching together until FAA troops allegedly sent to protect the protesters intervened. According to the protesters, the soldiers shot five civilians and left two of those with serious injuries. Following the protest, government authorities assured the people of Kitona and Pângala that a new turbine would be installed and functional within six months.

Around the same time, Angola's Department of the Interior installed a wing of the rapid intervention police (PIR) in the municipality at a cost of $350,000 to the local government (Mavinga 2003b). Authorities assured civilians that the PIR's mission in Soyo would be "to reduce the wave of illegal immigration" from the Democratic Republic of Congo (ibid.). Locals speculated that the specialized police force was installed to intimidate and repress potential protesters, especially those who would challenge the distribution of the costs and benefits of local oil extraction.

One year later, the government's promise to bring electricity to Kitona and Pângala remained unfulfilled. Similar protests in a sprawling community bordering the Kwanda oil base called Kikala Kiako resulted in the immediate installation of electricity, but Kitona and Pângala were farther down the road and apparently further down the new governor's list of priorities.[57] Kikala Kiako's proximity to Kwanda Base helped the community get electricity. Judging the disgruntled neighbors a potential threat to security, Sonangol partnered with the government to provide electricity.

Government officials and oil corporations operating in the country chose Soyo's developmental priorities strategically. They collaboratively prioritized development as an appeasement strategy for high-risk areas and wielded repression to subdue the remainder. Just as Sonangol responded to the potential threat in Kikala Kiako, Soyo's residents claimed that Chevron's development efforts in Cabinda represented a means of managing risk. One of the men in the focus group compared Chevron's disparate treatment of Soyo and Cabinda. He ventured, "They do it because of sabotage, I think. . . . I am fairly sure. But here, because people are peaceful, nothing is done. I really think this is the reason because in Cabinda they try to give."

Whereas sabotage officially occurred in both places, the act had a different meaning in Soyo than in Cabinda. To FLEC, sabotage—by blowing up pipelines or destroying corporate property—presented a means of threatening the government and Chevron, the occupying forces exploiting Cabinda's oil.[58] Apart from incidents attributed to UNITA during the war, Soyo's most common form of sabotage—pilfering and selling portions of tubing from well sites—represented a means of survival in desperate circumstances. After 2002, Soyo's oil industry registered only two cases of "attempted sabotage": the theft of metal pipes in December 2003 not far from Total's Quinfuquena base and the attempted robbery of tools, batteries, respiratory masks, lifesaving equipment, fire extinguishers, and storage containers from a platform in offshore Block 2 on May 12, 2004. Police arrested Macaia Mbinga and Chimba Komba, two middle-aged citizens of the Democratic Republic of Congo, in connection with the offshore burglary in 2004 and, despite police arrests of a few scapegoats from Quinfuquena, Total officials suspect that FAA soldiers from the military camp outside Pângala may have been responsible for the 2003 event.

Choosing Peace

António, a contemplative man born and raised in Soyo, contended that locals would never contemplate sabotage or violence no matter how desperate their situation.[59] He explained, "Sabotage or kidnapping does not occur here—it is different because this population is not too inspired by violence. They show their concern by talking on the radio, trying to negotiate with the government, and sending letters to companies." "We are not perfect," António continued. "If our government fails, we must be patient—we can react with words, but never violence."

Soyo's people experimented with words; they tried to express their grievances and to find ways to make claims to a greater share of oil's benefits. Nevertheless, they remained limited in their expression. All topics deemed "political" are taboo, for they are subject to repressive action. Almost anything—ranging from critiques of the government and discussion of protest events to simply estimating the population of a specific territory—may be labeled political.

During one of my first interviews in Soyo, I asked a war survivor how many people fled the municipality during the UNITA occupation. He responded uncomfortably, "I have colleagues who know, but they do not like to respond . . . they cannot respond . . . it is a little complicated to respond . . . politically." Pantomiming zippered lips, he shrugged awkwardly and I decided to proceed to the next question. When I asked about local resistance efforts in Pângala and Kitona, António warned me, "Look, I could lose my life for answering that." His friend Pedro jumped into the conversation saying, "They do not like the truth. I know that I am going to die, today or tomorrow, but I have to tell the truth. [We] lived for a long time under the single-party system." Pedro's friends coughed so as to cue him to stop his rant, but he continued: " . . . so no one had that courage. It was the fear of representing the truth. It is this same fear that lives within [us]. But for us it is worse [than Cabinda] because of the war. It was terrible. During the war with UNITA, the misery increased 200 or 300 percent. The misery increased . . . and the deaths increased. This was the worst. It was a grave situation. It was quite bitter." His friends groaned again, but he responded, "This is not politics or anything—this is the truth that we are telling. The people lived with bitterness. We saw things that we hadn't even seen in the colonial period. You know that this is the situation here, isn't it?" He nodded toward his friends and jeered playfully, "There are still people today that feel that democracy is a seven-headed beast."

Decades of war and repression instilled a fear of speaking out in Soyo. The war also diminished political alternatives for Soyo's residents seeking to voice their concerns. Giving credence to the popular Angolan aphorism, "The MPLA steals, UNITA kills," many ineluctably—albeit reluctantly— support the party of President dos Santos. Although both sides planted landmines in their fields and left their scars on the populace, Soyo's people tend to attribute their painful past to UNITA and to place their faith in the ruling party in hopes of a peaceful future.

SHALLOW BURIALS

Violence and degradation received a shallow burial in Soyo's sandy soils. The enduring effects of petro-violence have constrained local people's ability to effectively demand developmental benefits or compensation for damage to environmental and human health. Although many of Soyo's people privately condemn the MPLA's exclusionary politics, they lie trapped between a violent past with opposition parties and stiff government repression. Supporting the very system they despise remains the only path to economic advancement or a post in the oil industry. In a similarly convoluted sense, communities turn to the very oil corporations that have undermined local fishing and farming livelihoods as the best hope to overcome Soyo's chronic underdevelopment. Residents express renewed hope that LNG will fulfill oil's failed promises, but it seems unlikely that Soyo's latest extractive endeavor will undo or reshape the exclusionary patterns traced by the oil industry. The LNG plant's potential threats to human and environmental health could further compound the degradation of lands, fishing grounds, and livelihoods in the area.

Residents of Soyo expressed a preference for locating the LNG plant in Sereia, an environmentally sensitive area and local fishing beach, as opposed to Kwanda Base. It is unclear which motivations most influenced their choice—jobs, electricity, oversight, or even the possibility of compensation. They look toward Cabinda for clues as to how to gain compensation—but they do not yet recognize how, even in Cabinda, compensation has benefited only a select few and largely failed to offset the damage extraction has wrought on local ecosystems and livelihoods. No amount of money can compensate for the destruction caused by degradation, exclusion, and violence in the extractive zones. As a regional proverb cautions, "Only after the last tree is felled . . . the last fish is dead . . . the last river is poisoned, you will see that you cannot eat money."[60]

5. Unpalatable Compensation

Waves lapping at Fútila's blackened beach tell the story of the fishing community's relationship to oil. The community's proximity to offshore extraction and the Malongo base has rendered local livelihoods extremely vulnerable to pollution. Relying on the bounty of the sea, Fútila has grown poorer as workers from the neighboring base have exploited the rich deposits of oil beneath the seafloor.

At first glimpse, I found Malongo to be nothing more than an average industrial complex. It contains oil storage depots, a small refinery, living quarters, dining facilities, office blocks, and a company clinic. Standing outside its gates, however, I realized that Malongo's mystique owed primarily to the juxtaposition between the American way of life inside the compound and the weary sense of desperation in the surrounding area.

A Sonangol fuel truck emerged from Malongo and barreled toward Cabinda city, leaking gasoline onto the hot asphalt. A group of young boys slapped at the tinted windows of a shiny Toyota Land Cruiser parked next to the Teleservice security booth marked Gate 1. Kicking and elbowing one another, the boys jockeyed for the best position from which to shove their bulging Ziploc bags toward the driver.

They were selling *merendas*—snack bags provided free to oil workers, which are regularly smuggled out of Malongo base and resold at a premium outside the compound. Contents vary but each bag serves up a hearty American snack. A typical *merenda* includes a napkin and a very malleable plastic fork, three rolls of bread, an orange, a microwaveable cup of Hormel Kid's Mac and Beef, a small can of Prince's tuna, a small can of Spam, a package of peanut butter sandwich crackers, a Bluebird apple juice, a packet of Chips Ahoy cookies, and a quintessentially American Coca-Cola. This cornucopia of processed foods sold for around $3 on the

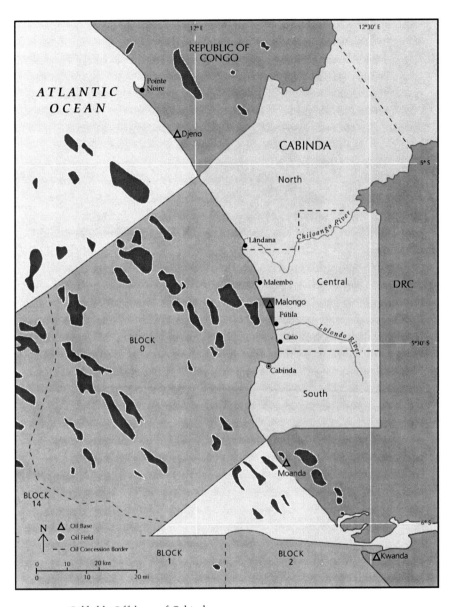

MAP 7. Oilfields Offshore of Cabinda

local market, an exorbitant price to most of Fútila's impoverished population, which subsisted mostly on locally sourced manioc, palm oil, and fish.

To borrow Frantz Fanon's phrase, Fútila is best described as "a town on its knees" turning "a look of lust, a look of envy" on Malongo (Fanon 1965:39). It is an ordinary Cabindan fishing community with just 1,754 inhabitants, but Fútila's proximity to Malongo stirs conflicting sentiments among the unemployed youth. Just twenty-five residents of Fútila hold coveted positions at the neighboring oil base—a lack of job alternatives leaves landless and undereducated coastal inhabitants few options besides fishing. Locals call Malongo "Little America" because all business within its gates is done in English; safety always comes first; there is always electricity, air conditioning, and running water; and the roads are well paved and free of dust (because they are regularly smoothed with waste oil).

In neighboring Fútila, most people speak Ibinda or Portuguese; underpaid and often drunk soldiers from the military base on the opposite end of Malongo harass locals; electricity is unreliable if it is available at all; the heat is suffocating; women carry water from communal standpipes when they function; and cars stir up a dull red dust every time they come rambling down the potholed road that splices the community down its center. The contrast between Fútila's deprivation and Malongo's excess sparks resentment among Cabindans: if this truly were their country, it would be their oil. Many Cabindans feel that the Angolan government has colluded with the American government and Chevron to exclude them from their own resource wealth. Malongo's concentric barbed-wire fences enclosing a corridor laden with land mines reinforce this aspect of exclusion.

Malongo, for its part, turns a look of aloof superiority and suspicion back at the rest of Cabinda. Although the Lulondo River traces a path from the highlands down to the coast near Malongo, Chevron's workers drink bottled water imported from Europe or mainland Angola and wash their hands in desalinated ocean water. The sanitized environment creates the illusion of separation, but offshore accidents occasionally pierce Malongo's bubble. On January 30, 2005, women in Malongo's laundry division noted the smell and tint of crude in their washing water and on their hands.[1] Offering little explanation, Chevron dismissed the launderers for two days. The source of the problem became apparent when it resurfaced the following month. This time, employees spotted an oil spill emanating from a pipeline near the intake apparatus of Malongo's desalination plant. The incident provoked a five-day hiatus in the laundry division. For urgent washing orders the laundry crew used bottled water.

Malongo can switch to bottled water, Fútila cannot. Fishermen and fish traders depend on the ocean's bounty for their livelihoods, yet they are not the only users of Cabindan seas. For weeks after the smallest of spills, children give up their favorite pastime of diving in the waves because they say the water feels prickly. An avid swimmer intimated that oily slicks had disrupted his daily dips and insinuated that Chevron might take a cue from Braspetro, which allegedly compensated bathers affected by an offshore spill in Brazilian waters.

Beachgoers and recreational fishers from Cabinda city also resent Chevron for degrading their weekend retreats. One city dweller, who enjoys driving up the coast on holidays, objected to executives in Malongo restricting his activities. He said, "We tasted oil and they told us not to fish. We felt itchy and they told us not to bathe in the ocean. Now we must wait 15 days or more until they say it is okay to eat or to swim." Ironically, oil spills have even circumscribed the pleasure activities of Chevron employees at their second homes on the coast or at Fútila Beach, a fenced-in private resort near Malongo.

This chapter examines the lives of artisanal fishers and fish traders, explores the socio-ecological costs of Angola's offshore oil industry on fishing communities, and assesses the value of Chevron's compensation programs intended to offset these damages. It begins in a similar vein as the previous chapter—by employing local narratives to elucidate resource users' grievances concerning exclusion and pollution associated with local oil extraction.[2] Whereas the previous chapter recognized how Soyo's residents failed to garner compensation due to repression limiting protest and a lack of political alternatives, this chapter demonstrates how local support for independence and protests from Cabindan resource users induced Chevron to compensate fishermen for losses associated with oil spills. Still, monetary payments fail to fully offset damage the oil industry exacts on ecosystems and livelihoods. Worse yet, populations most disadvantaged by extractive pollution in Cabinda have not received adequate compensation—or, in some cases, any recompense at all.

AN ENCLAVE OF NEGLECT

When President dos Santos declared peace in 2002, Cabinda's dilapidated infrastructure appeared almost decent in comparison with the most war-torn of Angola's provinces. Unlike UNITA, FLEC leaders had refrained from sabotaging targets like utilities and transportation corridors that would worsen Cabindans' quality of life; besides, FLEC's weapons arsenal was much less sophisticated. Decades of low-intensity fighting in Cabinda had wrought more psychological than structural damage to the province.

Neglect and lack of investment also account for Cabinda's degraded condition. Basic infrastructure, including roads, health posts, and schools need repairs. Of the 68,010 children between ages 5 and 14 enrolled in schools, the government expects only half to continue on to secondary school (GoA 2003b:7–8). Sanitation and electricity are confined mostly to the major towns. An overloaded, colonial-era sewer system—unfit to serve the estimated 160,380 inhabitants of the provincial capital—belches waste into Cabinda Bay. The electric company counts only 14,290 service addresses in all of Cabinda and outages are common (GoA 2003b:15). On top of all of these shortcomings, the cost of living is outrageously high. Due to Cabinda's outdated port, extra importation fees can make the cost of basic goods up to 66 percent more expensive than in Luanda (Heitor 2004b).[3]

Cabinda is an exclave of Angola, a detached province covering an area of 7,283 km² and containing a population of roughly 300,000. It comprises four municipalities: Cabinda, Cacongo, Buco Zau, and Belize. The municipality of Cabinda, host to the provincial capital of Cabinda city, is the most densely populated, with 68.5 persons per km² (GoA 2003b:1). Most Cabindans rely on subsistence farming, artisanal fishing, and trading on the informal sector to sustain themselves and their families. Chevron and a smattering of businesses supporting the oil industry employ a few hundred locals, but only 12 percent of Cabinda's population between the ages of 16 and 55 works in the formal sector (GoA 2003b:8).

Chevron's workers—known locally as *Malonguistas*—are the envy of Cabinda. *Malonguistas* are paid some of the highest salaries in Angola. They can afford to import American trucks and live in homes with electricity and running water. Almost everyone aspires to a job with Chevron, but only candidates with an excellent education and recommendations from influential individuals succeed. The chasm between the wealth embodied in Malongo and the poverty of Cabinda's masses fuels the independence movement headed by FLEC. Some Cabindans claim that Chevron invited FLEC members to take positions in Malongo during the 1990s so as to prevent attacks. One oilman reckoned that before 2002, 85 percent of *Malonguistas* were members of FLEC. Nevertheless, he conceded that the ratio was probably no higher than the proportion of people backing FLEC in the whole of Cabinda. "There are 300,000 people in Cabinda," he said, "they may not act with FLEC, but they support the ideals."[4] Since FLEC's founding in 1963, myriad internal disputes have provoked splinters and given rise to dozens of FLEC factions.⁵ Still, Cabindans continue to associate FLEC with a singular agenda: the pursuit of independence from Angola. However idealistic, they envision independence as the solution to Cabinda's exclusion and degradation at the hands of the Angolan government and Chevron.

Excluding Company

Cabinda Gulf Oil Company—first a subsidiary of Gulf Oil, then subsumed under Chevron's control in 1984, and hereafter referred to as Chevron—drilled Cabinda's first well in 1958. Portugal granted concessions prior to independence, but in 1976 Sonangol assumed the role of negotiator and concessionaire for all oil blocks. Chevron retained its operator stake in Block 0, comprising 5,500 km² of shallow water acreage, and entered a new contract with Sonangol in 1995 as operator of the 4,040 km² deepwater Block 14. Offshore discoveries multiplied and production increased exponentially over the 1980s and 1990s. By 2007, Chevron was producing 420,000 barrels per day from Block 0 and 200,000 barrels per day from Block 14 (De Sousa 2008).

Chevron ships half of the oil produced from Cabinda's offshore across the Atlantic to help sate the voracious American appetite for oil (Chevron 2002). Given Chevron's origins and the fate of the oil it extracts, Cabindans readily associate the corporation's installations with the United States. For example, a community fisheries coordinator explaining restrictions imposed by Chevron in the extractive zone sketched a map and explained, "It is prohibited to fish near the platform. There are limits. Let's suppose that *we* have the beach *here*. So, *there* are the *American* workstations—these are the platforms." Chevron's Takula platform sits about twenty-five kilometers offshore of Cabinda. The 6-story structure houses 180 workers and is equipped with telephones, running water, 24-hour electricity and satellite TV—amenities most Cabindans lack but readily associate with the wealth of America (Alfredo 2004). As with Malongo, Chevron restricts access to Takula and other platforms to employees, subcontractors, and registered guests. Just as Malongo's mined barbed-wire corridor guarded by Teleservice precludes uninvited locals from entry, patrol boats chase fishing vessels away from the platforms.

The platform moorings beneath the rippled ocean surface reportedly abound with fish, but Chevron prevents Cabindan fishermen from approaching. Safety regulations and post-9/11 anti-terrorist policy require fishers to keep their distance. The fisheries coordinator pointed to his hand-drawn map. "Where there are wells and pipelines, there is danger. We have a limit that cannot be trespassed—the danger zone—generally two miles, three, or one and a half," he warned. An informal survey of local fishermen revealed that few agreed on the actual distance of restriction. Some fishermen contended that Chevron had previously set the limit at 5,000 meters, yet a subset claimed that the corporation had increased it to 10,000 meters after 9/11. Others postulated a buffer zone of 10 nautical miles around each platform.

The fishermen also quarreled over the reason for their exclusion. A few claimed Chevron sought to avoid paying more compensation should fishermen's nets tear on underwater tubes. More believed that the corporation was worried fishermen could provoke a spill. A Chevron employee confided that corporate officials "think that people could take a bomb or something like that, maybe, to blow up a platform." The only such historical incident occurred when not a fisherman but a Chevron employee, said to be a member of FLEC, detonated a pipe bomb on an offshore heliport in an attempt to blow up the adjacent well, but succeeded only in exploding himself. Now, three Chevron boats, several helicopters, and a few fiscal police skiffs patrol the waters by day and AirScan surveillance planes monitor the area at night.

Cabindan fishermen seemed uncertain of the exact distance to keep from Chevron's offshore platforms, yet they clearly understood their exclusion from waters their ancestors fished long before oil's discovery. A seasoned seaman complained:

> There are areas where we used to fish that we can no longer fish because the man who exploits, our American, does not let us go to those areas where we once fished freely. Where there are petroleum wells, for example a platform where they work, we know that the fish congregate in these areas. They go there because it is a calm area and they eat the leftover food that they throw off the platform. Where there are humans, there is food. This [fish] is a being, whether a marine being, like any animal whether domestic or wild . . . where will it go? Where there is food. Would you like to live in an area where there isn't any food? Would you like to spend the whole day without eating? So, they need it, too.

The fisherman contrasts the extravagant lifestyles of excess pursued by platform workers with the constrained existence of artisanal fishermen. Revealing as much about artisanal fishermen's perceptions of exclusionary development and social change as about fish behavior, the narrative challenges the divisions between *Malonguistas* and the fraught lot of simple fishermen.

Much to the consternation of local fishermen, oil workers often fish from the offshore platforms during their twenty-eight-day offshore shifts. Sympathetic to the local fishermen, a former roughneck confided,

> This is really political, not letting the fishermen get closer to the platforms. It is political in the sense that people who have lived and gone offshore and fished as much as they wanted to do—they can no longer do that because [of] these artificial reefs, which are the platform structures where most of the fish now reside. There are lots of fish around those platforms. I have been there and seen a guy who throws in a hook and in a few seconds he gets a grouper. And he does it twice or three times and I say, 'This is not fishing, this is cheating!' So, all the fish are really in that area, that is why the fishermen want to go but they cannot go there. It is political.[6]

Surprisingly, neither Chevron officials nor artisanal fishermen cited health as a factor in distancing fishing activities from platforms. Nor did they seem concerned that toxic compounds released through flares, produced water, and drill cuttings may contaminate fish. Most dismissed the notion of standard procedures or chemicals regularly used to facilitate oil extraction as possibly damaging to fish. Only a well-educated man who had worked two decades offshore questioned the safety of eating fish caught near these "artificial reefs" "because of the residues." He commented, "I think the fish grow largest by the platforms—it's just that the use of chemicals hurts them."

Many fishermen dismissed dangers they could not see. As the former oil worker clarified, "We understand that there are chemicals there—but . . . you could catch a fish and see nothing!" Even fisherman far from any platform might unknowingly catch a tainted grouper for supper. "Generally, the fish are always circulating. There is one kind of fish that mostly stays in that area [around the platforms]—not permanently because it is not imprisoned and it has to leave a bit. And it goes . . . goes [away from the platform] and this is sometimes when it gets caught in a net." I asked what strategies fishermen might adopt to avoid capturing, selling, and eating contaminated fish. Leaning back, the old oilman sighed, "Once in a while there is some harm to us [from eating contaminated fish]." He clarified that the platforms are not the only sources of pollution; a network of pipelines and wells stretching across the seabed also leak and contaminate fish. Pointing toward the foamy waves, he remarked that "a little farther out there . . . even where there are no platforms there are many wells . . . and we might not discover it, but we are floating above them . . . this is a problem."

Motoring Offshore

Only a subset of fishermen with motorized boats can traverse the distance between the beach and offshore platforms. Artisanal fishermen navigate Cabindan seas in four types of crafts: *catrongas* (boats with internal motors), *chatas* (open wooden or fiberglass boats with outboard motors), *canoas com motor de popa* (canoes equipped with outboard motors), and *pirogas* (dugout canoes powered with paddles). Statistics from provincial fisheries authorities reveal that 79 to 84 percent of all fishing boats registered in Cabinda are non-motorized and nearly three-quarters of artisanal fishermen rely on *pirogas*. The romantic image of an artisanal fisherman standing tall in his *piroga*, silhouetted against a muted sunset and gliding across glassy waters, belies the onerous effort of paddling and the necessary chore of bailing water from these traditional canoes carved out of tree trunks.

Few fishermen in *pirogas* venture more than 500 to 1,000 meters from shore, yet they are no less affected by pollution than the fishermen who approach the offshore platforms. Instead, they insist that their lack of motors hampers their ability to escape the degraded waters hugging the coastline and to follow fish that have fled the contamination. One fisherman explained mournfully, "There used to be schools of fish here on the coast. To get our catch, the schools must come to the [coastal] zone. So, now there is practically no production because of the [polluted] waters."

During interviews, Cabinda's fishermen drew affectionate, respectful portraits of their quarry, depicting fish as discerning creatures capable of seeking out the best habitat with the healthiest, most food-abundant waters and shunning polluted areas. An animated fisherman flung his arms toward the horizon's edge, indicating the fleeing fish. He elaborated, "The waters circulate. When they are contaminated, no one stays there. If we are feeling cold, what will we do?" I shrugged, eager for him to continue. "We will find ways to wrap ourselves up. And when it is hot, we look for a shady place to escape the sun. Yes or no?" He waited for me to nod. "And the fish too. Where there is danger, they leave. And where there is none . . . that is where they go. Feeling the danger on the coast, they flee."

Another fisherman concurred, "The fish flee when there is a spill, they really flee. They go far, far away . . . and we, without the means to get there, are further hurt in terms of our catch." Traditional fishing grounds had become so polluted that fish avoided these areas. Now, only fishermen with motors could escape the degraded littoral zone. A few Cabindan fishermen with boats capable of navigating high seas traveled south to fish presumably less-polluted waters off Zaire province. Thus, the poorest of fishermen paddling dugout canoes suffered disproportionately from pollution, while wealthier fishers with fiberglass boats and outboard motors cruised off in search of cleaner, more abundant waters.

Fishermen with motors claimed that they were in no better position than the *piroga* fishers now that fuel shortages had stalled their operations. They had become dependent on irregular shipments from the Luanda refinery and, unlike Soyo, Cabinda's IPA office did not distribute subsidized fuel. One fisherman said:

> There are many days that we cannot get petrol to fish. There is no refinery here—the only one is at Malongo and that is only for internal use. Sonangol sends up a barge every 15 days from the Luanda refinery. It would be better if there were a refinery in Cabinda. I have spent two or three days looking for petrol. It is useless to try to fish in a canoe or without a motor because there are no longer any fish around here. The fish all left because of the pollution. I have this boat but no petrol.

As Angola awaits the opening of the Lobito refinery, consumers remain dependent upon the 39,000 barrels of fuel produced daily at the Luanda refinery and supplementary imports.[7] Domestic oil consumption hovers around 60,000 barrels per day; refined fuel shortages are common across the country (EIA 2008). Many interior towns suffer shortfalls due to Angola's poor roads, but Sonangol has fewer excuses for deficiencies in Cabinda because the shipments arrive by sea. Sometimes, and often without explanation, the expected barges do not appear, and Cabindans wait in queues stretching far from the filling stations, pushing their cars forward in line and hoping that they will reach the pumps before the fuel runs out. Cabindans also say FAA troops stationed in the region divert fuel shipments across the border into the Democratic Republic of Congo to earn extra cash.

Apart from shortages, central government cuts to fuel subsidies also hurt the motorized segment of Cabinda's artisanal fishing sector. As Luandan bureaucrats lowered subsidies on petrol, the fishermen with motors found filling their tanks increasingly difficult. After the first major subsidy cut in 2004, many Cabindans recommended that the government continue to keep local gasoline and diesel prices artificially low in the provinces where the oil is sourced. One Cabindan likened the proposed system to "how those who work in auto factories can buy the car at the base price." Others suggested that Chevron sell products locally from Malongo's small-scale refinery, which can produce up 16,000 barrels daily of various fuel grades

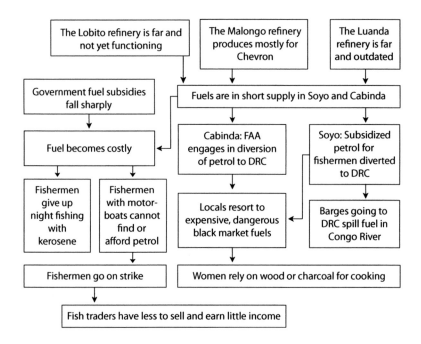

FIGURE 2. Fuel Shortages, Subsidy Cuts, Diversions, and Outcomes

ranging from aviation quality for its fleet of helicopters to diesel for nearly all other operations (Alfredo 2004). Despite these suggestions, however, the government and Chevron refused to make any concessions to improve fuel pricing or availability in Cabinda. Artisanal fishers looked for alternate employment; fishing required too many hours at sea and too many kwanzas for fuel to be considered a viable livelihood. Without fish, they questioned what their future might hold.

A FISHING HERITAGE

On a particularly scorching afternoon, I sought comfort in the cool halls of Cabinda's small cultural museum. A dusty exhibit featured a woven basket known as an *ndika*. It was kind of trap Cabindan fishermen once used when the waters teemed with fish. Now it sat in this museum under a shiny brass plaque commemorating the patronage of Chevron and its Block 0 partners in 1992. I found it irritating that Chevron was both the celebrated patron of Cabindan culture within these walls and the party responsible for the pollution destroying traditional livelihoods.

Joaquim Martíns, a Portuguese priest with a penchant for anthropological investigation, published cultural descriptions of the protectorate prior to independence portraying Cabindans as skilled fishers, relying on traditional ecological knowledge. Before fishermen could buy nylon nets, they wove *likonde* gillnets and *nkiti* seine nets from the fibers of baobab trees and fashioned buoys from the wood of *Sanga-Sanga*, the African Balsa, to keep their gillnets afloat (Martíns 1972:290). No seasoned fisherman would leave shore without the hard-shelled remains of a baobab fruit, or *mpusu*, to scoop out the seawater that would invariably penetrate his dugout canoe (Martíns 1972:291). Martíns even cited Cabindan proverbs that demonstrated the influential role of fishing on social norms, for example, "Let's divide the canoe; let's split the net," which he interpreted as "Without understanding, societies do not endure" (1972:343).

Long before Chevron arrived, Cabinda's coastal kingdom of Ngoyo depended on the sea for sustenance and strength. Historians described the population as "adventurous at sea and timid on land" (Franque 1940:56). Ngoyo leaders called upon traditional priests known as *nganga* to ensure not only good rains but also an abundance of fish (Serrano 1983:67–68). On moonless nights, Cabinda's coastal waters flickered with lamplight as fishermen hypnotized fish into entering their nets or even jumping aboard their canoes; the market teemed with fresh catch each morning (Carneiro 1949:195). Intrepid local fishermen even devised a strategy for catching sharks using neither hook nor net but an unusual wooden apparatus, which they lured the sharks into biting (Franque 1940:173–174).

Local fisheries fed the people of Ngoyo and fueled trade with the interior. A 1949 account of Cabinda described a custom in which inhabitants trading in palm oil and forest products from Mayombe demanded offerings of fish from traders as an "obligatory 'breakfast'" before engaging in commerce. They further stipulated that the offerings be "thick fish with brilliant scales" like croaker or smooth-skinned fish of predominantly "white-muscle and without oily traces" like shark (Carneiro 1949: 140–141).[8]

"We were always a fishing people—everything came from fish," a wiry old fisherman told me. He rubbed his rough hands together and reiterated, "Everything came from fish. Now, there are no fish." His words marked both a beginning and an end. His statement confirmed that the community's sustenance had depended upon fish, but it was also a way of saying, "fish were our everything and that everything is no more." The sun-wrinkled fisherman was hinting at ruptured cultural connections with the resource base by illustrating the profound attachments to the sea among

Cabinda's fishermen, fish traders, and coastal communities—whether for physical or spiritual sustenance.

Diminishing Catches

Fish were plentiful before oil extraction began in Cabinda. An artisanal fisher in his sixties recalled haltingly, "Back then . . . fishermen did not have to go a mile to catch fish. . . . a distance of a few meters [was sufficient] to get enough fish to your liking and after there was no one to buy them. So cheap . . . fish were abundant even in the bay." When dead fish first began to wash ashore in the late 1960s and early 1970s, Cabindans searched for the source of contamination. Those familiar with local, small-scale practices of using plant-based neurotoxins to paralyze fish first blamed venomous "trees along the [Chiloango] river that dropped their fruits" during the rainy season. Then, they noted that fish in the unbounded sea were dying and reasoned the waves and tides would have diluted the toxicity of any fruits floating down the river. It was only in hindsight that they suspected the oil corporation; the firm neither acknowledged any offense, nor relayed any health warnings, including cautions against bathing or fishing.

At first, Cabindans' environmental consciousness was weak and few people recognized oil as a hazard to human or ecosystem health. My friend Paulo confided, "You know I grew up in Malembo—I saw spills, I saw fish dying as a child." "Imagine growing up in the 1970s," he said, "there was nothing, especially in this part of the world, but the spills were there because the oil activities were there. Sometimes you would go swimming and you would come back with oil on your skin—you were stained with oil. You would sometimes see dead fish and in the 1970s we did not know what killed the fish." Even after independence "people noticed this layer of oil on the water—one that reached the shore." Other Cabindans also recalled how "the same coat of oil would stick" to their feet. Nonetheless, as one confessed, "We were unaware of the dangers . . . You know what we used to say? We would say 'Ah well, as the Americans are over there working, they must have washed out their tanks . . . They were washing their tanks—it was a normal task. But there was danger. At that time, dead fish appeared on the beach."

Fishermen eventually connected the spills with fish mortality, but repression was so severe they dared not speak out. Under Portuguese rule, Paulo remembered, "You could get in trouble by expressing any sentiments—by complaining about an oil spill." With the tumultuous transition to socialism after independence, no one dared denigrate Angola's top industry. Paulo reminded me, "In those days you could not talk much. Anything was interpreted as politics and you could be in trouble. Not from [Chevron's] side but from the government's side. Informants were all over. You would not dare speak."

Cabindans silently witnessed a multiplicity of devastating spills, developing an understanding of how weather and tidal patterns could exacerbate or minimize the impact of every drop of oil spilled offshore. Fishermen used their knowledge of the sea to anticipate the behavior of spills. For example, they recognized that rough seas encourage oil's dispersal into the water column, whereas blustery conditions or fast currents spread surface oil in wider slicks. Cabinda's fishermen spoke of the sea as both a sympathetic confidant and a raging adversary, infusing their stories with descriptions of its vicissitudes. They keenly illustrated how currents and directional winds could push pollution toward local fishing grounds. Moon phases and the corresponding moods of the ocean can also determine an oil slick's course. A fisherman in his sixties with bright eyes waxed poetic as he described how the water has four seasons that correspond to the phases of the moon. He began, "There are times when the water becomes rough during the new moon . . . and during the full moon it is resting—it is fuller, but has no strength." He continued, explaining that when the moon wanes "it is starving." A starving moon makes for rough seas. He joked, "When you are hungry, you become rough, no? Do you like talking with anyone when you are hungry? No. If you are hungry, you do not converse. You get angry."

A Confounding Problem

During my time in Cabinda, I found that most of my informants directed their frustration with local conditions toward the oil industry. Artisanal fishers presented innumerable testimonies attributing severely reduced fish stocks to Chevron. Pollution associated with the oil industry has undoubtedly undermined the health and productivity of local fisheries and fishing communities. Still, the long-term impact of marine contamination is confounded by poor sanitation and overfishing. Waste from Cabinda's growing provincial capital flows untreated into the bay (WB 2005:138). Heaps of scrap metal from long-dead factories rust on city beaches. Agricultural runoff clouds coastal waters and discarded plastics cling to the shoreline.

Chevron attributes the collapse of local fisheries to overfishing. Officials in Luanda issued permits to the USSR throughout the 1980s, which allowed Soviet trawlers to "scoop up everything in sight, including immature fish, threatening the future of the stocks"— so long as they sold a pro-

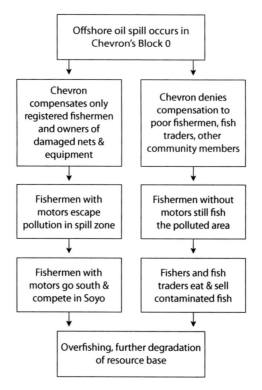

FIGURE 3. Pollution and Overfishing Combine to Exacerbate Degradation

portion of the catch in local markets (Gunn 1987:69). Cabindan fishermen also recalled how Spanish fleets equipped "with the type of nets used by the Russians" and assisted by "technology [enabling them] to take away everything down to the fish eggs" continued to sweep the coast during the 1990s. The government began to reassess its permitting strategy in 2004, yet the damage is not easily undone. Additionally, international fleets subsidized by the European Union and Chinese pirate fishers serving Asian, European, and U.S. markets regularly plunder Angolan waters (Salopek 2004).[9] Poor enforcement capacity prevents Angola from protecting its fisheries.[10]

Overfishing and pollution combine in feedback loops to undermine the ecological integrity of Cabinda's traditional fishing grounds. Whether by capture or contamination, both undermine the capacity of local fish stocks to reproduce sustainably. Artisanal fishermen also recognize their tragic role in the competition for dwindling stocks, including the capture and consumption of juvenile fish, but see few alternatives. A grizzled fisher from Lândana faulted the government for failing to limit industrial, semi-industrial, and artisanal captures of all commercial species. He lauded the constraints imposed by the Portuguese before 1975 and endorsed current species-specific limits on sardines and mackerel. Advocating for more stringent regulations and citing the need for more enforcement authorities, he declared, "the law has little force here—it needs to be more rigorous."

A LIMITED TRANSFORMATION

For decades, the government ignored successive spills in Cabinda's Block 0. Between 1990 and 1998, Chevron recorded 182 spills in Block 0 with an average of 33 barrels of oil released per spill. In total, Chevron accidentally spilled 5,984 barrels of oil—951,456 liters—in Cabinda's artisanal fishing grounds over this period (URS 2000). Justifiably, Cabinda's artisanal fishers and fish traders began demanding Chevron's accountability for oil pollution in the 1990s. On December 27, 1999, approximately 100 barrels—142,000 liters—of crude oil leaked from a Chevron offshore treatment facility and spread a dark slick over Cabindan waters (*Planet Ark* 2000). The spill hit Fútila hardest. The crude washed ashore and seventy people were treated for oil poisoning at a nearby hospital. Hoards of irate fishermen pulled their stained nets from the sea and marched them to Malongo. Crowding the gates, they demanded accountability and reparations from Chevron.

This spill marked a pivotal moment; the fishermen voiced their concerns and the corporation listened. Chevron responded to the protests and acknowledged fishermen's claims that oil pollution negatively impacted their livelihoods. The corporation distributed 505 gillnets and envelopes containing $2,000 to 149 artisanal fishermen as compensation for damaged nets and the six months during which they were unable to fish. Another 260 artisanal and semi-industrial fishermen filed claims against Chevron in the provincial tribunal and received $3,500 payouts for their losses.

Four shifts lead to this critical conjuncture. First, following the decline of Angolan involvement in the neighboring Congos and the intensification of internal battles with UNITA, the government had moved many FAA troops out of Cabinda. Second, incremental increases in freedom of expression in the late 1990s spurred protest movements—like the peaceful gathering of 300 Cabindan mothers in April 1999 to contest the drafting of their sons into the FAA. Third, alterations in the disposition and composition of workers in Malongo contributed to a new willingness to address community concerns. As the corporation replaced Malongo's "ex-marines and special breeds" with Californians and began to hire more locals, sensitivity to environmental concerns increased exponentially. Fourth, Cabindans recognized opportunities for greater freedom of expression in the late 1990s. Local protests proliferated as FLEC sympathizers began to openly express their hopes for a fully independent Cabinda (Maier 1996:64). To them, oil pollution exposed the government's indifference to the Cabindan people; so long as the oil revenues reached Luanda, leaders did not concern themselves with conditions in the extractive zones.

A smaller spill on March 8, 2001, dumped an estimated 14,000 liters of crude oil into Cabindan waters, which reportedly oozed onto local beaches (*Namibian Online* 2001). A newsletter published by the Angolan embassy in Washington related that "a valve on the petroleum drainage line was accidentally left open" and that "as soon as the leak was discovered, the Cabinda Gulf Oil Company [Chevron] promptly mobilized its emergency team that identified and locked the valve" (Embassy of Angola 2001). There is no official record of Chevron compensation to fishermen for this spill.

Cabindan discontent resurged when locals discovered an "insidious" long-term leak in the thirty-year-old Fox pipeline linking offshore fields to Malongo. They knew the leak contributed untold amounts of pollution but lacked the scientific means to prove their claims. Tubing systems installed in the late 1960s had corroded after decades of exposure to seawater, leaking a portion of Chevron's oil production into the sea. Corporate executives may have been aware of the situation yet deemed it more cost effective to lose a few barrels of oil than to invest the $108 million necessary to upgrade the tubes (BBC 2002).[11] Given that Chevron's concession contract was due to expire in 2006 and the corporation had not yet been assured its renewal, officials were loath to make costly infrastructural investments.

Chevron could no longer ignore the situation once the decrepit Fox pipeline provoked a visible, two-day spill that began on June 13, 2002. The relatively small spill of 9 barrels—1,278 liters—kept fishermen off the water for one to two weeks. Semi-industrial fishermen avoided damage to their equipment by motoring out far from shore, but artisanal fishers could not escape the slick zone. Chevron worked with Cabinda's Provincial Directorate of Agriculture, Fisheries, and Environment (henceforth Provincial Directorate) to devise a compensation plan for the fishermen affected by the spill. The corporation distributed 126 gillnets to replace damaged ones and dispensed $1,050 each to 372 artisanal fishermen.[12]

Simple compensation would not suffice. President dos Santos, convinced that the "Cabinda problem" was more social than juridical, made a show of responding to the relatively minor spill to win Cabindan hearts and minds. Authorities in Luanda demanded that the corporation replace corroded pipelines, pay $2 million in damages, and provide a laboratory with trained officials to independently monitor offshore water quality. Some Cabindans say that the government "overreacted" to the June 2002 spill and the national media "blew it out of proportion" for political purposes. A Chevron employee claimed, "It was very minimal, but they made it look like a big spill."

Why did Angolan leaders react so decisively in response to the relatively minor incident in 2002 after ignoring multiple spills of greater proportions? The government's reaction was meant to counteract critique on two levels. First, with Jonas Savimbi dead, Cabinda remained the only Angolan province suffering continued conflict. President dos Santos appealed to Cabindans to abandon their desires for independence. He needed to win their confidence. The fine was symbolic. It demonstrated that governmental power over Chevron could be leveraged to protect rather than exploit Cabindans.

Second, the government was keen to pass muster with the international environmental community at the 2002 World Summit on Sustainable Development in Johannesburg. At the time, the Angolan government had no environmental regulations to govern extractive operations either onshore or offshore. It had not even developed a national oil spill contingency plan (*Namibian Online* 2000a). In the heady months before the Johannesburg meeting, government officials promised to delineate regulations pertaining to oil pollution. Their rebuke of Chevron arguably served to earn them clout in Johannesburg.

Playing Reform

Despite the hype around Chevron's fine, it never amounted to much for Cabindans. The corporation translated the $2 million penalty into a public relations campaign and constructed a fisheries center in Buco Mazi equipped with freezers to conserve artisanal catches—an ironic form of recompense for an accident that killed or contaminated local fish stocks—but ignored a court mandate to establish an independent laboratory in Caio. Cabindans remain unable to monitor the environmental quality of their own waters and to back their claims against the corporation. The freezers have since broken and Chevron has neither repaired nor replaced them.

Although the merits and sustainability of its efforts in Buco Mazi were questionable, Chevron did respond to the public censure in 2002 by vowing to clean up operations in Cabinda. One of the corporation's Cabindan employees attributed the policy shift to the increasingly local composition of management staff like himself. He questioned, "Why would we put [oil] in the water? We are from here—our own relatives would be exposed." More pragmatic observers might point to the compensatory costs of pollution as a motive for reform. According to the Provincial Directorate's statistics, Chevron paid $1,598,600 in compensation for two incidents. Nonetheless, for an operation producing 460,000 and 431,000 barrels per day during the respective spill years of 1999 and 2001, compensation represented a relatively minor cost (IMF 2005).

The costs of condemnation by the Angolan government in 2002 were worse than the costs of compensation or the $2 million fine accompanying the censure. First, the penalty symbolized a government threat to Chevron's continued operations in Angola, including the renewal of the Cabinda concession, unless the corporation cleaned up its act. Second, Angolan leaders announced the fine just as Chevron representatives peddled their services to President Fradique de Menezes, leader of São Tomé and Principé, a rising oil producer in the Gulf of Guinea (BBC 2002).[13] Third, Chevron's public image was already suffering after its 2001 merger with Texaco when Amazon Watch launched the "ChevronToxico" campaign divulging Texaco's appalling environmental practices in the Ecuadorian rainforest.[14] Environmental justice advocates wearing "Chevwrong" t-shirts criticized its dirty operations from the Niger Delta to California's Richmond refinery. Chevron did not need another public relations disaster. Corporate officials decided to close the leaky pipeline to prevent further spills in Cabinda.

The Fox pipeline was not unique; much of the offshore infrastructure in Block 0 was damaged from the corrosive effects of seawater over decades of production. Chevron had delayed necessary repairs, given uncertainty over the renewal of its expiring concession contract. On March 26, 2004, the Council of Ministers formally guaranteed the extension of Chevron's concession on Block 0 through December 31, 2030. Without delay, Chevron committed funds to a series of infrastructural renovations. These improvements also serve as the backbone for $4 billion worth of investments in offshore field development (AE 2002).[15] Still, Chevron prioritizes its investments. For example, replacing faulty auxiliary pipelines servicing mature fields would necessitate multi-million dollar investments on reserves that may be depleted in a decade. The corporation weighs the costs of compensation versus renovation.

INCOMPLETE COMPENSATION

The government's renewal of the Block o concession and high gas prices provided Chevron with the opportunity to invest in infrastructure and technologies to reduce its impact on the local environment. An employee recalled how Chevron officials "were hiding" from the community during spills a decade ago. He acknowledged that his colleagues "did not communicate in a proper manner and people were infuriated." Now, Chevron "has become more proactive in preventing" local squabbles. A fisher from Fútila used a marital analogy to describe his community's expectations of Chevron. He said, "It is like a wife in the house with her husband. She might forget to do something for him, but the husband will forgive her. She will learn and she will not forget to do it again." People in Fútila and other fishing communities accepted Chevron's apologies and recompense in the hope that the corporation would learn from its mistakes. Unfortunately, further spills continue to push fish stocks and fishing communities toward the brink of collapse.

Many fishermen express frustration with Chevron for believing money could fully compensate for starved days and sleepless nights. Cynically, some Chevron officials reflect that, given the potential for compensation, Cabinda's fishermen are increasingly attuned to oil spills. One exclaimed, "Now everybody is praying for the next spill so that they can make it rich!" Local fishers disputed this myopic view, asserting that they would rather pursue independent livelihoods than remain beholden to parsimonious officials in charge of corporate compensation. Moreover, they declared that Chevron's disbursements barely compensated for the damages they incurred. To downplay or discredit their claims, some Chevron employees evoke the stereotype of fishermen as untrustworthy tellers of exaggerated "fish tales" or charge that "the fishermen come and they complain they have seen some oil sheen somewhere and they bring in nets—they've mixed them with [motor] oil—and then they ask for money."[16]

Compensation, originally conceived as a stopgap measure, is becoming a less reliable means for controlling discontent in Cabinda. Chevron appears to be reassessing its compensation strategy for three reasons. First, fishermen now register in far greater numbers to establish their eligibility for future reparations. At a large scale, compensation may not be financially feasible—at least not at the precedented rate set in the wake of the 1999 spill. Second, in recognition of compounded ecological effects of multiple spills, some fishermen expect more compensation for each successive incident. Third, the government has eased pressure on Chevron. President dos Santos did not earn the allegiance he desired from the Cabindan people for imposing the fine on Chevron in 2002.

Chevron continued to distribute payments to Cabindan fishermen after 2002, but the corporation began to employ a variety of techniques to limit compensatory disbursements. Based on an analysis of Chevron's responses to oil spills occurring between 1999 and 2006, the following six sub-sections describe the corporation's unspoken rules of engagement with local fishermen. The tactics enumerated are not part of any official Chevron policy; rather they add up to a blueprint for minimizing corporate responsibility for spills and compensation of Cabindan coastal communities.

Restricting Eligibility for Compensation

Most artisanal fishermen I interviewed agreed that Chevron overlooked the less powerful. An embittered fisherman mixed metaphors, contending that only "those who have godfathers in the kitchen receive compensation." Chevron's preferential disbursements for net owners provoked infighting and jealousy between those who fished for money and others who fished for subsistence. "To us, petroleum production is more for those who extract [oil] and more also for those who are in control," the fisher continued. "In the life of a fisherman, [there are] damages above all when there is a spill; fish are lost, nets are destroyed—and they do not give us compensation. In the city, yes, but not here—we are still waiting."

During another interview, an elderly fisherman wearing a bulky pair of eyeglasses smashed a silverfish into the tablecloth as he sorted through a heap of registration receipts on a wooden table. Finally, he pushed the receipts aside and fixed me with a set of elephantine eyes magnified by his thick lenses. Recalling the dark slick that spread over Cabindan waters in 1999, he stressed that he had not received compensation despite having registered as a fisherman with the local government. He stared blankly through his glasses. "That time that we were stopped [by the spill], we could not fish anymore and we could not eat fish," he said. "They only paid those who had nets in the water—I think $2,000—they did not pay everyone, but we all stopped [fishing], no?"

Chevron's compensation strategies are exclusionary, favoring wealthier *armadores* who own nets and registered, professional fishermen over the poorly educated, unregistered contract fishermen and day laborers. Another artisanal fisher told me, "Oil spills attack our seas and we cannot eat the fish. Chevron does not pay the people—it only pays those who own nets. There were times when we did not eat." In Buco Mazi, one of the coastal towns most affected by the 1999 oil spill offshore of Cabinda, Chevron compensated only nine of seventy fishermen. Fishermen complained that Chevron had unfairly distributed compensation, accounting for only 10 percent of artisanal fishers hurt by the spill. After similar complaints in 2002, the corporation responded by stipulating that it would henceforth only consider complaints from licensed fishermen and those who could prove damage to their nets. The passage of Angola's 1995 fisheries law and the implementation of associated regulations the following year required artisanal fishermen to register with the Provincial Directorate or Instituto de Pesca Artesanal (IPA).[17] Many fishers failed to register because they cannot read or are unable to afford the annual fees, which range between $17 for simple canoes to $30 dollars for medium-sized boats. Others do not bother to register because they see fishing as a temporary job until something better comes along.

Whether out of indolence, indigence, or ignorance, most artisanal fishermen fish without licenses. "The number of registered and actual fishermen is quite different," said Figueiredo, a representative of the Provincial Directorate, citing records that showed only forty-five licensed artisanal fishermen in Cabinda in 2002. Officials from IPA concurred. They carefully explained how to deduce the number of fishermen for a given year by the type and number of boats registered. In 2002, IPA registered 16 *catrongas*, 66 *chatas*, 9 *canoas com motor de popa*, and 956 *pirogas*. If each *catronga* holds six, *chata* four, *canoa com motor* three, and *piroga* two fishermen, then the total number of Cabindan fishermen in 2002 was roughly 2,299. Although Provincial Directorate records show that the number of licensed fishermen increased from 245 in 2003 to 800 in 2004, IPA's statistics reveal respective provincial totals of 2,317 and 2,335 fishermen in 2003 and 2004. Moreover, IPA officials admitted their extrapolations did not include an estimated 480 fishermen without boats who fish from shore with *banda banda* nets. Taking into account these calculations, if just 800 out of Cabinda's 2,815 artisanal fishermen were licensed in 2004, almost 72 percent were ineligible for compensation. Figueiredo supposed that oil spills contributed to exponential increases in registration. Even with gaps, Figueiredo said 1,797 fishermen registered with the Provincial Directorate in 2005.

A team of dedicated IPA officers set out to survey artisanal fishermen along Cabinda's coast in an effort to better understand their clients. In the first few months of 2005, they surveyed fishermen in twenty communities along Cabinda's coastline and estimated the number of provincial artisanal fishers as 2,746, excluding the three communities of Chinfuca, Tenda and Manenga they had yet to survey. The IPA data set showed that 9 percent of Cabindan fishermen are illiterate. Moreover, it revealed that roughly 94 percent of Cabindan fishermen with any education never attended secondary school. Based on a preliminary review of the figures, IPA officials suspected that education may account for variance in registration; they postulated, "Illiterates do not register as much." Thus, whether intentional or not, Chevron's strategy of only responding to claims made by registered fishermen disproportionately hurts those already most disadvantaged.

Chevron's compensation strategy not only implicitly divided claimants along educational boundaries but also gender lines. A compensation policy focusing solely on fishermen overlooks the wider reach of Cabinda's fisheries. Female traders buy the fish from fishermen when they disembark on the beach and resell them at fish markets or by walking around town with their trademark call of "Who wants fish?" When fresh fish is unavailable, these women sit idly on the beach fanning flies off yesterday's catch as it thaws rapidly in the hot sun. Oil spills undermine the quantity and quality of fish on the local market and fish traders suffer losses equal to those of fishermen, yet Chevron has never recognized their right to remuneration.

Three factors may have influenced Chevron's exclusion of fish traders: registration patterns, the women's reticence to acknowledge contamination of local waters, and their low social standing—in both gender and class. First, fish traders do not register with the government, and neither the Provincial Directorate nor IPA collects or retains records on fish traders. Second, fish traders' hesitance to publicly denounce pollution for fear of frightening potential buyers may explain why national media and Chevron officials have overlooked their claims, yet it renders them no less important. Third, whereas *armadores*, a wealthy subset of semi-industrial and artisanal fishers, exerted their influence to demand recompense from Chevron after the 1999 spill and thereby set a legal precedent for fishermen's compensation, fish traders have little legal or political clout.

Hiding Oil Spills from Local Communities

Residents of Cabinda's coastal villages assert that Chevron conceals spills through incomplete reporting practices and use of chemical dispersants. The 1999 spill allegedly spurred the creation of a stringent internal reporting rule. Chevron employees are allotted one hour to report spills to their superiors—if not, they will be fired for negligence. The rule does not require Chevron employees to share information about the spill to affected communities. During the first ten months of 2003, Chevron reported sixty-nine oil spills to the Ministry of Petroleum; it disclosed none of these to the public (Eviatar 2004). Cabindan fishermen complain that the corporation rarely informs them of spills. They also resent bureaucrats in Luanda for withholding information about pollution in Cabindan waters. One artisanal fisher said, "Do they inform us when there is a spill? We only hear about it on the radio or see it in the water. Chevron should help [inform us]; only the government knows this information."

Chevron keeps a close watch on its operations with helicopters by day and remote planes by night. The monitoring system enables rapid response to oil spills. Some fishermen worry that Chevron uses its technological superiority to detect and disperse oil spills without their knowledge. A middle-aged fisherman in a worn plaid shirt shrugged and said, "Whether the sea is good or whether the sea is bad, the variations of the sea are many . . . but the oil remains on the surface. From the moment when it sinks below and goes to the bottom, we cannot see it. We cannot see what is below the surface."

Fishermen express particular concern about Chevron's use of chemical dispersants, which can be more dangerous to the ecosystem than the oil itself. As I discussed in Chapter 3, dispersants prevent slicks from contaminating beaches by drawing oil from the surface into the water column, but little is known about their long-term or bioaccumulative effects in the ecosystem (Lindgren et al. 2001). Studies suggest that chemically dispersed oil is more toxic to aquatic organisms than oil physically dispersed by wave action. For example, a study of five dispersants including Inipol IP-90, a chemical dispersant used in Cabinda's offshore, showed that a combination of oil and dispersants proved more toxic to two types of coral than oil alone (Epstein et al. 2000). Dispersants appear to provoke greater absorption of polycyclic aromatic hydrocarbons (PAHs) in marine organisms. Research charting the PAH body burden—or concentrated build-up of PAHs—in polychaete worms showed that worms subjected to 1 to 10 days of exposure to chemically dispersed oil registered PAH levels 1.5 to 5.7 times higher than worms exposed to physically dispersed oil (Coelho et al. 1999).

Rather than letting a spill run its course and possibly confronting a costly beach cleanup, Chevron sometimes applies a chemical dispersant to slicks in or approaching shallow water. "The waves depend on the season, but if there are many waves they can push the spill towards the beach," explained an elder familiar with oil spills. "Then, Chevron will use buoys [to encircle the spill] and within [the buoy ring] they use dispersant." Chemical dispersants may not be visible to the eye, but fishermen contend that they are palpable to the touch. "We perceive its presence when we go fishing. We touch the water and note that it is stinging—it stings," fretted the middle-aged fisherman in plaid. He and others said that traces of a dispersant remain in the water long after its deployment, deterring the return of fish, so that "even when there is no spill or burst, there are no fish."

A young fisherman recalled his first encounter with dispersants. "The waters were prickly . . . prickly to the skin . . . and we were terrified. We spent four or five days like this [arms crossed] without fishing." The fishing community implored the tides to wash away the stinging waters. They awaited official news of a spill, but neither government nor corporate officials sent any alert. "We continued to test the waters," he said, "Putting in our hands, our feet, until the water no longer stung . . . until it had passed. Then we again took up our [fishing] activities." Without a laboratory, Cabindan fishing communities are unable to determine when invisible pollutants like dispersants no longer present a health risk. An older fisherman reasoned, "The slick disappears, you can't see anything—only water. So, in that context you may go test the water, but it stings. There is still danger. We were suspicious then and we remain suspicious."

Some fishermen suspect that the decline in local fish stocks may be linked not only to spills but also increased dispersant usage. They also question whether eating fish exposed to dispersants could be harmful to their health. A wizened fisherman squinted and said, "We cannot really say what harm the use of dispersants has provoked—even the type of dispersant should be analyzed." Cabindan fishing communities hope that the lab Chevron promised to build in Caio will provide unbiased answers to their questions. A fisheries consultant in Luanda confirmed that the excessive use of dispersants produces a long-term, negative impact on the marine environment. "The chemicals . . . to hide a spill will kill the microorganisms that eat oil; sometimes it is best just to leave it alone and let the microorganisms work because . . . they will not pass on harmful effects to the fish," he explained. "The half-life of these chemicals is much longer than that of oil—we do not even know [their] long-term impact . . . whereas oil is a natural substance." Fig.uereido, the aforementioned official at the Provincial Directorate, proposed a government study on the types of dispersants deployed in local waters. He wanted to know everything about the chemicals "down to the production year" so he could say to Chevron "use only this kind of dispersant" and tell fishermen "let's not go out there, let's stay away." Chevron refused to release information on local dispersant use to the Provincial Directorate; the corporation's contract outlines reporting requirements to the Ministry of Petroleum in Luanda only.

Waiting to Report Spills and Ignoring Wider Impacts

Fishermen claim that Chevron often minimizes the reported duration of oil spills by waiting to inform government officials. Minimizing the *actual* duration of spills helps everyone, but shaving a few days off the *reported* spill duration to save on compensation costs is irresponsible and unsafe. Chevron is required to report oil spills to the Provincial Directorate immediately. If government and corporate officials consider the spill of a magnitude sufficient to damage local fisheries, they may declare an area unsafe for fishing for a set period of time. Fishermen use the word *paralizado*, literally paralyzed, to describe this time period. They claim that the length of any suspension is always controversial, the remediation techniques are dubious, and the criteria Chevron and the Provincial Directorate use to determine the stoppage are unclear. Given compensation rates of $80 for each day an eligible fisherman is immobilized by a spill, Chevron has an incentive to keep the reported length of spills to a minimum. Thus, fishermen suspect that Chevron intentionally delays reporting spills to provincial officials.

With no independent laboratory, Cabinda's fishermen are unable to determine for themselves when the waters are contaminated or clean. Ultimately, local fishers and provincial officials alike are forced to trust Chevron to declare spills. Still, fishermen testified to frequently discovering oil in the water before news of a spill reached their community. Following one such slick, Chevron distributed $150 in compensation to each of 782 fishermen.[18] This spill began on April 4, 2004, and kept artisanal fishermen from Malembo to Mandarim off the water for fifteen days. The affected fishers calculated that Chevron avoided paying each fisherman an extra $1,050 in compensation by delaying the reporting process. Moreover, since neither government nor corporate officials formally recognized the spill or registered its duration, Chevron was not required to adhere to the precedented $80 daily compensation rate.

Additionally, Chevron only compensates fishermen for the time oil spreads dark slicks offshore. The company ignores the lag between net destruction and restitution.[19] Fish avoid a net contaminated with the slightest tinge of crude. So, after showing useless oil-contaminated nets to Chevron, fishermen see no recourse but to burn them and wait until the corporation distributes replacements. One fisherman pointed to his tangled net covered with bituminous clusters. He lamented that even after the oil dissipates, fishermen "are stopped [from fishing] for three to five months" for lack of nets.

As Chevron distributed compensation to fishermen with oiled nets, however, the corporation failed to see that the environmental and social characteristics of degradation spread beyond the contaminated sea. Residents of Fútila and Malembo say that offshore extraction caused their onshore crops to fail. Local women now walk for hours each day to reach more fertile farm plots in the interior. Corporate officials dismissed their claims to compensation as greedy, but it is possible that extractive activities—including reinjection and fracturing operations—provoked a breach of the aquifers along the coast. Salinization of local aquifers is a recognized externality of oil extraction. Studies of production sites evidence "death of proximal vegetation, stress on peripheral vegetation, salinization of surface and ground waters," and extensive salinization has occurred in Mexico's oil-rich Tabasco region (Kharaka and Otton 2003:4; Global Exchange 1996). In Cabinda, Chevron conducted "extensive waterflooding operations during 1993" that entailed injecting a daily stream of 376,000 barrels of seawater into 31 wells to force any remaining oil in the reservoirs to surface (EIA 1995). Chevron performed these high-pressured activities in "Area A" of Block 0, the portion of the concession running the length of Cabinda's coast and located closest to shore. Presumably, during its efforts to increase recovery from declining oilfields, the corporation created the conditions for saltwater intrusion in coastal aquifers and decreased crop production in community fields.

Pointing Fingers across International Borders

In February 2001, Chevron denied responsibility for an oil spill in Cabindan waters by insisting that the slick originated from the Congo River.[20] If the oil originated from production areas in or near the river's outlet, it may have come from operations in the sliver of offshore area belonging to the Democratic Republic of Congo (DRC) or Angola's Blocks 1 and 2. At that time, a Chevron subsidiary operated production zones offshore of the Bas-Congo province of the DRC and Texaco—later subsumed by Chevron—operated wells in Block 2. A fisherman familiar with spills reported, "The greatest pollution occurs during the drilling period" prior to well completion. Chevron completed the DRC Misato well in March 2001.[21]

Although there is no solid evidence to suggest that contemporaneous drilling in Chevron's holdings in the DRC perpetrated the February 2001 spill that spread northward into Cabinda, the scenario raises the question of whether Chevron's subsidiary in the DRC could be held responsible for environmental damage across international boundaries. On July 1, 2004, Chevron sold off the Muanda International Oil Company (MIOC), the corporation's wholly owned subsidiary with a 50 percent interest stake and operator rights to the 1010 km² concession offshore of the DRC (Alexander's Gas and Oil Connections 2004). A Chevron official refused to comment directly on any possible linkage between past pollution instances and the corporation's sale of their MIOC subsidiary. He did confirm, however, both the sale of corporate interests in the DRC and the Congo River's tendency to "push pollution up" toward Cabinda.

The Congo River forcefully propels water and sediments in all directions from its mouth, creating an alluvial fan reaching far across the undersea terrain. The Angola current also directs water flow southward along the Cabindan coast. Therefore, oil pollution from the Democratic Republic of Congo to the south and the Republic of the Congo to the north could threaten Cabindan waters. In late June 2004, a fifty-five-barrel oil spill leaked from the SNPC (Société Nationale des Pétroles du Congo) Emerald oilfield's dilapidated installations twenty kilometers offshore of Pointe Noire in the Republic of Congo (*Independent Online* 2004b). The Congolese slick spread over three kilometers, washing ashore on Pointe Noire's beaches, despite containment efforts by Chevron and Total (*Independent Online* 2004a). Jerome Moutou, Director of Production for the SNPC, claimed that the spill expanded once it combined with another emanating from Cabinda (*Independent Online* 2004b). Did Chevron take responsibility for the transboundary spill by cooperating with Total on containment efforts? Was Chevron's participation in controlling the slick intended to decrease the likelihood of its spread into Cabindan waters? Cabindan fishermen question why Chevron would get involved if it were not responsible for the slick, citing other occasions in which the corporation found it simpler to deny responsibility.

The incident raised the question of whether Chevron would be required to compensate local fishermen if one of its operations in the Congo spread into the Cabindan offshore. Another oil slick disrupted fishing activities along the northern Cabindan coast in December 2004. Fishermen from Lândana and Malembo submitted their nets to Chevron and demanded compensation. One recalled, "I tried to show them the oil [on my net], but they denied it, saying it was not theirs. So, we understood [the corporation] was maybe fleeing from responsibility—or what, I don't know. They said it came from Congo-Brazzaville. And it is only they who know." Oddly, Chevron denied responsibility but distributed a holiday greeting fleeced with $150 cash to a select number of Cabindan fishermen.

Disbelieving that the same corporation that routinely refused their claims would freely dispense money for no legitimate reason, the fishermen considered the payment both an informal admission of guilt and an unofficial form of compensation.[22] Some assumed that, as usual, the pollution emanated from Block o, and others speculated that the spill originated from one of Chevron's holdings in the Republic of Congo; perhaps Haute Mer, Marine VII, or the ZIC (Zone d'Intérêt Commun). Although the corporation merely possesses interest stakes in Haute Mer and Marine VII, Chevron's status as operator in the ZIC elicits new concerns. The ZIC contains a subsurface "oil-bearing structure with the potential to hold 500 million [to] one billion barrels of oil," yet it straddles deepwater Block 14 offshore of Cabinda and Congo's Haute Mer concession (AE 2006). In the event of a transboundary spill originating in the ZIC, presumably Chevron would assume the lead responsibility for remediation and compensation efforts in both Cabinda and Congo.

Giving Fishermen the Bait and Switch

Many Cabindans continue to criticize their neighbors in Malongo for environmental degradation and exclusionary policies, but a few desisted after receiving compensation from Chevron. One compensated fisherman said, "If I spoke poorly of Chevron it would be a sin because I have received something from them." Another downplayed the corporation's role in degrading the local marine environment by saying that oil spills "occur once in a while—[but] they are accidents. They always happen, but with minor impact—we cannot speak poorly of them." Although it transformed a few fishermen's opinions of the corporation, Chevron began to rethink the compensation model. A Chevron representative acknowledged that direct monetary distribution cost the corporation a lot and it ultimately failed to reach the wider community. He asserted, "$600 to $800 is not bad, but in terms of having to pay 800 fishermen it is a lot of money. Now what good does it do? I do not know that it does—it benefits only a few."

Rather than continue doling out compensation, a government official suggested Chevron could initiate "a joint cooperative effort, by bringing in training on conservation" and "subsidies for artisanal fishing material" so as to "create an environment [wherein] even when there is a spill there will not be any ill feeling." This optimistic official overlooked the degraded state of Cabindan waters for which Chevron is at least partially responsible, and his development scheme seemed likely to result in increased dependency on already-overfished waters. Nonetheless, he had stumbled upon a principle that would guide Chevron's community relations efforts: corporate social responsibility (CSR).

When the government fined Chevron $2 million in 2002 for environmental damages, the corporation responded by boosting CSR. It was a classic bait-and-switch tactic. Seeking exoneration for the damage incurred by successive oil spills, Chevron contributed money to local sea turtle conservation efforts, built an artisanal fishery center in Buco Mazi, and donated a few small boats to provincial fisheries authorities. "All of their efforts are nothing in relation to the scale of the effects of the spill," said a representative of the Provincial Directorate. With sad irony, he explained, "In reality, the environment, including the sea turtle habitat is being hurt by oil exploration activities, but they want to convince people that they want to help the turtles." His comment elucidates contradictions at the site of extraction wherein Chevron both threatens human and environmental health yet simultaneously plays the role of benefactor through CSR projects.

Inhabitants of Cabinda's resource-dependent communities affected by extractive pollution are skeptical of CSR. They point out that Chevron funneled monies into a fisheries center equipped with expensive industrial freezers but failed to find funds for constructing the independent environmental monitoring lab. A woman in Fútila saw Chevron's CSR programs as a diversionary means to gain access to local riches. "They invent little things just to commit robbery . . . may God help us remove these exploiters from here," she said. With regard to Chevron's duties to the community, many fishermen asked little more of the corporation than to keep the oceans clean. A fisher from Malembo said, "I only ask the people of good faith to save us from the toxics at least." CSR projects such as building health posts, constructing schools, and digging wells can all improve their standard of living by degrees, but they may never add up to the rounded whole of the livelihood lost.

Calling It Anything but Compensation

In the first two weeks of September 2005, nearly two dozen dead sea turtles washed ashore between Malembo and Lândana. Observers said that the turtles, due to lay their eggs in the region, may have become disoriented or even poisoned by an oil slick near the mouth of the Chiloango River. More dead turtles washed ashore between October 2005 and March 2006. Some of the carcasses bore the dark stains of oil. Many of the turtles appeared to have been mutilated by boat propellers, a fact that Chevron officials seized upon to declare the corporation's innocence. Nevertheless, a marine scientist working in Angola reasoned, "Oil may be affecting the turtles in a way which reduces their ability to avoid boats and their propellers."[23] A group of distressed fishermen in the towns of Malembo and Lândana confronted Chevron, blaming the corporation for the sea turtle mortalities.

They demanded up to $5,000 in damages, acknowledging the turtles as an ecological indicator species and declaring their deaths to be a clear signal of the toxicity of Cabindan waters.

Retaliatory rumors emanated from Malongo, painting the fishermen as extortionists who killed the turtles in a desperate attempt to collect more corporate funds. In official dispatches, Chevron representatives refused to concede responsibility and cited the corporation's previous efforts to protect sea turtles in the region (e.g., suspending seismic activities during seasonal nesting cycles and funding local NGO Grémio ABC's turtle conservation projects, including nest protection efforts on Cabindan beaches). Ultimately, Chevron acceded to monetary settlement, paying 600 fishermen $1,500 each (though the corporation began negotiations at $250). Still, Chevron officials continued to deny responsibility for the sea turtle mortalities. They emphasized that the payment represented a "contribution" in solidarity; it was not to be construed as compensatory. By calling these disbursements anything but compensation Chevron could deny responsibility while pacifying outraged fishermen.

As oil-poisoned turtles washed ashore, Cabindans questioned whether Chevron's model was failing to compensate for the true costs of extraction on the marine environment. By paying off select groups of resource users, Chevron was essentially inducing them to allow the damages to their environment without dispute and to passively accept the degradation of their livelihoods. As individual fishers fought over compensation, coastal communities atomized. Rather than finding solidarity in their struggle to protect the sea, fishermen competed for the remaining fish and exacerbated the crisis of degradation. "We need to change the mentality of the government, communities, and companies; this partial compensation is not enough, it is not something that can be valued in money," said a representative Grémio ABC. "What is environmental is social as well and we must take the two together."

In May 2006, an oil slick plainly originating from Chevron's operations offshore of Malembo halted fishing yet again. The corporation reportedly agreed to pay affected fishermen $2,000 apiece for the six-month interruption of their activities. Nevertheless, true compensation would consider the foregone earnings of fishers and fish traders, costs of destroyed equipment, and harm to human health in subsistence fishing households at the time of the spill, as well as the long-term economic and ecological impacts of oil pollution. A graying fisherman confided that he had witnessed oil pollution's negative "influence on plankton levels." Did Chevron compensate for these losses? He recalled a time in his youth when Cabindans would walk to the sea with baskets to harvest shimmering schools of sardines, but intimated that the fish had disappeared since Chevron's arrival. Given that oil spills can kill fish eggs and fry, did Chevron consider the consequences on future generations of fish? A fairer compensation scheme would assess the wider range of social and ecological impacts associated with oil industry activities, including the release of toxic byproducts like mercury-tainted barite, the damages from seismic testing, the deleterious impacts of chemical dispersants, and the effects of pollution on local cultures and livelihoods. As a corporation beholden to its shareholders, however, Chevron must externalize these environmental and social costs because fair compensation would likely exceed the profits from oil production.

CHASING COMPENSATION

Offshore oil spills can spread in slicks across vast distances. The effects of pollution associated with offshore oil extraction are similarly far-reaching; everyone in coastal communities suffers. The 1999 spill increased Cabindan fishermen's awareness of the connection between local environmental deterioration and oil extraction, heightening their demands for compensation. They learned to recognize the "coating of oil" on the water's surface as a sign of a spill, to associate pollution with fish die-offs, to organize associations, and to take their claims to the Provincial Directorate and the local IPA office. Fishermen also learned how to successfully demand compensation. Nonetheless, Chevron's policy of compensation fails to offset the true ecological and social costs of oil spills and reinforces patterns of socio-economic differentiation. By limiting monetary reparations to the wealthiest of fishermen and excluding illiterate fishermen and female fish traders, the corporation deepens class and gender rifts.

A struggling group of fishers still haul their nets onto the stained sands of Fútila beach. They maintain that offshore oil spills created the swathe of black sand hugging the shoreline, whereas Chevron attributes the dark patches to sedimentary deposits from the Congo River carried northward on oceanic currents. Without an independent laboratory, the fishermen in Fútila, Malembo, and other Cabindan fishing communities have no evidence to contest the corporation's claim. After each spill, fishers and fish traders slip back into their lives, tracing the shape of the ordinary. They have no futures to chase, save those tied to the crude industry destroying their livelihoods.

Luanda has largely refrained from regulating the oil industry in Cabinda—

with the exception of fining Chevron in 2002. Still, the Angolan government imposed the $2 million penalty for reasons arguably more political than environmental. The gesture failed to impress Cabindans. Why should the people of Cabinda trust President dos Santos and his government as their protectors? In their view, Angolan leaders had stolen their independence, enriched themselves on Cabinda's oil wealth, and disregarded the suffering of Cabindans from the coast to the interior. Cabindans continued their calls for independence, leaving dos Santos to explore other ways to capture their attention.

6. Militant Territorialization

From an altitude of around one thousand meters, the waves tumbling toward Cabinda's coast appeared frilled and tame . As the plane made its final descent, my perspective shifted and the waves took on a new character—slamming against the shore with great force. The plane taxied to the terminal, and I pulled the in-flight magazine of Angola's national airline from the seatback pocket.[1] A colorful article accompanied by a set of glossy photos depicted a peaceful Cabinda. The author described the nightly "shows" from the offshore oil installations where "dozens of flares from the ocean light up the night sky" (Piçarra 2005). He rattled off a fulsome tally of "signs of growth" in Cabinda. Finally, the piece ended with this sanguine appraisal:

> A feeling of calm is settling over the province after many long years of armed conflict. Crime rates are dropping, migrants are returning home, and the city center is getting back to normal. Today, people can travel by car without an armed escort as far as the equatorial forest of Mayombe. This immense forested area, stretching far beyond Angola's borders, is one of Cabinda's tourism highlights. The flora and fauna of this enveloping green mantel are living proof of the incredible power of nature. Surely this is the postcard image of the whole region, outshining even the impressive night display of burning oil flames.

The idea of tourists flocking to Cabinda to gaze at the offshore flares or to track gorillas in Mayombe seemed absurd. Violent waves of troops washed over the province—from Yabi to Mayombe—as part of a military campaign that began on October 11, 2002. Recognizing FLEC as a risk to onshore oil development, the government directed the army to quash the Cabindan movement for independence. Only months after winning the war with UNITA, Angolan President and Chief of the Armed Forces

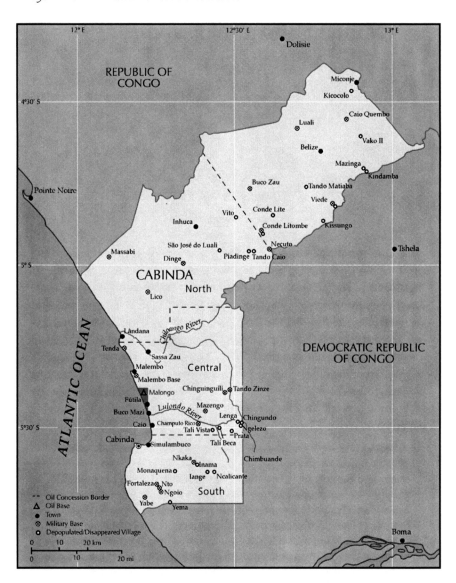

MAP 8. The Militant Territorialization of Cabinda

José Eduardo dos Santos commanded up to 50,000 troops in Cabinda, including his own "special second military brigade."[2] Their mission was to definitively establish control over Cabinda and its resources through use of force against all FLEC fighters, members, and sympathizers.[3] During the two-year military campaign, the soldiers extended state influence over the Cabindan territory by terrorizing the population into submission. The campaign officially ended in October 2004, but up to 30,000 FAA soldiers remain stationed in Cabinda (Stratfor 2008). Their presence instills fear in the populace and serves as a reminder of the dreadful power of the petro-state.

This chapter investigates the Angolan government's disproportionate use of force as part of a carrot-and-stick strategy to territorialize Cabinda. Complementing James Ferguson's analysis of Angola (discussed in earlier chapters), in which *private* security companies protect the interests of oil corporations, I demonstrate that *national* militaries still play a strong role in the extractive zones. Specifically, I explore the government's use of FAA troops to destroy endemic resistance and secure onshore oilfields in Cabinda as a form of petro-violence. In this chapter, I employ the optic of territorialization to emphasize the violence inherent to the petro-state and the extent to which the state's pursuit of resource control drives military objectives.

According to Vandergeest and Peluso (1995), territorialization is a geographic resource control strategy that uses threats or acts of violence to delineate who has access to natural resources and who is excluded. This chapter focuses less on what territorialization is than how territorialization is achieved and what effect it has on the territorialized. Michael Watts (2004:57) and Nikolas Rose (1999:34) draw on William Connolly's observation of the etymological linkage between *territory* and *terrere*—a root word suggesting exclusion, terror, and fright. Connolly infers that "to occupy territory, then, is both to receive sustenance and to exercise violence" and that "to become territorialized is to be occupied by a particular identity" (1995:xxii). Using Connolly's twin definition, I examine the FAA's campaign of terror as part of a government strategy to eradicate or co-opt anyone that might jeopardize its control over oil revenues—the lifeblood that fuels the Angolan petro-state.

The petro-state prioritizes concession contracts over the social contract, using force to extend enough control over oil-rich territory to exclusively collect the resource rents. Recalling Weber's defining feature of the state as the monopoly on the legitimate use of violence within a given territory, Coronil contends that the petro-state is characterized not only by a monopoly on the use of force but also a monopoly on the natural wealth of a territory (1997:4). The Angolan government extends its control over oilfields by means of violent territorialization—a resource control strategy that "works by proscribing or prescribing specific activities within spatial boundaries" (Vandergeest and Peluso 1995:388).

Oil concessions reflect one of the clearest examples of state territorialization as a resource control strategy. Concessions are actualized on the ground through extractive activities, but their legitimacy resides in the contracts negotiated between transnational oil corporations and the Angolan government. These contracts are essential to the territorialization process; they structure the allocation of resource revenues from set geographic areas to corporations and the government. The foundation of Sonangol in 1976 laid the foundation for territorialization, but the process continues with the signing of each concession contract, which grants formal access to resources within the lines drawn on a map in Luanda. These claims must be actualized on the ground or out at sea. Flags raised on a deepwater oil platform far offshore may constitute territorialization, but this chapter outlines the far more violent measures required to territorialize Cabinda's onshore oilfields.

GROUNDS FOR EXPLOITATION

Roc Oil Company (ROC) Limited, a mid-sized Australian firm, garnered the operator stake of Cabinda's South Block in October 2001 and announced plans to begin onshore exploration in 2004. At ROC's General Meeting in 2005, one of the copious PowerPoint presentations included a slide picturing a cup of cappuccino entitled, "The frothy bits are always the first to go" (ROC 2005). An apt metaphor for the worldwide scramble for petroleum concessions, the slide insinuated that while supermajors grabbed the most favored areas, the hype over these "frothy" concessions did not always bear out, and more discerning firms could realize substantial gains by focusing on undervalued reserves. The presenter used the cappuccino metaphor to illustrate his firm's "sensibly contrary approach to the oil and gas business" (ROC 2000). ROC looked to Cabinda's terrestrial South Block, which energy analysts noted, "for a variety of historical and non-technical reasons, has not been subjected to any exploration since the early 70s" (Alexander's Gas and Oil Connections 2001).[4]

Gulf Oil—since subsumed by Chevron—explored Cabinda's onshore before settling offshore. The corporation received a concession in 1957 for three years of exploration and fifty years of exclusive exploitation in the Cabindan territory and offshore (Hedberg 1958:1644).[5] In 1958 and 1959, the onshore wells Ponta Vermelha-1, Bucomazi-1, and Malembo-1 yielded oil shows, but Gulf considered none of them significant enough to develop. The corporation continued exploration with more geophysical surveys and geological mapping in 1960. Gulf drilled ten wells and abandoned them all, despite oil shows at four.[6] In 1961, the oil corporation commissioned the Western Geophysical Company of America to undertake seismic activities in the offshore portion of the concession (Rabanit 1963:1358). Five years later, Gulf Oil celebrated the completion of seven successful offshore exploration wells in the Iabe formation and the negotiation of a new contract with Portuguese authorities to extend the concession in Cabindan waters to the edge of the continental shelf (Saint et al. 1967:1591–1593).

Gulf Oil focused its attention on Cabinda's offshore. The corporation ultimately relinquished its onshore holdings in 1972, having drilled only ten wildcat wells in the concession spanning 1,080 km² (ROC 2005).[7] Whether conflict leading up to Angola's independence in 1975 influenced Gulf's decision to turn its back on Cabinda's onshore fields is unknown. After Cabinda was denied independence separate from Angola, further violence ensued. In January 1977, FLEC militants kidnapped nine French and Congolese engineers near the Congolese border with Cabinda. They used the incident to demand ransom and draw attention to the Cabindan independence cause, later releasing the hostages without injury. In the same month, FLEC claimed responsibility for an attack on Malongo, which caused some property damage but no injuries. On July 31, 1979, FLEC bombed a pipeline near Cabinda city and a police unit, resulting the death of eighteen officers (GTD 2007).[8]

Confronting Compromise

The socialist government in Luanda vacillated between confrontation and compromise with FLEC. President dos Santos took a hard line in 1981, sentencing six suspected FLEC members to death and four others to twenty-four years in prison on charges of bombing economic targets, hospitals, and schools in mainland Angola (IRIN 2003a). Two years later, he offered FLEC fighters unofficial amnesty. Chevron overtook Gulf Oil in a merger in 1984, the same year that UNITA began targeting the corporation's holdings in the Cabindan territory. Responding to UNITA's presence in Cabinda, falling oil prices, and Mobutu reopening the Zairean border, the government negotiated a short-lived ceasefire with FLEC in 1985.[9]

Internal disputes divided FLEC into FLEC-FAC (Forças Armadas de Cabinda) and FLEC-R (Renovada); however, both FLEC factions cooperated with UNITA to tackle military and corporate targets.[10] In August 1990, UNITA attacked a five-vehicle convoy, resulting in twenty-three fatalities. FLEC perpetrated a series of kidnappings in 1990, culminating in the October 19 abduction of a Chevron mechanic, Brent Swan.[11] Government troops responded with violence; they burned civilian homes, killed six people, and wounded more than twenty protesters the following year during a peaceful demonstration (AI 1992a).

After fifteen years protecting the MPLA's interests, the last Cuban soldiers departed Cabinda in 1991.[12] As part of Angola's transition to democracy, President dos Santos prepared the country for elections and pledged to resolve the "Cabinda problem."[13] Cabindans hoped that the political and economic changes in Luanda would strengthen their chances for independence and threw their full support to FLEC.[14] President dos Santos proposed only limited autonomy backed by an economic plan to boost the proportion of oil revenues spent on Cabinda from 1 to 10 percent, contingent upon his success in the 1992 elections (Tati 2002; Maier 1996:66–67). FLEC and Bishop Dom Paulinho Fernandes Madeca rejected dos Santos' offer, encouraging Cabinda's faithful pursuit of autonomy.[15]

Violence on both sides continued in the months leading up to Angola's 1992 presidential and parliamentary elections. FLEC-R abducted three Portuguese construction workers in Cabinda's Belize municipality on July 5, while an alternative faction, FLEC-FAC, kidnapped two French businessmen on July 14 and another Portuguese worker in Lândana on August 20; all were later released uninjured (MIPT 2005). The deliberate shooting of the oil worker João Evangelista Mbathi by local police for his suspected support of FLEC contributed to the toll of three deaths and several injuries after a weekend of political turbulence at the end of July (AI 1992b). At the start of September, the month of the elections, FLEC kidnapped a Frenchman in Cabinda city and the provincial director for law and order in Lândana without injury (GTD 2007). Two weeks before the polls opened, FLEC attacked Cabinda's main prison, incurring property damage (ibid.).

Cabindans boycotted the elections on September 29–30, 1992, citing their linguistic, ethnic, geographical, and cultural differences from Angola. Of the province's 84,000 eligible voters only 16,079 (19 percent) registered to vote—most of whom were government bureaucrats, police officers, and soldiers—and of these just 9,948 (12 percent) actually voted (Maier 1996:67; Tati 2002).[16] President dos Santos ignored the obvious political statement, but historians saw the electoral boycott "as a referendum for independence on the part of the Cabindans" (CR 2004). The concept of independence provided a way for Cabindans to envision a different reality and a means to protest their subjugation. Likewise, FLEC represented a political alternative to the repressive rule of the Angolan government. Villagers fed the soldiers their surplus produce and concealed them during government raids in the hopes that they would wrest the territory from Angola's grip.

Young men with few employment options swelled FLEC's ranks; fighting for Cabindan independence became a rite of passage to manhood. Journalists considered FLEC fighters a ragtag bunch, ill equipped in comparison to MPLA forces and "badly in need of haircuts and a good scrubbing" (Maier 1996:66). Still, FLEC forced the government to suspend onshore contract timelines with oil corporations under *force majeure* in the 1990s. In 1992, FLEC militants halted buses filled with Chevron employees, evacuating and burning the vehicles. Several months later, FLEC attacked a convoy of eight vehicles belonging to an American corporation, resulting in four fatalities and one injury (GTD 2007). In 1994, Chevron registered an injured employee as a result of a FLEC assault on Malongo with explosives and an Italian sawmill reported three workers abducted by FLEC (ibid.).[17]

Capturing Cabinda

As the war with UNITA in mainland Angola wound down, the government began to pursue a calculated strategy to territorialize Cabinda. Angolan leaders prepared the post-war offensive well before sending troops to the region. In the late 1990s, officials in Luanda began bribing high-ranking FLEC leaders with funds and positions in the army or police force in an effort to induce them to abandon armed conflict (HRW 1999).[18] For example, after a shake-up in the leadership of FLEC-R in January 1997, a number of high-ranking exiled militants surrendered to government authorities. The same men reemerged two years later in stable, high-paying posts in the police and civil defense units—working to eradicate their former allies.[19] Ousted FLEC-R leader José Tibúrcio Zinga Luemba also abandoned armed struggle, joining government authorities in October 2001 in advocating political negotiations and calling for other FLEC fighters to follow his lead.[20]

Meanwhile, President dos Santos replaced FLEC sympathizers in the provincial government. Between 2000 and 2002, he substituted Cabindan officials holding strategic provincial posts—relics of past détentes and negotiations with FLEC—with MPLA loyalists hailing from mainland Angola. First, he targeted the posts of provincial delegate to the Ministry of the Interior, the provincial police commander, and the provincial chief of information.[21] Then, he replaced the regional directors of RNA and TPA (the government radio and television networks), top officers in the Service on Migration and Foreigners and the director of the provincial port authority. José Aníbal Rocha, then-governor of Luanda, replaced Cabindan José Amaro Tati as governor of Cabinda.[22] Substitutions in the military followed; then the government pressured oil corporations operating in Cabinda to fire their local staff (Luemba 2008).

After Savimbi's death in February 2002, Cabindans hoped that their province might be given a chance for more autonomy; they never expected Angola's peace would bring a virtual takeover by officials from Luanda and full-scale war to Cabinda.[23] With Chevron pumping nearly 600,000 barrels per day from Blocks 0 and 14, two-thirds of all Angolan oil originated from Cabindan fields in 2002 (Chevron 2002). In the wake of a relatively minor oil spill in June 2002, President dos Santos styled himself as Cabinda's protector by imposing a $2 million fine on Chevron. Even so, Cabindans refused to embrace dos Santos' leadership or relinquish their hopes for independence. Angolan leaders vowed to extinguish FLEC and reopen Cabinda's onshore oilfields for exploration and production. In October 2002, the government mobilized 50,000 troops as part of a campaign to territorialize Cabinda.[24] The FAA referred to the campaign as *Operação Vassoura* (Operation Broom) or *Operação Limpeza* (Operation Clean-Up). These euphemistic titles suggested FAA's aim "to sweep all the FLEC combatants" from the province (VoA 2004a). Considering the stated mission, 50,000 soldiers was disproportionate if not excessive; the estimated strength of the remaining factions—FLEC-R and FLEC-FAC—stood at not more than 2,000 militants (Gomes Porto 2003:9). The FAA squadrons scattered throughout the territory, forming dense concentrations in the traditional FLEC strongholds of the interior. The government soldiers quickly dismantled Nzita Tiago's FLEC-FAC operations. Two months after their arrival, the soldiers destroyed FLEC-FAC's Kungo-Shonzo operational base in Buco Zau (Gomes Porto 2003:8). FLEC-R's "true guerrilla" tactics allowed Bento Bembe's military apparatus to remain intact for a few months longer despite the FAA's discovery of the faction's arms cache 10 kilometers from Cabinda city in December 2002.[25]

Sweetening Surrender

Well-armed, battle-hardened FAA troops devastated FLEC strongholds, inducing FLEC militants to surrender. On May 11, 2003, FLEC-FAC's Chief of Operations Miguel Zamba and Administrative Secretary General Celestino Paca turned themselves in to FAA's command in Buco Zau (*Agora* 2003). The following month, FLEC-FAC Chief of Staff Francisco Luemba, and six more of the faction's high-ranking officers surrendered to government authorities, including Training Director Zeferino Mabiala, Logistics Chief of Staff Joaquim Jimmy, and Counter-Intelligence Chief Jorge Gomes Macaia "Vasco" (Gomes Porto 2003:8; Chitata 2003b). A few months later, FAA Lieutenant Colonel António da Conceição "Lacrau" and his battalion of 708 *caçadores especiais* declared control over Necuto, the site of a major FLEC-FAC base (Suami 2003).[26] By October, FAA General Agostinho Nelumba "Sanjar" announced the integration of eighteen more ex-combatants from FLEC-FAC and FLEC-R into the Angolan army, referring to the occasion as "a sign of hope and confidence of Angolans in a future of peace and harmony" (*Jornal de Angola* 2003e).

The government announced a demobilization program as part of a strategy to encourage FLEC militants to abandon armed struggle. According to government officials, each FLEC combatant participating in the program was eligible to receive Angolan citizenship documents (i.e., ID card and birth certificate), $300 in contingency cash, six months' worth of food (including rations for up to six family members), access to medicine and treatment at a local military hospital, construction materials (e.g., zinc roofs, lumber, and nails), a small business or agricultural starter kit (i.e., seeds and tools), and reintegration counseling and skills training.[27] Higher ranking FLEC fighters were eligible for additional benefits. Displaced fighters and their families would also be transferred to the area of their origin. Whereas this attempt was largely successful, it was not without hiccups. Over 2,500 ex-FLEC combatants enrolled in the demobilization campaign, substantially more than expected, prompting concern that charlatans from the Democratic Republic of Congo were attempting to exploit the program (Taty and Massanga 2004). After rumors surfaced that some former combatants had sought to upgrade their packages by falsely declaring higher rank, former FLEC-R Chief of Staff Francisco Rodrigues and former Lieutenant Colonel of FLEC-FAC Alberto Nkuanga called on all demobilizing FLEC militants to furnish accurate details about their roles in the war to government authorities (Capita 2003). After six months, the demobilization campaign officially drew to a close.[28]

Where bullets and demobilization programs failed to induce surrender, the government encouraged FLEC fighters to lay down their arms with more enticing offers. Cabindans spoke of government operatives using bribes to infiltrate FLEC and offering gifts or money to family members who surrendered a wanted individual. According to one account, security officials kidnapped the son of a suspected FLEC collaborator and interrogated him at the Hotel Simulambuco for over two hours about his father's daily routine. The interrogators dangled keys to a flashy new car and promised to put a duffle bag stuffed with money into the trunk if the teenager divulged the contacts and activities of his father.[29] Although the son remained loyal to his father, the remaining FLEC combatants were fighting a losing battle—only a handful of FLEC militants continued to stalk FAA soldiers in the Mayombe forest. FLEC's final attack on the Angolan

Armed Forces took place in early 2004. The most adamant FLEC sympathizers refused to believe reports of FLEC's defeat, but most Cabindans accepted that FLEC would not win their independence militarily.[30]

The government paid former FLEC fighters to encourage their obstinate counterparts in the bush to surrender. When the FAA captured Cornélio Tando, a FLEC-FAC militant who had spent half of his life in armed struggle, news sources reported his unequivocal plea to remaining guerrillas to lay down their arms and embrace the government's peaceful resolution to the "Cabinda problem" (Ibinda 2004d). Government forces also widely distributed a pamphlet featuring eleven former FLEC militants entreating, "It is your turn, abandon the bush, join us. We are for peace and understanding among Angolans. Do not suffer in the bush" (*Jornal Digital* 2004a).[31] The ex-FLEC guerrillas' shared call to surrender echoed the work of Portuguese propagandists in their 1962 leaflet to UPA sympathizers, which promised, "If you approach the troops or a post and say that you want to be good again, everything will work out happily" (Marcum 1969:346).[32] Still, the 2004 Angolan pamphlet contained darker sentiments. It issued an eschatological judgment on FLEC while hinting at a possibility of amnesty by stating: "FLEC has given you nothing. . . . Nzita Tiago and Bento Bembe will not give you anything but disgrace and death. Your salvation is the Government of Angola" (*Jornal Digital* 2004a). Among its closing statements was the same line the Portuguese had used decades ago: "Present yourself without fear." To surrender themselves, however, FLEC combatants would need to face their deepest fear: surrendering the dream of independence.

Engendering Terror

In their violent sweep across Cabinda, government troops destroyed villages in Buco Zau, Necuto, and Belize as they burned fields, looted homes, and displaced or killed their inhabitants (AI 2004). Some survivors sought refuge in the neighboring Congos; the remainder rebuilt their lives, reseeding their gardens and constructing temporary homes of mud and thatch (Congo et al. 2003). Accustomed to the ebb and flow of past battles between FLEC and FAA, Cabindans said they had never considered that government soldiers would remain in their villages, monitoring their every move. One villager told me in low tones, "Soldiers will watch your house—when you come and go, wake and sleep—they will put a knife to your wife's throat and kill your children for a television, a satellite dish."

Despite the dwindling number of FLEC militants, the government maintained an alarmingly high ratio of soldiers to civilians in Cabinda; there were at least four soldiers per square kilometer of the forested

Mayombe region (Heitor 2004b). Given FLEC's wide appeal among the populace and the integration of its bases within communities, FAA troops treated all Cabindans as FLEC allies, especially those from villages in the interior. The villagers, in turn, viewed the soldiers as occupiers and considered their brutal tactics part of a plan to terrorize the province into submission. As I conducted interviews in FAA-controlled villages, informants eyed their surroundings—and me—with suspicion. My introduction from a local human rights advocate, coupled with their desire to reveal the abuses in Cabinda to the wider world, encouraged them to take a chance on me. "We cannot talk," confided a young man. Cocking his head to one side, he said in a low voice, "We are not at peace—they control everything." The young man turned a slow circle as he motioned obliquely towards local FAA posts. "There are five here, five there, five more over there, and even more in the bush—who knows how many."

Governor Rocha claimed that the troops sent for the "pacification of Cabinda" would cement an "alliance between FAA and populations" (*Jornal de Angola* 2004m). Cabinda's population was extremely vulnerable; a 2003 study counted within its borders 13,658 internally displaced persons, 6,606 handicapped persons, 1,267 orphans, and 16,476 recently returned refugees (GoA 2003b:6). Foreign correspondents and human rights groups noticed that rather than aiding the vulnerable population, FAA troops were abusing Cabindans. Rafael Marques commented, "The propaganda that is broadcast through the state media shows the FAA in Cabinda delivering social assistance to those in need when, in reality, the FAA are the perpetrators of the tragedy" (Marques 2003b).

During Operação Vassoura, FAA soldiers used terror tactics to territorialize—or in the words of Governor Rocha, "pacify"—Cabinda. According to the human rights activist Agostinho Chicaia, it was to be "a war without witnesses, [each] deliberately silenced with the finality of annihilating the adversary to the last breath and imposing dictatorship on the vanquished" (Ibinda 2004i). FAA troops harassed, beat, and sexually abused civilians under their control, preying upon local women as they washed clothes or tended crops; gangs of soldiers raped mothers and daughters simultaneously, or raped a girl as her father was beaten (CADHC/CRTC 2002; Congo et al. 2003).

Human rights advocates detailed hundreds of arbitrary detentions, scores of summary executions and rapes, and even evidence of internment camps in Cabinda since the commencement of Operação Vassoura (CADHC/CRTC 2002; Congo et al. 2003). Still, statistics fail to capture the terror in the eyes of the half-nude, sixteen-year-old Amélia Teco Luemba as she attempted to flee the FAA soldiers preparing to rape her, or the unimaginable suffering of Tiago Macosso as he was summarily executed at the Angolan army's Necuto base when troops burned a gasoline-soaked tire around his neck (CADHC/CRTC 2002). Tallies of rape victims fail to note how government forces abducted Judite Mavungo in November 2003 and held her for six weeks at a military outpost where soldiers habitually gang-raped her at gunpoint and left her to sleep outside in the rain each night (Marques 2004d). Figures fail to demonstrate how FAA troops attacked the vulnerable, such as visibly pregnant women or prepubescent girls. In May 2003, soldiers raped five young girls: ten-year-old Teresa Simba from Buco Zau, eleven-year-olds Marta Pedro of Buco-Cango and Alice Matsuela from Panga-Mongo, and twelve-year-olds Maria Lourdes Mataia and Odília Muanda from the respective towns of Caio II and Buco Zau (Congo et al. 2003).

On balance, human rights reports covering Operação Vassoura described FLEC's wrongdoings but revealed far more violations perpetrated by FAA soldiers than FLEC militants.[33] Nevertheless, the government attempted to blame violence against civilians on FLEC. Angola's "state-controlled radio called on soldiers and members of the paramilitary Rapid Intervention Police to 'mercilessly annihilate' FLEC fighters, claiming that they had murdered, maimed and tortured civilians, and 'press ganged' and 'used them as slaves'" (AI 2004). Many Cabindans denied these allegations, claiming that the civilians living in or near FLEC bases were neither captives nor slaves but supporters and relatives of the fighters. They suggested that the government simply attributed to FLEC the abuses that its own soldiers perpetrated.[34]

Recycling Maneuvers

As I reviewed the terrible details of the reports on human rights abuses in Cabinda and spoke with occupied communities in the interior, I began to recognize a pattern. The soldiers used terror tactics learned from their experience in Angola's twenty-seven-year war. Even the campaign's name, Operação Vassoura—and its alternate title, Operação Limpeza—nodded to a tactic designed to cleanse a territory of enemy forces. During the civil war, FAA soldiers routinely undertook *limpeza* operations both to "root out possible UNITA supporters and to recruit able-bodied men for civilian militia groups"; soldiers also raped, beat, and harassed civilians in UNITA-held zones, assuming them to be "rebel supporters or collaborators" (HRW 2002). Since the Angolan army now focuses more on demobilizing than recruiting, locals told me that Cabindan boys are generally safe from forced conscription—but not from beatings. "When they get drunk," a young man asserted, "the FAA [soldiers] say 'you are FLEC' and they beat you." A woman at his side nodded and confirmed that locally stationed troops had threatened her son too. Once masters of their agricultural domain, she and other women said they now feared venturing to the fields. Sexual assaults by FAA troops stationed in the area were still common and impeded local food production. Unwilling to watch their families die of starvation and emboldened by their hunger, the women formed protective groups and bravely set out to tend to and harvest their crops. As one woman told me, "we go in groups, but we walk with fear."

Hunger was the best weapon of the FAA troops in their fight against UNITA; *limpeza* operations razed farmers' fields, forcing them to flee to government-controlled areas in search of food. Cabindans said that government forces now targeted FLEC and FLEC sympathizers through *limpeza* operations limiting food production. Government troops "accompanied villagers to their fields, impeding their work and increasing food shortage" (AI 2004). Father Púcuta, a Catholic priest in Buco Zau, testified that "in each field there is a military presence" and that FAA soldiers "regularly ambush civilians" going to the fields because the troops fear that the people will "bring supplies to the guerrillas in the bush" (*O Apostolado* 2004b). Government forces threatened to cut off the hands of women married to FLEC combatants if they went to the fields (HRW 2004a). In Dinge, FAA Commander Santos allegedly ordered his unit to kill any civilian found in the fields until locals turned in twenty-five FLEC militants known to patrol the region, thereby severing the flow of sustenance to the communities of Lico, Weka, Liambaliona, Ikazu, Bichekete, and Chapa (Ibinda 2004b).

The tactics FAA soldiers employed to territorialize Cabinda also recalled the influence of UNITA. For example, the appalling case of Judite Mavungo's gang rape by FAA soldiers who held her captive for six weeks evoked UNITA's practice of abducting women and girls and using them as sexual slaves (HRW 2002). A number of UNITA and FAA soldiers who committed atrocities in the past may now be responsible for similar abuses in Cabinda. In 2002, a few months after the government declared a general amnesty for all military crimes perpetrated during the civil war, the FAA integrated thousands of UNITA troops into its ranks.[35]

Former UNITA militants—largely of Ovimbundu ethnicity—constitute a significant proportion of the FAA troops in the province (Moore 2003). Rumor circulated in Cabinda that the government had tricked the Ovimbundu soldiers into fighting there, so they expressed their frustration by abusing locals.[36] The rumor explains the former UNITA soldiers' predicament as follows: First, FAA commanders promise the war-exhausted soldiers from Huambo retirement posts in Luanda or uncomplicated missions protecting Cabinda's oil installations but transport them deep into the dark heart of Mayombe instead.[37] The Ovimbundu, accustomed to the sweeping grasslands and pastoral vistas of Angola's central highlands, find the dense humidity of the forest oppressive. The soldiers contemplate desertion but the terrain is unfamiliar and most inhabitants of Mayombe speak only Ibinda, so the native Umbundu speakers cannot communicate. Moreover, leaving Cabinda requires crossing international borders, and they are well aware that FAA tightly controls all of these. After a few weeks of training, groups of five to ten soldiers take their posts in rural villages and are tasked with eradicating FLEC. The troops are well equipped with arms and ammunition yet have few rations and little cash. They suspect villagers of sustaining their quarry with food and support. The FAA fighters eventually make no distinction between FLEC militants and their sympathizers: both become the enemy.

The rumor—whether fully accurate or not—contains a kernel of truth. FAA soldiers eye villagers with suspicion, abusing them in lieu of their evanescent enemy. Facing resentment from the villagers under their control, they import Congolese wives, marry outcasts, or force local women to wed under threat of death and by shame of defilement (HRW 2004b).[38] Using extortion and violence, the soldiers attempt to construct lives and livelihoods out of their posts. Faced with a seemingly insuperable mission for an indeterminate period, getting drunk becomes an escape mechanism.

Extortionary Gatekeeping

Government reports at the time of my visits to rural Cabindan villages proclaimed the free movement of goods and persons in the province.[39] Despite the government's claims, FAA troops stationed in Cabinda's interior restricted not only the cultivation but also the distribution of produce.[40] As I traveled from one village to the next, their inhabitants' ability to freely cultivate and distribute their produce varied widely. I encountered emaciated villages with fearful, hungry-eyed inhabitants separated only ten kilometers from communities so plentiful with fruits that the pineapples bundled in palm-woven sleighs and readied for market rotted under the searing sun for lack of transport.

Community members attributed variations to the demeanor of the soldiers posted to the area. A resident of a dusty rural village offered me two of her pineapples, explaining that the earnings from the freshly picked pineapples could not offset both the costs of transportation and the beer to assuage the local FAA gatekeepers. Farmers in other villages offered me bananas; another community gave me some green oranges and a few guavas; and a big-hearted family heaped three coconuts and six ears of corn in my arms. The gifts of food were not only a testament to the generosity of rural Cabindans but also the perishable nature of all they had. Military checkpoints and gatekeepers precluded sales of surplus foodstuffs to neighboring communities and markets, as soldiers tended to loot goods at the checkpoints or demand cash for letting them pass unscathed. Without access to markets, Cabindans could not earn the currency necessary for purchasing basic items like soap and clothing.

Gasoline was also an issue. An indignant inhabitant of a town on Cabinda's eastern edge looked wistfully at his ripening bananas and said, "The tanker trucks pass by all the time—they should be filling local posts, but they go right over the border." Worse than the lack of transport for his bananas, the man said that for lack of gasoline members of his community had been forced to balance a woman in labor across two bicycles to bring her to a health post several kilometers away. Many Cabindans blamed FAA troops for fuel shortages.[41] Allegedly, soldiers collude with Sonangol to divert gas tankers to the Democratic Republic of Congo, sharing a portion of the proceeds with their commanding officers and the border guards.[42] "They are duping us—it is a complete fiasco," said one man.[43] "Who can bring gas to the border? Not me, not you, but the one with the stars on his shoulders. He gets a Congolese [guy] to work for him—a Cabindan could not do this job . . . no, you would dirty your criminal record."

To investigate the illegal fuel trade, I decided to follow the flow of fuel through Yema, a dismal border town on Cabinda's southern border with the Democratic Republic of Congo. The area between Cabinda city and Yema was highly militarized; en route, I passed a military camp near Fortaleza, the Second Brigade's training facility at Nto with a display of rocket launchers and tanks at the front gates, and the entrance to N'goio's FAA barracks flanked with combat vehicles. Apart from a series of depopulated towns, the only other notable features in the area were the Yabi prison and Cabinda's sprawling garbage dump.[44]

It was around one o'clock on a torrid Saturday afternoon when I walked into no man's land. The Ministry of the Interior pass around my neck declared Yema neutral terrain, yet the Angolan army clearly controlled this zone along Cabinda's eastern border with the Democratic Republic of Congo. A trucker from Kinshasa told me that I had arrived too late to witness FAA soldiers directing their regular shipments of Cabinda's gasoline to Congolese middlemen, but he pointed me down a dusty path toward a makeshift bar. There, I found a dozen inebriated soldiers under a canopy.

Kizomba music blared from a boom box in the corner. Semi-automatic rifles leaned uneasily against a painted bamboo partition. A poster pasted on the flimsy wall read: "Turbo King: *Une affaire d'hommes.*" I took the only available seat—across from an imposing commander keeping a blind eye on his recruits. Dressed in khaki and camouflage fatigues, the men crowded around plastic tables overloaded with chinking beer bottles. A half-dozen of them were doubled over, laughing at one of their lewdly dancing counterparts. With glazed eyes and stumbling steps, the drunken soldier swayed to the rhythm, sloshing Turbo King beer on the toes of his combat boots.

When I emerged from the bar, I saw a pack of young boys sorting through piles of empty Skol, Turbo King, and Primus bottles, dropping them into crates bound for refills at breweries in the Democratic Republic of Congo.[45] By spending their earnings from the illicit fuel trade at this makeshift bar on the border, the soldiers were essentially trading truckloads of Cabinda's gasoline for their liquid weight in Congolese beer.

Harried Homecomings

In the wake of Operação Vassoura, waves of conflict, deprivation, and misery pressed more than 23,000 Cabindans to seek refuge in the Democratic Republic of Congo and Republic of Congo (Heitor 2004b). The endemic violence also created massive internal displacement. Residents from embattled sections of the interior fled to safer coastal villages, larger towns, and the capital. On a visit to a community not far from the DRC border, a local schoolteacher recalled that he once had a shortage of chairs in his classroom; now most sat empty because so many families had left.

Operação Vassoura displaced 45,000 rural villagers (Moore 2003). Many villages in the interior disappeared altogether, their former inhabitants escaped or dead. An independent newspaper reported the disappearance of twenty-two villages from the municipality of Buco Zau, between October 2002 and January 2004 (*Semanário Angolense* 2004c, 2004d). North of Buco Zau in the municipality of Belize, seven villages suffered severe depopulation or abandonment over the same period (Congo et al. 2003). The inhabitants of a number of the abandoned villages in the region were often forcefully removed as part of a government territorialization strategy. FAA troops forced 500 families from Alto N'Sundi, a FLEC stronghold in Belize, to resettle in Necuto (*O Apostolado* 2004b). As Operação Vassoura spread terror across Cabinda, fifty-nine villages suffered depopulation or even disappeared as they were abandoned by inhabitants or razed by the FAA.[46]

After government soldiers exerted their control over most of the Cabindan territory to ensure access to onshore oilfields, FAA Chief of Staff General Armando da Cruz Neto made an announcement. He declared that "the operation launched to restore peace in Cabinda [had] reached a positive phase" and revealed plans to pursue "the development of border control mechanisms so as to prevent FLEC forces from regrouping and returning" (Gomes Porto 2003:9). At the same time, the FAA ran cross-border campaigns to force the return of Cabindan refugees. Under the assumption (or pretext) that Cabindan refugees in the neighboring states were supporting FLEC, Angolan forces thwarted international law, crossed into the neighboring Congos, and attacked refugee settlements. In May 2004, correspondents revealed how FAA troops had invaded the villages of Ngunga, Mbubisi, Ngeba, and Manenga across the Republic of Congo (Brazzaville) border in an attempt to forcibly return Cabindan refugees to Cabinda (*Jornal Digital* 2004b). Four months later, a similar report accused FAA of forcibly repatriating Cabindans in Kimbianga, Sekizola, Lundu Matende, and N'fuike in the Democratic Republic of Congo and Komi in the Republic of Congo (*O Apostolado* 2004b).[47]

The Angolan Social Welfare Ministry (MINARS) attempted to lure Cabindans back to the province with guaranteed housing and food security. Once they had crossed back over the border, the agency reneged on many of its promises. One year after their return to Cabinda, 278 repatriated families in the MINARS Zôngolo camp petitioned Governor Rocha to make good on the zinc roofs, lumber, and materials the agency had promised them for constructing their homes (Cuteta 2003b).

To better understand the dynamics of government-sponsored repatriation, I made an informal visit to a MINARS settlement in July 2004. Luvula was an isolated village where 45 families, returned from Congo-Brazzaville, packed into unfinished mud-brick houses constructed by the government. Each house featured a living room and three small bedrooms; MINARS assigned families of up to twelve persons to each house. A returnee in a frayed brown hat told me that the government had neither provided cement to reinforce the brick structures nor drapes to offer privacy. I glanced toward the houses, fixing my eyes on the open windows. A few families with a spare *pane*, the bright cloths that Cabindan women tie about their waists and heads, had fashioned makeshift curtains. The returnee in the brown hat said that there was little fabric or anything else to spare in Luvula; the soil was poor and their subsistence was uncertain. He regretted returning to Cabinda and wished he could reunite with his family members who had refused to leave Congo-Brazzaville. Taking off his frayed hat, he confided that he originated in a village in Cabinda's interior but remained in Luvula so as not to be associated with FLEC. "If we go back to the village," he said in a low voice, "they say, 'You are with them' and we will be in danger."

In September 2005, MINARS halted the fourth and final phase of an organized repatriation program for 3,000 Cabindan refugees from Congo-Brazzaville after just 286 people had returned (ReliefWeb 2005).[48] Although the Ministry cited technical difficulties as the cause of the stoppage, Cabindans explain that their compatriots likely resisted relocation. In March 2005, the United Nations High Commission on Refugees (UNHCR) took representatives of Cabindan refugee groups on a tour of three of Cabinda's municipalities to encourage them to return. The representatives "were concerned about the massive presence of the Angolan military and lack of infrastructure," "said they would be reluctant to come home unless conditions improved," and returned "to the Republic of Congo (Brazzaville) to tell their fellow refugees what they saw" (IRIN 2005a). One refugee representative doubted that Cabinda was really at peace, for "all we saw were troops, troops, troops"; however, UNHCR officials tried to explain that the FAA troops "were there to establish and provide security for all citizens" (ibid.). The refugees disbelieved the UNHCR officials; abuse by the soldiers was exactly the trouble that had forced many of them to seek refuge outside of Cabinda.

Allowing Abuse

For decades, police and soldiers had mistreated Cabindans in retribution for FLEC strikes against their forces, with Luanda's tacit acceptance or clandestine approval.[49] On a few occasions, the government openly acknowledged abuses by FAA troops undertaking Operação Vassoura. Military leaders admitted to some "indiscretions" on the part of "undisciplined soldiers" but denied any intent to terrorize the populace and implied that Cabindans had manufactured most of the charges. Cabinda's Deputy Governor João Santos de Carvalho Mesquita admitted, "The provincial government is aware of these reports and the accusations made against the army, but I must point out that these are isolated incidents and not institutionalized behavior" (IRIN 2003a).[50]

Bureaucrats in Luanda might not have explicitly promoted the violent tactics employed by FAA soldiers in Cabinda, yet they played the role of enablers. The combination of poor discipline, abysmal wages, and low morale among soldiers with a history of civilian abuse and psychological damage created the conditions for atrocities.[51] Far from home, scattered throughout rural communities, and with no clear objective other than to seek out the FLEC guerrillas camouflaged under dense forest canopy or disguised in mundane occupations, many of the soldiers became frustrated. Even after declaring victory over FLEC, the Ministry of Defense set no clear timeline for the troops' departure; FAA soldiers increasingly performed security detail, protecting the interests of transnational oil corporations like Interoil, Devon Energy, and ROC, as well as their Angolan counterparts Sonangol and Force Petroleum.[52]

Government officials in Luanda also set a poor example for the soldiers by publicly articulating their disdain for Cabindans. Fearful of loosening the clenched grip on the territory and its resources, the government often depicted Cabinda as volatile and painted its people as disobediently flouting the rule of law. As peaceful protests against FAA abuses gained traction in Cabinda, Minister of Interior Osvaldo Serra Van-Dúnem warned, "We have a state of law in Angola, governed by valid laws and principles, and where there are disturbances in the normal state of living, there are forces tasked with acting in conformity [with the law] . . . in Cabinda, the same as in Benguela or in Luanda" (Ibinda 2004f). This government strategy of portraying regions on the geographical fringe as unruly to justify state-sponsored violence to establish order and preserve national peace is not uncommon (Kirsch 2002). Still, it is a dangerous game. If the government deems FLEC a terrorist organization whose goal of Cabindan self-determination is considered threatening to Angola's political and territorial integrity, then all FLEC sympathizers are painted as traitors. FAA soldiers took this one step further, treating all Cabindans as FLEC sympathizers with the disdain reserved for traitors and subjecting them to rape, torture, and execution.

RESISTING TERRITORIALIZATION

As Operação Vassoura spread across Cabinda, the FAA's cruel tactics discouraged civilians from taking up arms; however, they failed to force Cabindans into submission. On the contrary, Cabindans responded to the atrocities with activism. Human rights advocates compiled accounts of abuses perpetrated by soldiers. Survivors of rape and torture joined in protest with families mourning victims lost to extrajudicial executions. Civil society and the clergy organized conferences and marches. Rather than subjugating Cabinda, Operação Vassoura inspired a renewed call for Cabindan self-determination.

Osvaldo Serra Van-Dúnem, the minister of the interior, challenged civil society and church members' protests against military abuses, asking a journalist, "Why is there this tendency of people in Cabinda to favor independence and for some missionaries to react to all the government says and all the government does?" (Ibinda 2004f). Van-Dúnem construed Cabindans as ungrateful to the MPLA for their liberation from Portuguese colonial rule, portraying them as unwilling to share their resource wealth with the rest of the suffering country. The Cabindan attorney Francisco Luemba countered, "No one gives or refuses what he does not have." He reminded critics that "the natural resources of Cabinda are not in the hands of its people"; rather, "Cabinda's resources are at the mercy of the strongest or most audacious and Cabindans are reduced to the condition of servicing the fields of those resources" (Luemba 2002).[53]

Both sides accuse the other of an insatiable thirst for oil: leaders in Luanda suggest that FLEC's clamor for independence corresponds only to a narcissistic desire to be the so-called "Kuwait of Africa," and Cabindans maintain that the government's interests in their territory are purely extractive. Regardless of the aspersions and ambitions ascribed to FLEC, independence means more to the Cabindan people than control of the oil deposits. They envision independence as a chance to free themselves of violent incursions, chart an alternate diplomatic course emphasizing regional trade relationships, and direct their own economic development in a manner that does not compromise local ecosystems.

Cabindans cite the 1885 Treaty of Simulambuco (discussed in Chapter 3) as juridical proof of their right to independence, while the government discounts any legal claims in the document. To Cabindans, the quest for independence is as much a reflection of a belief in their legal right to self-determination as a protest against a repressive government that has mismanaged its oil wealth. Still, Cabindans rally around provocative petro-claims. The government's failure to bring basic services (e.g., electricity, sanitation, etc.) to Cabinda begets speculation on what might be improved if Cabindans were to control the revenues from offshore oil extraction. Cabindans know that Block o has produced more oil than any block in Angolan history and recognize that they have not received benefits proportionate to the resources extracted from their province, though they have borne the burden of oil spills and decades of environmental degradation. Using petro-claims has helped Cabindans gain traction in the global media. Even news reports on military abuses perpetrated by the troops in Cabinda implicitly recognize the relationship between the violent acts and the quest to control Cabinda's oil wealth.[54]

Oil attracts media attention to the FAA's violent territorialization of Cabinda, yet the strategic value of oil has dissuaded FLEC's few diplomatic allies from confronting the powerful Angolan government.[55] Even East Timorese Prime Minister Mari Alkatiri, who paid a diplomatic visit to

Angola in the same month Operação Vassoura began, refused to acknowl-edge the situation. FLEC-FAC's José Maria Liberal Nuno, cognizant of Alka-tiri's description of Cabinda as "Lusophone Africa's East Timor" during his exile in Portugal, reportedly encouraged the prime minister to broach the subject of state-sponsored violence in Cabinda during his meetings with President dos Santos (RFI 2002). Alkatiri suppressed his sentiments on Cabinda as he negotiated bilateral accords for oil sector cooperation with what he called a "politically stable" Angola and graciously accepted dos Santos' pledge to be "totally available" in assisting East Timor's "great chal-lenge" of reconstruction after the long decades of the island nation's occupa-tion by Indonesia (LUSA 2002).

Aiming for Autonomy

During the first few months of Operação Vassoura, top government offi-cials promised dialogue as FAA troops stalked Cabinda in search of FLEC militants (Tati 2002). Then, in January 2003, FLEC-FAC leader Henriques Nzita Tiago entered into talks with the Angolan government in Paris. Nzita Tiago refused to consider any solution for Cabinda short of inde-pendence; the dialogue yielded no solution.[56] Cabinda's Deputy Governor João Santos de Carvalho Mesquita likened acceding to Cabindan demands for independence to succumbing to a contagious disease. He worried that "granting independence to Cabinda may set a precedent for other prov-inces" and asked rhetorically if "the people of Cuando Cubango decide one day that they want independence, should the government also agree to that?" (IRIN 2003a).

President dos Santos repeated the old MPLA slogan *de Cabinda à Cunene* and denied the possibility of granting Cabinda independence.[57] As an alter-native, the government signaled a willingness to negotiate greater auton-omy for Angola's northernmost province (IRIN 2003d). Abel Chivukuvuku of UNITA ruled out Cabinda's independence under the Organization of African Unity's precept that the borders inherited under colonialism be maintained so as to prevent state fragmentation but agreed that autonomy might be an option (IRIN 2003a; Chivukuvuku 2002). He warned that an independent Cabinda, small in population and territorial size with "few physical attributes to guarantee its sovereignty," would risk falling "vic-tim to the greed of various international interests" (Chivukuvuku 2002). Even UNITA leader Isaías Samakuva—who guaranteed Nzita Tiago's FLEC faction continuing assistance after Savimbi's death—advocated a system of autonomy in which Angola would negotiate a pact with Cabinda similar to Portugal's arrangement with Madeira and the Azores.[58]

Journalists and human rights activists observed that all the banter on Cabindan autonomy lacked any definition. Rafael Marques declared, "It is important for the government to clarify to all parties what it means by autonomy—if this is, in fact, up for serious discussion. There is uncertainty around how this concept will actually work, which has led to mistrust among all concerned" (IRIN 2003a).

As I conducted interviews across the province, I also discovered a great deal of mistrust of the government's commitment to resolving the "Cabinda problem." Some Cabindans even grudgingly accepted that the government had firmly imposed its rule on their territory according to *"a sorte do mais forte"* (literally, "the luck of the strongest"). A young man called Marco elaborated on the government's iron-fist strategy for winning the prize of Cabinda's oil as he pointed to a poster of Arnold Schwarzenegger from the 1985 film *Commando*. He laughed, insinuating that as a Californian living under Schwarzenegger's governorship I should know something about *a sorte do mais forte*. "We live in hell," Marco asserted in a matter-of-fact tone. Cabinda may be a beautiful, resource-rich territory, but he felt exhausted from living in a climate of overwhelming suspicion, fear, and desperation. Though cognizant of the repression suffered in mainland Angola, Marco contended that in Cabinda "with petroleum in the lead, we continue to be tortured—it cannot compare with what is done in Luanda." Like many other Cabindans, Marco distrusted the government and discerned the role of oil behind its efforts at territorialization.

Envisioning Peace

The atmosphere outside the Chiloango Cultural Center was tense but energized on July 8, 2003. It was the first morning of *Uma Visão Comum para Cabinda*, a conference to define a shared outlook for Cabinda's future. Attendees chatted excitedly, brushing up against Open Society posters with the NGO's bold catchphrase: *Paz sem democracia é fantasia* ("Peace without democracy is imaginary"). I took a seat inside the air-conditioned theater and marveled as hundreds and hundreds of people filed in to hear speeches on Cabindan identity and the Treaty of Simulambuco. They filled every aisle and corner. Outside, people crowded around the windows and doors. Some waved FLEC flags, singing the refrain, *Separar, separar, separar . . . Separar Angola e Cabinda . . . Nós queremos independência total* ("To separate, separate, separate . . . To separate Angola and Cabinda . . . We want total independence"). In all, some 1,500 people attended the conference, representing over 150 political and social organizations concerned with Cabinda's future (Pasipanodya 2003).

Father Congo, a towering Catholic priest from the Immaculate Conception parish, presided over the conference. The Cabindan clergy has long advocated for peace and suffered the consequences.[59] Church leaders first spoke out publicly against the violation of Cabindans' rights and liberties on February 10, 1975 (Luemba 2008). Since the mid-1980s, under the leadership of the compassionate Cabindan Bishop Dom Paulino Fernandes Madeca, local Catholic priests have developed a homegrown version of liberation theology.[60] Although Madeca veiled his sympathies because of his position, Father Raúl Tati and Father Jorge Casimiro Congo are two of the most outspoken priests, challenging the government's extractive and repressive presence in Cabinda.[61] At the conference, Father Tati cited the poverty, hunger, and misery of Cabindans, exacerbated by pillaging, torture, and violence at the hands of government soldiers. Creatively coining a new phrase to describe the repressive powers in Luanda, he insisted, "We have to assume a critical role as a means of change. . . . Angola is not a democratic state, but a *demonocratic* state. . . . I defend [Cabinda's] self-determination in the sense of total independence" (Heitor 2004b). Father Congo seconded the Church's role as the people's advocate by pursuing "a peaceful solution to the Cabindan problem" and ensuring that the government respects "the legitimacy of the concerns and desires expressed by Cabindans" (IRIN 2003a).

The guest speakers and attendees confronted the "Cabinda problem" by recognizing the motive and the means by which Angola exerted control over the territory. The celebrated intellectual Justino Pinto de Andrade asked the audience what Cabinda had gained from petroleum. "Nothing!" they yelled. Pinto de Andrade shook his head and reminded them that extraction had brought pollution, unemployment, and war. Attorney Francisco Luemba added that Chevron's promised "American Way of Life" had not materialized; rather, Cabinda suffered from the "American Way of Strife"—wherein inhabitants of the extractive region had neither the expected benefits of jobs and electricity, nor even access to refined petroleum products.[62] Manuel Monteiro, a politician from the Portuguese *Nova Democracia* party, distinguished between Angola's military agenda and Cabindans' emphasis on the Treaty of Simulambuco, saying, "The state has the reason of force, but we have the force of reason."[63] José Marcos Mavungo claimed that with the signature of the Alvor Accords Cabinda had become a servant to Angola, living off Luanda's table scraps and obeying under threat of violence. He questioned whose interests the FAA troops represented. "Angola . . . Chevron . . . America," came the mixed replies from the crowd. One person suggested Angola could simply "take all the oil and leave us alone." Another called out, "We will give George W. Bush all the petroleum he wants in exchange for our liberty." Audience members argued over whether abandoning the natural resource wealth was a viable strategy until Francisco Luemba wisely interjected, "Liberty can neither be bought nor sold and having a ceasefire is one thing, but we also have to stop this psychological war and the environment of persecution."

At some point during the speeches, the conference center's electricity went out—an occurrence regarded by the attendees as a signal of the local government's displeasure with the event. Despite the stuffy surroundings, people animatedly leapt forward when Father Congo announced the time for the audience members to express their thoughts onstage. One speaker rattled off a series of pithy quips advocating Cabinda's separation from Angola: "We are a stone in the shoe of Angola and we ask that the government take off its shoe and free the rock; we are a mathematical equation waiting for a solution; we are waiting for the Angolan government to hit the space bar on the keyboard." Other respondents deplored the extreme militarization of Cabinda. "It is easier to go to the U.S. than it is to go to Mayombe—I was stopped by seven military officers on the way to my village," said one. Another decried the government's complicit acceptance of abuses committed by FAA soldiers as flouting its patriarchal obligations to all citizens. He asked, "Does a good father hurt his child? Then why does the Angolan government torture us and kill us?" The speaker deduced his conclusion before a roaring crowd: "Cabindans are not Angolans and never will be," he said triumphantly.

Inventing an Interlocutor

I found many of the impassioned speeches during the conference quite moving, especially a gendered perspective on the FAA occupation delivered by a member of the Mães Cabindesas, the Cabindan Mothers association. As an outside observer, however, I was most surprised by the audience's poor reception of FLEC representatives. I had naïvely assumed that Cabindans supported FLEC without reservation, but the crowd booed José Tibúrcio Zinga Luemba of FLEC-Nova Visão and likewise expressed displeasure at the reading of a letter sent from Paris by Henriques Nzita Tiago's FLEC-FAC faction.[64] Cabindans had grown skeptical of FLEC. The various factions had failed to deliver on their promise of an independent Cabinda. For decades, government officials in Luanda discounted dialogue with a fractured FLEC and promised to initiate peace talks as soon as a "singular, valid interlocutor" could be found. The promise was merely a stalling tactic; this interlocutor was "understood in advance to be non-existent" (Mabeko-Tali 2004). Cabindans almost unanimously supported the broader goal of independence from Angola, but many of them resented FLEC's history of splintered infighting.

Worse yet, Cabindans felt excluded from the negotiating table. For example, former FLEC-R leader José Tibúrcio Zinga Luemba jumped at the chance to promote the government's ill-defined plan for autonomy; he formed FLEC-Nova Visão as a mediating body but alienated civil society leaders and clerics by claiming that they stalled the negotiations process (*Jornal de Angola* 2003i).[65] Given "the bipolar politics" of "political elites be they of the MPLA or of FLEC," explained Father Tati, "civil society and independent voices have been shut out or made subordinate to those of the main parties" (Tati 2003). Father Congo agreed, "Cabindans have come to rely on those leaders who have remained in Cabinda instead of hoping that exiles would deliver their freedom to them [and] in many ways, this means that there are individuals who command a lot more support than the individual FLEC factions" (IRIN 2003a). During the July 2003 conference, participants encouraged FLEC to remain accountable to Cabindans—the people all factions claimed to represent. The attendees also elected a six-member board charged with forming a Cabindan civil society organization. Unsurprisingly, the people nominated Father Tati and Father Congo.[66] The government had consistently dismissed dialogue as a viable means to seek resolution of the "Cabinda problem" for "lack of a valid interlocutor," but Cabindans hoped that this new civil society organization could represent their interests more effectively than the backbiting FLEC factions. Father Congo recognized, "I think Cabindans are tired of other people sorting out their problems [and] they are standing up for themselves now, which is perhaps a lot more problematic for the government" (IRIN 2003a). Cabindan civil society's gathering strength also presented a threat to FLEC leaders in exile. Rafael Marques ventured that FLEC's overseas "political leaders fear losing total control of the situation by being militarily defeated and losing their moral grip on Cabinda, so they are rushing to negotiate" (IRIN 2003b).

President dos Santos reached out to FLEC's spectral fringes in an attempt to cobble together an autonomy agreement before Father Congo and Father Tati had a chance to form a civil society organization representative of all Cabindans. In August 2003, the government invited Luís Ranque Franque—one of FLEC's founding members—to participate in peace talks concerning Cabinda but denied him permission to travel outside of the capital.[67] During his stay, Tibúrcio pressured Ranque Franque to join Francisco Xavier Lubota, ex-leader of the long-defunct FLEC-Lubota, in signing onto

Cabinda" (IRIN 2004g).[73] Shortly thereafter, Minister of Interior Osvaldo Serra Van-Dúnem confirmed, "There is no war in Cabinda" and called local inhabitants' allegations of repression "fictitious and imaginative."[74] Father Tati cited a contemporaneous skirmish between FAA and FLEC militants, retorting, "The government cannot say the war is over when there is so much insecurity in the province" (IRIN 2004g). Most Cabindans shared Tati's perspective. An elder I interviewed seethed, "The war is not over. It cannot be over—how can so much [extraction] be done without us getting any benefit? [They say] we have to shut up. Shut up? How? . . . He who lives with hunger, he who lives deceived. . . . How will he sleep? Does one who is hungry sleep? Does one who has been tricked sleep? . . . So the war is not over. We have been tricked and we are hungry."

President dos Santos discounted the notion of Cabindan independence again in May 2004, announcing a regional autonomy plan for the province and declaring his intention to "discuss the terms of autonomy with everyone, including the most radical sectors of civil society and the churches" (Costa 2004). Later that month, he claimed to have held "discussions with representatives of all sectors of the Cabindan population" but Father Tati rejoined, "If there has been any dialogue, then it must be secretive because neither the Church nor the civil groups are aware of any talks" (IRIN 2004g). Mpalabanda leader Agostinho Chicaia lamented, "It is quite clear from the government's statements that they will not allow us to decide our future. This will only make the situation even worse. Right now the only solution, it seems, is to get the authorities to commit to serious talks" (ibid.).

Cabindans popularly declared Mpalabanda the singular, valid interlocutor to represent their interests; however, Interior Minister Serra Van-Dúnem denied Mpalabanda the role. Chicaia fumed, "The litany 'independence no, autonomy yes, lack of a valid interlocutor, FLEC divided, let's talk, the Constitution does not allow referenda' is a refrain that does not rhyme with reality and thus loses its resonance. In the end, the war continues at a Machiavellian pace."[75] He understood that Mpalabanda's mandate to "give voice to those without voice [was] uncomfortable for some, certainly for those who thought one day Cabinda would quiet down" (Ibinda 2004i).

Governor Rocha diminished the significance of civil society protests in comparison to the strength of MPLA militants, blithely stating in an interview that he lost no sleep over Mpalabanda (*Chelapress* 2004a, 2004b).[76] Still eager to disprove allegations that he feared Mpalabanda, Rocha approved the organization's right to march on Cabinda city in July 2004. Tens of thousands of Cabindans flooded the streets in peaceful demonstration carrying signs emblazoned with slogans like "The People Want Peace," "Stop the War" and "Dialogue Now!"[77] Some emboldened civil society activists reaffirmed their nonviolent partnership with FLEC in the struggle for independence. One demonstrator said, "FLEC cannot advance without the people; nor can the people take initiative without the assistance and collaboration of FLEC." From his residence in France, an exiled Henriques Nzita Tiago declared Cabinda's independence "a historical inevitability" (Heitor 2004a). During a meeting in Holland the following month, Henriques Nzita Tiago of FLEC-FAC and António Bento Bembe of FLEC-R fused their factions into a single FLEC.[78] The united FLEC joined members of the Cabindan Church and civil society in creating the Fórum Cabindês para o Diálogo (FCD), a representative body to serve as a singular, valid interlocutor in discussions with the government (IRIN 2004a).

The government had successfully delayed dialogue on the "Cabinda problem" for decades by inciting fractures between FLEC factions and citing the divides as evidence that a singular, valid interlocutor could not be found. Now Cabindan civil society and a united FLEC jointly declared a desire for independence from Angola. How would the government respond? FAA Brigadier Henrique Futi eyed the fused FLEC with suspicion. He threatened, "If they unite to help consolidate the peace in Cabinda then this unification is welcomed, but if they unite to disturb the peace the Government will assume the responsibilities of the State to guard and protect the populations and to defend sovereignty and territorial integrity" (Taty and Massanga 2004).

Cabindans worried that the government would subvert the FCD. One interviewee told me, "At present, as in the past, the Angolan government wants only to manipulate, divide, and buy time. It has no intention of resolving the problem through earnest, transparent, and open negotiations." He viewed the government's negotiations with the FCD as a ruse. "For Cabindans, the problem is not the choice between a legal or peaceful solution and a military solution. The people want their freedom. If it were possible to achieve this freedom without sacrifices and without recourse to conflict, everyone would accept this path. But it is not possible—neither in the past nor now: the Angolan government does not want . . ." My interviewee trailed off, leaving the truth of the matter unsaid: the government does not want to grant Cabinda independence.[79]

To underscore Cabindans' desire for independence, Mpalabanda organized a march commemorating the 120th anniversary of the Treaty of Simulambuco.[80] An estimated 10,000 Cabindans took to the streets in remembrance of the treaty, shouting slogans like "Cabinda is ours, Angola out."[81] Other chants demanded a fair share of resource revenues, like "We want the money from our petroleum and not the crumbs."[82] As the demonstrators marched toward Simulambuco carrying signs demanding peace they passed under a banner reading, "With the spirit of February, Angola will triumph."[83] The government had strung the banner in commemoration of the February 4 uprising that began the war against colonial oppression, but the triumphalist threat now seemed directed at Cabindans. The significance was not lost on the demonstrators; they saw the FAA's violent military campaign in Cabinda as a symbol of Angolan colonization. As they marched to Simulambuco, the protesters recalled that—whereas the Portuguese once colonized Angola—the Treaty of Simulambuco defined Cabinda as a protectorate of Portugal. Only after Portugal granted Angola independence did Angola colonize Cabinda and impose a brutal form of subjugation founded on resource extraction.

Mpalabanda organized the Simulambuco anniversary demonstration to coincide with the release of "Cabinda: The Reign of Impunity"—the third report on human rights abuses in the territory. Mpalabanda's Raúl Danda cited continuing FAA abuses against Cabindans; he suggested that "instead of talking with guns" leaders should "speak with their mouths" (Eisenstein 2005). In a preemptory press conference, General Agostinho Nelumba "Sanjar" denied the continuing allegations of FAA brutality. Claiming that his soldiers acted dutifully "from Cabinda to Cunene," General Sanjar told reporters that troops stationed in Cabinda were there to "neutralize instances of banditry" and that their activities "have no political substance whatsoever" (*Jornal de Angola* 2005c). Still, many Cabindans avoided the Simulambuco anniversary protest for fear of persecution—not just by the military or government but in the private sector as well. A successful businessman confessed that he avoided the demonstration despite supporting Mpalabanda. "If you go to that demonstration you could be blacklisted. . . . I mean, I sympathize but I would not go," he confided.

Targeting the Triumvirate

The FCD represented a united front in favor of Cabindan independence comprising delegates from the civil society organization Mpalabanda, the Catholic and Evangelical clergy, and FLEC. The coalition promoted direct negotiation with the government, a ceasefire, and granting Cabinda a special status (IRIN 2006c). Recognizing the formidable threat posed by this union, the government intensified efforts to weaken the FCD's constitutive parties so as to force them into accepting its plan.

Two months after the Simulambuco march, the provincial government increased the number of PIR officers stationed in the streets of Cabinda city. Mpalabanda members informed me of their precarious safety; soldiers loitered at their doorsteps and anonymous callers threatened their lives. Consumed with anxiety, they divulged suspicions that the government wiretapped the telephones in their homes and that secret police monitored their behavior.

If they do not show support for the government or ruling party, Cabindans—particularly Mpalbanda members—are presumed sympathizers of FLEC. On Angolan Women's Day, an exhausted baker told me she had marched all day on behalf of OMA, the women's group of the MPLA, holding a banner emblazoned with the slogan *A vitória é certa*.[84] The only victory of which she had been certain that afternoon, she related bitterly, was that of the mostly male grouping of top MPLA officials who helped themselves to steaming plates of food while the women marching received only water. She traded complicit smiles with a few of the women from her workplace. None of them supported the MPLA, but if any woman refused an invitation to march on this important holiday she would be investigated.

One outspoken Mpalabanda supporter I interviewed—before his arrest on the grounds of alleged ties to FLEC—made the prescient remark that dissenters "are seen and treated like informants" by the government, "blacklisted," and "at one moment or another possibly kidnapped." Similarly, Mpalabanda leader Agostinho Chicaia knew that his work endangered him. After receiving numerous death threats, he allegedly went into hiding by late 2005. He emerged in March 2006, announcing he would submit a request to the International Criminal Court calling for the investigation of atrocities committed by FAA soldiers stationed in Cabinda (IRIN 2006d). Mpalabanda released the fourth report on the human rights situation in Cabinda the following month. Entitled "Cabinda: Between the Truth and Manipulation," the report compared military *limpeza* in Cabinda to ethnic cleansing in Rwanda and the former Yugoslavia, advising the international community to "act before it is too late" (Mpalabanda 2006:6). Mpalabanda received word in June 2006 that the government had initiated judicial proceedings aimed at extinguishing the organization (Ibinda 2006). Chicaia called on human rights advocates and friends in the Church to help save Mpalabanda. His colleagues in the clergy, however, were embroiled in their own battle.

Nearly all Cabindans are Christians—whether belonging to Evangelical or Catholic denominations—and many claim that the government infiltrated church groups as a means to manipulate civil society (*Jornal Digital* 2004b). For example, José Marcos Mpaca, an ex-FLEC guerrilla turned government operative masqueraded as a pastor, penetrated the ranks of the Evangelical Church in Cabinda and barred choirs from participating in one of Mpalabanda's demonstrations (Ibinda 2004k). The government reached far deeper into the Catholic Church, where Cabinda's outspoken Bishop Dom Paulino Fernandes Madeca was due for retirement.[85] The diocese in Luanda chose Filomeno Vieira Dias, a cousin of President dos Santos' most trusted military adviser—General Manuel Hélder Vieira Dias "Kopelipa"—as Madeca's successor in February 2005. Protesters accosted Administrator of the Cabinda Diocese Father Eugénio Dal Corso, demanding the nomination of a native Cabindan, and the police allegedly quelled the crowd with tear gas. Dal Corso retaliated by closing Immaculate Conception church, the site of the protest, and suspending parish pastor Father Jorge Casimiro Congo.[86] Father Congo even received notice that he was under criminal investigation and was not allowed to leave the country.[87] Cabindan priests, including Father Raúl Tati, suspected Dal Corso's hand in the debacle. They sent a letter to the Vatican demanding his resignation— but Dal Corso responded to the missive himself by dismissing Father Tati from his post as General Vicar of Cabinda.

As the Church and Mpalabanda struggled against government interventions, FLEC also received a severe blow. FLEC Vice President António Bento Bembe became the target of a U.S. extradition request in Holland; Interpol sought Bembe in connection with the 1990 kidnapping of the Chevron contractor Brent Swan.[88] Under pressure from the United States, Dutch authorities detained Bembe on August 24, 2005, and released him on bail in October.[89] When Bembe did not report under the terms of his bail and could not be found by police, the Dutch court officially denied the extradition request on the grounds that Bembe was no longer within jurisdiction.

Bembe resurfaced in Angola after his mysterious disappearance from Holland (Luemba 2008). Angolan authorities presented Bembe with an ultimatum: either he could capitulate to their plan for Cabinda, or he could face extradition and a prison term nearly as long as Angola's civil war. Bembe chose the former. He signed off on a July 2006 ceasefire agreement with FAA Deputy Chief of Staff General Sachipengo Nunda and acceded to a government plan for "special administrative status" but *not* autonomy in Cabinda. Under the deal, FLEC officials received six key posts in Sonangol (two non-executive directors, a deputy director for Cabinda, and three administrative advisers); four positions in the national government (one undefined minister to the government and three deputy ministers in the areas of petroleum, interior, and forestry); as well as places in the

Cabindan provincial government (including deputy provincial governor and a few other provincial director posts). The plan to which Bembe acceded was nearly identical to a previous plan offered by the government. FLEC had rejected this plan complete with its $20 million sweetener in 2003; yet, under duress, Bembe accepted it three years later (*Africa Confidential* 2006). The United States seemed to forget the warrant for Bembe's arrest and expressed strong support for the deal, saying the agreement signaled "the promise of economic development and increased political influence" (IRIN 2006e).

The FCD's remaining members dismissed Bembe from the coalition, denounced his actions, and discounted the agreement. Delegates from the civil society organization Mpalabanda, the Catholic and Evangelical clergy and FLEC reaffirmed their commitment to the principles of direct negotiation with the government, ceasefire, and granting Cabinda a special status (IRIN 2006c). FCD spokesman Raúl Danda condemned Bembe's unilateral action. He cautioned, "Bembe is not representing Cabinda's aspirations. The Angolan government insisted on negotiating with him, but they have given him money and he doesn't represent the people of Cabinda" (IRIN 2006e). Danda viewed Bembe's weakness as the lynchpin in the government's plan to dismantle the FCD. FAA troops had already raided Mpalabanda's office, interrogated Danda and his colleague Agostinho Chicaia, and ultimately extinguished Mpalabanda in June 2006 (IRIN 2006a). Bishop Filomeno Vieira Dias cast a shadow over activists in Cabinda's Catholic Church and the desertion of Bembe's men reduced the strength of Nzita Tiago's FLEC loyalists.

The government awarded António Bento Bembe the rank of general in the Angolan Armed Forces and induced hundreds more former FLEC-R militants to join the national police and FAA contingent in Cabinda in their shared mandate to quash dissent.[90] Despite Mpalabanda's extinction, soldiers and police officers continue to harass Mpalabanda members with arbitrary arrests, threats of torture and death, and travel restrictions to the extent that several Mpalabanda activists fled Cabinda (OPHRD 2006). Amnesty International reported that Cabinda remains "rife with egregious violations of human rights" and lamented that the government's ban on Mpalabanda meant that many of these violations would go unreported (AI 2006b).[91] Police arbitrarily arrested Raúl Danda and detained him for almost a month for possession of documents containing statements "injurious to the President of the Republic" and advocating for Cabinda's secession from Angola (AI 2006a). Provincial Secretary of the FCD Mateus Massinga received a five-month prison sentence and two-year suspension from politics on charges of "insubordination and incitement of violence" following his attempt to distribute a document promoting Cabindan autonomy (HRW 2008b). José Fernando Lelo, a former Voice of America correspondent and outspoken critic of the Angolan government, received a sentence of 12 years imprisonment on "politically motivated" charges of armed rebellion following an unfair trial (AI 2008a). Government authorities even cracked down on foreigners investigating abuses in Cabinda; they detained Global Witness campaigner Sarah Wykes for three nights in a Cabindan jail and threatened her with charges of espionage.[92]

On August 10, 2007, President dos Santos visited Cabinda for the first time in six years. In the days before his arrival, police teams—of up to twenty officers each—searched the homes of the Mpalabanda activists Gabriel Bilongo, André Luemba, Julho Paulo, and Xavier Soca Tati. On the day of President dos Santos' visit, intelligence officers encircled the homes of the Mpalabanda activists Margarida Cabral, João Baptista Neto, and Xavier Soca Tati, holding them under house arrest from 2 A.M. until 7 P.M. when the head of state departed Cabinda.[93] Many Cabindans criticized dos Santos' visit to Cabinda as a publicity stunt, as he presided over the opening of a supermarket and the refurbished airport. Others saw his visit as an assurance of security to investors preparing to place bids on Cabinda's onshore blocks in the December 2007 licensing round. Former Mpalabanda President Agostinho Chicaia declared, "For Cabindan people, the president is not welcome because we don't have peace in Cabinda, we have a lot of problems and our priority is dialogue" (BBC 2007). Chicaia's words recalled the incompleteness of territorialization efforts in Cabinda; the militant campaign could never reach into the hearts and minds of Cabindans—where a longing for independence remained.

A ROCKY RELATIONSHIP

Since 1975, the Angolan government has used threats and acts of violence to suppress the endemic independence movement in Cabinda. Operação Vassoura signaled a new means of dealing with the "Cabinda problem"—a militant territorialization campaign aimed at securing the territory for onshore oil extraction. FAA troops fanned out across Cabinda, spreading terror in their wake. Whether the army's abuses were part of a strategic plan to subdue the populace or merely attributable to lack of discipline, they provoked a backlash.[94] Cabindans documented the atrocities and organized reports for internal and international circulation. Resistance to the militant territorialization campaign strengthened civil society, reviving calls for self-determination and a more equitable distribution of local oil revenues. Challenging their subjugation by a violent and corrupt government, Cabindans revisited the 1885 Treaty of Simulambuco as justification for their continued struggle for independence. Leaders from civil society, FLEC, and the clergy searched the globe for support. The Angolan government pursued every means to debilitate all forms of resistance, which it perceived as threatening to onshore oil investments in Cabinda. It used disproportionate force against the citizenry and toppled the three pillars of the FCD one by one, denying Cabindans a fair chance for dialogue.

Before I left Cabinda, I returned to the home of the first Cabindan elder I interviewed almost two years before. He graciously welcomed me back as I asked for his opinion on the prospects for peace in Cabinda. To him, President dos Santos' peace plan appeared to consist of a two-part strategy to territorialize Cabinda: first annihilate FLEC and terrorize all sympathizers, and then offer a compromise to the trembling remainder of the Cabindan populace. "It is like this," he cried, "A child is asking for bread and they give him a stone." Louder still, he exclaimed, "The child is crying 'give me bread' and they give him a stone!"

The elder's metaphor of a stone handed to a child represented the degraded relationship between the government and the Cabindan people. Cabindans demanded tangible benefits from the oil extracted from their province, but their petitions were met with stony silence and their indictments with obdurate repression. Then, during the Carnaval parade, the tables turned for an instant. Governor José Aníbal Rocha, who had long ignored Cabindans' cries for bread, suffered the blow of several stones thrown from the crowd.[95]

7. Corporate Territorialization

The gloss of gasoline produced iridescent swirls on the surface of Cabinda Bay. Like the gleam on the water, Chevron has spread the sheen of development in its wake. Corporate social responsibility (CSR) projects dotting the Cabindan landscape reflect waves of corporate influence. Investments in Cabinda's capital city and the coastal areas near the offshore sites of extraction seek to simultaneously extend Chevron's "social license to operate" and cut production costs, while oil-backed development investments in the interior contribute to territorialization. As Angolan Armed Forces (FAA) soldiers destroyed separatist FLEC strongholds, Chevron's development projects lured the terrorized populace into government-held territory. Father Raúl Tati of Cabinda said, "The people indeed want bread, but they want bread with dignity" (Tati 2003). Cabindans had demanded greater investment in local development, but they did not foresee how the government would use Chevron's CSR investments as part of its campaign to territorialize Cabinda.

This was a carrot-and-stick territorialization strategy; Chevron dangled oil-backed development schemes (e.g., building health posts, water wells, and schools) as the government applied terrorizing military campaigns and repressive policing. Sandra Barnes (2005) contends that Big Oil's CSR projects represent an effort to win the hearts and minds of local people, while Anna Zalik (2004) counters that such developments essentially function as a disciplinary tool to extend control over the populace. Drawing on CSR's persuasive and disciplinary strengths, I contend that the government and corporations use oil-backed development as part of a broader strategy of implementing and maintaining exclusionary patterns of resource control.

James Ferguson's "Angola model" rightly describes how capital skips over unusable spaces; likewise, CSR jumps to strategic locales while ignoring

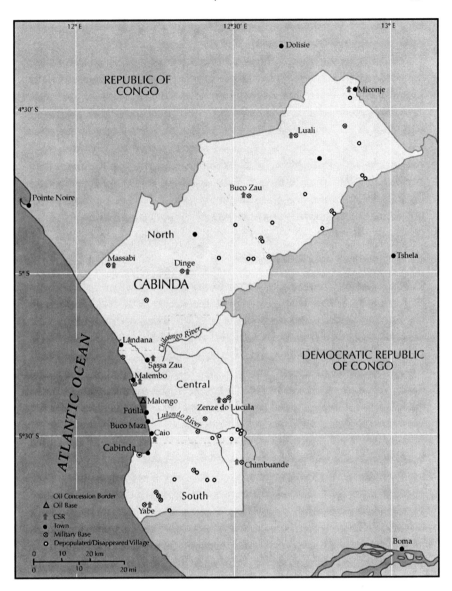

MAP 9. The Corporate Territorialization of Cabinda

less valuable sites within both Cabinda and Zaire provinces. The "Angola model" also explains how Chevron continued to operate in Cabinda despite the military incursion; however, I argue that the model's focus on the role of private security firms in securing the enclave obscures both the function of national military in the wider extractive zone and the role that transnational oil corporations play outside the boundaries of the enclave, specifically through CSR interventions.

Precisely by obfuscating the petro-capitalist underpinnings of Angola's developmental void, reconstruction efforts afford oil corporations a unique opportunity to rewrite the history of oil. As Africa's rising oil producers look for a positive model, oil corporations like Chevron are keen to endorse extraction as a legitimate development strategy and promote their successes through CSR. This chapter explicates the myriad roles Chevron plays outside the enclave of Malongo. It examines Chevron's CSR programs to demonstrate how these initiatives have deepened community dependence on the corporation. Finally, it explores the role of CSR as a substitute for government social services and the political implications therein.

RESPONSIBLE PARTNERSHIPS

It was a cool July morning as I awaited my guide for a tour of Chevron's CSR projects. I was staring blankly at the smoke of dawn fires thick on the horizon when a short, muscled man approached with a bulky plastic sack. He shook two porcupines from the sack onto a nearby concrete block, smearing their blood in dark streaks across the pavement. A potential customer arrived to inspect the animals. The two men bargained briefly and agreed on a price. At the buyer's approval, schoolgirls in white smocks and elegant sandals gathered around to pluck the porcupines. As the seller was showing me how Cabindan women traditionally use porcupine quills to unbraid their hair, a shiny black SUV with flashy hubcaps and tinted windows rolled up. I excused myself; it was my ride.

The vehicle belonged to Nobre, the Chevron official responsible for orchestrating oil-backed development projects in Cabinda. Whether financed independently or jointly under the auspices of the Block o or Block 14 consortia, Chevron-sponsored developments dot the Cabindan landscape. Nobre had offered to show me a smattering of them—from the refurbished Lândana mission school and vocational facility to the Sassa Zau health center opposite Malongo. Believing Chevron's generosity would improve the standard of living and encourage stability in Cabinda, Nobre spoke glowingly of the corporation's collaboration with the provincial government to improve health and educational facilities. Still, he conceded that government authorities had failed to uphold their end of the agreement on a few occasions. For example, Chevron constructed the $400,000 Sassa Zau Health Center, but it remained unused because the provincial government had yet to equip the facility with running water and medical supplies.

As we entered Malongo, a monkey dashed in front of the car. Nobre swerved, proudly exclaiming that monkeys escaped from hunters in the surrounding areas by seeking refuge on the oil base. To me, their presence here and absence there seemed less a symbol of Chevron's commitment to conservation than a reflection of the desperation beyond Malongo's barbed-wire perimeter. Outside of the provincial capital, most Cabindans have neither running water nor electricity in their homes. Health and educational facilities are mostly in a state of disrepair. Chevron is investing millions of dollars in developmental funds in the province, building new health posts and schools, and supporting local agricultural development. Chevron and its idealistic employees envision corporate philanthropy as a means to spread peace and development from the coastal regions to the interior; they publicize development initiatives as evidence of corporate responsibility.

Rising CSR

Transnational corporations invented corporate social responsibility (CSR) in response to pressure from governments, financial institutions, and civil society organizations (Swanson 2002a).[1] Transnational oil corporations increasingly embrace CSR, not only as a gesture of goodwill but also as a business strategy for increasing long-term profitability proportional to the investment (Orlitzky et al. 2004). CSR advocates refer to a "triple bottom line" encompassing economic, environmental, and social sustainability (Elkington 1994; Henderson 2001).

Investments in "strategic philanthropy" and "corporate social development" are not random acts of kindness. By investing in strategic areas such as education and health, CSR responds to shareholder interests, deflects the demands of international watchdog groups and local activists, and creates a more stable, profitable operating environment. Recognizing these advantages, corporations positioned themselves as leaders of "sustainable development" at the 2002 World Summit in Johannesburg, embraced "corporate citizenship" as essential to African development at the 2002 African Economic Summit, and promoted "partnering for security and prosperity" at the 2004 World Economic Forum.

International financial institutions' encouragement of neoliberal policies has bolstered the CSR trend. These policies, which gear the development agenda toward privatization and liberalization, constrict government's developmental role to merely creating a good environment for foreign direct investment (Stiglitz 2004; Korten 1995). Firms in the extractive industries, especially oil corporations, eagerly step in to fill the void.

Oil companies use CSR as a "social license to operate" and to counter critique of their operations in underdeveloped or politically sensitive areas, especially in Africa, where extractive industries accounted for more than 50 percent of exports and 65 percent of all foreign direct investment in the 1990s (Gary and Karl 2003:5). As oil corporations struggle with the financial fallout of their own negligence in Nigeria, they seek to find a replicable model for community engagement to facilitate extraction. Shell and Chevron have leveraged CSR as a disciplinary tool in the Niger Delta by building community centers, post offices, and schools (Zalik 2004).

During the Extractive Industries Review, NGOs launched protests against World Bank support of extractive industries claiming that they "can do more harm than good by entrenching a destructive and predatory elite" (Beattie 2004). Transparency coalitions such as Publish What You Pay actively encourage corporations to report their payments of taxes and royalties to governments with opaque accounting practices, like the Angolan government, in hopes that transparency will encourage development. BP's good intentions of publishing its payments to the Angolan government in 2001 were met with severe reprisal. Angola nearly revoked BP's production contract for violating the confidentiality clause.

Caught between the Scylla of publishing their payments and Charybdis of international critique, transnational oil corporations operating in Angola turned to CSR as a means to earn legitimacy and divert attention from their dealings with a notoriously corrupt government. They even sought to bolster their reputations by collaborating with international NGOs as well as bilateral and multilateral aid groups like USAID and UNDP on joint development programs.[2] Still, oil corporations may not be able to dissociate their contributions to development from the government.

Oil corporations are obligated, under the terms of their confidential contracts with the government, to contribute to the development of Angola. Sonangol originally allocated portions of signature bonuses to community development projects, but during the late 1990s the national oil company began demanding social bonuses, in addition to signature bonuses, from consortia submitting concession bids. The consortium awarded the block forms an association and pays the social bonus fund to Sonangol, which decides how to invest the money. Corporations can suggest investment avenues, yet Sonangol plays a forceful role and often favors pet projects or organizations with political ties to the government, like ADPP and FESA. Ultimately, all projects tied to the block must receive approval from all members of the consortium as well as the government.[3] One Chevron official admitted, "This ties our hands a lot," because politically controversial projects are rejected along with anything "perceived by the government as undermining them." Government officials discourage oil corporations from contributing to civil society or human rights programs. "Oil companies know that if they support civil society, in the future they won't receive new petrol blocks," said Benjamin Castello of the advocacy group Jubilee 2000 (quoted in Eviatar 2004). Another human rights activist backed Castello's statement; all of his organization's proposals for funding had been rejected, too.[4]

ECONOMIC INCENTIVES

Oil corporations leverage contributions to development in Angola as "cost oil" or as tax write-offs, but they can manipulate CSR to improve their profitability in myriad ways. A survey of CSR in the Angolan oil industry revealed an overwhelming majority of initiatives related to activities that increased corporate profits (Wiig and Ramalho 2005). Likewise, many of the initiatives Chevron publicizes as CSR improve the corporation's bottom line. For example, Chevron celebrated a commitment "to eliminate routine flaring from its operations in Angola" (Chevron 2003). After the government extended Chevron's Block 0 contract in 2004, Chevron pledged to invest $1.5 billion to reduce and eventually eliminate flaring from select fields in its concessions by 2006 (Alfredo 2004). Director of Production Operations Daniel Rocha said Chevron's effort evolved from "a certain responsibility to improve the well-being of the communities around us" and a desire "to do our best to not damage the environment" (*Jornal de Angola* 2004i).

Chevron's announcement coincided with natural gas prices soaring to record highs. The commodity once burned in noxious flares off the Cabinda coast had become "the next prize" (Yergin and Stoppard 2003). The corporation had previously used Block 0's associated gas as fuel for offshore installations; and, in Malongo, Chevron had reinjected the gas into reservoirs to aid production or store it, or produced it as liquid petroleum gas (GPC 1999). The remainder, including all hydrogen sulfide (H_2S) gas, was flared.[5] As the value of the associated natural gas rose, Chevron expressed greater interest in responsible management and advanced the Sanha Condensate and Takula Gas Processing Platform projects, estimated to reduce flaring by 9.9 million cubic meters per day (Chevron 2003).[6] Associated "gas management" modifications on the Takula, Nemba, Lomba, and Malongo fields would further reduce flaring by processing some of the natural gas liquids and reinjecting produced natural gas into the reservoir.[7] Reinjected gas would be recovered once infrastructure existed to facilitate its transport to the Soyo LNG plant.

Chevron will reap substantial economic benefits while cutting greenhouse gas emissions through the implementation of no-flare technologies; however, it is unlikely that the corporation would have voluntarily instituted measures to decrease air pollution in the absence of a strong natural gas market. Profit incentives undergird most CSR expenditures, sometimes to the extent that the banner of social responsibility becomes muddled. The following sub-sections explore a range of economic underpinnings for Chevron's CSR efforts in Angola, recognizing social shortcomings associated with a few of the programs.

Using Angolans

Angolanization changed the face of Angola's oil industry. During the 1980s, Chevron employed only a few nationals for menial posts. One Chevron executive said, "In 1982, you could not dream of being an African and doing the type of job I have been doing now." At that time, Malongo segregated cafeterias for expatriate and Angolan staff. Chevron became Angola's largest oil industry employer in 2001 (Chevron 2002).[8] Angolans now comprise 88 percent of Chevron's national staff and 75 percent of the executive and supervisor posts in Angola (ANGOP 2008d). Roughly 2,000 Angolans and 300 expatriates work in Malongo (Alfredo 2004). The integrated lunchroom serves some 1,500 meals per day to expatriates and nationals alike. Chevron's advances in hiring Angolan staff may be partially attributed to the corporation's support of training efforts in Angola as well as employee scholarships for study abroad at U.S. colleges and universities.[9]

The government encourages foreign firms to hire Angolans through statutes on Angolanization, and since nationals are often paid less than expatriates, corporations are amenable to hiring Angolans. A former Chevron employee explained that "if you have a good strategy [and] a good school over here to train people for the future, then hiring a local employee [becomes] cheaper than hiring a foreign employee where you are going to spend millions of dollars." Local workers find the disparate pay scale unfair. "We might be paid 170 times less and why?" asked the former Chevron employee. His estimate is exaggerated but reflects a valid concern for disproportionate compensation levels. "For the same duties, equal competence and identical regime of responsibility, the American earns four or five times more than his African counterpart" (Luemba 2003). Angolan supervisors receive $1,425 per month, substantially less than the $5,000 to $7,000 salary of foreign supervisors. Likewise, the senior grade base salary of an African Chevron executive is around $4,250 per month, whereas Americans in the same position might earn a monthly salary of $8,000 to $12,000. High-level national employees sometimes earn less than subordinate expatriates.

Cabindans argue that Chevron discriminates against locals, choosing mostly mainland Angolans with political connections to fill open positions. They criticize Chevron for hiring Luandans or even Bakongo from Uíge and Zaire provinces. Moreover, they claim that mainland Angolans benefit from better working conditions, higher wages, exceptional training facilities, and more opportunities for promotion (Luemba 2003). Chevron's low-level employees from Cabinda earning $280 per month argue that their Luandan counterparts receive 25 percent more. Attorney Francisco Luemba has noticed a pattern among Cabindans passed over for promotions. He writes, "The Angolan personnel are admitted at salary grade 12, with a contract for an indeterminate time, and they are rapidly and easily promoted; the Cabindans enter at grade 8 or 9, and have a fixed term contract and they only obtain employment stability after they have given plenty of evidence of their value, competence and suitability. They are rarely promoted and then with difficulty" (ibid.).

Many Cabindans feel that Chevron has excluded them from important roles within the corporation and distanced them from decision-making processes. "Malongo is ours; it does not belong to the Americans," fumed one Cabindan. He resented that the American corporation chose to work with mainland Angolans rather than locals. "We have people coming from Luanda and the two Congos to work here—but the petroleum is ours. How are we not getting the jobs? Even those of us from Fútila!"[10]

Sourcing Local Content

Transnational oil corporations retain ample control over their global supply chains; thus, they are well positioned to shift to local procurement patterns (Swanson 2002b). Chevron operations in Cabinda infused $230 million into the Angolan economy through the corporate supply chain, exceeding local content targets by 275 percent in 2003 (Chevron 2003). Chevron lists these statistics alongside charitable contributions in the corporation's annual CSR reports, but sourcing goods locally also cuts procurement costs. Chevron started a Business Development program in 1996, helping local firms like S&N Pump, Cabestiva, Servemar, SPL, and Empebat get their feet on the ground. Idealistic employees like Nobre hoped Chevron's support of local businesses would help to create a middle class that could offer stability in Cabinda and diffuse the sharp divide between *Malonguistas* and the indigent masses. Nobre said, "Instead of Chevron taking money from this place and then sending it outside of the country, the money stays here and then it helps the local business grow; it helps those businesses give more jobs to people." Although he acknowledged the profit incentive for local content development, Nobre emphasized the initiative's societal benefits. "It cuts costs, but the most important thing is to see your neighbor change," he said.

Chevron contributed $3 million to USAID and Agriculture Cooperative Development International/Volunteers in Overseas Assistance (ACDI/ VOCA) for a five-year, $20 million Agribusiness Development Project in Cabinda (Coelho 2004; Casimiro 2004). Chevron's prior partnerships with ACDI/VOCA helped reduce catering costs.[11] Corporate officials expressed hope that the $20 million program would obviate the corporation's need to import produce from South Africa or at least trim down the massive greenhouse operations in Malongo.[12] Still, Chevron's director for public and governmental relations focused on the initiative's potential to reduce poverty in Cabinda by increasing family income for 3,000 small farmers. Meanwhile, local farmers point to influential Cabindans—like former governor Amaro Tati—benefiting from the program.[13]

There are limits to sourcing local content within Angola. As a transnational oil corporation, Chevron sources goods in four demand categories: super-high-tech, high-tech, quality-regulated, and lower-end. Chevron procures higher-tech items from countries with a strong manufacturing base like South Africa and South Korea, whereas Angola supplies the corporation with lower-end articles. Chevron and the Angolan government are also working to develop quality-regulated goods through local investment and training initiatives. Unfortunately, officials have expressed concern that Angolan companies in the supply chain are not following health, safety, and environmental standards; they cited cases of welders not using eye protection and disposal procedures entailing little more than pouring toxics down the drain.

Preventing AIDS

As Nobre and I toured Malongo, he pointed to a colorful poster on the wall and outlined Chevron's proactive measures to combat AIDS among the staff and wider Cabindan populace. AIDS prevention is a strategy like any other health and safety standard meant to keep workers productive, saving Chevron the costs of missed workdays and sick leave. Chevron leads a $1 million annual effort to promote HIV/AIDS awareness, education, and treatment among the corporate workforce and in Cabinda on the whole.

Moreover, the corporation sponsored a state-of-the-art blood bank with technology to screen for hepatitis, HIV, and other infectious diseases. Nobre declared, "In the last five to eight years, there was too much disease contamination through blood transfusions, but now there's more control. I can say there is *zero* contamination now."

AIDS is a serious problem in Cabinda. It is the third-largest cause of adult mortality behind malaria and anemia (Ibinda 2004g). In the first trimester of 2004, AIDS accounted for 14 percent of the deaths among patients at Cabindan hospitals, and the Chevron-sponsored blood bank found 120 of the 1,207 blood donors to be HIV positive (GPC 2004b). Many Cabindans blame prostitution on Congolese women slipping across the borders; however, representatives of Grémio ABC's AIDS education project told me local women also engage in prostitution out of desperation. Soldiers and oil workers create most of the demand for prostitution in Cabinda; they are said to contribute to the spread of AIDS. The men operating Chevron's platforms remain offshore for three to four weeks at a time, working long hours and enduring stressful conditions. When they return to land, many seek the pleasures they are denied offshore: particularly booze and women.

Prostitutes with a regular asking price of around 1,000 kwanzas ($12) for sex using a condom will accept offers of $100 in hard currency for unprotected sex.[14] Chevron's employees earn high salaries in hard currency, and some Cabindans say *Malonguistas* use their wealth to get what they want—whether from sex workers or impressionable teenage girls. A young man described the relationship between AIDS and glaring disparities in wealth between oil workers and the remainder of the Cabindan population:

> We have two classes here: the superior class working in Malongo and using American money and the rest. Working in Malongo provides people with a different social base. If they work there they get a special attitude because they are "full of money." Prostitution becomes a problem. The *Malonguistas* have money and the girls always follow behind them. What young woman would not want to go out with a guy who would buy her a nice new dress? . . . In the *feira* at 7 P.M. the girls will go to sell their bodies for 500 kwanzas. Their parents are hungry and they will not ask where the sack of rice the girl is carrying came from . . . 28 days on, 28 days off and with different girls every time. AIDS has become a problem.

I asked a *Malonguista* about these allegations. Naturally, he denied that he and his colleagues had any part in spreading sexually transmitted diseases. He dismissed the rumor as having originated in a rivalry between *Malonguistas* and Cabindans living on lesser state salaries. He claimed, "They created this story to scare the girls away from us—they are jealous." Nevertheless, when I mentioned Chevron's efforts prevent the spread of AIDS to a group of young Cabindan women, they responded that it was only natural for Chevron to become involved—the promiscuity of *Malonguistas* contributed to the burgeoning problem. Some Cabindans even suspected that Chevron funded the blood bank as a measure of controlling the information about its employees' role in the spread of AIDS. One young man ventured, "Something like 33 percent of the population around the base has AIDS." Only Chevron knows for sure. "They have the statistics because they collect the blood samples," he said.

CONTROLLED DISSENT

Constructed in 1968, Malongo was originally a simple base of operations. Employees lived in Cabinda city, integrated with the rest of the population. After independence, Gulf Oil requested—for security reasons—that all Americans working for the corporation live in Malongo and that local employees reside on the base during their shift, for some up to twenty-eight days at a time. By 1979, the transition was complete. A former Gulf employee remembered, "So the relationship with the community became a distanced relationship—very distant—people are not really neighbors because they are two worlds apart and there is not much interaction going on."

As the MPLA pursued a socialist path to development, the disparities between Malongo and the rest of Cabinda became increasingly evident. Shortages of staple goods plagued downtown shops while Malongo received copious shipments of imported wines and cheese. Some locals developed suspicions about *Malonguistas*. A former Gulf employee recalled, "There was a revolution going on—there were a lot of inspired Marxists—if you had one dollar in your pocket those days, you were labeled an imperialist." He recognized the potential role of the MPLA in ushering the profligate expatriates into Malongo. "It was a communist time, maybe it was [a function of] not letting the Americans go out and show the good things that the West had—you know, a nice pen could take you to jail," he said.

The threat of violence also fueled Chevron's isolationist path. Expatriates and local staff transited by bus from the airport and their homes to Malongo for their shifts until 1984, when FLEC saboteurs bombed a section of the Cabinda Gulf Oil (CabGOC) pipeline near Chimbolo. During the same year, CabGOC became a subsidiary of the Chevron Corporation through the merger of Gulf Oil and Standard Oil of California (Socal).[15] After the attempted bombing of the Malongo storage tanks by UNITA's South African Captain du Toit in 1985, Chevron installed a set of concentric barbed-wire fences on the perimeter. MPLA and Cuban troops laid landmines within the fenced corridor and took up defensive positions around the base. Chevron began ferrying expatriate employees from the Cabinda airport to Malongo by helicopter and forbidding all but a few American workers, including the aircraft mechanic Brent Swan, to travel by road in Cabinda. FLEC's kidnapping of Swan—one of four Petroleum Helicopters, Inc. (PHI) employees permitted to drive from the oil base to Cabinda city for a shift at the airport—further increased Chevron's withdrawal into Malongo.

Reaching Out

The Angolan government encouraged Chevron's seclusion in Malongo until the country shifted to a liberal democracy. After the transition, the corporation began to pursue community development projects—including building a school in Fútila. During our tour of oil-backed development along the Cabindan coast, Nobre recalled how Chevron's interest in CSR coincided with "the changes that started to take place in the country . . . the openness, the free market economy . . . moving away from communism and becoming more open-minded." Ultimately, Chevron found its Government Affairs department inadequate in its capacity to serve new community outreach projects and created a Public Affairs division.

Conflict and government oversight constrained the new development agenda. "You could not undertake [community development projects] in the whole territory," said Nobre. Neighboring Fútila seemed a safe place to begin. By 1994, Chevron development efforts had sprouted in many of the coastal villages on Block o's fringe. Violence and government restrictions prevented Chevron's outreach to communities in the interior until 1995. "As soon as we got the green light," Nobre told me, "we went out."

Why would Chevron be interested in implementing development projects in communities so far from its operations? Nobre responded, "We found many, many infrastructures destroyed and abandoned . . . in areas like Dinge, Buco Zau, and Belize. Of course the people would leave those villages and come into town. We wanted to help people to stay there . . . to encourage them to stay—to live there in their areas [with] sustainable infrastructure like health posts and schools for the kids." Government neglect of interior towns created more migrants, increasing the number of desperate job seekers on Malongo's doorstep.

Chevron also used development projects to prove to disgruntled Cabindans that oil extraction could bring benefits. According to Nobre, the government soon "realized that these types of initiatives were important." Provincial officials even began to partner with Chevron on some of the development initiatives. The national government began to leverage corporate contributions to development; President dos Santos even extracted donations from Chevron for his personal foundation, FESA, and his friends at ADPP.

Disciplining Cabinda

In 1994, Chevron donated $415,000 to ADPP to fund the organization's child aid projects, a vocational school, and a teacher training facility—the *Escola para os Professores do Futuro* (EPF).[16] ADPP founded the EPF in 1998 under the auspices of a government contract charging the organization with responsibility for training teachers for Cabindan schools.[17] Over a period of two and a half years, each graduating class of sixty teachers learns how to work in rural areas and to undertake community projects like creating HIV awareness programs or digging latrines.[18] "This is all made possible by the oil companies," said one ADPP volunteer. According to her, Chevron contributes 46 percent of the funding for the EPF and the government provides another 50 percent.[19]

Cabinda's teacher training center "is the only EPF school in Angola to get funding from the national and provincial governments" and benefits from "electricity 24 hours a day from Malongo" (Jason 2006). Why did this one school receive so much attention from Chevron and the government? Following Zalik (2004), the school may serve a disciplinary function. One of the school's representatives admitted that ADPP was "aiming to change people here," and that the EPF encouraged Cabindans to integrate with a cohort of "very patriotic" colleagues from Luanda and learn to have an "open mind."[20] By shaping the minds of teachers—important agents of social discipline in Cabindan society—ADPP's curriculum is likely to have a widespread influence in Cabinda.

A TITHE FOR DEVELOPMENT

As in Zaire province, 10 percent of the revenues derived from taxation of profits from oil produced in Cabinda are earmarked for return to the governor's office for the purpose of provincial development. Nevertheless, Cabindans cast doubt on the 10 percent rule and Governor José Aníbal Rocha's investment of oil monies. One man exclaimed that Governor Rocha "has five cars in the backyard and $100,000 in his pocket, but the town of Tando Zinze has no water and atrophied children have to walk kilometers to get it."

Rocha has pursued a very narrow version of development in Cabinda, funneling petrodollars into patronage. For example, the Provincial Government of Cabinda financed the construction of 350 homes built by Chinese and South African firms in the Cabassango neighborhood (Buela 2004). The homes, intended for MPLA loyalists and government officials, possessed sanitation and electricity standards unknown in the rest of the province. Cabindans protested the governor's investment in well-appointed homes for the few while the rest of the population suffered from a lack of sanitation and electricity. Rocha did not appreciate the continuous stream of complaints on his development decisions. He told the press:

> I think there are no reasons to complain . . . I will give you an example: now I am giving a school snack to more than 80,000 children, from Yema to Miconje, from Massabi to Zenza Lucula; so, all the children who are in the school system are receiving a daily snack. That is 80,000 and not 80 children; this year we made and distributed 200,000 smocks and all the students are receiving two smocks each; I gave free books to all these children and next month I will give out a school kit comprising a backpack with notebooks, pencils, color pencils, an eraser, etc. to more than 80,000 children! I do not know where the complaints are founded. I do not know of another province in the country that does this.
> (*Chelapress* 2004b)

Rocha's rant demonstrates two major shortcomings of the development model he employs in Cabinda. First, the system of rule is personalized, as evidenced by the governor's persistent use of the first person to describe all government initiatives. Second, the approach to development is haphazard and inequitable; a few schoolbooks and uniforms are handed out arbitrarily to a subset of children while schoolhouses crumble. This fosters dependency on the government rather than creating solid foundations for education. In the words of Rafael Marques, Angola's leaders "are not developing a nation but developing personal interests" (Marques 2004b).

Cabinda's provincial government released a censored version of their budgetary expenditures in the wake of the transparency scandal in 2004. Surprisingly, Rocha and his cadre did not find anything embarrassing in the figures they did publish, including $120,000 spent on lawn maintenance at the governor's palace, $449,000 in furniture for government offices, $80,000 in toys, and $85,000 for the Miss Cabinda beauty contest (Marques 2004b; *Ngonje* 2004a). Other questionable expenses included $900,000 in Christmas gifts for loyal supporters and $124,000 paid to a local pastry shop. The provincial government's largest single expense in 2003 was the $1.34 million cost of feeding the army and police stationed in

Cabinda—paid to Ecoserv, the military catering firm owned by President dos Santos (*Ngonje* 2004a). The budget painted a picture of provincial officials gorging themselves on pastries and gawking at beauty queens while the Cabindan masses struggled to endure militant repression.

Trading Freedom

The government's carrot-and-stick approach to territorializing Cabinda recalled Portugal's strategy in the late 1960s and early 1970s. As the military distributed leaflets calling for surrender, Portuguese administrators sought to win the Cabindan people's favor with development projects. In 1965, the Portuguese government opened a "profusion of schools" in Cabinda, including a high school (Lelo-Tubi 1980:9).[21] They paved roads from Cabinda city to Lândana, Dinge, and Buco-Zau, and even appointed a Cabindan *mestiço* to the post of undersecretary for education (Wheeler and Pélissier 1971:222).[22] Meanwhile, the Portuguese betrayed the FLEC leaders that had once collaborated with them against the MPLA and FNLA. After a 1971 independence protest, authorities deported Nzita Tiago to the Bay of Tigers and placed Alexandre Taty under house arrest in Luanda.

Four decades later, the Angolan government tried the carrot-and-stick approach to combat the continued movement for Cabindan independence. They paved roads to the interior, facilitating military transport into the region. As FAA forces terrorized the populace, the provincial government strung up signs around Cabinda city with slogans like: "The most important [thing] is to resolve the problems of the people."[23] They aimed to pacify Cabindans through social programs aimed at hunger reduction, agricultural regeneration, infrastructure rehabilitation, and demobilization and reinsertion of former FLEC combatants and their families (*Jornal de Angola* 2003d). As part of the plan, the provincial government promised to invest $370 million in development projects over six years; they promised to construct a new Superior Technical School offering high-level coursework and even a provincial Petroleum Institute (Fragoso 2004a, 2004b). Government officials touted the plan as a means to improve employment opportunities and promote progress in virtually every other sector, including energy, water, health, education, transportation, fisheries, industry, environment, and tourism.[24]

A keen reporter from the independent weekly *Semanário Angolense* observed that by assigning a $370 million budget for practically all of Cabinda's development needs over the next six years, the government "implicitly admits that Cabinda does not receive the total percentage of petroleum revenues to which it theoretically has a right" (*Semanário*

Angolense 2004a). If Cabinda is entitled to 10 percent of the taxes on oil from its oilfields—a sum accepted as $6 million per month during Governor Amaro Tati's administration—then considering this monthly figure for six years would return a total of $432 million. Assuming that the value of taxes to which Cabinda is entitled has not increased apace with oil production rates since 2002 and the government did not contribute *anything* from its general budget, the six-year development budget of $370 million falls $62 million short of what Cabinda is legally owed. Even presupposing that the plan would *not* cover Cabinda's administrative costs, the remaining $62 million would provide roughly $10.3 million for each of six years. This is still $3 million more per year than the provincial government's self-reported annual rate of fixed costs.[25]

Neglecting Health

As provincial government officials devise new ways to divert oil revenues into patronage schemes, pastries, and personal interests, Cabinda's health infrastructure crumbles. Three types of facilities make up the health sector: (1) hospitals with internment facilities, a pharmacy, and at least one doctor on staff; (2) health centers largely run by nurses and with minor pharmaceutical capacity; and (3) health posts staffed by nurses or trained community members and occasionally stocked with basic medicines. Of the 113 health facilities in Cabinda, whether hospitals, health centers, or health posts, 40 (35 percent) are functioning, 47 (42 percent) are deficient, and 26 (23 percent) are closed. The area around Cabinda city counts the highest proportion of functioning health facilities given its population density. As the unwell make their way to the capital, however, they are likely to find no better conditions than in rural areas. The provincial hospital in Cabinda city is filled beyond capacity and sick patients are forced to share beds (*O Apostolado* 2004d).[26]

The provincial government and Chevron took a few steps toward improving the ailing system, but some of their efforts appeared to be limited to the usual channels and interests. Chevron, through the Block 0 Association, is contributing to ADPP's efforts to expand the Malembo health post. The president's personal foundation, FESA, contributed medications and supplies to the overbooked provincial hospital through a program designed, in part, to "diminish the transfer of patients to the central hospitals" in Luanda (Gonçalves 2004). The government opened a second hospital in the neighborhood of Cabassango, near the housing development for its officials, featuring a thirty-eight-bed internment facility and obstetric technology capable of preventing HIV transmission from mother to child (ANGOP 2004b).

TABLE 1. Cabinda's Degraded Health System

Municipality	Commune	Population	Condition of Health Facilities
Cabinda	1. Cabinda	133,014	2 functioning hospitals, 5 functioning health centers, 11 functioning health posts; 2 deficient health centers, 8 deficient health posts
	2. Malembo	6,408	1 functioning health post; 2 deficient health posts; 2 closed health posts
	3. Tando Zinze	20,958	1 functioning health center, 5 functioning health posts; 1 deficient health post; 8 closed health posts
Cacongo	1. Cacongo	10,324	1 functioning hospital, 3 functioning health posts; 6 deficient health posts; 2 closed health posts
	2. Dinge	4,453	2 functioning health posts; 3 deficient health posts; 3 closed health posts
	3. Massabi	3,293	1 functioning health post; 1 deficient health center; 3 closed health posts
Buco Zau	1. Buco Zau	23,279	1 functioning health post; 1 deficient health center, 6 deficient health posts; 1 closed health center, 3 closed health posts
	2. Inhuca	649	1 functioning health post; 2 deficient health posts
	3. Necuto	10,593	2 functioning health posts; 1 deficient health center, 6 deficient health post
Belize	1. Belize	6,182	2 functioning health posts; 1 deficient hospital; 5 deficient health posts
	2. Miconje	7,132	3 closed health posts
	3. Luali	1,948	2 functioning health posts; 1 deficient health post; 1 closed health post
Provincial total		228,233	n=113; 40 (35%) functioning; 47 (42%) deficient; 26 (23%) closed

SOURCE: Provincial Government of Cabinda.
NOTE: Population statistics from 1999; health facilities figures as of March 2005.

TERRITORIALIZATION BY DEVELOPMENT

Cabindans told me that the provincial government restricted Chevron's developmental activities in FLEC strongholds. Chevron, recalled an elder in a village near Tando Zinze, offered to put in a well but "the government prohibited it because it thinks that FLEC will consume the water." The man sniffed, "But does FLEC not drink from the river?!"

As I mapped out Chevron's contributions to development in Cabinda, I began to see shadows of the militant territorialization campaign. Government officials sanction all of Chevron's development projects, and I wondered whether the government was using Chevron to further its anti-FLEC agenda. Chevron built community projects at key geographic sites in the fight against FLEC, including a house for nurses in Zenze do Lucula, a health post and house for nurses in both Yabe and Massabi, and second- and third-level schools and a teacher's residence in both Luali and Miconje. All of these projects were sited in FAA-controlled towns. Many were located close to borders, perhaps in an effort to gain the confidence of refugees or lure them back from the Congos.

Chevron also positioned projects in government-held towns near FLEC strongholds. A school and municipal market in Buco Zau hinted at a strategy of providing development near strategic nodes of strong popular support for FLEC. The pattern of development suggested a progression; Chevron made its first foray into the interior in Dinge with construction projects in 1995 and 1996, later plunged into Massabi in 2000 and 2001, and followed the wave of military stabilization in the interior with projects near Luali in 2003 and Miconje in 2004. By 2007, FLEC's historical stronghold in the Mayombe region was secure enough for Sonangol P&P to announce its operator stake and 20 percent interest in the Cabinda North Block.

Oil-backed development plays a role in providing critical services and bringing weary FLEC sympathizers under government control. Terrorized inhabitants of nearby villages destroyed by government soldiers wander into the nearest large town seeking food, shelter, and healthcare. Chevron's role as service provider may be new, but the strategy is rooted in previous battles; the government used a similar combination of scorched-earth tactics and development assistance to lure people into FAA-controlled areas during the war with UNITA (Pearce 2005). Recognizing the similarities, Cabindans question whether Chevron has made other strategic contributions to territorialization beyond the scope of CSR.

Affecting Ignorance

From roughnecks to top executives, oilmen knew that revenues from their operations underwrote military campaigns from Cabinda to Cunene. Still, they denied Chevron's role in fueling war—whether in Cabinda or mainland Angola. Isolated in Malongo, Chevron employees saw little of the brutality financed by the oil they extracted. During the civil war, some employees expressed regret that the conflict had continued for so long. Louisiana native Terry Hurst said, "The war has been going on for many years and it's a shame. But it's just not on our minds. We're just too darn busy" (PU 1999). Nigel Baker, a Texan and boss of the Nemba platform, seconded Hurst. "Out here, we know about the war," he said, "but we're not part of the trouble" (Lovgren 1999). Chevron employees diverted their gaze seaward, toward Blocks 0 and 14, turning their backs on the Cabindan territory.

Oil workers even ignored the battles between FAA and FLEC just beyond Malongo's perimeter. Occasionally, fragments of the war permeated the divide. Cabindans alleged that the corporation knowingly allowed intelligence service agents and FAA soldiers to infiltrate Teleservice, the private security firm protecting the base (Tati 2003). One employee intimated a high level of distrust within Malongo; the management considers all Cabindan workers potential members of FLEC and monitors their emails and telephone calls for suspicious activity. Human rights activists in Cabinda condemned Chevron for allowing Angolan police to conduct interrogations and surveillance of suspected FLEC sympathizers in Malongo (CADHC/CRTC 2002).

Chevron addressed the interrogations issue in its 2002 Corporate Responsibility Report, which declared the corporation was "troubled by this allegation" and defended accommodating the police in Malongo. The report stated, "It is not unlike finding a police station within an airport or a large train station, providing civil law and order for, in this case, thousands of employees living and working in Malongo" (Chevron 2003). Although Chevron has been careful to publicly detach itself from national security forces, employees say the corporation collaborates with the government security apparatus at the highest levels (i.e., FAA generals up to President dos Santos).

Territorializing Energy

Three flags fly on the oil platforms offshore of Cabinda, two national and one transnational: American, Angolan, and Chevron. Each holds a stake in the oil extracted. As a powerful corporation with an interest in promoting regional security, Chevron employs private security firms like Teleservice and AirScan to protect its operations. These security companies are deeply entwined with Angolan and U.S. national security interests. The linkages between Teleservice and top FAA brass are apparent—but what of AirScan, the American outfit that flies remote-operated surveillance planes over Cabinda's oil installations?[27] AirScan's founders John Mansur and Walter Holloway are former U.S. Air Commandos—an elite division of the U.S. Air Force—and the leader of surveillance operations in Cabinda, Retired U.S. Brigadier General Joe Stringham, earned his stripes in Special Forces counter-insurgency operations in El Salvador in the 1980s (Campbell 2002).[28]

AirScan's public statements reference contracts with Sonangol and Chevron subsidiary Cabinda Gulf Oil Company "to protect personnel, environmental resources, overseas high-value oil field production facilities, pipelines and pumping stations" through "airborne data and intelligence gathering and interface with security and maritime security personnel and ground security" (ibid.). AirScan has assisted military objectives in other countries.[29] Did AirScan, while working under contract to protect Cabinda's oil installations, also provide intelligence to the Angolan military? On Chevron's recommendation, Angolan officials hired AirScan to conduct aerial surveillance of Cabinda's offshore oilfields only weeks before FAA troops launched an invasion on Congo-Brazzaville in October 1997 (O'Brien 1998). At the same time, an unnamed American defense contractor shipped nearly 500 former U.S. Special Forces operatives to Cabinda (AI 1998b). By extending Angola's influence over Congo-Brazzaville, a country that habitually harbored FLEC and UNITA forces, the invasion served both Angola's and Chevron's interests.

Conspiring against Us

One evening, I visited the home of a FLEC sympathizer who had shuttered his windows both to keep the mosquitoes from buzzing in and his words from floating out into the night air. We paused our conversation to catch the hum of an AirScan drone overhead. The man leaned close and confessed a belief that AirScan's surveillance planes helped chase down Savimbi. He also claimed AirScan's Israeli operators collaborated with the FAA in efforts to track FLEC militants, who escaped detection only under Mayombe's dense canopy.[30]

Other rumors circulating in Cabinda portrayed Chevron and the government as co-conspirators in genocidal plots. For example, after an underground storage tank leaked gas in 2001, reports circulated connecting Chevron and the government in a plot to unleash a "dense toxic fog" in Cabinda city. A separate rumor implicated former Minister of Interior Osvaldo de Jesus Serra Van Dúnem in the suspected poisoning of FLEC militants by way of rivers and streams running through FLEC territory. Proponents cited Chevron's refusal to draw its drinking water from local streams in support of their theory; instead, the corporation preferred the costly process of desalinating ocean water. Another rumor charged the government with attempted genocide by introducing a potentially poisonous type of manioc that grows up to twice as fast as the original variety, anticipating that FLEC guerrillas and Cabindans in general would attempt to eat the raw form of this manioc and die.[31] Even if exaggerated or totally untrue, such stories reveal the depth of Cabindans' distrust of Chevron and the government.

FLEC also portrays Chevron and the Angolan government as co-conspirators; FLEC activists posted a series of mock warrants for the arrest of top government leaders and Chevron officials on the Cabinda.net Web site in May 2004.[32] The Wild-West style warrants offered $1 million and $500,000, respectively, for Chevron's Chairman David J. O'Reilly and Vice Chairman Peter J. Robertson, charging the executives as "accomplices in all raping, torture and murders of innocent civilians in Cabinda carried out by the MPLA Army." Additionally, the warrants condemned O'Reilly and Robertson as "responsible for arming and financing the occupation of Cabinda by the MPLA since the beginning in 1975." Under the names of each man, a caption read, "Considered Armed and Extremely Dangerous: This man has no scruples neither has he any form of conscience one day he must answer to God and we pray that, may his soul burn in Hell forever." The Mpalabanda leader Raúl Danda called the warrants "a joke in poor taste" and noted that, even if the posting had been of a serious nature, FLEC "does not have the money to offer" (VoA 2004a; Paulo 2004). Offensive humor aside, the episode revealed the extent to which FLEC viewed Chevron as complicit in suppressing Cabindan independence.

Coercing Compromise

A fiery Cabindan elder and his son appealed to President George W. Bush to terminate relations with Angolan President José Eduardo dos Santos. The elder associated American demand for oil with violent repression in Cabinda; he saw Chevron as a proxy for U.S. interests and as a corporation with significant influence on the Bush administration.[33] "Ask George Bush to send for at least one Cabindan to speak with him. I will go speak," he offered. The would-be diplomat announced his plan: "We will give George W. Bush all the petroleum he wants in exchange for our liberty!"

His son nodded grimly and said, "We have seen what happens when oil companies rule a country—look at yours—we do not want that."

At the time I spoke with the old man and his son, U.S. Secretary of State Condoleezza Rice was attempting to extradite FLEC's António "Bento" Bembe for his involvement in the 1990 kidnapping of the Malongo consultant Brent Swan. Observers questioned whether Rice's previous affiliations with Chevron influenced her actions.[34] After Bembe failed to report to Dutch police under the conditions of his bail, the Netherlands dismissed U.S. demands for his extradition. In a suspicious twist of events, Bembe later turned up in Angola, renounced his lifelong pursuit of Cabindan independence, and announced his accession to the government's plan for Cabinda.

U.S. authorities had already captured Artur Tchibassa, another FLEC militant involved in Swan's kidnapping, in the Democratic Republic of Congo on July 11, 2003. Tchibassa was one of 330 people "charged as a result of terrorism probes in the three years after the September 11, 2001 attacks" (*Washington Post* 2005; Eggen and Tate 2005).[35] U.S. authorities had sought Tchibassa for over a decade. The day after his capture, the U.S. District Court of Washington, D.C., unsealed indictments against Tchibassa filed on September 25, 1991. The court precluded an affirmative defense of necessity and a jury convicted him of hostage-taking and conspiracy, while the district judge ordered Tchibassa to pay Brent Swan $303,957.34 in restitution and sentenced him to 293 months in prison.[36] The presiding judge stated his hope that the harsh sentence would "serve as a warning to those who will kidnap Americans abroad" and declared it *"entirely appropriate* for the type of actions that occurred here in depriving Mr. Swan not only of his freedom for two months, but basically of his life" (USCA 2006). Interestingly, the United States no longer appears keen to extradite José Tibúrcio Zinga Luemba, Maurício Amado Zulu, and even António Bento Bembe—all of the former FLEC militants sought in connection with Tchibassa for Swan's kidnapping—since they committed to compromise with the Angolan government.[37]

DEVELOPMENT BY CHEVRON

Although many Cabindans express disdain for Chevron's collaboration with the government, they have come to depend upon Chevron as a purveyor of development assistance. Residents of Caio, Fútila, Lândana, Malembo, and Cabinda city said they would ask Chevron rather than the government for development projects. Referring largely to Chevron as "the company," they expressed a multitude of reasons: "The work of the government is [dealing with] the company, the government does not work with the people, it does not look our way" . . . "Chevron, they are the ones governing our province" . . . "We are close to Malongo but denied jobs and as a consequence there is great unemployment and poverty" . . . "We women have to walk 3 hours to and from our fields and our husbands spend far too long out at sea because of the pollution" . . . "We ask the company to please have a conscience." A few said that they would ask the government, but only as an intermediary to reach Chevron. A man from Malembo dismissed any hope of dealing with provincial officials. "The government is a dictatorship," he said. A fisherman in Lândana said he would neither contact the government nor Chevron because "the two are flour from the same sack."

Many Cabindans still submitted claims to the corporation even though it had not made good on development projects promised years ago. A man from Caio said that his community had been waiting for Chevron to repair the local health post—which he referred to as "the only place we have to drop dead"—for four years. Women in Malembo claimed that Chevron agreed to build a school three years prior and delayed progress on an unfinished health center for two years. They lamented, "What we ask for is not given." In Lândana, where fishermen complained of poverty and violence, the corporation pledged to provide the fishers with boats and build a new school. Not one person ever mentioned Chevron's denial of a project—only delays. A man in Malembo summed up the situation with a witty turn of phrase, saying, "I cannot say that they reject [our proposals] . . . just that they do not cement them, but everyone in the community still goes to [Chevron]."

I asked Nobre whether Chevron ever turned down proposals for development. He responded, "We do not say 'no' to the communities; if we cannot do it we go to the government and say 'the community needs X.'" The government had also come to rely on Chevron to provide community development, and they failed to hold up their responsibilities on joint development projects. Recently constructed health posts lacked nurses and medicines, while new schools suffered from a dearth of teachers and desks. Five months after Chevron inaugurated the health center in Sassa Zau, the government still had not delivered on its pledge to provide water to the facility. Under pressure from the local community, corporate officials were induced to undertake the water project themselves—just what the government had anticipated.

Nobre admitted that Chevron often helped out the government and that their overtures were greeted with ingratitude. "We send our trucks here

TABLE 2. Chevron's Oil-Backed Development Projects

Project	Location	Funds
Capital		
Dom Paulino Madeca High School extension	Cabinda city	$1,214,000
Cabinda Genderal Hospital Blood Bank	Cabinda city	$250,000
Evangelical Mission School rehabilitation	Cabinda city	$200,000
Cabinda Catholic Mission Cemetery repair	Cabinda city	$100,000
Coastal		
Lândana Male Mission Vocational School	Lândana	$500,000
Cabinda Agriculture Project	Coastal villages between Caio and Malembo	$420,000
Village upgrades (new roofs, paint, improved water supply and drainage)	Fútila and Malembo	$400,000
Lândana Female Mission School rehabilitation	Lândana	$300,000
Interior		
Luali School and teacher housing	Luali	$450,000
Lucula Zenze Mission School	Zenze do Lucula	$445,000
Sassa Zau Health Post	Sassa Zau	$400,000
Lucula Zenze Health Center	Zenze do Lucula	$350,000
Miconje School and teacher housing	Miconje	$300,000
All Cabinda province		
Support to Provincial Water Department	Cabinda province	$200,000
Educational health programs	Cabinda province	$200,000
Cabinda Malaria Fighting Program	Cabinda province	$150,000
Support to local environmental NGOs & seminars	Cabinda province	$130,000
Summer Jobs for Youth	Cabinda province	$110,000
Promotion of traditional arts and culture	Cabinda province	$80,000
Child Education and Activities Program	Cabinda province	$80,000
Promotion of youth sports	Cabinda province	$80,000
"Pela Vida" AIDS Project	Cabinda province	$50,000

SOURCE: "ChevronTexaco and Africa: Community Development Examples," Angola 2001/2002.

and there. We pumped sewage from the Cabinda prison and paid for it just because they needed our help; for municipal services like this we have minimal funds," said Nobre. "It would be nice if they even just sent a letter of thanks . . . but nothing," he finished, bearing his empty palms in exasperation. Dependence on Chevron was not limited to Cabinda; Angolan leaders also requested the corporation's assistance with development outside the extractive zones.

Postwar Positioning

Angola's twenty-seven-year civil war killed 1.5 million people and displaced between 2.5 and 4 million more, necessitating a massive influx of humanitarian aid. From 1990 to 2004, U.S. emergency aid to Angola totaled approximately $844 million (USAID 2004b). During the 2002 fiscal year, the U.S. government contributed $122 million in assistance to Angola, including $20.6 million in funding for critical needs through the Office of Foreign Disaster Assistance (USAID 2004a). Two years after Jonas Savimbi's death and the final peace accords, emergency funds dried up and international donors began to downsize or discontinue assistance efforts. USAID's humanitarian assistance to Angola dropped to $45 million during fiscal year 2004 (USAID 2004b).

Despite Angola's persistently appalling development indicators, donors cited contingency of future development funding on two factors: free and fair elections and increased government transparency. Donors argued that transparency of the negotiations and agreements set forth in oil contracts and payments made to the Angolan government by transnational oil corporations would foster greater accountability for the use of those revenues. To this end, many donors and NGOs working on behalf of Angolan civil society backed one of two transparency initiatives: the Publish What You Pay (PWYP) coalition, forcing oil companies to publish their net taxes, fees, royalties, and other payments to governments on a country-by-country basis, or the Extractive Industries Transparency Initiative (EITI), obliging governments to publish the revenues earned from extractive industries.[38] Even the International Monetary Fund promised to withhold funding until the Angolan government passed a Staff Monitored Program with minimum transparency and accountability standards.

To compensate, the same transnational oil corporations sworn to opacity under the terms of their Angolan production contracts began contributing directly to NGOs through the Global Development Alliance (GDA). The GDA patches together public-private development alliances to complement USAID's meager budgets and vast expertise with corporate funds as well as to match strategic U.S. policy interests with corporate investment objectives. These alliances are sealed through informal agreements or formal memoranda of understanding (MOUs) facilitated by USAID's capacity to accept conditional gifts and offer tax deductions through its 501(c)3 status. In 2003, USAID combined $250 million in public funds with $1 billion in private sector partnerships in 100 new and continuing alliances.

Qualifying neither for disaster assistance nor Millennium Challenge Account funding, USAID's Angola mission suffered a decline in U.S. government support. Nevertheless, funding shortfalls and the presence of transnational oil firms with a strategic interest in encouraging CSR efforts that can decrease risk and maximize returns on their investment, proved Angola to be a model country for the GDA. As USAID began to look for an exit strategy from Angola, it saw an opportunity to transfer responsibility for development to private sector entities with long-term interests in Angola, like Chevron.

Going National

In the face of intractable oil-backed debts, their resulting insolvency, and some intransigence when confronted with the international transparency ultimatum, the Angolan government encouraged oil corporations to wear their development hats outside the extractive zones. In 2002, President José Eduardo dos Santos called on Chevron, the largest single private investor in Angola, to make a "significant contribution" to postwar reconstruction efforts. He urged the corporation to contribute to a broader development agenda targeting provinces not already benefiting from corporate initiatives associated with oil production. The timing of the president's appeal was strategic—a series of oil-backed loans negotiated during the last decade of the Angolan war had effectively mortgaged existing oil production. Additionally, he made this request at an exceedingly opportune moment: just prior to the negotiations for an extension on Chevron's Block 0 concession.[39] Chevron responded with the Angola Partnership Initiative, a $25 million contribution to development spanning five years.

Not only was Chevron's pledge a response to dos Santos' petition, it was also a reply to the shareholders and transparency watchdogs who questioned what good the corporation was doing by operating in a corrupt country. In an effort to sidestep the usual corruption and bribery circuits in Angola, Chevron negotiated a five-year agreement with USAID as part of its Angola Partnership Initiative. USAID and Chevron each committed

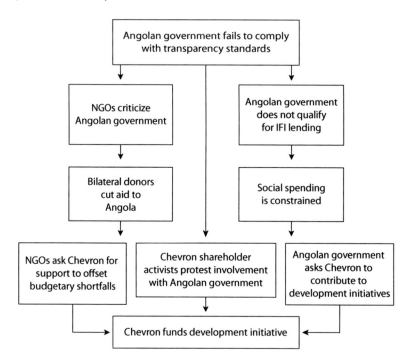

FIGURE 4. Pressure for Oil-Backed Development

$10 million to a joint effort to increase food security in four provinces in Angola's highland breadbasket: the Planalto.

USAID and a consortium of NGOs began strategizing on the Planalto agricultural development project in July 2002, but USAID did not announce to its NGO partners that Chevron would provide a substantial portion of the funding until November. A representative of Catholic Relief Services (CRS) said the announcement threw his organization "into a tailspin." USAID had neither consulted nor informed the collaborating NGOs regarding their negotiations with the oil firm. CRS and CARE wrestled with the idea of taking money from one of the oil companies they had criticized for impeding transparency. CRS refused the funds so as not to compromise the credibility of the organization's *Bottom of the Barrel* report, which critiqued the role of transnational oil corporations in supporting corrupt and unaccountable governments. Thus, in the second month of its fiscal year, CRS embarked on an emergency fundraising campaign.[40]

Donors hoped that their funding embargo—coupled with the temporary insolvency of the government preceding an anticipated jump to production rates of nearly two million barrels per day by 2008—would compel Angola to adopt more transparent accounting in order to gain access to World Bank credit (ANGOP 2004e). By providing development assistance at this critical juncture, Chevron weakened the donor boycott, legitimated the government's lack of transparency, and indirectly undermined the developmental success of the farmers targeted in the agricultural development program. These were likely unintended consequences; Chevron was merely complying with government demands to ensure the successful renewal of its Block o concession agreement (ANGOP 2003,2004g). The corporation's generosity also resulted in some intended consequences: the $10 million contribution to the USAID Planalto project advanced Chevron's renewal of the Block o concession and it was also tax deductible.

Chevron strived to associate itself with American democratic values despite contributing to an autocratic regime in Angola. The corporation appeals to Americans with color-saturated representations of fertile hope in postwar Angola The ad firm Young and Rubicam developed a Chevron advertisement featuring a handful of golden corn kernels grown on the Planalto. Around the time of the ad's release, Chevron spent $4,426,382—a figure representing almost half of its contribution to the five-year budget for agricultural development—on placing ads (not even creating them) in just five months.[41] In contrast to operations and advertising costs, Chevron insiders confessed they considered the money they spent on CSR projects to be "chump change."[42]

Voting for the Oiligarchy

I traveled to the Planalto to speak with beneficiaries of Chevron's agricultural iniatiative.[43] Corn stalks stretched in rows out toward the horizon, impeded in their expansion only by remaining minefields. During an interview with a local *soba*, I was surprised to learn that he understood the MPLA to be the source of the local seeds, tools, and developmental assistance. It is not uncommon for credit to be assigned to undeserving actors or for scheming pretenders to take undue credit for the charity of others, especially in the more remote regions of Angola. Justin Pearce describes a similar scenario, wherein a rural villager gave the government credit for the World Food Program's distributions. He wrote: "The government? The only conclusion to be drawn was that he thought the WFP was an agency of the Angolan government. It was an understandable mistake for a peasant farmer whose experience of a functioning state was no greater than his knowledge of the United Nations. The government-issued ration cards did nothing to dispel the impression that the food was a gift from Luanda rather than from foreign donors" (2005:81).

In this case, however, there was no innocent misunderstanding. The *soba* and village residents confirmed that after distributions, MPLA supporters had visited the area and claimed to be responsible for the donation. The president's party seemed to be leveraging Chevron's contributions for political support. I wondered whether President dos Santos had encouraged Chevron to contribute to postwar reconstruction efforts in the Planalto— UNITA's stronghold—with the notion of the MPLA usurping the rewards of the project.[44]

For the first time in sixteen years, Angola would hold elections: parliamentary elections in 2008 and then presidential elections in 2009.[45] The MPLA was aiming for a two-thirds majority by doling out favors through its "well-oiled system of clientelistic legitimacy" (Messiant 2008:120).[46] During his August 2007 visit to Cabinda, President dos Santos distributed to loyalists 200 radio cassettes, 200 televisions, 40 motorbikes, 30 refrigerators, 50 stoves, and 1,500 pieces of fabric (Coelho 2007). MPLA boosters in the provincial government offered cars to Cabindan trade union leaders loyal to the president's party, while trucks flying the MPLA flag distributed water, sacks of grain, agricultural tools, motorcycles, televisions and refrigerators across the country (HRW 2008a). The MPLA was buying allegiances with appliances; voters abandoned democratic principles for a chance to win prizes.

A few months before the parliamentary elections, Angolan leaders ordered out the UN Office of the High Commissioner for Human Rights under criticism for "political motivations" and lack of transparency (HRW 2008c). The government devised a group of national human rights institutions to perform perfunctory obligations of overseeing human rights. Human Rights Watch expressed concern that "without an independent human rights body, civil society organizations are at risk of government intimidation" (HRW 2008c). A few months later, Amnesty International reported, "The authorities are attempting to shut down one of Angola's most active human rights organisations, the Association for Justice, Peace, and Democracy (AJPD)" (AI 2008b). The AJPD played an instrumental role in supporting civil society, investigating injustices, and exposing human rights abuses during the 2008 election cycle.[47]

According to Human Rights Watch, a lack of accountability by law enforcement agencies enabled patterns of political violence including "sporadic assaults by local MPLA supporters, sometimes involving traditional authorities and local MPLA leaders, against local UNITA party members and their property and party symbols" and even cases of intimidation against civil society election monitors like the AJPD (HRW 2008b). Threatening violence, MPLA supporters prevailed upon *sobas* to "prevent UNITA [from] developing party activities in villages"; thirty MPLA militants beat traditional leader Pedro Pomba for flying the UNITA flag in his village of Bongue Kandala in Benguela province (HRW 2008b).

Bias toward the president's party reached deep into the electoral machine. MPLA supporters dominated the agency conducting voter registration and determining the location of polling centers; government officials restricted independent access to the voter registry and refused to commission an external audit of the register (HRW 2008b).

Despite legal provisions requiring equal allocation of media resources, the MPLA benefited from biased media reports and a disproportionate amount of airtime on state television. While some partial reports emphasized the MPLA's good works, others dwelled on UNITA's previous sins. Human Rights Watch (2008a) observed, "On September 3, the last day of the election campaign, the state-owned Angolan Public Television broadcast footage of a woman weeping as she recalled how she had suffered due to UNITA during the war. She also accused the current UNITA leader Isaias Samakuva of lying when he said UNITA had changed since the war ended. This item bore no evident relationship with current news, and appeared to have been broadcast expressly to discredit UNITA."

Widespread irregularities marred election day on September 5, 2008 (including late delivery of ballot papers and failure to check names against voter rolls to prevent multiple votes) and official obstruction of the accreditation of national electoral observers, especially those from independent civil society organizations (HRW 2008a). A variety of organizational problems, whether intentional or not, received redress when officials added a second day of voting on September 6; however, other irregularities marked a blatant disregard for free and fair polling standards. International electoral observers witnessed hordes of soldiers outside polling stations in Cabinda and members of the ruling party standing outside polling booths while voters marked their ballots (BBC 2008). A European Union observer even alleged cases of vote rigging in Cabinda; he claimed MPLA supporters bussed voters from Congo-Brazzaville and lavished them with government-funded gifts, food, and comfort in exchange for sympathetic votes (ibid.).[48]

In a landslide vote on September 5–6, 2008, the MPLA won 191 of the 220 seats in the legislature, whereas UNITA held on to only 16 seats (IRIN 2008a). After initially demanding a fresh ballot, UNITA leaders conceded defeat though they deemed "it was not possible" to judge the elections free and fair (IRIN 2008b). Observers from the African Union, European Union, and U.S. Embassy acknowledged media bias, organizational insufficiencies, and procedural problems; however, they accepted the election results (ibid.). The MPLA handily exceeded the two-thirds majority required to change Angola's constitution according to President dos Santos' wish that parliamentarians elect his successor rather than the populace (Corkin 2009).[49]

Peaking Interests

An oil boom preceding the 2008 parliamentary elections underwrote the massive infrastructure projects and social spending of which the MPLA boasted during the campaign.[50] Social spending jumped from 12 percent in 2003 to 30 percent in 2006, keeping pace with a 400 percent increase in the value of oil exports since 2002 (IRIN 2006b; Russell 2007). On the eve of elections, the government pledged to use oil revenues to improve public welfare, apportioning 31.7 percent of the 2008 budget to social spending—more than double the 14.6 percent designated for defense and security (ARB 2008).[51]

While oil prices remained high, Angola strove to meet production targets of 2 million barrels per day by the end of 2008 (ANGOP 2008f). Officials announced a five-year, $100 billion capital injection for Angola's oil sector and Chevron publicized a $1 billion investment to increase production from Block 14 by 100,000 barrels per day (Aimurie 2008; ANGOP 2008e). Analysts projected Nigeria and Angola would capture $3.5 trillion in cumulative oil and gas revenues from 2006 to 2030 (Ikokwu 2008). When violence in the Niger Delta interrupted extraction, Angola surpassed Nigeria as Sub-Saharan Africa's largest oil producer.[52]

Once oil prices fell, OPEC fixed Angola's production quota at 1.9 million barrels per day, setting annual oil production forecasts at 711 million barrels (OECB 2007).[53] Angolan Oil Minister Botelho de Vasconcelhos accepted the 99,000-barrel-per-day production cut mandated by OPEC in the hopes that decreased supply would improve oil prices (ANGOP 2008b). An additional quota reduction cut Angola's production to 1.517 million barrels per day by January 2009 and operators adjusted their production schedules to reflect the change (ANGOP 2008b; Quinlan 2009).

Economists predicted a severe contraction of Angola's economy—from $86 billion in 2008 to $69 billion in 2009—resulting in drastic government spending reductions, fewer job opportunities, and a large deficit (Mendes and Theunissen 2009; IMF 2009).[54] Angolan authorities announced plans to sell $9 billion in bonds to finance budgetary priorities (Mendes and

Theunissen 2009). The World Bank also pledged $1 billion in loans to assist with economic diversification, despite Angola's failure to comply with transparency obligations (Corkin 2009).[55] Accustomed to an expansionary economy afforded by rising oil production windfall profits since the war's end, government officials sought assistance from all sides. How would Angola leverage CSR to fulfill budgetary shortfalls this time, despite prevailing on corporations to reduce production rates?

A RESPONSIBLE LEGACY

How many health posts and schools are needed to compensate for a repressive regime and lack of government accountability? CSR advances a mutual interest between government and corporate officials: consolidating political control. By using tandem tactics of violence and oil-backed development as complementary means to territorialization, leaders in Luanda preserved their exclusionary control over and access to Cabinda's resource revenues. Similarly, provincial government leaders in Cabinda depend on Chevron's strategic interventions to manage dissent and sustain their personalized system of rule.

Chevron produced 770,700 barrels of oil per day from Cabinda's Blocks 0 and 14 in 2008 (ANGOP 2006a). The corporation's CSR initiatives rose in proportion to a $2.2 billion oil and gas investment in Block 14. Oil, however, is a non-renewable resource. Fields in shallow water concessions are declining and production is shifting to deepwater Blocks 14, 15, and 17, as well as ultra-deepwater Block 31. Angolan oil production capacity is expected to peak between 2011 and 2013 (EIA 2008). OPEC-mandated production cuts may forestall peak oil by a few years, but only discoveries of new reserves could radically alter Angola's outlook.[56]

Once the oil runs out, what legacy will Chevron leave behind? Who will repaint the schools or restock the health posts? The ultimate test of corporate responsibility will surface once Chevron and the other firms have moved on. Then, the government will no longer be able to task oil corporations with fulfilling social obligations and advancing territorialization schemes.

Conclusion

Converging Shores

An oil slick rippled across calm waters. As the spill spread its toxic shadow across the bay, tar balls spattered local beaches and the corpses of 1,800 oil-fouled seabirds washed ashore (Schreiber 2008). Authorities closed more than fifty coastal recreation areas and ordered a halt to all fishing activities. Halfway around the world from Fútila, this spill hit close to home.

More than 200,000 liters of bunker fuel oil had gushed into the San Francisco Bay after the *Cosco Busan* collided with the Bay Bridge on November 7, 2007. The slick spread west through the fabled Golden Gate into the Gulf of the Farallones and Monterey Bay National Marine Sanctuaries and east toward the wetlands of Richmond. County officials warned of health hazards posed by contact with the spilled oil, but locals critical of the slow official response in their area organized volunteers to collect oiled waterfowl and clean up Richmond's thirty-seven-kilometer shoreline (Heredia and Fagan 2007). Coast Guard officials attributed their lapse, in part, to an agency-wide shift away from safety and environment and toward security detail, including guarding LNG tankers against terrorist attack (Helvarg 2009:56–57).

The spill in San Francisco Bay heightened the mounting frustration with oil dependence at a time of rocketing fuel costs, implosion in Iraq, and increasing awareness of global climate change. Many Bay Area residents long recognized oil's role in the convergence of degradation, violence, and exclusion on a global scale, but the oil spill offered this privileged community a rare glimpse into the local dynamics of degradation. Could experiencing even a fraction of what communities like Fútila continuously endure help engender the solidarity necessary to will the end of oil dependence? Catastrophic incidents can induce episodic global-local convergences, and alliances with communities experiencing environmental injustice offer long-term opportunities for building solidarity. To understand the costs of oil dependence to human and environmental health, however, San Franciscans had only to look across the bay. One of the largest refineries in the United States, currently operated by Chevron, has spewed toxics into Richmond's backyard since 1902.

FAMILIAR SHORES

The residents of Richmond are both familiar with oil's toxicity and attuned to environmental injustices in their midst.[1] Chevron refines 240,000 barrels of crude oil per day and releases 900 metric tons of pollutants each year at the Richmond facility (BADA 2008).[2] With the refinery's emissions, ranging from hazardous compounds including dioxins, benzene, and xylene to noxious gases like sulfur dioxide, cancer rates in Richmond exceed regional, state, and national averages (Smith 2005; BADA 2008).[3] Richmond's asthma rates are five times the state norm (Amazon Watch 2008). "The asthma and cancer rates are very high in North Richmond and a lot of people have died from it. We made the connection, even if the doctors didn't, between the air pollution and the health problems," said Amadia Thomas, co-founder of Richmond's West County Toxics Coalition (WCTC 2005:7).

The West County Toxics Coalition represents the interests of Richmond residents at the Environmental Justice Advisory Committee of the California Environmental Protection Agency (Sherman 1996). Richmond's population of 100,000 is largely composed of minority and low-income families; 17,000 residents live within 5 kilometers of the Chevron refinery, including those in the Triangle Court and Las Deltas public housing projects (BADA 2008).[4] Ugochi Nwadike lives in a public housing facility near the refinery. She says her children suffer from chronic asthma, skin rashes, recurring nosebleeds, headaches, and coughing attacks. As a nurse who neither smokes nor drinks and has no history of asthma, Nwadike worries, "The poison from the refinery is killing these children" (Flournoy 2000).[5] West County Toxics Coalition's Henry Clark agrees: "When people live in a toxic environment, it compromises their immune system" (WCTC 2005:13).

Chevron executives distance themselves from Richmond's toxic environment. Chevron's corporate headquarters is fifty kilometers away in San Ramon. Although both cities are located in Contra Costa County, San Ramon is an overwhelmingly white city with an average household income of $95,856, while Richmond's primarily minority population has a median household income of $44,210 (U.S. Census Bureau 2000).[6] Even within Richmond itself, residents argue that minorities are far more likely to live next to the refinery and whites at the opposite end of town.[7]

Accidents at the refinery are common.[8] Chevron recorded 304 accidents between 1989 and 1995, from major fires, spills, leaks, and explosions to toxic gas releases, flaring, and other forms of air contamination (Sherman 1996).[9] From 1991 to 1999, the aged refinery emitted ten "serious chemical releases" (Smith 2005). Residents still recall a particularly terrifying explosion at the refinery at 2:28 P.M. on March 25, 1999, when a series of blasts thrust 8,100 kilograms of sulfur dioxide far into the sky.[10] Prevailing winds pushed the pollution toward Richmond's homes and schools; the smoke "killed trees, burned the fur off squirrels, and sent hundreds of temporarily blinded, vomiting residents to hospitals" (ibid). Blast victim Cherron Holmes recalled, "I lost my voice for six weeks. And I threw up a lot. Everybody did" (Flournoy 2000). Authorities ordered 10,000 residents to "shelter in place" and remain inside with windows and doors shut until 8:30 P.M., but more than 1,200 people rushed to nearby hospitals seeking medical attention (Flournoy 2000; Tansey et al. 1999). According to a local news story, thirty-one-year-old Tamara Sexton visited the hospital with concerns about the effect of the fumes on her unborn child. "I'm in my first trimester, which is more dangerous. That's when the baby starts forming. Of course I'm worried. I don't even know what the toxin was," she said (Tansey et al. 1999).

Environmental justice advocates from the West County Toxics Coalition and Communities for a Better Environment employed various strategies to hold Chevron accountable for hazardous releases including direct negotiation, lobbying public officials, mobilizing concerned citizens, and allying with legal and scientific experts (Sherman 1996). They even joined the Bucket Brigades: Denny Larson's group, which employs low-tech air sampling buckets to test for eighty-one different compounds.[11] Community advocates celebrated a number of victories against Chevron. Their pressure helped shut down Chevron's incinerator, fertilizer plant, and "landfarms"— essentially open-air dumpsites for toxic chemicals like benzene, toluene, xylenes, chromium, lead, vanadium, nickel, and hydrocarbons—from which emanated fumes that burned the leaves off nearby trees (Smith 2005). Activists celebrated a 1998 settlement in favor of the Environmental Protection Agency for $540,000 as compensation for Chevron's toxic releases in violation of the Clean Water Act associated with the refinery's bypass of wastewater treatment systems between 1991 and 1995 (EPA 1998). Media attention drawn by community groups also pressured Chevron to reduce flaring; Chevron flares released up to twenty metric tons of sulfur dioxide per day prior to activist interventions (CBE 2004; WCTC 2005).

Chevron ranks among California's top five chemical polluters (Smith 2005). Despite the battles won by activists, the EPA cited the Richmond refinery for "significant noncompliance" and reported 300 pollutant spills from the refinery from 2001 to 2003 (BADA 2008). On January 31, 2002, accidental releases of sulfur dioxide, sulfur trioxide and hydrogen sulfide at the refinery activated twenty-two warning sirens indicating that residents should "shelter in place," but twenty local residents were forced to seek treatment at area hospitals for associated symptoms like dizziness or burning eyes and throat (CCHS 2007).[12] Similarly, warning sirens sounded after a release of sulfur dioxide on January 15, 2007. Community activists still struggle to hold Chevron accountable for accidents and clean up operations at the refinery.

Aligning Strategies

Corporate spokeswoman Marielle Boortz assured reporters after the 1999 explosion at the Richmond refinery that Chevron "would never do anything to intentionally create an unsafe situation" (Flournoy 2000). Her words echoed the sentiments expressed by Chevron's management in Cabinda following oil spills. As in Fútila, Chevron's accidents in Richmond are often attributable to preventable conditions or decrepit infrastructure (CBE 2004). Activist Denny Larson charges, "It's no accident that dangerous fires, explosions, and toxic spills continue to increase when refineries are calling the shots and monitoring themselves" (Smith 2005).[13] Larson's statement nods to a weak regulatory environment as well as Chevron's unsavory manipulation of Richmond city officials with petro-capitalist pet projects in exchange for overlooking hazards. For example, when Richmond's planning commission approved Chevron's retrofit plans contingent upon the corporation's $50 million contribution to a refinery disaster claims fund requested by the West County Toxics Coalition, Chevron appealed to the commission, dropped the claims fund, and invested $6 million in corporate social responsibility (CSR) projects—including the Martin Luther King Jr. Health Center, police athletic leagues, and community beautification (Johnson 2008; Sherman 1996).[14] Chevron's strategy in Richmond recalled the corporation's actions in Buco Mazi described in chapter 5, when the corporation ignored a court directive to build a laboratory and diverted settlement monies into a community fisheries center.

Chevron draws tactics for deflecting accountability and suppressing dissent from a common quiver, whether operating in the United States or

Angola. The corporation's CSR contributions provoke similar disciplinary effects in disparate environments. Much as Cabindans benefiting from CSR projects hesitated to criticize Chevron, Richmond school administrators found themselves reluctant to speak ill of Chevron for fear of losing valuable corporate donations.[15] Chevron also bet—to the tune of $1 million in the 2008 campaign cycle—that politicians would refrain from critiquing the source of their campaign contributions (CRP 2009b).[16]

Spilling Over

Three days after oil from the *Cosco Busan* spill washed ashore in Richmond, protesters converged on Chevron's refinery. Chevron had nothing to do with the spill in San Francisco Bay, but the incident underscored U.S. dependence on fossil fuels and drew attention to the environmental hazards entailed in an "upgrade" to the Richmond refinery that Chevron was proposing.[17] The protesters, however, did not limit their grievances to local issues; instead, they underscored Chevron's role in petro-violence around the world. Demonstrators denounced Chevron's lack of accountability in the Ecuadorian rainforest, where subsidiary Texaco dumped 68 billion liters of toxic waste (Amazon Watch 2008).[18] They accused Chevron of supporting a repressive military dictatorship in Burma, war profiteering in the Middle East, and complicity in killings of peaceful protesters occupying its oil platforms in Nigeria.[19] Antiwar advocates blockaded the entrance to the Richmond refinery, condemning Chevron for processing one million barrels of "stolen" Iraqi crude per month (BADA 2008).[20]

Protesters also lambasted Chevron—the second-largest oil firm in the United States—for exerting pressure on the political system. Chevron posted record earnings of $23.9 billion in 2008—a nearly $7 billion increase from 2006.[21] Demonstrators chided the corporation for wielding undue influence over Republican lawmakers to protect its soaring profits when Democratic members of Congress threatened to revoke subsidies to Big Oil or tax windfall profits accruing to the five largest American oil firms. They admonished Chevron for spending $38 million to defeat Proposition 87, a California ballot measure proposing to impose a per-barrel tax on crude oil to fund renewable energy development, and lobbying against California's Global Warming Solutions Act (AB 32), a progressive bill to limit greenhouse gas emissions (Thompson and Hubbard 2007).[22]

Earning profits in the oil industry requires externalizing costs to human health including (but not limited to) increasing cancer risks, rising asthma rates, and surging methylmercury levels.[23] Transnational oil corporations also profit by externalizing environmental damages, including oil spills, releases of noxious gases, and global warming. Activists developed a campaign to elucidate the true costs of Chevron's financial returns from operations in Angola, Burma, Canada, Chad, Cameroon, Ecuador, Iraq, Kazakhstan, Nigeria, the Philippines, and across the United States, focusing on "the lives lost, the wars fought, communities destroyed, environments decimated, livelihoods ruined, and political voices silenced" (Juhasz et al. 2009:1).

The oil and gas industry's six supermajors are all implicated in various configurations of violence, degradation, and exclusion: Total along with Chevron for abuses of the Karen in Burma; ConocoPhillips for bribery in East Timor and ignoring environmental impacts of a pipeline in Georgia; BPAmoco for a refinery explosion in Houston, Texas, and dealings with the U'wa in Colombia; Shell for egregious human rights violations of the Ogoni in Nigeria; and ExxonMobil for the Exxon Valdez disaster and military violence in the Aceh territory of Indonesia.[24] For conscious consumers, boycotting particular brands of filling stations has little impact; independent stations regularly sell surplus fuel from other brands, including the supermajors.[25]

Neither transnational oil corporations nor corrupt host governments accept accountability for the true costs of oil production. Partnerships between the government and transnational oil corporations provide the structural foundation for the enclave economy, which enables the twin dynamics of petro-capitalism and petro-violence. As the various chapters of this book have sought to demonstrate, the constitutive forces remain the same; however, they wash ashore in different configurations. Patterns of violence, degradation, and exclusion converge and generate self-sustaining feedback loops: violent actions repress civil society, whereby members cannot effectively protest their exclusionary condition, wherein cultural and environmental degradation is condoned. The scope and intensity of their reach is inversely related to the legal safeguards in place for human and environmental health, equal protection for all persons, and sustainable use of natural resources—as well as the government's willingness to enforce the rule of law.

CRUDE DEPENDENCY

The shared curse of oil in more developed countries is our dependency—and thus our complicity in petro-capitalism and petro-violence. Entire economies hop to the roaring rhythm of combustion. Conventional agriculture thrives on petroleum-based fertilizers. Fossil fuels drive most modes of transportation from automobiles to airplanes. When oil prices set a new record at $147.27 per barrel in July 2008 and the cost of gasoline hit an all-time high, American consumers briefly recognized the enslaving power of oil in their lives. They pawned gold jewelry and electronics, golf clubs and musical instruments for reasons as inescapable and mundane as financing their daily commutes (Munro 2006; Edelhart 2008).[26]

Oil dependency in Angola is of a different nature; government leaders are more addicted to oil's power in terms of the wealth it brings. They maintain access to oil revenues through petrodollar patronage and violent exclusion, diverting social spending to buy constituents and mortgaging future oil production to procure weapons. Oil disproportionately powers lives and livelihoods, enriching some and weakening others. For as long as government leaders, transnational oil corporations, and consumers of petroleum products fail to value the lives of people in the extractive zones, those fishers and farmers, mothers and fathers, sons and daughters are constrained to endure a crude existence.

Notes

1. Technically, a subsidiary of Chevron (Cabinda Gulf Oil) runs the oil base and produces oil in Angola, but I refer to the transnational oil corporations extracting Angola's oil by the names of their parent corporation rather than their subsidiary titles to emphasize the transnational character of their operations. Likewise, following Suzana Sawyer (2004), I recognize Chevron's headquarters in San Ramon, California, and Total's main offices in Paris, France, as the respective *matrizes* of each firm, the places where business strategies are conceived and formulated before their implementation worldwide.

2. Figure based on Block o and 14 production rates of 420,000 and 200,000 barrels per day, respectively, out of total rate of 1.9 million barrels per day in 2007 (De Sousa 2008).

3. Distinct from a multinational corporation that styles operations according to the national identity in each country where it operates and establishes independent production and sales systems, a transnational corporation is more flexible, relying on integrated subsidiary structures and global supply and distribution chains. According to David Korten, transnational corporations are designed "to produce where costs are lowest, sell where markets are most lucrative and shift the profits to where tax rates are least burdensome" and, as such, effectively tip "the balance of power from the local human interest to the global corporate interest" (1995:126).

4. See HRW 1994, 1996b; and GW 1999.

5. Hodges produced a seminal work on Angolan petro-politics in 2001 entitled *Angola from Afro-Stalinism to Petro-Diamond Capitalism*. An updated edition in Portuguese was published in 2002 as *Angola: Do Afro-Estalinismo ao Capitalismo Selvagem* and in English in 2003 under the title: *Angola: Anatomy of an Oil State*.

6. Here Apter is referring to Nigeria, but the statement is equally appropriate for Angola.

7. Transparency International, in rating the level of corruption in Angola,

gave it a score of 2.2 in 2006. A score of 10 denotes a highly clean country and 0 the most corrupt. Countries near Angola in the rankings included Congo, Kenya, Kyrgyzstan, Nigeria, Pakistan, Sierra Leone, Tajikistan, and Turkmenistan. See www.transparency.org.

8. This is Aihwa Ong's model of "graduated sovereignty."

9. So long as the mangroves, which are highly susceptible to oil spills, are not affected.

10. The political geographic division of the Angolan territory is organized in a hierarchy of provinces, municipalities, and communes. Zaire province is divided into six municipalities: Mbanza Kongo, Soyo, Nzeto, Tomboco, Noqui, and Cuimba. Each municipality possesses a number of communes. The municipal seat and town, also called Soyo, was known as Santo António do Zaire during the colonial period.

11. The Cabinda province contains four municipalities: Cabinda, Cacongo, Buco Zau, and Belize.

12. The Ministry of Fisheries' Technical Council recommended a ban on *banda banda* fishing along Angolan coasts in August 2004 (*Jornal de Angola* 2003c). Pesnorte and local authorities enforce the ban in Soyo. On one occasion I witnessed artisanal fishermen using *banda banda* techniques in Cabinda. Studies indicate that *banda banda* is rarely if ever used in Cabinda and Zaire (Agostinho et al. 2005).

13. In northern Angola, fish traders from the Republic of Congo or the Democratic Republic of Congo are further discriminated against by fiscal police and other local fish traders resentful of the competition.

14. On occasion, fish traders with access to freezers also sold frozen fish.

15. By comparison, Angolan men typically work eight to ten hours a day (IFAD 2002a). In addition, an assessment of how Angola's extended conflict influenced gender roles indicates that, as their husbands and sons left to fight, the women undertook "activities that used to be performed by men such as providing for the household, disciplining male children, building and repairing houses, dealing with community leaders and government officials, and fulfilling religious and social obligations" (ibid.).

16. I collected survey data on use of fuels for domestic and artisanal fisheries use and knowledge of local oil extraction from 23 leaders from 19 villages along the coast. (The villages in Zaire province included Tulombo, Bocolo, Kimpula, Moita Seca, Pângala, Quinfuquena, Kungo, Lucata-Ntampa, Kipai, Kivanda, Manga Grande, Quinxia, Nsikisilu, Mukula, Nzeto, Kinssamba, Kissando, Kinssukulo, and Musserra.)

17. I conducted twenty in-depth interviews on experiences of degradation and several focus groups on petro-violence.

18. Traditional authorities are persons, predominantly men, who retain customary authority over a given community. A *soba, regedor,* or *rei do povo* may be described as a traditional authority. Still, some prefer to think of a *rei do povo* as the only traditional authority—because he inherits his title whereas a *soba* or *regedor* (sometimes the leader of all of the *sobas* in a given

area) is generally appointed by the Angolan government. This framework is grounded in the colonial system of indirect rule. Portuguese colonials used the term *soba* in reference to any chief, king, or community leader officially recognized by the colonial government, employing these authorities (and sometimes producing them) to implement their policies. Luandan officials continue to wield influence over faraway territory through *sobas*.

19. This was fortunate because my team of research assistants dwindled from eight to two as we surveyed eighty-eight people in communities along the coast. These communities included Malembo, Lândana, Fútila, Buco Mazi, Caio, and Praia dos Pescadores.

20. I conducted thirty-five additional in-depth interviews in these coastal villages as well as communities in the interior.

21. These names were inspired by the national soccer team's 2006 World Cup roster.

CHAPTER 2

1. A World Bank report estimated that 38 percent of Angola's urban population lacks access to sanitation. Only 40 percent of Angolans have access to sanitation countrywide, and just 27 percent in rural areas (WB 2005:15). Wartime physical and economic insecurity coupled with military operations designed to herd people into government-controlled areas drove innumerable Angolans to urban centers. By 2002, 57 percent of Angolans lived in provincial capitals and urban centers (WB 2005:13). Despite hopeful predictions by the Angolan government that most Luandans would pack up for the countryside following the end of the war in 2002, Luanda's population jumped from 3,100,000 to 4,110,000 between 2000 and 2005, meaning the proportion of all Angolans living in the capital increased from 23.6 percent to 26.9 percent (Colaço 2004). Government security agents forcibly evicted 20,000 people, destroyed 3,000 homes, and expropriated numerous small-scale cultivation plots between 2002 and 2006 (HRW 2007). The evictions in prime neighborhoods like Boavista made way for construction of new offices and apartments for oil corporations and their executives.

2. Shaxson addresses governance problems in oil-rich countries. He says, "This is like saying of a heroin addict with criminal tendencies that there is no drug problem, just a criminal problem. They are wrong: the heart of the matter is not rulers corruption or companies' misbehavior but oil and gas itself." (2007:235).

3. Outside of the oil and diamond industries, the next-largest industrial project in Angola is the Coca-Cola bottling plant in Luanda (Marques 2004d).

4. Isabel dos Santos is a partner in Ascorp, which was overtaken by Sodiam/ LKI.

5. The rounded imperial divisions are as follows: shallow water (up to 1,000 feet), deepwater (1,000 to 5,000 feet) and ultra-deepwater (5,000 to 8,000 feet).

6. Ratified in 1994, the United Nations Convention on the Law of the Sea ruled that coastal nations could claim as part of their territory an exclusive economic zone (EEZ) stretching two hundred miles offshore. Angola's EEZ extends over 160,000 square miles of the adjacent Atlantic, a watery domain 44 percent of the size of terrestrial Angola (Cuteta 2003a).

7. Gunn proposes four reasons for transnational oil corporations' predilection for Angola: low production costs, high discovery rates and reserves, the low sulfur content of Angolan oil, and the reliability of Angolan contracts (1987:56).

8. Production sharing agreements divide produced oil into cost oil and profit oil. The sale of cost oil, also called cost recovery oil, is used to pay back the concession partners for all of the costs for exploration, development, and operating costs of the operation. The revenues from the sale of remaining oil, called profit oil, is shared between the partners and the government according to a proportion determined by production rates and concession agreements. "Profit oil can be based on cumulative production or internal rate of return, but in either case the state take grows with production volume" (Lyle 2007). Bhagavan reported that under the terms of most PSAs in Angola "exploration costs are to be recouped from the 'cost oil' component of production, while 'profit oil' is usually shared 70–30 percent, rising to 95.5 percent in line with cumulative production" (1986:29). Sonangol also reserves the right to place a price cap on the profit oil, which enables it to claim windfall profits.

9. During an interview, one oil executive suggested some indiscretions in the bidding process wherein Sonangol the concessionaire favored consortia including Sonangol P&P over competitors. The Angolan government is considering creating a national oil agency to separate Sonangol from regulatory activities and improve transparency of oil accounts (AOJ 2007a). Sonangol P&P is also expanding its influence abroad. Cobalt International Energy invited Sonangol's U.S. subsidiary (Sonangol Exploration and Production International) to take a 25% working interest in 11 deepwater concessions in the Gulf of Mexico (Upstream 2009).

10. The threshold of "commercial quantities" has as much to do with the amount of oil in the deposit as the cost of recovering it given the configuration of world oil supply and demand. License renewals and relinquishments can be politically charged. According to the Economist Intelligence Unit (2008), "In 2004 the government refused to renew Total's licence for shallow-water Block 3/80, and in 2005 it forced the company to relinquish unexplored acreages in its prolific ultra-deepwater Block 17, where the company has made some of the richest discoveries in the region, forcing it to rebid for the block and relinquish some of its Angolan assets in return." Relinquished portions of blocks are presented as new blocks at bidding rounds, where Sonangol requests additional signature and social bonuses. These blocks are named according to their block of origin and the year of the bidding round in which they were redistributed. For example, a list describing portions of blocks distributed to new operators in Angola's 2006 offshore bidding round included: 1/06 Tullow Oil, 5/06 Vaalco

Energy, 6/06 Petrobras, 15/06 ENI, 17/06 Total, and 18/06 Petrobras (De Sousa 2008).

11. In 2003, oil industry analysts estimated nearly 150 billion barrels of potential deepwater recoverable reserves worldwide of which only 50 to 60 billion had been discovered and 3 to 4 billion extracted (Moritis 2003). The most optimistic estimates on undiscovered reserves proved unrealistic once geologists realized the confinement of prolific zones to the submarine fans around river mouths. Deepwater developments accounted for approximately 30 percent of the planned production increase among the seven largest transnational oil corporations between 2002 and 2008 (Copin 2003:85).

12. Whereas continental erosion buries shallow water reservoirs to depths of 3000 meters below the mudline, the top of deepwater reservoirs may be only 1200 meters from the mudline (Gazaniol 2003:40). Despite the increased proximity of deepwater wells to the mudline, their depth below the ocean's surface complicates extraction.

13. By way of comparison, the industrial average "cost to find, develop, lift and transport a barrel of oil from the deep waters" in the Gulf of Mexico was $3 to $4 per barrel in 2002 when oil earned $25 per barrel (Banerjee 2002). Keep in mind that the aforementioned Gulf of Mexico production cost is an average—across all deepwater zones from 300 to 1500 meters—while the figure for Angola's production costs is at the deepest end of the deepwater spectrum. On the whole, Angola is a cheaper operating environment than the Gulf of Mexico—Hodges claims that "exploration success, along with the relatively low operating costs in Angola's offshore industry, meant that even the steep decline in world oil prices in 1998–99 did not dent the enthusiasm of the international oil companies" (2003:145). Given the rising price of oil between 2001 and 2008, however, oil corporations reprised development plans for fields previously considered too costly.

14. Henry L. Williams constructed Summerland's offshore oil wells accessed by piers in 1896. The "cost of a typical well including derrick, tubulars and drilling expense was $552.65" with prices of $1 per barrel and Williams's "net return on initial investment was $459 per year" until harsh storms in 1932 stalled operations and a tidal wave one decade later terminated them (*World Oil* 1980b).

15. BP towed the Greater Plutonio FPSO to Angola from Korea in 71 days (BP 2007b).

16. The *Instituto Nacional de Petróleo* (INP) was founded in 1983. It boards 360 mid-level and 164 professional-level students and offers training in petroleum drilling and production, geology and mines, general mechanics and maintenance, computer science, welding, heating and cooling, refinery operations and English (Tomás 2003). The INP is located in the hills above Sumbe, a town of 140,000 in Kwanza Sul province (WB 2005:138).

17. The text quoted refers to Article 54 of Angola's Law of Private Investment (Law No. 11/03 of May 2003).

18. The Sonangol Group comprises multiple joint-venture subsidiaries.

These include Petromar (a petroleum equipment construction and maintenance joint venture with Saipem founded in 1984), Sonatide and Sonasurf (operators and providers of boats for assistance to offshore oil operations developed in association with Tide Waters in 1997 and Surf SA in 1999, respectively), Sonawest (a seismic data processing and storage joint venture with WesternGeco and Schlumberger created in 1998), Sonamet/Sonastol (a provider of platforms, hydrocarbon transport systems, Remote Operated Vehicles [ROVs] and drilling assistance founded in 1998 as a joint venture with Stolt Offshore and World Assistance Petroleum Operations [WAPO] International), Sonamer (a drilling firm operating on the continental shelf created in 1998 as a joint venture with Pride Foramer), Sonaid (a supplier of drilling and production equipment with interests in environmental restoration activities developed in 2002 in conjunction with Foraid and Kitona), Sonangalp (a fuel and lubricant distributor formed in 1994 with Petrogal), Sonils (a logistical service provider created in 1995 with Intels), Sonasing (an oil treatment and storage firm working mainly with floating production, storage, and offloading units formed in 1999 with SBM Production), Sodispal and Sonadiets (food service enterprises developed in association with Catermar Angola and Dietsmann, respectively), Kwanda Ltd. (the firm operating the logistical and operations support base in Soyo founded in 1982 with DHL, ESAP, and Sangemetal Ltd.), Technip Angola (an engineering company formed with Technip Group in 1999), and Angoflex (a producer of umbilical tubing created with Technip Angola in 2002). Sonangol has also created subsidiaries in important markets (Sonangol USA) as well as key sectors such as civil aviation (Sonair), maritime transportation (Sonaship), and logistics (Sonalog). See the Sonangol Web site at www.sonangol.co.ao for more information.

19. Personal communication, November 21, 2004.

20. Between 1997 and 2000, the government spent more on scholarships for foreign universities than on higher education within Angola—a greater amount than any other country in Africa (Sogge 2006). Pitcher and Graham (2006) also note the Angolan government's interest in subsidizing gasoline for 4x4s rather than fixing the ubiquitous potholes in the streets. Gasoline and diesel subsidies help to fuel the imported Volkswagen Touaregs and Phaetons sold to Luanda's elites for $84,000 to $154,000, as well as upper-class families' generators humming through the city's regular power outages (*Folha 8* 2004c). Nevertheless, as chapters 4 and 5 will show, Angola's wider populace also depends on gasoline subsidies.

21. The original figure in LaFraniere is 12 cents per gallon. In 2001 only 4.3 percent of Angolans benefited from functional systems to pipe water into their homes and 3.8 percent more from backyard standpipes (de Carvalho 2004). Nearly 59 percent of Angolans secure their water needs from a spring, river, lake, or well, 25 percent carry water from a neighbor's faucet or a public fountain to their homes, and 5 percent rely on the mobile trucks that sell water to peri-urban families. A Christian Aid report entitled *Fuelling Poverty* recounted the Victorino family's struggle to raise $2.75 each morning to

buy the minimum 180 liters of water needed each day (Melby 2003). A 2006 article in the *New York Times* by LaFraniere reported a cholera outbreak that infected 43,000 Angolans and left 1600 dead in the span of little more than three months, noting that the poorest of Luandans suffered most from the epidemic. LaFraniere notes that part of President dos Santos' plan to combat cholera is "moving Luandans out of the most appalling slums" like Boa Vista, where the epidemic first hit, but fails to report the government's pursuit of any opportunity to reclaim Boa Vista's valuable real estate. See Justin Pearce's insights into the government's forced removal of Boa Vista residents in his 2005 book, *An Outbreak of Peace.*

22. The lottery's current name, *Raspidinha da Sorte*, roughly translates to "Lucky Little Scratcher," as each ticket features scratch-off panels. The lottery was originally called *Rapidinha da Sorte* in reference to the rapid gains of winners—but the word *rapidinha* also carries the lurid colloquial connotation of a brief sexual encounter.

23. Angolan currency is measured in kwanzas. Although the kwanza is relatively stable now, the government released several variations on the kwanza, which it successively devalued in an effort to check inflation throughout the 1990s. The treasury introduced the new kwanza in 1991, the readjusted kwanza in 1995, and the current kwanza in 1999. At the time of my fieldwork (2004–2005), US$1 typically bought between 75 and 85 kwanzas.

24. Dependency theory developed as a critique of modernization theory, which tended to accept that all countries follow a similar path to development. Frank (1966) argued instead that richer, more powerful nations "underdevelop" poorer regions. Cardoso and Faletto (1979) built on this proposition by demonstrating how primary commodity export patterns and an endless influx of cheap imports reinforced underdevelopment and perpetuated poverty.

25. State policies attempting to diversify the economy—for example, by "sowing the oil" and investing oil wealth back into the ailing agricultural sector—merely transform independent landlords into a type of *rentier* class dependent on oil subsidies (Coronil 1997). See also Auty 2004.

26. Shaxson (2007) actually suggests the direct distribution of oil revenues. He cites a figure of $400 each. The $1,000 figure is based on revenues of $16.807 billion and a population of 15.9 million (IMF 2007). Angola increased the national minimum wage from $50 to $100 per month on April 1, 2007.

27. I borrow the term "fiscal centralization" from Watts (2005).

28. Cabinda's governor, Aníbal Rocha, exemplified the single-minded allegiance to the MPLA encouraged by this system by proclaiming himself "a party militant" and pledging his service to the party whenever he is called or wherever he is appointed (*Chelapress* 2004b).

29. Wage figure based on personal communication with *sobas* in 2004 and 2005.

30. Sonangol had granted preferential stakes in Angola's offshore concessions to company affiliates of arms traders, such as Pierre Falcone, and private military allies of the MPLA during the war. In 1993, the French leader François

Mitterand received a plea for military assistance from President dos Santos, whose army was severely weakened by UNITA's post-election war campaign. The French president's son, Jean-Christophe Mitterand, allegedly skirted official channels for military assistance, passing the task to Pierre Falcone and his Russian partner Arcadi Gaydamak, who supplied $633 million in arms to Angola from 1993 to 1994 and $44 million more one to two years later through a Slovakian company called ZTS-Osos (GW 2002). Watchdogs suspect that dos Santos financed these arms purchases by negotiating oil-backed loans through Parisian Banque Paribas and distributing stakes in offshore oil Block 33 to Pro-Dev, Naptha, and Falcon Oil—three companies more experienced in arms deals and private security than oil exploitation (HRW 1999). Although not officially registered under his name, Falcone is said to manage Falcon Oil in league with António "Mosquito" M'Bakassi, the same accomplice who assisted President dos Santos in importing a shipment of Audi A6 cars earmarked for each of the President's allies in Parliament (Le Billon 2001a).

31. Aware of the upcoming licensing round for smaller onshore opportunities in the Congo and Kwanza Basins, the elites had formed domestic firms for oil exploration and service provision.

32. These are the "Old Creoles" with names and positions of power inherited from members of the Portuguese and Dutch upper class (Birmingham 1998). Birmingham called attention to this fact that when *Semanário Angolense* published the list of the fifty Angolans "who had each accumulated more than fifty million dollars of oil money it was noted that only one of the new tycoons had an African name" (2004:10). The remaining forty-nine had Portuguese and Dutch surnames. The Dutch occupied Luanda in 1641 when Spain took over Portugal. After the occupation diminished slave exports to Brazil, a Brazilian force led by Salvador Correia de Sá ousted the Dutch in 1648, but their descendants remain.

33. The Law on Crimes against the Economy is listed as law No. 6/99 of September 3, 1999.

34. Intermediaries included Abalone Investment Limited and Brenco Trading Limited, companies linked to arms dealer Pierre Falcone. Abalone Investment Limited also functioned as an intermediary in the 1996 to 2000 rescheduling of Angola's debt to Russia, but Global Witness reported that only $161 million of the total $774 million paid to the Abalone account in Geneva was transferred to another account labeled "Russian Finance Ministry" (GW 2004). The Prosecutor-General of Geneva froze the related Swiss accounts and later ruled that the transfers through Pierre Falcone's business appeared legal, but French courts issued a global warrant for his arrest in January 2004 on charges of illegal arms trading. Falcone's lawyer attempted to invoke diplomatic immunity to protect the arms dealer, citing his post at the Angolan Embassy in Paris as Angola's representative to UNESCO.

President dos Santos threatened to discontinue or delay the operations of French oil firm Total in Angola if French courts did not clear Falcone and his Abalone partner, Arcadi Gaydamak, of charges, for, as one Angolan diplomat claimed, "The judicial persecution of Pierre Falcone is the judicial persecution of the Angolan State" (Neto 2004, 2005). (It appears that France ultimately *did* recognize Falcone's diplomatic immunity, and Sonangol allowed Total to proceed with developments in Block 17 after 6 months of delays.) Nevertheless, Total's negotiations with Sonangol for the sale of the Luanda refinery were reportedly damaged by the Falcone scandal.

Total could not afford to lose its business in Angola. The corporation was still reeling from investigations in 2003 that found André Tarallo (a.k.a. "Mr. Africa") and other employees of the French oil firm Elf, since subsumed into Total, guilty of using corporate funds to bribe officials across Africa, including in Angola. In all, the businessmen diverted $346.8 million from state-owned Elf Aquitaine for use as bribes during contract negotiations from 1989 to 1993 with various countries in Africa, Asia, Europe, and South America (Deutsche Welle 2003).

35. Reasoning that Angola's production rates of 246.5 million over the course of 2004 with oil prices at $30 to $35 would generate over $8 billion in government revenues fails to consider the proportion of cost and profit oil claimed by transnational oil corporations. Costa's misunderstanding alarmed Angolans because he is expected to know how the oil sector functions not only as the country's minister of petroleum but also as a joint partner with Alberto de Sousa in Somoil, a newly founded private entity dedicated to petroleum exploration.

36. FESA's board boasts the most powerful business and political leaders in the country including Sonangol CEO Manuel Vicente, National Director of Fisheries Dr. Maria Antónia Nelumba, and Deputy Minister of Education Pinda Simão. Local subsidiaries of transnational oil corporations such as BP Amoco BV, British Petroleum Exploration LDA, Elf Exploration Angola, Texaco Panama Inc., and Norsk Hydro Angola held places on the foundation's General Assembly (Fundação Eduardo dos Santos 1999).

37. President dos Santos' former press secretary José Gonçalves Martins Patrício landed an executive position with BP (Silverstein 2004).

38. Minister of Energy and Water and former Minister of Petroleum José Maria Botelho de Vasconcelos worked his way up through the ranks of Chevron, Total, Shell, and Sonangol before dos Santos appointed him as Minister of Petroleum. Likewise, Minister Joaquim da Costa David first worked for a subsidiary of Petrofina, Texaco, and Sonangol before President dos Santos appointed him as Minister of Finance and later Minister of Industry. Many executives stay in the oil industry rather than return to the government, for, as one official said, "With the companies, you can get a Mercedes right away if you want one. You will not wait until the government gives you an Audi!" (Personal communication, July 2003).

39. Le Billon asserts that "even the innocuous 'wining and dining' of government officials by companies so often characterising contract negotiations bears the risk of promoting a 'lifestyle' that local officials can later on sustain only through corruption" (Le Billon 2001a).

40. A 1996 "financial 'phantom' scandal" revealed government ministry payrolls included some 100,000 "phantom workers" in the civil service due to shifty accountants inserting false personalities or failing to erase the names of deceased employees (UPASC 1997a).

41. Despite recognizing ancestral ties to the Kongo kingdom, Cabindan nationalists drew linguistic boundaries between Kikongo and the local Ibinda language and ethnically dissociated themselves from the Bakongo. The Basolongo also acknowledged their ties to the Bakongo, but many recalled Soyo's autonomous coastal trading history and threw their support to the local MNA liberation front rather than Holden Roberto's FNLA.

42. The FNLA alienated Bakongo Catholics who opposed the appointment of a Protestant king to the Kongo throne, while the MPLA had many Catholic supporters but shunned the Church for its association with the Portuguese (Kapuściński 2001:137; Stockwell 1978:64–65).

43. The effects of a wave of Portuguese immigrants to Angola's urban centers during the first half of the 20th century shifted relations in Benguela and Luanda. The mostly male contingent of settlers had intermarried with African women and produced mixed-race offspring called *mestiços*. By the middle of the century, these *mestiços* had earned positions in the colonial bureaucracy, thus displacing members of the "Old Creole" elite whose forefathers had earned influence through the slave trade (Birmingham 1998). The "Old Creoles" recovered their high status in the armed forces, but they continued to reserve animosity for *mestiços*. Likewise, stark disparities between the *assimilados* and the class of *indígenas* angered the latter, who comprised ninety percent of the Angolan population and were subjected to colonial forced labor requirements and suffered violent repression. Under the Portuguese colonial assimilation policy, nonwhite Angolans who espoused Portuguese cultural values; could read, write, and speak Portuguese; demonstrated proper use of flatware at mealtimes and used a bed at night; and were able to afford the administrative fees could be granted a form of honorary whiteness. Black Angolans could obtain this *assimilado* status, but most *assimilados* were *mestiços*. Although the economic disparities between white employers and their African workers ranged between tenfold to one-hundredfold, bosses rarely had more education than the employees they paid seventy-five cents a day (Bender 1980:226). Twenty-five percent of Angola's privileged white population in 1950 was illiterate (de Figueiredo 1961:127).

44. Discrimination also existed between the *assimilados* schooled in the Belgian Congo and those educated in Lisbon (Messiant 2006:419).

45. Neto appealed to Fidel Castro for support and met with a group of Cubans on August 11, 1975, to discuss a plan "to portray the situation in Angola as a crucial struggle between the two systems—Imperialism and Socialism—in order to receive the assistance of the entire socialist camp" by claiming that "the FNLA and UNITA represent reaction and world imperialism and the Portuguese reactionaries, and the MPLA represents the progressive and nationalist forces" (Argíelles 1975). The Cuban-MPLA partnership is commonly attributed

to a shared faith in Marxist principles. Castro indoctrinated his "internationalist" recruits to believe that a shared set of socialist ideals bound them to assist their Angolan brothers, but some Cubans questioned the depth of the MPLA's ideological commitment. A high-ranking officer in the Cuban army recalled his frustration when he left his family and country in 1976 to serve the MPLA, only to find indifferent government officials like the minister of finance jetting off to Portugal for a month-long vacation (personal communication, February 2006). He claimed some MPLA leaders paid more attention to the status reports of their Mercedes imports than to key battles. Meanwhile, soldiers on the ground encountered hordes of starving children who begged for a portion of their monthly rations.

On battlegrounds ranging from verdant forests to thorny scrubland, Cuban soldiers shared the misery of their MPLA counterparts: they suffered insect stings and snakebites, dodged bullets and shells, tolerated dirty days without baths, endured hungry nights with no food, and many lost their lives. The British journalist Xan Smiley wrote: "There is a steady stream of coffins returning to Havana. It must be a miserable life for Castro's young conscripts, fighting a remote African war whose international (let alone tribal) ramifications they cannot understand" (1983).

Cuban support gave the MPLA a clear military advantage. As of September 1976, the Cuban-backed MPLA controlled twelve of Angola's sixteen provinces, principally those bordering the Atlantic coast stretching from Namibe to Cabinda (Risquet Valdés 2005). The borrowed Cuban soldiers and their 122mm rockets contributed to staggering MPLA successes against the FNLA in northern Angola (Stockwell 1978:215). Kapuściński claims that the Cuban presence demoralized the opposition—that they turned and ran at sight of Cuban uniforms (2001a:120). Some scholars even say that the MPLA capitalized on the fears of its enemies by developing a strategy wherein Cuban troops led the advance and challenged the opposition while MPLA units remained to stabilize towns after the fighting (Watson 1977:76).

46. Oil revenues underwrote the MPLA's war effort in addition to Soviet financial and Cuban military support. When the market for cash crops collapsed under the weight of war and rural people turned to subsistence farming, the MPLA increasingly used oil revenues to finance food imports in the capital.

47. Covertly supported by the Soviet Union, Alves and his conspirators killed several powerful MPLA mestiços, among them Minister of Finance Saydi Mingas. Alves' racialized protest even involved "a number of pro-Soviet whites" (Smiley 1983). MPLA officials questioned whether Soviet and Cuban ambassadors with whom Alves had maintained close contact had collaborated in the coup attempt and fired them on suspicion of the fact that they had not forewarned the Luandan government (Marcum 1986:19).

48. The MPLA abandoned the slogan Poder Popular (People Power) following the 1977 coup attempt and shut down most of its populist action committees and activist groups.

49. Upon receiving long-awaited authorization from the Ford administration, Gulf Oil disbursed $125 million in tax and royalty payments owed to Angola on March 9, 1976, renegotiated its contract with the government, and recommenced operations in Cabinda the following month (Stockwell 1978:241; Gleijeses 2002:343; Bignell 1977:1747). Although dos Santos maintained relations with the Soviet Union, he opened Angola to Western capital by negotiating concession agreements to exploit Angola's natural resources including oil, iron ore, and shrimp; hired the American firm Arthur D. Little as a government-contracted consultant on financial issues; and wrangled $200 million in financing for Sonangol through American private banks (Marcum 1986:22).

50. This was due, in part, to a decline in output from some of Cabinda's older oilfields (Bhagavan 1986:29).

51. Bhagavan notes that in 1983 one kilogram of fish at a government shop might cost 100 kwanzas (roughly $3.33), in contrast to 500 kwanzas ($16.66) on the informal market (1986:62).

52. In 1983, the official exchange rate was US$1 = 30 kwanzas, while the informal rate was US$1 = 1,000 kwanzas (Bhagavan 1986:62). Smiley proposes a less extreme, but still desperate, scenario of an informal to formal exchange rate ratio of fifteen to one and states that the "price of a cabbage of a couple of eggs sometimes exceeds the daily wage" (1983). Gunn claimed that "five small and rather anemic tomatoes" on the *candonga* cost $30 given official currency exchange rates (1987:68).

53. Boosted oil production would generate export revenues. The MPLA earmarked 50 percent of these revenues for defense, 30 percent for imports of essential foodstuffs and consumer goods (with distributional priority for the armed forces), and the remaining 20 percent for servicing war-weighted debts (Bhagavan 1986:85).

54. Seeking to consolidate his power in the military, dos Santos shrewdly distanced himself from pro-Soviet elements, including his Russian wife, and narrowed the MPLA by disavowing the *mestiço* forefathers who had cultivated the party's "cosmopolitan and anti-tribalist image" (Smiley 1983). By 1987, dos Santos had delivered the government into the hands of a dozen "Old Creole" families from the powerful colonial military caste and had ostracized the idealistic MPLA contingent that had led the country to independence.

55. The late intervention of the World Bank and the IMF in Angola was unusual for a developing country with mineral wealth. International financial institutions often back the development of extractive sectors from the start, but Soviet support had allowed Angolan leaders to delay joining the World Bank.

56. The World Bank and IMF, formed through the Bretton Woods agreements in 1945, originated in an effort to finance both postwar reconstruction in Europe and development around the world. The World Bank comprises the International Bank for Reconstruction and Development (IBRD), International Finance Corporation (IFC), International Development Association (IDA), Multilateral Investment Guarantee Agency (MIGA), and International Centre

for Settlement of Investment Disputes (ICSID). The World Bank and IMF prescribe a similar set of conditionalities in nearly every country.

57. Crude oil, the unprocessed petroleum extracted from underground fields, is classified by sulfur content into the categories of sweet (less than 0.5 percent sulfur) and sour (at least 2.5 percent sulfur). Sweet crude is easier to refine and earns higher prices on the world market, yet the specific gravity of the oil also determines its commercial value. The American Petroleum Institute created the API gravity measure to divide crude oil into three categories: light (greater than 31.1° API), medium (between 31.1° and 22.3° API), and heavy (between 22.3° and 10° API). Angola's top six grades of oil are as follows: Cabinda (32.5° API), Girassol (31–32° API), Kuito (19° API), Nemba (38.7° API), Palanca (38.6° API) and Soyo (39.5° API). All of these are considered sweet except Kuito (0.68 percent sulfur). The sweetest crudes typically sell at a premium: "Palanca grade oil sells at a premium in relation to Brent, but Cabinda 32° API normally sells between $0.75–$1.50 lower, depending on market fluctuations" (Aguilar 2001:40). For more information in a global comparative context, see *The Crude Oils and Their Key Characteristics*, a report published online by the Energy Intelligence Group and available at www.piwpubs.com.

58. I am grateful to Carlos Leite for pointing out this correlation.

59. The International Monetary Fund (IMF) required that Angola submit to a Staff Monitored Program (SMP) before delineating a lending package in order to gauge the Angolan government's commitment to the IMF's loan conditionalities (a series of economic reforms usually involving currency stabilization, privatization of state industries, and slashing government expenditures). The team of IMF economists tasked with monitoring Angola's progress on the SMP refused to approve a loan package for Angola, in part, because of the government's reticence to comply with transparency standards.

60. Some 123 legally recognized political parties exist in Angola (CR 2004). The following parties also won National Assembly seats in 1992: Partido Renovador Social (PRS) with six seats, Frente Nacional para a Libertação de Angola (FNLA) with five seats, Partido Liberal Democrático (PLD) with three seats, Partido Democrático para Progresso—Aliança Nacional Angolano (PDP-ANA) with one seat, Partido Renovador Democrático (PRD) with one seat, Partido da Aliança da Juventude, Operários e Campesinos de Angola (PAJOCA) with one seat, Aliança Democrática de Angola (AD) with one seat, Fórum Democrático Angolano (FDA) with one seat, Partido Social-Democrata (PSD) with one seat, and Partido Nacional Democrático Angolano (PNDA) with one seat.

61. Foreign Investment Law No. 15 of Sept 23, 1994, and Decree 12 of May 5, 1995.

62. The rising price of oil prior to the global financial crisis of late 2008 has been attributed to four factors: the expansion of the American, European, and Southeast Asian economies; the failed liberalization of energy, which under Enron spurred a crisis in California; the implementation of environmental standards, which led to a shortage of tankers; and Saudi Arabia's inability to

increase short-term production at that time (Aguilar 2001:23). Poor Angolans struggled to feed their families as market prices shifted to reflect the rising price of crude. Prices of basic agricultural staples such as manioc, bananas, beans, corn, sweet potatoes, and peanuts increased 100–500 percent between 2000 and 2002 alone (GoA 2003a).

63. Commercial banks offered an alternative to the conditionalities imposed by the IMF: oil-backed private loans. These loans, accounting for one-third of Angola's total external debt, effectively mortgaged the country's future oil production at high interest rates while enabling an opaque and exclusionary system (Gary & Karl 2003:33).

64. Many of the same NGOs that praised the IMF's push for transparency and accountability in Angola had long demanded more transparency and accountability from the IMF and World Bank themselves. Recognizing the degenerative effects of extractive industries on the economic and political strength of developing countries, these watchdogs critiqued the Bretton Woods institutions for financing oil, gas, and mining projects. The Africa Initiative on Mining, Environment and Society criticized the World Bank and IMF for their liberalization policy prescriptions, which "pry open the extractive sector for the benefit of transnational corporations at the expense of national economies, workers, local communities, the poor and vulnerable groups on the continent" (AIMES 2004). The financial institutions responded by initiating the Extractive Industries Review (EIR) in 2000 under the leadership of Dr. Emil Salim, an Indonesian coal tycoon and former Environmental Minister in the Suharto administration. The participants agreed that responsible oil and gas development could help to combat poverty, but they also concluded that the World Bank must fight global climate change by supporting renewable energy alternatives and phasing out funding for fossil fuels by 2008 (Beattie 2004).

Sir Mark Moody-Stuart, chairman of mining giant Anglo-American and former chairman of Shell Oil, rebuffed the EIR's conclusions and criticized Salim. "I consider the job of an adviser is to give advice which might be adopted. Giving extreme advice which will be rejected is not doing your job," he said (Beattie 2004). NGO leaders and human rights advocates, however, celebrated the EIR's results. Six Nobel laureates sent a letter to World Bank President James Wolfensohn in February 2004, encouraging him to accept the EIR's recommendations and to cease funding extraction of fossil fuels. Wolfensohn, presumably recognizing that investments in extractive industries comprised the most lucrative set of loans in the International Finance Corporation's portfolio, rejected the recommendations of the Nobel laureates and the EIR (Gary & Karl 2003:15). As an alternative, he promoted the use of transparency measures as social safeguards to improve extractive lending. Under this rationale, the International Finance Corporation justified its involvement in the Baku-Tbilisi-Ceyhan pipeline running from the Caspian Sea through Georgia to the Mediterranean.

65. War had displaced 1.3 million Angolans—10 percent of the population—by the end of 1998 (Pike 2003). Reductions in social spending further

complicated their lives. For example, from 1991 to 1998 government contributions to the health sector plunged from 8 percent to 2.8 percent of total spending despite rising oil revenues (Swarns 2000). The government counted on the compassion of international humanitarian organizations to provide the social services the populace so desperately needed. Millions of dollars funneled through international NGOs, making Angola's humanitarian sector one of the largest employers in the country by 1995 (CR 2004).

66. U.S. President George W. Bush refused to encourage transparency and may have even privately assured dos Santos during talks in November 2003 that he would try to get the IMF to ease reporting requirements (Dynes 2003a).

67. Eximbank's first loan was intended to finance the rebuilding of the Benguela railway from the Zambian border to the port of Lobito (*Angola Peace Monitor* 2004). Eximbank offered the second loan at the low interest rate of 1.7 percent over 17 years and later extended and refinanced the loan with interest lowered to 0.25 percent (Corkin 2007). Other lenders to Angola include but are not limited to Portugal, Brazil, Spain, and India. See Campos and Vines (2008) for an excellent overview of China-Angola relations, including concerns about the opaque management of Chinese credit.

68. The Angolan government agreed to participate in Article IV consultations and technical assistance, but dismissed all formal agreements with the IMF and any associated conditionalities.

CHAPTER 3

1. In their analysis of environmental violence, Peluso and Watts emphasize the "ways in which specific environments, environmental processes, and webs of social relations are central parts of the ways violence is expressed and made expressive" (2001: 25).

2. Ten years after the anniversary of his brother Ken's death, Owens Wiwa said, "As long as oil provides 90 percent of the foreign exchange, there will continue to be injustice and violence in the Niger Delta. Oil needs to be removed from the equation" (Wiwa 2005).

3. Hodges even draws a link between Cabinda's shape and endemic violence by describing the Cabindan territory as "pistol-shaped" (2001).

4. The struggles over oil in Nigeria have spurred ethnic conflicts over entitlements to revenues and generated "economies of violence" where identity plays a key role in negotiating the chaotic forms of governance exerted through the spaces of chieftainship, indigeneity, and the nation-state (Watts 1999, 2004).

5. The Portuguese presented claims to contemporary Cabinda, citing the treaties of Chinfuma of September 29, 1883, and Chicamba of December 26, 1884. Still, authorities at the Berlin Conference denied formal acknowledgement of Portugal's exclusive claim on the Cabinda territory, granting only recognition for the lands south of the Congo River. The Portuguese eagerly negotiated the Simulambuco treaty to solidify their claims in Cabinda and the

local rulers accepted Portugal's offer for protection from would-be colonizers England and France.

6. Martin states, "The arrangement was finally sealed only after the Portuguese agreed to pay substantial monthly pensions to the principal signatories of the treaty" (1977:54).

7. See Lelo-Tubi 1980. Luemba (2002) states that previously, under the 1933 constitution, Portugal had recognized Cabinda and Angola as two distinct overseas territories *(territórios ultramarinos)*.

8. The União Social dos Maiombes de Luali and the Comunidade Cabindense also formed around this time, but their support was limited to a small number of traditional leaders (Wheeler and Pélissier 171:168). Portuguese forces reacted severely to a 1960 protest for independence in Cabinda city: MLEC reported that police killed 5,000 demonstrators (Marcum 1969:173).

9. Mayombe shared a limited history with the remainder of Cabinda. Although traders from the coastal kingdoms once exchanged sea salt and dried, salted fish for forest products and slaves from the interior, Ngoyo monarchs never ruled the Mayombe region (Franque 1940:141–143).

10. Wheeler and Pélissier confirm, "Both intellectually and materially they were better treated by the Portuguese than their brother Bakongo" (1971:168).

11. The newly formed Organization of African Unity confirmed admitted Cabinda, apart from Angola, as the 39th African colony slated for decolonization in 1964. Angola was registered as the 35th African colony on OAU lists (Tati 2002).

12. Portuguese authorities hired the Cabindan Alexandre Taty, formerly aligned with the FNLA and the Minister of Armaments to the Governo Revolucionário de Angola no Exílio (GRAE), both to encourage Cabindan refugees in the Congos to return to the enclave and to bribe anticolonial FNLA and MPLA soldiers with salaries, food, and clothing if they agreed to defect (Marcum 1978:176). Although FLEC's guerrillas did little more than harass the soldiers, the MPLA and FNLA both abandoned the Cabindan front in 1966: the MPLA redirected most of its troops to "Neto's big obsession" in the Dembos region or its new front in Zambia while the FNLA retreated to its bases in Kinshasa and battlegrounds south of the Congo River (Gleijeses 2002:178; Ignatyev 1977:51).

13. The MPLA's military capacity was inferior to the FNLA prior to receiving training and troops from Cuba. MPLA forces had tried to open a battlefront against colonial forces in the forested Dembos and Nambuangongo, but twenty out of twenty-one men died at the hands of rival anti-colonialists of the FNLA during such an attempt in late 1961; a subsequent mission in early 1963 was equally dismal, leaving all thirty soldiers dead (Gleijeses 2002:175). Gleijeses writes that Holden Roberto had ordered FNLA troops to "destroy any MPLA column entering Angola" (2002:175). On January 20, 1963, a group of fifty-six MPLA soldiers embarked on their first mission in Cabinda: they attacked the Portuguese post at Massabi killing nineteen of its guardians before succumbing to the colonial forces (Marcum 1978:40–41).

14. With the loss of allies in Leopoldville after Mobutu's rise to power, the MPLA was fortunate to find support from the rising Massemba-Debat regime in Brazzaville, who authorized the first arms delivery to the MPLA's base at Dolisie in July 1964 (Guimarães 2001:73). Guimarães suggests it is no coincidence that the MPLA began a shift toward a Marxist line at this time. Roughly 300 MPLA soldiers, some of whom had trained with Algerian rebels at FLN bases in Ghana and Morocco, were stationed at the camp (Gleijeses 2002:82; Guimarães 2001:60). Savimbi's 1964 assessment was less rosy, claiming that only thirty men occupied the base and "there was no real fighting going on," just scattered raids of five or ten men entering Cabinda at a time (Guimarães 2001:78). The MPLA hoped to increase the severity of its attacks with the import of Cuban soldiers to the Cabinda front. Six Cuban soldiers arrived in May 1965, and by December around forty Cubans were training the MPLA forces for "Operation Monkey" (Operação Macaco) (Gleijeses 2002:175).

15. Operação Macaco was the first joint Cuban-MPLA mission and it failed miserably. On December 25, a team of one hundred MPLA guerrillas with forty Cuban soldiers intending to attack the Sanga Planicie fort in northeastern Cabinda panicked, some leaving their artillery behind, when Portuguese forces ambushed them not far from their target (Gleijeses 2002:177). The operation's failure and the disdain of the Cabindan populace who resented the MPLA's intervention in their territory diminished the soldiers' enthusiasm for the Cabinda front. In a letter to the head of Cuban intelligence, Manuel Piñeiro, military commander Rolando Kindelán noted the Cabindans' "indifference, even hostility, to the nationalist project' and its effect on the MPLA guerrillas who "don't want to do anything because they don't consider Cabinda their own country" (quoted in Gleijeses 2002:177–178).

Pepetela addressed the self-doubt and resentment for Cabindans among the MPLA's soldiers stationed in Cabinda in his book *Mayombe*. In the story, one of the characters asks: "Why is the war progressing in other Regions and always falling back here? Because we have not been up to the mark, we, the Movement. The blame is put on the people, for treachery. An easy excuse! Are the people here treacherous or are we incompetent? Or both?" (1987:7).

16. As Martin (1977) recognized, Cabinda has historically maintained a sizeable emigrant and exiled population, which has exerted influence on Cabindan politics. Thousands of Cabindan refugees had scattered to the neighboring Congos to escape the fighting, but a portion came home after the announcement (Marcum 1968:174;1978:205). Cabinda Gulf Oil sent ripples through the starved local economy, spending $20 million for goods and services in Angola and $76,000 on its local payroll in 1972 (Marcum 1972:12).

17. FLEC laid the groundwork for future collaborative options with governments in Brazzaville and Kinshasa by setting up a revolutionary committee in Pointe Noire and a government in exile in Tshela. Marcum notes that these dual authorities might have been envisioned as the foundation of federative alliances with the Republic of Congo or Zaire (Marcum 1978:205).

18. Gulf Oil loaded the first tanker of Cabindan oil on November 26, 1968,

and recorded a total of 1,351,293 barrels produced by the year's end (Castelo Branco and Schaefer 1969:1728–1736). By October 1971, Angola had become the fourth largest oil producer in Africa, with Cabindan fields pumping out 150,000 barrels per day (Marcum 1972:12).

19. Figure from Laidi cited in Guimarães (2001:234). By 1973, oil had over-taken coffee as the source of the greatest proportion of export earnings, at pro-duction rates of 140,000 barrels per day (Hodges 2003). The United Church of Christ condemned Gulf Oil's role in bolstering Portuguese forces against the liberation fronts and the Netherlands boycotted Angolan petroleum and coffee in a show of solidarity with the anti-colonial movements (Marcum 1972:12; 1978:232). Marcum criticized the oil company's response to charges that its operations were detrimental to people living under Portuguese rule and their aspirations for liberty: "The Gulf Corporation nonetheless maintained that an investment that was 'transforming [the] economic outlook in Angola' repre-sented a 'politically neutral' act. Gulf asserted that—presumably regardless of the political system—people 'always profit' from the extraction of their oil. 'Invariably,' it argued, 'because a foreign company is doing business in a devel-oping nation, the citizens of that nation are better off than before.' Of course, the foreign activities of multi-national corporations, with enormous capital resources and technical expertise such as Gulf has, have inevitable political consequences—not always salutary. They often deal with governments either too weak, corrupt, repressive or unrepresentative to be able or willing to see to it that all or most of their citizenry do indeed 'profit' from the exploitation of their country's wealth" (1972:12).

American-based Gulf Oil remained unflinchingly rooted in Cabinda. The U.S. government, determined not to lose the Air Force base in the Azores, continued to support Portugal and followed President Kennedy's 1969 decision not to support Angola's liberation movements. Watson contends that the U.S. policy toward Angola up to April 25, 1974, relied on a 1969 review (NSSM 39) "which assessed the nationalist groups as not 'realistic or supportable' and questioned 'the depth and permanence of black resolve'" (1977:66).

20. As president of the Portuguese Republic, General Spínola declared a ceasefire between Portuguese and the liberation armies in Angola and began plans for decolonization of the overseas territories under Decree 203, which stated, "the populations of the *Ultramar* should decide their future with respect to the principles of self-determination."

21. The proposed arrangement would last for twenty years, during which all Portuguese and transnational corporations operating under Portuguese protection at the time of independence would receive continued or expanded rights to exploit natural resources in the Zaire-Angola-Cabinda configuration (Ignatyev 1977:105). Marcum claims that Spínola intended to set up a provi-sional government "with twelve ministers: two each from the FNLA, UNITA and MPLA and six from various ethnic and white movements" wherein the two "MPLA ministers were to be Daniel Chipenda and Joaquim Pinto de Andrade" and Neto's faction would be excluded (Marcum 1978:251).

22. According to Harsch and Thomas, Admiral Rosa Coutinho considered Neto the only valid leader of the MPLA, the movement he viewed as "more progressive" than the FNLA and UNITA (1976:59).

23. According to Luemba (2008), FLEC's military wing was composed of two groups. The first, Jeunesse, was a group of young soldiers trained in the Republic of Congo (Brazzaville). The second, the Tropas Especiais, was a Special Forces unit of Cabindan guerrilla fighters who had originally fought for the MPLA and FNLA but became disillusioned in addition to militants the Portuguese had co-opted to combat MPLA forces in Cabinda between 1965 and 1974.

24. Luemba (2008) notes that the statement on Cabinda was not spontaneously conceived at the Alvor Accords, but was a pre-fabricated product of negotiations between UNITA, MPLA, and FNLA leaders from a meeting the preceding week in Mombasa, Kenya.

25. Watson (1977:13) states the terms of the Alvor Accord as: "a) A transitional government consisting of a Council of Ministers, a National Defence Council, and a Presidential Council, was to be established immediately; b) Representation on these councils was to be shared among the nationalist parties and the Portuguese; c) Each Ministry held by one of the nationalist groups would have two Secretaries of State, one from each of the other groups. Each ministry held by a Portuguese would have three Secretaries of State; d) A National Army of 26,000 Portuguese troops and 8,000 from each party would be responsible for security during the transitional phase; and e) Elections to a constituent assembly would be held no later than the end of October 1975." Since the Alvor Accords only recognized the MPLA, FNLA, and UNITA as participants in the legislative elections, "the many white, Bakongo, Cabindan, and other organized or nascent political groups would have to aggregate within or about one of the three" (Marcum 1978:255–256).

26. Omar Bongo, the President of Gabon, "expressed his—and it was widely assumed, French—support for the proposition that oil-rich Cabinda constituted a 'separate entity'" (Marcum 1978:254). Tati (2002) notes that Uganda, Zaire, and Congo also supported FLEC's call for Cabindan independence. Congo's President Ngouabi even delayed a shipment of Soviet arms to MPLA forces in August 1975 "hoping FLEC might use the time to revitalize itself" (Marcum 1978:438).

27. FLEC guerrillas, collaborating with Mobutu's CIA-armed Zairean soldiers and a dozen French mercenaries with ties to Elf, confronted the MPLA forces in November 1975. A force of 1,000 MPLA and 232 Cuban soldiers repelled the attack (Stockwell 1978:164; Gleijeses 2002:312). Gleijeses claims that the French mercenaries were "sent by the notorious Bob Denard, who had been a leader of the CIA's 'White Giants' in Zaire, to give the FLEC some backbone" (2002:312). Harsch and Thomas contend that "several FLEC leaders were thought to have close contacts with the French oil company ELF" and that, perhaps in relation "Jacques Foccart, a key French intelligence figure in Africa for years, was reportedly supplying arms and money—and had promised mercenaries" to FLEC (1976:108).

28. Professor Douglas Wheeler, a respected scholar of Angolan history, wrote in a November 30, 2005, email to the H-LUSO-AFRICA listserv that he would suggest the term "internationalized civil war" to describe the post-1975 conflicts in Angola and Mozambique.

29. When a mercenary scandal undermined Holden Roberto's credibility, the U.S. transferred its anti-communist support to UNITA by pledging Savimbi $1 million in military and financial aid (Stockwell 1978:234–235). Following successive defeats, the FNLA had realized that its Zairean allies could not stand up to the MPLA's Cuban counterparts. Roberto decided to hire mercenaries, but even they would fail the FNLA. Attractive offers drew poor and unemployed young men out of Europe to fight in the company of the anti-communist FNLA, but this rag-tag bunch "hired from pubs" were soon "being cut to pieces by Cuban forces" (Gleijeses 2002:339). The FNLA's call to arms also attracted a dishonorably discharged ex-paratrooper from Leeds by the name of Costas Georgiou. Adopting the alias Colonel Callan, he took up the post of field general for Holden Roberto (Stockwell 1978:226). Increasingly frustrated with the FNLA's defeated and retreating position, Georgiou stripped and gunned down fourteen men from his own unit in retribution for their mistaken identification and subsequent attack on an allied defense post. In February 1976, MPLA troops captured Georgiou and arrested him along with a band of mercenaries composed of nine Britons, two Americans, and one Argentine. The MPLA used their capture and trial to criticize the intervention of mercenaries in Angola, juxtaposing condemnations of Georgiou's soulless pursuit of monetary gain with praise for the ideologically driven Cuban and MPLA soldiers. An interview published by Cuba's Friedrich Engels Press for Propaganda revealed that Georgiou received £150 per week from the FNLA; but the mercenary described himself as 'apolitical' and admitted that if the MPLA had offered him double he would have changed sides (Valdes Vivo 1976). The tribunal in Luanda sentenced Georgiou and two of the other mercenaries to death by firing squad and the remainder to prison terms.

30. "Oil production was not a stated target" for UNITA *(World Oil* 1993: 104). Some Cabindans attribute the explosion to poor pipeline maintenance, while others blame UNITA. More than two decades later, survivors of the blast are seeking compensation for their losses (personal communication with Francisco Luemba, December 2008).

31. Fidel Castro seized the opportunity to comment on the tragic irony of the situation: "So what were they going to do, the associates of the United States, Reagan's friends, the CIA's friends? They were going to destroy the oil installation in Cabinda, the primary source of Angola's revenue. The curious thing about this, the amazing thing, which points to the hypocrisy of both South Africa and the U.S. Government, is the fact that this installation is owned by a U.S. transnational company, the Gulf Oil Company. The things that the U.S. Government does! The things that the CIA does! The things that the fascist South African Government does! In order to attack Angola and affect its economy, they wanted to blow up the oil installation of a U.S.

company. It would be good if newsmen would comment on the meaning of these things" (Castro 1985).

32. The Reagan administration had once lauded Chevron's contribution to its policy of constructive engagement with communist governments, yet by early 1986 officials counseled Chevron to mind national security interests in its business dealings and abide by new U.S. economic policy discouraging support of "Angola's ability to earn foreign currency and thus fund its war against UNITA until the government of Angola demonstrates clear intent to reach a negotiated settlement on Namibian independence and in that context Cuban troop withdrawal" (Gunn 1987:61). The journalist Karl Maier visited Malongo in 1986 and spoke with Chevron's "American workers, most of them from Louisiana and Texas, who in their long southern drawls repeatedly accused Ronald Reagan for being 'full of shit' for failing to open full diplomatic relations with the MPLA government" (1996:63).

The French oil corporation Elf (now part of Total) coveted Chevron's holdings, but Chevron was reluctant to abandon its interests in Cabinda and the highly favorable production terms it had negotiated with the MPLA in the late 1970s (Gunn 1987:64). Gunn points out that, ironically, if Chevron had pulled out, the MPLA-led government would likely have been able to increase its share of revenues by negotiating a new contract with another firm (ibid.).

33. Other oil corporations including Conoco, Petrofina, Texaco, Elf Aquitaine, British Petroleum, Braspetro, Total, Cities Services, Mitsubishi, and Marathon held stakes in Angola's offshore blocks; investment by Sonangol and foreign firms would increase by 46 percent that year (Gunn 1987:55).

34. With the collapse of the Soviet Union and the independence of Namibia, socialist allies abandoned the MPLA, while U.S. and South African aid to UNITA plummeted.

35. The few hundred U.N. peacekeepers in country proved quickly overwhelmed by nearly 150,000 armed Angolans taking to violence on the streets of Luanda (MacQueen 1997:226). Although the Bicesse Accords had weakened UNITA forces by ordering the integration of some regiments into the Angolan Armed Forces (FAA) under the direction of the recently elected government, Savimbi had strategically retained his best fighters. The MPLA-led government's newly formed Rapid Intervention Police (PIR), popularly known as the "Ninjas," reacted to the UNITA uprising with crushing force, igniting the second phase of the Angolan conflict.

The FAA and police teams exploited ethnic associations with opposition parties during Luanda's 'Three Day War' from October 30 to November 1, 1992, which claimed the lives of some 10,000 Ovimbundu and Bakongo (CR 2004). The perpetrators actively targeted Bakongo not only for their affiliation with UNITA as with the Ovimbundu, but also for their ethnic ties to the Zairean population, whom they saw as active supporters of UNITA. Resentment peaked again on January 22, 1993, with the "Bloody Friday" massacre of twenty to sixty Bakongo by armed civilians and the wounding and looting of dozens more in Luanda's open-air markets in response to government reports that

Zairean mercenaries had assisted UNITA in its attack on Soyo (AI 1996b). The violent months following the elections through the close of 1993 left 100,000 dead in what Angolans called the 'war of the cities' (Pitsch et al. 2002).

36. Commenting on a parallel resource war, Justin Pearce notes that the wartime practice of FAA generals appropriating lands seized from UNITA as personal property and rendering a cut of their earnings to Luanda "echoed the colonial past" when a system of "primitive extraction" allowed colonial officials "to grab what they wanted from the earth or from the people of the conquered territory, provided that they rendered a predetermined tax to the Portuguese crown each year" (2005:155). Bosom buddies of the president and partners in the Simportex arms trading firm—General "Kopelipa," Angolan Intelligence Chief Fernando Miala, Pierre Falcone, and António "Mosquito" M'Bakassi—profited handsomely from the wartime weapons boom; Sonangol even rewarded Falcone and M'Bakassi with stakes in ultra-deepwater concessions (GW 1999). Global Witness suggests that dos Santos himself even profited by purchasing the CADA (Companhia Angolana de Distribuição Alimentar) firm as the resumption of war in 1998 necessitated a $720 million, five-year contract for feeding the government troops (ibid.).

37. I owe thanks to an anonymous reader for pointing this out.

38. This runs counter to scholars' contentions that offshore oil production is insulated from violence (see Hodges 2001, 2004; Le Billon 2001a). Elf understood the threat to its operations and reportedly paid off UNITA to protect its installations in Soyo. Residents suspected Elf's collusion with Savimbi when UNITA spared the French corporation's property in early attacks. One recalled, "There was some suspicion of Elf—that they were befriending UNITA." Loïk Le Floch Prigent, Elf Aquitaine's CEO from 1989 to 1993, penned a memoir during his Angolagate prison term in which he described his role as "to keep the equilibrium between Savimbi and dos Santos in Angola, in order to prevent either from winning" and later admitted: "Elf's problem in Angola was that some of the company's installations in the country are located in regions that regularly change hands. We therefore negotiated with Savimbi to protect our materials and personnel. In the end, we gave money to him" (Lallemand 2002). Drawing on this thread, Global Witness reported that Angola's "spectacular growth of cooperation with France in the area of oil" in the early nineties may be attributed to French desistance from duplicitous dealings and illicit assistance to the MPLA (GW 2002).

39. This is an ironic twist, given the MPLA's previous criticism of the FNLA's use of mercenaries. A British partner to Executive Outcomes, Branch Energy, won a contract to protect two of the government's most vulnerable extractive zones: the Soyo oilfields and a government-controlled mining town in Lunda Norte (PU 1997). In a cunning move, the government also financed and/or incentivized the defense of the Lunda Norte diamond fields from UNITA capture by granting the regional mining concession to a firm known as DiamondWorks, of which Branch Energy's Tony Buckingham owns one-quarter of

the shares (PU 1998). Buckingham helped Executive Outcomes to secure a $40 million deal from the Angolan government "to help train its army," but UNITA forces discredited this pretext in July 1994 when they downed a planeload of South Africans and detained two EO operatives belonging to a group of 100 mercenaries instrumental in the government capture of UNITA's diamond-mining stronghold at Cafunfo (PU 1998; Maier 1996:159). Director Eeben Barlow, like many of the estimated 500 to 4,000 EO fighters in Angola, possessed an intimate knowledge of UNITA's tactics through personal experience: these men had allied with Savimbi during their service for apartheid South Africa's 32 Battalion in the 1980s as "regional warriors against communism" (Pike 2003; PU 1997; Maier 1996:159). Executive Outcomes, tasked with gaining and maintaining control of Angola's oil and diamond fields, relied on its affiliate Strategic Resources Group to shoot down UNITA supply planes, conduct intelligence forays, and "intercept flights for the Angolan government in 1994" (PU 1998). South Africa's deputy president at the time, Thabo Mbeki, perhaps remembering his imprisonment under dos Santos, painfully acknowledged the existence of 500 South African mercenaries fighting for the regime and sighed with disdain, "Those people ought not be there" (Maier 1996:159). Meanwhile, President Nelson Mandela facilitated negotiations between the embittered leaders of the Angolan government and UNITA: both dos Santos and Savimbi refused to personally assent and relegated the November 20, 1994, signature of the Lusaka peace accord to subordinates.

40. Maier notes that Ango-Segu, headed by "a former colonel in the Israeli security agency" Mossad who was "linked to senior members of the MPLA government, including a former Minister of the Interior," was charged with "passing sensitive military intelligence to UNITA" after a raid on its warehouses revealed "hundreds of illegal weapons" in December 1993 (1996:157–158). For more information on Executive Outcomes see Bunker and Marin 1999. U.S. President Bill Clinton pressured dos Santos into hiring Military Personnel Resources Incorporated (MPRI), an American private security firm run by high-ranking former soldiers, to protect oil installations both onshore and offshore in 1997 (O'Brien 1998; Mason 1999). In the same year, another U.S. firm called AirScan won a contract to monitor Chevron's offshore installations in Cabinda.

In accordance with the law, the State Department Office of Defense Trade Controls regulates the activities of U.S.-based private military and security firms. Critics worry that these private companies act as "the covert wing of U.S. foreign policy, going into regions of the world where the U.S. government is unwilling to become overtly involved" (O'Brien 1998). Given the strategic value of oil, securing oil installations is a simultaneously local, regional, national, multinational, and global effort often achieved through the joint efforts of national armies and American private security firms (Dunning and Wirpsa 2004).

41. Rafael Marques commented, "The Angolan government is one of the main defenders and beneficiaries of this mechanism, which allowed it to weaken

the rebel forces and help put an end to the armed conflict" (Marques and de Campos 2004).

42. The intense desperation originates in both the disempowerment of Angolan women, who on average give birth to seven children, and the lack of livelihood opportunities in an economy suffering from 60 percent unemployment (IRIN 2004k; Kairos-Africa 2002).

43. Strategic minerals exhibit price inelasticity, wherein demand remains even despite price increases. As the purveyors of a strategic, nonrenewable natural resource, transnational oil corporations have an operational reach that reflects global geopolitics as well the location of reserves. A map of Chevron's worldwide operations in February 2002 depicted the corporation's interests all across the globe except areas where the United States held little influence: the Sinai Peninsula, Cuba, North Korea, Iran, Iraq, Libya, Ethiopia, and Somalia. President George W. Bush explicitly referred to three of these countries (Iraq, Iran, and North Korea) as part of an "axis of evil." Two more—Libya and Somalia—had shaky relations with the United States. Four years later, in 2006, Chevron's map reflected further shifts in U.S. policy. Chevron had gained ground in Iraq, Libya, Somalia, and the Sinai Peninsula while North Korea, Iran, and Cuba remained out of reach. Although the United States was thoroughly embroiled in the deepening conflict in Iraq, President Bush had begun talking about a military option in Iran. The corporation had also pulled out of Greenland, Sudan, New Guinea, Mauritania, Djibouti, Gabon, Sierra Leone, the Gambia, Guinea, and Eritrea. While Chevron's departure from Sudan was likely motivated by U.S. divestment campaigns associated with the genocide in Darfur, the other changes may relate to shifting extractive priorities. See http://www.chevron.com/operations/worldwide.

44. Following the September attacks, oil extraction in the United States also took on greater significance. James H. Dupree, BP's former vice president for Gulf of Mexico deepwater production, portrayed his team's work as a matter of national security. He said that "right after September 11" his crew "wanted to go to New York and dig people out of the rubble. But I told them that the country needed them here" (Banerjee 2002).

45. Eager to gain access to their oil, the United States has shown great interest in all of these countries since the events of September 11, 2001. Secretary of State Colin Powell visited Gabon and Angola in 2002, President Bush himself traveled to Nigeria in 2003, and in 2006 Secretary of State Condoleeza Rice called Equatorial Guinea's dictator Teodoro Obiang Nguema "a good friend" of the United States (*Washington Post* 2006).

46. Angola is the second-largest supplier of crude oil to China, at rates of 650,000 barrels per day (EIA 2007). China is also pursuing military cooperation with Angola. Ding Jin Gong, Deputy Director General of the Office of Foreign Affairs for China's Defense Ministry, visited Angola in March 2007 to negotiate "an accord of technical cooperation aimed at the supply, by the Asian country, of military equipment to the Angolan Armed Forces" (ANGOP 2007).

47. During an October 2003 congressional hearing, Assistant Secretary of State for African Affairs Walter Kansteiner explained that "in order to stabilize the African country and advance human rights, the United States 'engagement with the Angolan armed forces will need to increase'"(Moore 2003).

48. The heads of state discussed transparency issues, the timetable for elections, and possible military cooperation between the United States and Angola (*Jornal de Angola* 2004e).

49. Nongovernmental sources contend that the Angolan government spent as much as 32 percent of the 2004 budget on defense and security (CR 2004).

50. DISA (Direcção de Informação e Segurança de Angola) was the intelligence and security apparatus of the MPLA during the socialist period. The agency received mentoring and tactical instruction from the KGB. Older Angolans even recall the Portuguese secret police force, known as PIDE (Polícia Internacional e de Defesa do Estado), which arrived in Angola under Salazar in 1957. PIDE forced the budding liberation movements, which were banned by the state, to either go underground or go abroad, but the first option still left the organizations vulnerable to infiltration and the second could weaken a movement's ties with its supporters by distance (Wheeler and Pélissier 1971:160–161).

51. The incident took place on November 22, 2003. Rafael Marques noted with dreadful irony in his discussion of the tragedy that MCK's song declares that whoever "speaks the truth ends up in a coffin" and reported that the presidential guard supplied the coffin for the funeral in addition to three trucks to carry mourners, food, and ten armed soldiers (Marques 2003a).

52. The title (*O baton da ditadura*) may also be translated as "The Big Stick of Dictatorship" in a reference to a police baton (AI 2000). The article admonished President dos Santos for "the destruction of the country" and "for the promotion of incompetence, embezzlement and corruption as political and social values" (Marques 1999; CPJ 2000).

53. The UN Human Rights Committee responsible for monitoring the compliance of signatories to the International Covenant on Civil and Political Rights determined that Angola violated the covenant through the arbitrary arrest and detention of Marques, failure to inform Marques of the charges against him in a timely manner, denial of his right to legal representation during the ten days he was held incommunicado, and the imposition of a travel ban on Marques (OSJI 2005).

54. The other officials included the MPLA's coordinator of business interests Mário António, MPLA Secretary General Paulo Julião Dino Metros, the Minister for Administration of the National Territory Fautimo Muteca, and Chairperson of the African Investment Bank Mário Palhares (MISA 2004). In June 2008, Angolan courts sentenced Campos to a "six-month prison sentence and ordered him to pay $90,000 in damages following his conviction in three separate libel cases filed by government officials"; Campos appealed the decision (HRW 2008b).

55. An Angolan vice minister's salary is usually around $19,200 annually

(*A Capital* 2004). I assume that ministers do not make astronomically greater sums than vice ministers and becoming a millionaire would entail significant engagement in peripheral activities.

56. Many cosmopolitans use their satellite access for little more than to enjoy episodes of *Dallas* and *Friends* on South Africa's DSTV channels or *telenovelas* on Brazil's Globo Internacional, which Rafael Marques referred to as "the opiate for the fortunate and literate in Angolan society to cast a blind eye to the dire reality of the country" (Marques 2004c).

57. See *Notícias Lusófonas* 2006. This article features Angola's Minister of Defense Kundy Paihama opening a meeting on peacekeeping with UN, AU, and NATO officials from the United States, France, the UK, and Russia in March 2006.

58. Oil corporations demonstrate more concern for a stable policy environment to uphold their concession contracts than a steady political environment (Frynas 1998).

59. The environment is an "arena of contested entitlements," which can be deciphered through their political-economic, cultural, and power-laden contexts (Peluso and Watts 2001:25). Natural resource users refer to institutions mediating resource tenure and access to explicate their entitlements (Peluso 1996). The socio-cultural relationships of farmers to land are analogous to the claims fishers and fish traders stake in the offshore. Fishing communities use complex tenure, regulatory, and arbitration systems to control access and use of fisheries, which are equal to terrestrial policies in their scope and depth (Durrenberger and Pálsson 1987; Olomola 1998).

60. Corporations may plan accordingly. Bassey (2000) claims transnational oil corporations concerned with local resistance or intent on evading environmental standards may prefer offshore developments "removed from the immediate view of local communities."

61. In imperial measure: just one pint of oil spilled in water can cover an acre of surface area (EPA 2000).

62. Original figure in imperial measure: 2,000 tons.

63. This pattern may also be attributed to the decreasing diameter of the hole as drilling proceeds (Patin 1999).

64. Also known as barium sulfate, drilling-grade barite must have a specific gravity of at least 4.20 g/cm^3. It is used as a weighting agent in ground form with particle sizes between 3 and 74 microns. Bentonite, a clay mineral compound, is also commonly used in conjunction with barite during the drilling process.

65. Original figure in imperial measure: 1 billion pounds.

66. The FDA limit is 1.0 parts per million, but the agency cautions that pregnant women and children should adhere to a lower limit.

67. Original figure in imperial measure: 120 tons. Oil service companies Prodoil and Schlumberger announced plans to assess the feasibility of exploiting barite deposits in Kwanza Sul province (Mayer 2003).

68. The Canadian Public Health Association explains, "Similar to the bub-

bles arising from carbonation when a soft drink is opened, solution gas bubbles to the surface of the oil when oil reserves are brought to the surface" (CPHA 2000). For decades, oil corporations have burned (flared) or simply released associated natural gas without burning it (called venting).

69. The original figures are in imperial measurements, inserted as follows: Estimates suggest that flaring increased from roughly 140 billion cubic feet in 1998 to almost 230 billion cubic feet in 2000 (ESMAP 2001:15). Chevron's Block o alone flared approximately 300 million cubic feet per day in 1999, including up to 60 million cubic feet of hydrogen sulfide gas (H_2S) in Area A nearest the Cabindan coast (GPC 1999:22).

70. Original figure in imperial measure: 14.8 million tons.

71. Portuguese sailors were the first foreigners to learn of asphalt deposits and oil seeps in Angola; Lisbon analyzed samples of oil from the region in the 1790s (Koning 2002; Wheeler and Pélissier 1971:142).

72. Informants actually described the chronic leaks as *insidiosos*.

73. Holing claims that English sole are known to "develop cancerous tumors when exposed to oil" (1990:29).

74. Riki Ott's (2005) work depicts the debilitating effects of these chemical agents on the cleanup crew.

75. Inipol IP-90 is distinct from Inipol EAP 22 but is produced by the same manufacturer: the French firm Société CECA, S.A., part of the Atofina chemical branch of Total, manufactured Inipol EAP 22 and currently produces and markets Inipol IP-90. Scientists' concern based on personal communication with two fisheries experts visiting Luanda in 2003 and 2005.

76. See HalliburtonWatch 2005 and the Halliburton Watch Web site for more information at http://www.halliburtonwatch.org.

77. See the International Oil Tanker Owners Pollution Federation Web site at http://www.itopf.com/stats05.pdf .

78. The 460 million gallons of oil discharged into the Persian Gulf in 1991 during the Iraqi invasion of Kuwait and resulting Gulf War, considered at least partially intentional, ranks as the worst spill in history. The International Oil Tanker Owners Pollution Federation distinguishes oil discharges associated with shipping accidents by tankers, carriers and barges from spills incurred by acts of war. See http://www.itopf.com/stats05.pdf.

79. Executive Decree 8/05 of January 5, 2005, regulates refuse disposal; Decree 12/05 of January 12, 2005, pertains to the management of operational discharges; and Decree 11/05 of January 12, 2005, outlines procedures on notification of government following oil spills.

80. Decree 39/00 of October 10, 2000.

81. Personal communication, June 2003.

82. Personal communication with an affiliate of the Ministry of Petroleum in July 2003.

83. This shift is the central foundation of environmental justice movements (Bullard 1993:203).

CHAPTER 4

1. Soyo is both the name of the town and the surrounding municipality.

2. During periods of regional instability, a portion of the provincial government authorities relocated from Mbanza Kongo to Soyo (GoA 2003a).

3. Sonpetrol now operated this rig for Total and it remained the only rig owned by Total worldwide until the corporation sold its stake in Fina Petróleos de Angola to Sonangol.

4. Petrofina conducted explorations through the firm Carborang; Petrofina held 70 percent of Carborang's stock (Boavida 1972:92).

5. Portugal established the *Companhia de Petróleo de Angola* (Angoil) in Lisbon in 1922 (Wheeler and Pélissier 1971:142). It appears that this prospecting firm faded for lack of capital or technical capacity as Petrangol's star rose. The Belgian Société General held 15 percent and Petrofina 45 percent of Petrangol's capital (Boavida 1972:97).

6. Saint et al. reported that "Pinda-1 found production at about 6,700 feet and was tested at 450 barrels per day for 30 degrees gravity crude" (1967:1591–3). Neighboring wells Pinda-2 and Pinda-3 showed no oil, only saltwater.

7. Soares de Oliveira states, "Sonangol reportedly hired Executive Outcomes at the behest of Chevron, Elf, Petrofina and Texaco, initially to secure the important onshore Soyo facilities from a UNITA takeover." (1997:116). Shankleman (2007) cites differing accounts indicating that the oil corporations may have brought Executive Outcomes to Soyo before the private military company contracted with the government.

8. Specifically, the FAA retook Sumba, Kikandi, Kinzau, Manga Grande, Nenga, and Kelo on November 29, 1995.

9. Luango and Quinguila North fields dominate the FS concession, while FST comprises the fields of Cabeça de Cobra, Ganda, Lumueno, N'Zombo, Quifuma, Quinfuquena, Kinguila, and Sereia). At the time of research, Sonangol held a 51 percent stake in FS and FST. Fina Petroleum of Angola was operator of both concessions and maintained a 49 percent stake in FS and 32.6 percent in FST—leaving Texaco Angola Exploration and Production with 16.4 percent. For more details on Total's cession of Fina Petroleum of Angola holdings to Sonangol, see Buffery (2007) and AOJ (2007b).

10. Nearly a century after the U.S. instituted antitrust regulations and used them to dismantle Standard Oil, the world's oil corporations merged into gigantic conglomerates like ExxonMobil (which also includes Esso), Total (swallowing Fina and Elf), BP (subsuming Amoco and Arco), Royal Dutch Shell, Chevron (including Texaco, Caltex, and Unocal), and ConocoPhillips (incorporating Union 76 and Phillips 66). These vertically integrated private sector oil and gas corporations are known as "supermajors." The supermajors conceal the process of industry consolidation from the public by condensing their merged names to hide their heft and maintaining a plurality of names at pumping stations.

11. Personal communication with Total official, October 2004.

12. Dick Cheney infamously told the crowd at the 1998 meeting of the Panhandle Producers and Royalty Owners Association, "You've got to go to where the oil is. I don't think about it very much" (quoted in Christian Aid, ed., 2003).

13. Displaced families and individuals filtered back to Soyo, but homes and businesses rebounded more slowly than the oil industry. People began from scratch: UNITA had robbed them of all consumable or saleable items from goats and manioc to shoes and tin roofs. A local government official commented, "Normally their houses in the villages are not inhabitable. If one wall stands, another is knocked down . . . the houses have neither doors nor roofs. Usually they have only two or three roof panels on top of a wall and little else. So they are making bricks of mud and those without money to buy zinc roofing materials use straw."

14. Considering that a statistically average Angolan woman has 7.2 children over her lifetime (UNICEF 2003), the assertion that the influx of returnees over the last forty-odd years could all be blood relatives of those who had previously staked out land in Soyo seems plausible.

15. Many Basolongo fled to the Belgian Congo during the colonial period in reaction to forced labor policies and expropriation of their traditional lands for sisal and palm oil plantations. It is likely that the resettlement scheme aimed to repopulate the area with laborers. Across northern Angola, expropriation of land and labor had generated an emigration of Bakongo to the neighboring Belgian Congo so great that plantation owners imported an estimated 180,000 Ovimbundu workers from the south of Angola to compensate for labor deficiencies (Kaure 1999:12).

16. Portuguese colonial policy pressed men into service for concession companies and compelled women to cultivate specific cash crops by taxation or threat of force. The colonial government also required households unable to pay their taxes to serve as laborers. Forced labor pushed many from northern Angola to the Belgian Congo.

17. See Reed 2008 for further discussion.

18. Total usually uses a "pig" device equipped with brushes or cups to remove internal paraffin buildup from the uniform sections of pipeline, but is limited to using chemical injections to clean its patchwork pipeline.

19. On July 14 and December 19, 2003.

20. The records specifically referred to remediation efforts at waste pits corresponding to LM-17 and LM-12 on the Lumueno field in 2003 and 2004.

21. ENI and partners won residual exploration acreage in Block 15 in 2006 for a bid offering a $902 million bonus payment and commitment to drill five exploration wells starting in 2007.

22. Just as I referred to Fina Petroleum of Angola by the name of its parent Total in the previous section regarding onshore oil, I will use the names of the supermajors owning the subsidiaries operating in Angola at the time of research to elucidate the transnational relationships at work. In official documents, ExxonMobil of Block 15 is known as Esso Exploration Angola Ltd., Agip of Block 1 is registered as Agip Exploration Angola BV, Chevron in Block 2

is recognized as Texaco Panama Inc., and BP is referred to as BP Exploration (Angola) Ltd. After Block 1/06 was relinquished by ChevronTexaco, Tullow Oil won a bid in the December 2005 licensing round and assumed the role of operator (and 50 percent interest stake) with partners Sonangol (20 percent), Prodoil (20 percent), and Force Petroleum (10 percent). Although Chevron retains a 20 percent interest stake in Block 2, Sonangol assumed the operator role (and 52.5 interest) in 2006. Petrobras holds the remaining 27.5 percent interest stake in Block 2.

23. The fisherman marks his fish with a personalized pattern (e.g., two shallow slices of a knife above the tail) so he can reclaim the fish as his when the boat reaches shore.

24. ExxonMobil's deepwater Block 15 loomed far enough off the horizon to remove it from public scrutiny, but not from local people's curiosity. The Kizomba A and B fields in Block 15 boast reserves of 2 billion barrels and production rates of up to 520,000 barrels per day in 2007 (De Sousa 2008). Despite the distance from shore, ExxonMobil's operations contribute to pollution of Angolan waters. ExxonMobil accidentally released nearly 225 barrels of non-aqueous drilling fluids into the marine environment in Block 15 over the course of 2004 (ExxonMobil 2005).

25. A liter of gasoline on the informal market in Ndalatando, Kwanza Norte, cost 100 kwanzas (Fontoura 2004). In Mbanza Kongo of Zaire province price increases were not as steep but still problematic: the price for a liter of kerosene *(petróleo iluminante)* doubled to 50 kwanzas *(Jornal de Angola* 2004p).

26. Gasoline rose from 12 to 20 kwanzas per liter and diesel from 8 to 14 kwanzas *(O Apostolado* 2004g). The government also cut utilities subsidies, resulting in rate increases of approximately 40 percent on electricity and water *(Agora* 2004c).

27. Prices reached roughly 17 cents and 24 cents per liter of diesel and gasoline, respectively *(Agora* 2004c). If one U.S. gallon equals 3.785412 liters, then a gallon of gasoline would cost nearly 91 cents and diesel would be about 64 cents a gallon. Figures based on an exchange rate of 84 kwanzas to $1 in May 2004.

28. Only 1 percent of households in the northern region of Angola use butane gas to cook their meals, in contrast to the 48 percent of households using firewood and 49.6 percent using charcoal (GoA 2002).

29. Executive Decree 25/98, in accordance with the Angolan constitution, guaranteed that Sonangol would provide IPA representatives with fuels subsidized at a rate of 40 percent to bolster artisanal fisheries (Paiva 1998:418).

30. Figures for March 2005 based on exchange rate of 87 kwanzas to US$1 and gasoline prices of 22 kwanzas per liter for fishermen and 40 kwanzas at Sonangol filling stations.

31. Each drum holds 200 liters of fuel—as opposed to a barrel, which contains 158 liters.

32. The figure of 22,362 tons is based on six months at rates of 3,727 tons per month (Cristóvão 2004).

33. This figure is based on a price of 380 Congolese francs per liter and an exchange rate of 470 Congolese francs to US$1 at the time.

34. Estimate considers normal profit margin of $2 per barrel for retailers.

35. Maintenance activities induce regular electricity cuts on alternate weekdays, but unscheduled power outages are common and often last from a few days to an entire week. Carlos, a neighbor, once explained that the outages lasted so long because spare parts were hard to come by in Soyo and had to be sourced from Luanda. As I cleared out the fillets and shellfish from my rapidly thawing freezer during one such outage, I suggested that the utilities commission might consider advance planning and stockpile a range of spare parts for such occasions. Nodding toward the adjacent illuminated houses occupied by a former military commander and Sonangol officials, I hinted to Carlos my suspicion that government officials had few incentives to fix the energy grid if they, too, used private generators.

36. *Ensino de base* is Angola's primary level of education, akin to kindergarten through middle school in the United States.

37. Personal communication with a Total official, October 2004.

38. I was always keen to visit the *praça*—even in the rainy season when the open-air market's aisles turned into muddy wallows that sucked at the flimsy soles of my flip-flops. Despite the official linguistic divide of the Congo River once imposed by colonial powers, merchants speaking Kisolongo and Lingala found similarities in their shared Bantu heritage. One linguistic battle I found particularly fascinating: Fruit sellers squabbled over which pineapples met the local standard for the Portuguese label *abacaxi* and which would be relegated to the French *ananas*. Both *ananás* and *abacaxi* mean pineapple in Portuguese, while the French term for the fruit is *ananas* (note the lack of an accent mark). At the Soyo market, French-speaking fruit merchants from the DRC used the term *ananas* for all of their pineapples, but Portuguese speakers seemed to refer to their pineapples as *ananás* or *abacaxi* in relation to each fruit's relative size and value. Did their terminology indicate a bias that even Angolan pineapples are superior to the pineapples grown in the DRC (or even those sold by Congolese merchants)?

39. The *Jornal de Angola* featured an article entitled "Go, Soyo Awaits You!" in which a spirited young journalist explored Soyo's boundless supply of two complementary products: beer and prostitutes. After ranking brews from both Congos, including Turbo King, Skol, Primus, and Simba, along a scale of manliness and capacity to boost sex drive, the reporter turned to the "young, pretty and attractive" sex workers from the Democratic Republic of Congo, noting the convenience of "beds for occasional couples" at the local nightclub Moyo a Mutu for the $10-an-hour gals and marveling that with just $27 "you will have a congolesa for the night" (Chitata 2003a). The article cited rates of 700 kwanzas per hour and 2,000 for a full night. Figures in dollars are based on June 1, 2003 exchange rate of 73.63 Angolan kwanzas to US$1 (UN 2003).

40. Many positions, especially offshore, require employees to leave home and devote themselves entirely to work for weeks at a time in a cycle; perhaps

eight weeks working followed by a four-week break or equal shifts of five, four, three, or two weeks on and the same amount of time off.

41. In 2002, Soyo registered 685 workers in the oil sector and 25 of these were expatriates (GoA 2003a).

42. Total employees who had participated in a strike before the UNITA occupation were not hired back when operations resumed. One of the strike's participants claimed that he was blacklisted and now he "cannot work, for having defended justice." This is not uncommon in both Soyo and Cabinda. The rights to form a union and to strike are not recognized by many oil corporations operating in Angola (Cafussa 2004a; Luemba 2005b).

43. Refers to Law 10/04 of November 12, 2004.

44. The refinery project was originally a joint venture between Sonangol and Sinopec; however, the partnership collapsed in early 2007 due to disagreements over the proportion of refined products to be distributed domestically versus exported to China. In December 2008, Sonangol signed a construction contract with KBR linked to the Lobito Refinery.

45. Energy analysts predicted increased demand "with LNG trade in the Atlantic basin alone forecast to triple, from 30 million tonnes per year in 2002, to 100 million tonnes per year by 2010" (Sonangol 2004c). The top ten African oil and gas producers are expected to increase gas exports, primarily in the form of LNG, from 21.6 billion cubic meters in 2006 to 130 billion cubic meters in 2030 (Ikokwu 2008).

46. Chevron officials originally said that inclusion of gas from Blocks 0 and 14 offshore of Cabinda would be contingent on continued strong world demand for LNG and overcoming engineering feats, such as crossing the undersea Congo Canyon.

47. Original figure in imperial measure: 33 million gallons.

48. The remaining fifteen percent of natural gas is either reinjected into the well to facilitate oil recovery or extracted in the form of liquefied petroleum gas (EIA 2006).

49. Original figure in imperial measurement: 75 million standard cubic feet daily (*Jornal de Angola* 2004i). The World Bank, citing the "depressed international fertilizer market," disparaged prospects for an export-oriented ammonia/urea plant with a capacity of processing 50.6 million standard cubic feet per day (UNDP–World Bank 1989:xi). It made no mention of production for the domestic market, possibly betraying the financial institution's export-oriented bias and/or recognizing conflict in Angola's most productive agricultural zones in 1989.

50. He specifically referred to new well sites on the Vuandembo field.

51. According to a representative of Total, government officials opposed the corporation's proposal to install new water pipes to Bairro Fina for fear that its residents would begin selling water from their homes or that the surrounding neighborhoods might become jealous.

52. Literally, "Se você quiser crescer um bocado na vida económica, arranja amizade com um rico."

53. He acknowledged their neediness but recalled with a chuckle how Sonangol representatives had also come with a request; they tried to pressure Total to donate $5 million to sponsor a local soccer team.

54. ADPP stands for "Ajuda de Desenvolvimento do Povo para o Povo" (Development Aid from People to People). Oddly, a map on the Humana German Webpage on ADPP Angola (http://www.humana-de.org/05_ang/aointro .html) referred to a program in Zaire province for Refugee Aid (Flüchtlingshilfe), but made no mention of Soyo's Escola dos Professores do Futuro or any teacher-training program. Chevron and ExxonMobil's support for ADPP presents part of a worrying trend whereby corporate contributions are leveraged in support of personalized or partisan projects. ADPP, a subsidiary of Denmark's Humana People to People and the cultish Tvind network, funnels millions of dollars in corporate contributions and earmarks from Sonangol's Social Bonus Fund into projects like teacher training schools in the provinces of Cabinda, Bengo, Huambo, Zaire, Luanda, and Benguela. While ADPP's stated objective is to "improve and develop the conditions for basic human development in cooperation with local populations," the organization is strongly allied with the MPLA and FESA, the personal foundation of President dos Santos. Rikke Viholm, ADPP's representative in Angola, sits on the FESA board. Could ADPP's teacher training schools be creating educators with a bias for the MPLA? Will these teachers inculcate their students with a loyalty to the MPLA and a disdain for all opponents?

The organization began working in Angola's Bengo province in 1986, forming a school in Caxito. Fifteen years after its founding, UNITA kidnapped sixty children from the ADPP school. The incident prompted comment that UNITA might have seen ADPP's links to the MPLA as "sufficient justification for its kidnap raid on the town" (Pearce 2005:9). (UNITA's July 2000 kidnapping of twenty-one boys from ADPP's Quissala Orphans Village in Huambo province may have been similarly motivated.)

The management of ADPP monies is also suspect. Watchdog groups like TvindAlert have called attention to Tvind's network of offshore bank accounts and holding companies, as well as some unorthodox accounting and fundraising methods. As an arm of Tvind, ADPP collected clothing donations in Europe and, under an exclusive agreement with the government, sold these in Angola at a profit of $30,000 a week in 1995. Rather than fund projects, ADPP sent the proceeds to accounts in Denmark to cover administrative costs. Meanwhile, the organization solicited funding from oil corporations in hard currency, including administrative costs in the budget—thereby creating "a hidden surplus" that "never showed clearly in the books" according to a former ADPP officer (Tvind Alert 2006).

In 1998, ADPP earned $4.6 million in clothing sales and accepted more than $1.1 million from the Chevron-led Cabinda Association as well as Sonangol's Social Bonus Fund for Block 18 (ibid.). Criticized for their contributions to ADPP's questionable efforts in Angola, oil corporations are increasingly opting to undertake development projects on their own or limiting their contributions to suspect organizations to indirect funding through the Social Bonus Fund.

55. Although a Total official refused to discuss the Well 41 incident, he claimed that local government officials regularly pocketed half of the compensation funds intended for illiterate community members.

56. I once spied a boat near Cabeça de Cobra bearing the Kisolongo name *Uizayla*, which my companion Fabrício roughly translated as a taunt of "I dare you" to corporations operating offshore. Fabrício suggested that by naming this boat in such a manner as to taunt oil corporations the owner might have contemplated the potential profit of a spill more than he considered the damage.

57. A local informant explained, "The country goes like this: one goes and takes everything and the next has to start from zero. The first one says 'the money ran out' and the next says 'I will not make promises because the promises made by my predecessor were not kept.' He plays on the past—so many promises and nothing done."

58. Total officials presumed UNITA responsible for a spate of sabotage in 2000 targeting the Cabeça de Cobra pipeline, Luango's LN-01 and LN-02 wells, Kinguila's GN-23 and GN-11 wells, and Lumueno's LM-11 well.

59. Even still, 500 Teleservice security officers, equipped with guns and bulletproof vehicles, protect Soyo's oil installations.

60. Translated and adapted from the saying, " Só depois de: A última árvore ser derrubada, O último peixe ser morto, O ultimo rio envenenado, vocês irão perceber que dinheiro não se come!" published on the front page of *Folha 8* on February 5, 2005. In the spirit of this aphorism, a small group of Soyo's residents formed the Conselho de Acção para a Protecção do Ambiente e a Saude Pública (Action Council for Environmental Protection and Public Health), an independent organization concerned with the anticipated environmental and social impacts of the LNG plant.

CHAPTER 5

1. Incident related by an employee of Malongo in February 2005.

2. Narratives on environmental degradation enable communities to articulate the struggles over the uneven distribution of oil's costs and benefits. In Nigeria, "pollution of natural ecosystems and environments provided the language for opposing historically specific forms of economic alienation and political dispossession throughout the nation, as rentier-capitalism and prebendal politics privatized the state and undermined the public sphere" (Apter 2005:122).

3. For example, shipping a twenty-ton container from Europe to Luanda might cost $3,000, including customs and port-related fees, while an equal shipment bound for Cabinda would ultimately cost $5,000 after it had passed through Luanda and proceeded up to the Cabindan port (da Assunção 2004).

4. The exact number of inhabitants in Cabinda is unknown. The last time the government carried out a census in the province was in 1988, yielding a

total of 114,000 inhabitants (ANGOP 2004d). In a 2004 article, a government-controlled source cited a population of 170,000 in Cabinda, but this minimal population increase over sixteen years is unlikely (ANGOP 2004c). Even by the government's own early estimates of population growth from approximately 134,000 in 1985, the 2005 figure would reach 260,000 (Setas and da Rocha Junior 1991). On the other end of the spectrum, Cabindan independence sympathizers estimate the province's population at 500,000 inhabitants and perhaps more if Cabindan refugees in the neighboring Congos are included (*Folha 8* 2005a; Heitor 2004b). I follow Human Rights Watch in accepting population estimates of 300,000 (HRW 2004b:4).

5. These included: Aliança do Maiombe, Comité de Acção da Unidade Nacional de Cabinda, Comité Comuniste Cabindais, Comité para Independência de Cabinda, Comando Militar de Libertação de Cabinda, Comité dos Nacionais de, Cabinda, Comité de Redynamisation du FLEC, Comité Révolutionnnaire Cabindais, Fórum Cabindês para o Diálogo, Front Démocratique Cabindais, Frente de Libertação do Enclave de Cabinda—Original, Frente de Libertação do Enclave de Cabinda—Forças Armadas de Cabinda, Frente de Libertação do Enclave de Cabinda—Lubota, Frente de Libertação do Enclave de Cabinda—Posição Militar, Frente de Libertação do Enclave de Cabinda—Renovada, Forum dos Nacionalistas Cabindas, Frente Unida de Cabinda, Grupo de Reflexão de Cabinda, Junta Militar de Reconciliação Nacional, Movimento de Libertação do Enclave de Cabinda, Mouvement de Libération de Cabinda, Mouvement Populaire Cabindais, Movimento Popular de Libertação de Cabinda, Movimento de Resistência para a Independência Total de Cabinda, Partido Democrático dos Povos de Cabinda, União Democrática dos Povos de Cabinda, União Nacional de Libertação do Enclave de Cabinda, and União Nacional de Libertação de Cabinda.

6. Whether pursuing aims of resistance or subsistence, a few intrepid Cabindan fishermen admitted fishing near the platforms under cover of night. One explained, "There are restrictions, but this is where the fish congregate most." When asked whether he feared detection by Chevron's security personnel he shrugged and said, "If they catch us, they take us to Malongo and we stay there for a while."

7. A report from SADC (2006) noted plans to increase the Luanda refinery's production capacity to 100,000 barrels per day. Sonangol acquired ownership of the Luanda refinery when Total ceded its Fina Petroleum of Angola holdings to Sonangol.

8. Easily dried for preservation and transport, shark meat became an essential ingredient of the local dish of cooked manioc leaves called *sacafolha*, especially in the interior. Wealthier families often use more expensive fish in their recipes.

9. Angola's fishing sector is also struggling to cope with pirate fishing. While pirate ships may not fly the Jolly Roger, the sight of them instills fear in the hearts of industrial fishers. Armed with weapons and trawling gear, these modern-day pirates violate international law by fishing in Angola's EEZ without authorization. These unlicensed and unauthorized ships are devastating

the marine environment offshore, and the Angolan government does not have the surveillance or enforcement capability necessary to eject them (Salopek 2004). Pirate fishing boats compete with industrial fishermen for high-value pelagic species. Industrial fishing near Benguela accounts for 31,000 metric tons of fish annually, roughly 45 percent of Angola's total catch (AllAfrica 2004).

10. Pirate fleets and overfishing may also accelerate the extinction of local wildlife. A 2004 study demonstrated that poor fish supply in West Africa, induced by over-fishing from European Union–subsidized fleets, corresponded to an increase in poaching within protected areas as locals sought an alternative source of protein (Brashares et al. 2004). The booming bushmeat market from Cabinda's Mayombe forest may be connected to the trend of diminishing fish stocks offshore. Chevron even sponsored a program that trucked 1,035 goats to Mayombe in an effort to reduce local demand for bushmeat.

11. On October 15, 2008, Chevron recorded a seven-barrel oil spill in Block 0 between Zenga and Massabi Lagoon (ANGOP 2008c). The corporation attributed the spill to a pipeline rupture and acknowledged damage to fishing nets in the vicinity (ANGOP 2008d). Chevron attempted to limit the spread of the slick through mechanical diffusion techniques, but wind and wave action pushed the oil toward the shore (ANGOP 2008c). This spill was wholly unrelated to the April 2008 pollution events attributed to operator negligence on the Takula platform, which sent allegedly eight to ten barrels of oil into the flare and created a fireball visible from shore (Moeen 2008).

12. This included 151 fishermen from Lândana; 153 from Malembo; 50 from Tenda, Muba, and Bêmbica; and 18 from Lombo-Lombo.

13. Although speculations persisted as to whether the news colored negotiations in the small fisheries-centered and tourism-dependent nation, two years later Chevron announced the acceptance of Chevron JDZ Limited's $123 million exploration bid as operator with a 51 percent stake in Block 1 of São Tomé's joint development zone with Nigeria.

14. The campaign Web site (http://www.chevrontoxico.com) alleges that Texaco "disposed of toxic formation waters into the pits, swamps creeks and rivers during its period of operations in Ecuador from 1964 to 1992" and that "the amount of crude dumped [in the region] was thirty times greater than that spilled during the Exxon Valdez disaster." The website also claims that "a comprehensive clean-up will cost at least $6 billion" but "this amount is a fraction of the total profits of $30 billion Texaco extracted from Ecuador."

15. To implement the repairs, Chevron reduced daily production in Block 0 by 12,000 to 55,000 barrels per day (African Energy 2002; BBC 2002). Despite the decrease, Chevron still managed to produce 157 million barrels of oil from Cabinda's offshore fields in 2002 (IMF 2005).

16. Such attempts to undermine claimants' credibility are not uncommon to relationships between oil corporations and local communities. In 1996, Claude Ake recognized that Shell Petroleum Company of Nigeria "insists defiantly that it will not change its ways and denies any part whatsoever in the environmental

degradation of the Niger Delta, which it blames on indigenes conniving at oil spills to collect compensation" (quoted in Robinson 1998:46).

17. These figures reflect numbers of coastal fishermen; only in 2005 were fishermen of interior lakes and rivers required to get licenses.

18. From Lândana and its outskirts, 489; 234 from Malembo and Chinfuca; 42 in Zenga; 10 from Bêmbica; and 7 from Tenda.

19. As fishermen quickened their pace in demanding compensation, Chevron officials charged with investigating oil spills began to drag their feet. A member of Lândana's association recalled, "Even though they arrived a little late, I could still show them a net that was affected so they could take a sample to the laboratory. If they had come [one or two days earlier], they would have seen the slick on the water."

20. Rádio Ecclesia reported that Chevron "denied responsibility" for the spill. In the piece, Chevron's representative, Timoteo de Almeida, claimed it "had dissipated and had not washed ashore." Rather, he maintained, "The stain near [Chevron's] operation was oil and plants coming from the Congo River" (Cabinda.net 2001). Experts from Chevron, Angola, and the Democratic Republic of Congo examined oil-stained patches of beach in Cabinda, took samples of the oil near the mouth of the Congo River, and hypothesized that "the pollution was caused by petroleum derivatives or by unidentified agents such as waste from shipping, which can linger for a long time" (*Namibian Online* 2001). Similarly, in February 2000 a Namibian news source reported that a "mystery slick of an 'oily nature' killed fish and other marine life and forced many fishermen in northern Angola to stop working for five days" (*Namibian Online* 2000a). Some wondered whether the phenomenon could be linked to natural oil seeps offshore (*Namibian Online* 2000b). Natural seeps, however, more often yield tar-like bitumen, not surface slicks.

21. *World Oil* (2002) announced that Chevron's Misato "exploration well tapped a marginal oil discovery" on DRC's continental shelf, adding that the wildcat "was completed as an oil well and brought into production in March 2001."

22. After Shell offered cash payments to locals "as a gesture of goodwill" while denying responsibility for the Ebubu oil spill in Nigeria activists questioned, "Why would Shell offer to compensate the villagers if they were truly not at all responsible for the spill?" (Robinson 1998:46)

23. Personal communication, April 2006.

CHAPTER 6

1. TAAG— Linhas Aereas de Angola (Airlines of Angola)—is the country's national flag carrier.

2. An estimated 12,000 to 15,000 troops were stationed in Cabinda prior to the start of the military campaign in October 2002 and during the height of the campaign that number rose to nearly 50,000 (Luemba 2008). In a September 2003 interview with Radio France Internationale, FLEC-FAC spokes-

man Alexandre Bati claimed, "The government has about 42,000 FAA soldiers deployed in the central and northern regions of the country [Cabinda] alone" (quoted in Kairos-Africa 2003). An independent newspaper estimated the total number of FAA soldiers in Cabinda as 45,000 (*Semanário Angolense* 2004b). Regarding the special brigades, see *Jornal Digital* 2004b.

3. Comprising military forces and political entities, FLEC factions enlisted guerrilla fighters, registered members, and counted the majority of Cabindans as sympathetic supporters.

4. ROC holds the operator stake and a 60 percent interest in the Cabinda South Block with partners Force Petroleum (20 percent) and Sonangol (20 percent).

5. The Portuguese granted three years of exploration by Decree 41,180 of July 1957 and fifty years of exclusive exploitation by Decree 41,374 of December 1957. Boavida reported, "The Gulf Oil Co, Mexican Gulf Oil, Chase National Bank and the City Bank of New York constitute the major subsidiary shareholders in the Cabinda Gulf Oil Co. Corporate capital already subscribed to this company is in the order of 1.5 million dollars" (1972:96).

6. A 1961 review of Cabinda's activity record only three of these wells showed oil (Mandjeno-1, 2 and 3), but more recent industry maps add oil shows at Tamba-1. Both agree on a lack of shows on wells Lucula-1, Lucula-2, Maconga-1, Cota-1, Bonde-1, and Vongo-1.

7. Drilling wells according to a hunch on where oil might be, rather than extensive scientific data, is called wildcatting. Thus, wildcat wells are those drilled in the hopeful expectation that oil may exist in a specific location but without advanced geological evidence.

8. FLEC usually targeted infrastructure rather than people, particularly civilians. For example, on January 15, 1977, FLEC attacked a Zaire railway, exploded several bridges and kidnapped three Frenchmen whom they released uninjured after two weeks without ransom payment (MIPT 2005).

9. Despite mutual assurances in 1985 by dos Santos and Mobutu that neither Zaire nor Angola would undermine the other's authority by harboring subversives, Mobutu welcomed FLEC and in 1986 he began channeling American arms in and smuggled illegal diamonds out for UNITA (Gunn 1987:60–61). The MPLA responded by asking Castro to send more Cuban troops.

10. Many Cabindans told me that FLEC agreed to cooperate with UNITA on the condition that Savimbi's men agree not to harm civilians. According to Cabindans, FLEC was their protector. They cite one occasion in which FLEC accidentally fired on a civilian vehicle in Bulo, resulting in four fatalities and six injuries (GTD 2007). This occurred in June 1999.

11. The other kidnappings included the abduction of thirteen French and ten Congolese employees of Elf in the Republic of Congo in April and two Portuguese aid workers in Angola in September 1990 (MIPT 2005). FLEC-FAC condemned the April kidnapping, claiming that a dissident faction had perpetrated the attack.

12. In just over a decade, some 300,000 Cuban troops fought in the Angolan war, including the 2,077 soldiers who died. An additional 50,000 Cubans

served in Angola as civilian volunteers in the fields of medicine, education, and journalism (Castro 2005).

13. Meanwhile, violence on both sides continued in the months leading up to the 1992 elections. FAA soldiers summarily executed Deacon Arão, an activist from a local protestant church in Necuto, on suspicion of harboring FLEC affiliates after guerrillas carried out attacks in the area in January 1992 (AI 1992a). FLEC-R abducted three Portuguese construction workers in Cabinda's Belize municipality on July 6, while alternate faction FLEC-FAC kidnapped two French businessmen on July 14 and another Portuguese worker in Lândana on August 20; all were later released uninjured (MIPT 2005). The deliberate police shooting of the oil worker João Evangelista Mbathi for his suspected support of FLEC contributed to the toll of three deaths and several injuries during this turbulent weekend at the end of July (AI 1992b).

14. Captain Bonga Bonga, a twenty-year MPLA veteran, deserted and joined FLEC's armed forces division in 1991, saying, "I came to see that as a Cabindan, I had no choice but to fight this year, but it has to be for complete independence" (Maier 1996:68).

15. Maier quotes the Bishop of Cabinda as saying "If I asked my congregation to pray for autonomy, they would hate me. They are suffering as never before and they see autonomy as a continuation of their current misery" (1996:66–67).

16. The territory held only 160,000 inhabitants at the time, but Cabindans claimed that some 100,000 of their compatriots had fled to the neighboring countries (Vicente 1995a:17). Many returned during the peace to join the independence cause, although MPLA soldiers at the border detained those who spoke only French under the presumption that all Angolans should speak Portuguese (Maier 1996:53).

17. During this period, FLEC also targeted government military installations. For example, on March 18, 1995, FLEC militants killed ten FAA soldiers during an attack on a military barracks (GTD 2007).

18. FLEC militants continued kidnappings and attacks during the negotiations with the government. On March 10, 1999, FLEC-R kidnapped two French and two Portuguese employees of Bouygues, a firm working for Chevron out of Malongo (GTD 2007). The following year, authorities suspected FLEC's involvement in the kidnapping of one Angolan and three Portuguese construction workers (ibid.). No injuries were reported in either kidnapping, however, FLEC allegedly killed Angola Public Health Ministry official Luís Filipe Gomes during an assault on a government vehicle on June 10, 2000 (ibid.). FLEC was also presumed to be responsible for the kidnapping of five Portuguese nationals and their Angolan driver without injury on March 9, 2001 (ibid.).

19. Victor Jorge Gomes, former chief of staff for FLEC-R, became second commander in Cabinda's National Police squad and ex-FLEC militant Marcelino Tubi earned a post as counsel to the Ministry of the Interior offices in Cabinda (*Jornal de Angola* 2004j).

20. FLEC-R continued to carry out attacks. On January 31, 2002, the fac-

tion claimed responsibility for killing twenty-one FAA soldiers in an attack on Chibodo (GTD 2007). Likewise, FAA troops continued to abuse civilians in retaliation for FLEC assaults. FAA troops responded to FLEC-R's capture and execution of a government soldier in July 2002 by venting their frustrations on the village of Champuto Rico where the soldier was taken. The soldiers allegedly "kicked a 13-year-old girl in the stomach, beat other villagers with their fists and guns and subjected one to a mock execution" (AI 2003).

21. Charged with international security, officers of the Angolan National Police are accountable to the Ministry of the Interior, but the provincial chief of information, the top provincial post in the intelligence service, reports to the Office of the President.

22. José Aníbal Lopes Rocha was born in Uíge province, but lived in Mbanza Kongo for most of his childhood. He served on the Zaire provincial committee for the MPLA-PT from 1979 to 1986, became governor of Zaire province from 1986 to 1992, and served as minister of territorial administration and governor of Luanda before taking his post in Cabinda. José Amaro Tati, a relative of Alexandre Tati and likewise part of the Cabindan noble lineage, also renounced separatism in favor of a political career upon joining the MPLA. Tati helped to found one of the first Angolan NGOs in 1990, known as ADRA (Acção para o Desenvolvimento Rural—Action for Rural Development). A highly effective NGO, ADRA works to rehabilitate infrastructure, revive agricultural production and recreate trade in the most war-damaged provinces while prioritizing service to the most needy, including displaced persons, children, and women heads of households. Following his departure from Cabinda, Tati became governor of Bié province.

23. Nearly 7,000 refugees hoping for a lasting peace had returned to Cabinda after Savimbi's death (IRIN 2005a). A convoy of American oil workers in Cabinda suffered a grenade attack in May 2002, but no injuries were reported (State Dept. 2003). FLEC did not claim responsibility for the incident. Some Cabindans suspected that the government had colluded with local security firms employed by Chevron to create a pretext for increased militarization of the province. The relatively minor attack still did not seem like enough to justify the massive influx of FAA troops.

24. Rafael Marques chided the government for promising peace but unleashing violence on Cabinda. He contended that "FLEC, as a guerrilla movement, does not represent and never represented a threat to dialogue and to political accord" and that by "steering away from broad and inclusive dialogue . . . the authorities chose the path of impunity, arrogance and bellicosity in such a way as to set themselves apart from the rest of society (Marques 2003b).

25. Informants used the phrase *verdadeira guerrilha*. The insinuation here is that FLEC-R integrated itself seamlessly into extant communities whereas FLEC-FAC developed sprawling bases hidden in the forested interior. The strategies served both groups well until the commencement of Operação Vassoura. FLEC-FAC fared worse with the wholesale destruction of its once-covert bases, but FLEC-R simply faded back into the host communities.

26. The *caçadores especiais* are a special forces division of the FAA. The term literally means "special hunters."

27. By way of comparison, the Angolan government spent $160 million on the reintegration of 105,000 former UNITA soldiers and their families, supplying each ex-combatant with $100 contingency cash and a seventy-five-item kit with a street value of $500 and providing them with transportation to resettlement sites.

28. Despite the expiration of the six-month demobilization program, the provincial government continued to provide assistance to FLEC combatants surrendering in late 2004. Ex-FLEC Colonel Estêvão Bungo Alberto, his fifty-one men, and their families (nineteen wives and thirty-seven children) received soap, blankets, and rations of cornmeal, garlic, and salt as part of a demobilization effort (GPC 2004a).

29. The father beamed proudly as he revealed to me that his son refused to comply, offering his story as proof that love is stronger than greed. He commented, *"Os Angolanos são tão egoistas que vão sempre no bolso de uma pessoa."* This literally translates as something to the effect of, "The Angolans are so egotistical as to always go into a person's pockets"—referring to their propensity for bribing as a means of obtaining information.

30. One committed supporter contended that FLEC forces continue to eliminate upwards of fifty FAA soldiers a day in the dense Mayombe forest and that the army, ashamed of these deaths and unwilling to concede the losses to FLEC, flies the corpses by helicopter to Luanda.

31. This occurred just after General Marques Correia Banza announced that troops stationed in Cabinda would begin training "patriotic educators" as both part of an effort to promote the FAA's mission and a form of psychological combat against remaining FLEC factions (ANGOP 2004h).

32. The colonial army (comprising Portuguese and conscripted Africans) used airplanes as a "potent physical and psychological weapon" to drop both bombs and leaflets that appealed to African laborers to renounce the UPA (a liberation movement predating the FNLA) and return to the coffee fields (Marcum 1969:230). The Portuguese were desperate to salvage their coffee: the 1961 crop "was worth about $55 million and accounted for forty percent of Angola's foreign exchange earnings" (Harsch and Thomas 1976:33). The entire Portuguese flyer read:

> Can't you see the women and children starving and dying in pain? The UPA is lying to you. Your money was taken by the people in the UPA who live well and are abandoning you. The U.P.A. is lying and taking you off to war to die. When there was no confusion, all of you worked in the coffee fields. You went to the store to sell it and you had money with which to purchase cloth, shoes, jackets, shirts, food and wine. Don't make war anymore. The coffee must be picked in order to have money and food and clothing. The whites know that the blacks were deceived. The whites continue to be your friend and are forgiv-

ing when the blacks come back to their jobs and take care of the fields. Coffee brings in money. If you approach the troops or a post and say that you want to be good again, everything will work out happily. The troops will not harm you and will help you against the U.P.A. The Army will defend you if you do not want war any longer. The authority will not punish if the black returns to his senses. (quoted in Marcum 1969:346)

33. Specifically, the report documenting the summary executions and assassinations, sexual abuse, torture, arbitrary detentions, and disappearances of Cabindans during the first year of Operação Vassoura revealed an instance in May 2003 in which FLEC guerrillas executed a civilian for collaborating with the government (Congo *et al.* 2003).

34. Cabindans often cited government reports on government radio or television programs blaming FLEC for the capture and killing of civilians as false, asserting that the secessionist militants would not harm their own base of support. One observer commented on the aforementioned incident in which FLEC opened fire on a civilian vehicle in Bulo (near Miconge), killing four of the vehicle's occupants and injuring six others, on June 13, 1999 (HRW 1999). He remarked that the military and police force often used civilian vehicles and noted that the reports on the incident made no mention of whether the ten occupants in the vehicle were civilians. Likewise, he questioned statements made by the FAA in May 1999 that charged FLEC-FAC with kidnapping some seventy "young men of military age" for their operations in the enclave (ibid.). Challenging the validity of the FAA reports, he recalled his own youth when "the greater part of youths passed through FLEC" and suggested that the youths probably joined willingly.

35. Pearce describes the integration as follows: "On 1 August 2002, the 5,000 UNITA soldiers whom the FAA had selected from volunteers in the quartering areas were officially drafted into the national army. The next day, 30 UNITA generals were allocated their new positions in the FAA with UNITA's Commander-in-Chief, General Kamorteiro, taking the title of Deputy Chief of Staff. The UNITA army that had once controlled most of Angola was signed out of existence" (2005:108). Rafael Marques asserted that by signing Law 4/02 of April 4, 2002, government authorities "were seeking to avoid, at any cost, the establishment of a mechanism that would investigate who might be responsible for wartime actions, and consequently, a formal means of reconciliation and pardon" (Marques 2003b).

36. A variant of the rumor explained that high-ranking FAA officials devised Operação Vassoura as a scheme to kill off two of President dos Santos' least favorite ethnic groups—Ovimbundu and Cabindans—by sending Ovimbundu soldiers to terrorize Cabindans, condensing two ethnic cleansing operations in one.

37. Dissident soldiers told journalists that they had received assignments to protect oil installations in the enclave, but upon reaching Tando Zinze they

realized how far they were from the extractive zone and refused to proceed (*Jornal Digital* 2004b).

38. *Congolesa* might refer a woman from the Republic of Congo (Brazzaville) or the Democratic Republic of Congo (Kinshasa)—though Cabindans also called people from the DRC *Zairenses*. During my research, people in Soyo and Cabinda made few references or generalizations about people from the Republic of Congo, but spoke more often of citizens of the Democratic Republic of Congo—and rarely in the positive. The most common statement I heard about the Congolese that the women consenting to marriage with FAA soldiers were either Congolese or "without pride." The insinuation was that any self-respecting Cabindan woman would not submit to serving the occupying forces. A handful of informants suggested that forced marriages between Cabindans and FAA soldiers from the Angolan mainland were part of a government plot to create a new generation of mixed-ethnicity Cabindans who would campaign for the enclave's full economic and political integration after a few decades of relative autonomy.

39. As early as September 2003, a government spokesman claimed that "FAA are doing everything to bring peace to the region, to permit the free circulation of persons and goods" (Suami 2003).

40. The FAA exerted their influence mostly in rural villages as opposed to coastal towns, where women cited financial constraints as their greatest impediment to marketing produce.

41. Fuel is not the only commodity FAA soldiers profit from routing across Cabinda's borders. During my trips into the interior, I saw swathes of Mayombe cut clear of trees and countless trucks hauling timber out of the forest. Government officials had expressed keen interest in the estimated 200,000 cubic meters annual exportable yield of tropical lumber from Mayombe, and I wondered whether the top military brass was receiving a cut (*AngoNotícias* 2003). Locals claimed that the troops had often used their access and influence to profit from the illicit timber trade—selling Mayombe's valuable wood at the price of $80 to $100 for a truckload of around ten massive trees. Although FAA soldiers patrolling the region detained fourteen illegal loggers (two from Malaysia and eleven from Congo Brazzaville) and confiscated their equipment, critics claimed that the arrests were a publicity stunt, staged to lend credibility to FAA's forest patrols (Ibinda 2004h).

42. Government-appointed authorities called *regedores* may also profit from the illicit fuel trade by diverting subsidized barrels of fuel apportioned to them by Sonangol. A *regedor* outranks a *soba*: each *regedor* is responsible for a group of *sobas* in a given geographic area, such as a *comuna* (the sub-division of a municipality). The rural fuel subsidies are part of a government effort "to stem cross-border smuggling and price racketeering" and to keep fuel affordable in rural areas (Piçarra 2005). Sonangol allows the *regedores* to retain one percent of the transaction value on every sale of fuel to local residents, but the *regedores* can realize a much larger margin by selling the fuel to FAA.

43. The man literally described the situation as a complete *confusão* (con-

fusion). Kapuściński defined *confusão* as "a state of absolute disorientation" (2001:114). Nodding to Kapuściński's definition and describing his own experience, the journalist Justin Pearce explained, "*Confusão* can signify anything from a minor misunderstanding to a massacre" (2002a:220).

44. Also spelled Iabe, Iabé, or Yabe.

45. Bralima (Brasseries, Limonaderies et Maltières du Zaïre), originally founded by Belgians in 1923 under the name Brasserie de Léopoldville, brews Primus and Turbo King, while Bracongo (Brasseries du Congo) produces Skol beer.

46. The villages are Alto N'sundi, Binga Grande, Binga Pequena, Buco Lite, Caia Lite, Cata Buanga I, Cata Buanga II, Cata Buanga III, Cata Chivava, Chienze Lite, Chimbenzi I, Chimbenzi II, Chingundo, Conde Lite, Conde Litombe, Conde Lintumbo I, Conde Lintumbo II, Conde Mbumba, Ditadi, Finho, Iange, Inama, Khengue, Khoyi, Kicololo, Kimbede, Kindamba, Kingubi, Kissungo, Kungo Butuna, Lenga, Mazinga, Mbata-Banga, Miconje Velho, Monaquena, Mongolu, Ncalicante, Ngelezo, Nkandikila, Ntaca, Piadinge, Prata, São José do Luali, Seke Banza, Sigundo, Simobe, Tali, Tali Beca, Talivista, Tando Caio, Tando Ibulassi, Tando Matiaba, Thando, Tsuka-Kingubi, Vako II, Vemba Chionzo, Viedi, Vito, and Yema. (Data from Mpalabanda and *Semanário Angolense* 2004c, 2004d.)

47. Cabindans claimed that the Angolan government, aware that dispatching full battalions into the DRC was both against International Humanitarian Law and capable of generating bad press, began to adopt a more creative strategy to repatriate Cabindans from the DRC. According to them, FAA troops trained soldiers from the DRC in tactics aimed at forcing the refugees back into Cabinda. Allegedly the Congolese soldiers, first stationed in Povo Grande for training attracted too much local attention, so they were transferred to the more discreet Chinga military base.

48. The UNHCR had estimated only 1,750 Cabindan refugees remaining in the Republic of Congo at that time (IRIN 2005a).

49. Amnesty International reported several egregious instances of such retribution, including but not limited to a May 1996 event wherein government soldiers and police "acting in reprisal for the murder of a policeman" drove around "the Povo Grande area of Cabinda City for over four hours shooting indiscriminately, killing one woman and wounding several other people"; a series of extrajudicial executions of "dozens of unarmed villagers" including a pregnant woman and an elderly man perpetrated by FAA soldiers after a set of attacks by three FLEC factions in February and March 1997; an December 1997 incident in which a FAA officer "killed seven people and wounded eleven others because a driver refused to give him a lift"; and a January 1998 raid wherein government troops, enraged by the loss of two high-ranking army officers to the recent explosion of an anti-tank mine, beat civilians while looting and burning their homes (AI 1998f). A 1998 report on the Cabindan conflict prepared by Amnesty International detailed "the atrocities committed by government security forces in the context of a war which has been ignored for

far too long by the international community" and charged that the adjudicating "authorities' consistent failure to investigate killings and torture by both police and soldiers and bring the perpetrators to justice strongly indicates that the perpetrators are acting with the acquiescence, if not the complicity, of the government" (AI 1998e).

50. A report by the U.S. State Department Bureau for Democracy, Human Rights and Labor obliquely suggested that Angolan security forces, comprising the Angolan National Police, the Angolan Armed Forces (FAA), and internal intelligence service, may have consciously engaged in human rights abuses against civilians. Two sentences mentioning the role of the FAA in counterinsurgency operations against FLEC in Cabinda proved especially telling: "The civilian authorities maintained effective control of the security forces. Members of the security forces committed human rights abuses" (BDHRL 2005). The report's pairing of these two seemingly contradictory sentences could be interpreted to mean that the government knowingly allowed, if not encouraged, the security forces to violate the rights of civilians in Cabinda.

51. A civil society activist in Luanda likened FAA abuses in Cabinda to police demanding the petty bribes known as *gasosas* in the capital—just another manifestation of corruption and abysmal wages. "The undemocratic government causes all Angolans to suffer," he said. "You will see it in Luanda just as you see it in Cabinda: there is no housing, potable water or circulation of goods anywhere across Angola."

52. Occidental and Devon Energy declared *force majeure* as operators of Cabinda's North and Central Blocks, respectively, during the civil war. Once *force majeure* was lifted, Sonangol claimed the operator stake on Cabinda's North Block. Despite estimated potential reserves of 250 million barrels of oil, Cabinda's Central remained unclaimed in Angola's 2007–2008 licensing round (Lyle 2007). As the operator of Cabinda's South Block, ROC (2001) refers to its consortium partner Force Petroleum as a "privately owned company based in the UK" in a way that implies it is a British firm, but *Africa Confidential* (2006) recognized Force as an Angolan company.

53. Francisco Luemba the lawyer is a distinguished professor at the Cabinda campus of Lusíada University and author of *O Problema de Cabinda Exposto e Assumido à Luz do Direito e da Justiça*. He is not to be confused with Francisco Luemba the former FLEC military chief of staff. Luemba is a common Cabindan surname.

54. A BBC article entitled "Angolan Army Accused of Abuses in Cabinda" notes the proportion of Angolan oil produced from Cabinda (2004a).

55. Marino Busdachin, secretary general of the Unrepresented Nations and Peoples Organization (UNPO), sensed the international community's apprehension regarding Cabindan independence. He clarified, "Cabindans are not necessarily calling for independence, they are looking for dialogue, the right of self-determination, human rights and an element of democracy" (IRIN 2006d).

56. Reports later surfaced that FLEC-FAC's Nuno collaborated with Ango-

lan officials to create a plan for eventual autonomy in the enclave complete with a $20 million bribe for Nzita Tiago (*Agora* 2003). Nzita subsequently sent a letter to the government proposing a ceasefire, but Angolan officials claimed to have never received any such correspondence. Following the incident, Nuno defected from FLEC-FAC. Sources conflict on whether Nzita Tiago fired Nuno or whether he left of his own accord. An article in *Agora* (2003) says Nuno was dismissed; the *Jornal de Angola* (2003j) says he left on his own. Governor José Aníbal Rocha pledged to unveil an alternate proposal to FLEC and Cabindan civil society groups the following month, yet his plan never materialized (SADOCC 2003).

57. The MPLA leaders adopted the catchphrase "from Cabinda to Cunene" in imitation of their former colonists who spoke of Portugal as extending "from Minho to the Algarve" or the Lusitanian empire as stretching "from Minho to Timor"—a territorializing claim, to be certain.

58. Savimbi once provided military support to FLEC. After Savimbi's death, Isaías Samakuva became his elected successor. Observers note that given UNITA's lack of "capacity to militarily help the Cabindan rebels, one might infer that the continued help that Samakuva promised Nzita Tiago could be just financial and political-diplomatic" (*Semanário Angolense* 2004b).

59. Amnesty International and Human Rights Watch reports detail the way in which government authorities have violated the rights of outspoken clerics; a few examples follow. Government troops fatally shot Bernardo Kebeki, a man from Cabinda City, in August 1997 when they mistook him for a Protestant pastor living in the same neighborhood (AI 1998f). During two separate raids near Necuto in January 1998, FAA soldiers killed Jorge Bitiba Ndembe, a Catholic catechist, and twenty-one members of an Evangelist church, including Deacon José Adriano Bitiba (ibid.). After criticizing the government for intervening in the war in the neighboring Democratic Republic of Congo in an August 1998 radio interview, the Protestant minister Afonso Justino Waco was arrested in Cabinda City and beaten with electroshock batons (Luemba 2008; HRW 1999). He was the former leader of the Comité dos Nacionais de Cabinda, one of Cabinda's earlier civil society groups. In November 1998, UNHCR helped Minister Waco attain political asylum in Denmark (Luemba 2008).

60. In October 1984, the Diocese of Cabinda formed under the leadership of Bishop Madeca; previously an auxiliary Bishop of Luanda presided over Cabinda, maintaining a residence in the enclave (Luemba 2008). Even as Bishop, Madeca was not immune to threats: in September 1998, he received a warning from António Maria Sita, a Cabindan and provincial delegate to the Ministry of the Interior, after Father Congo mentioned FLEC in his homily (HRW 1999). The charismatic clergy and its powerful message won converts in unexpected places, like Angolan Catholic Bishop Dom Manuel Franklin da Costa who backed a referendum on Cabindan independence (GPF 2001).

61. Father Tati is the son of FLEC founder Francisco Andre Tati. Under pressure, Madeca published an "Easter Message from the Binda Church" on April 7, 2004. The missive clarified that "the sentiment of independence never

was official discourse of the Church" and encouraged parishioners "not to confuse individual opinions in the heart of the clergy with the official position of the Church" (*O Apostolado* 2004c).

62. Luemba eloquently opined, "If everything that represents American prestige, technology and values suggests the 'American way of life' and transports the so-called American dream, then ChevronTexaco's presence in Cabinda is still not an opportunity or blessing for the Cabindans; because instead of the 'American way of life,' it imposes on us what will be instead perhaps, a type of 'American way of strife' which transforms the 'American dream' of freedom, equality of rights and opportunities, justice and dignity into a nightmare" (2003).

63. Following the conference, General Secretary of the MPLA João Lourenço attacked Monteiro for his support of Cabindan independence. Lourenço claimed that Monteiro's defiance of Angolan sovereignty was tantamount to the idea of an Angolan traveling to Madeira to defend its independence from Portugal (*Jornal de Angola* 2003f).

64. Tibúrcio emphasized that FLEC-Nova Visão is *not* a liberation movement, but a "political instrument" with the aim of acting as the valid interlocutor in discussions with the Angolan government over Cabinda's future (Zinga Luemba 2003).

65. Willfrid Pena Pitra, the spokesperson of Luís Ranque Franque's mostly defunct FLEC faction, claimed Tibúrcio's organization "was in reality created by the Angolans, with the aim of destabilizing and discrediting the legitimate Cabindan movements" (ACD 2003).

66. The six persons elected to the board were Father Jorge Casimiro Congo, Father Raúl Tati, Martinho Nombo, Agostinho Chicaia, the lawyer Francisco Luemba, and José Marcos Mavungo. Many of these respected members of Cabindan civil society had contributed to the 2002 "Terror in Cabinda" report. They would later form the organization known as Mpalabanda.

67. Meanwhile, Cabinda's Governor José Aníbal Rocha clearly threatened any would-be dissidents as he made a show of visiting the enclave's new criminal lab and Polícia de Intervenção Rápida (PIR) unit near the Yabi prison in Cabinda's southern region (Manje 2003).

68. The government appointed former Justice Minister Paulo Tjipilica as the country's first justice ombudsman in January 2005. The appointment encouraged hopes that FAA atrocities in Cabinda would be investigated. It also drew criticism: the Angolan government had not followed the protocol outlined in the Paris Principles, which entails interchange with civil society not only on the proposed appointee but the functionality of the entire institution (IRIN 2005e).

69. Registration in *Diário da Republica*, III Série, no. 96, December 5, 2003.

70. According to Mpalabanda, government authorities barred some 3,000 supporters from attending the first scheduled inaugural celebration on February 1 at the Immaculate Conception parish and prevented a group of 4,000

from entering the soccer fields at the Higher Seminary of Philosophy on March 6 when Mpalabanda tried to announce its formation a second time. The U.S. Department of State's Bureau of Democracy, Human Rights and Labor presented an alternate version, claiming that the government prohibited 1,500 Mpalabanda supporters from entering a soccer stadium to inaugurate the organization in February (BDHRL 2005).

71. Mpalabanda is the local name for a savanna tree, *Hymenocardia acida*, with an extremely durable root system, which is almost impossible to extract from the earth.

72. The number of attendees is disputed: Mpalabanda claims 6,000 were present, other sources claim 3,000.

73. A few members of opposition parties resented the denials of war in Cabinda. In June 2003, UNITA's Isaias Samakuva declared, "Listen, if Cabinda is at war and we say Angola is at peace that means that Cabinda is not Angola" (*Semanário Angolense* 2003d:7). His statement acknowledged how top government officials' bipolar strategy of shouting military orders and proclaiming peace in all of Angola only served to distance Cabindans and even support arguments for the enclave's separation.

74. The minister of interior's words in Portuguese were *"fictícias e fantasiosas"* (Ibinda 2004f). As Cabindans protested the minister's statement, oil corporations celebrated the prospect of a secure operating environment in Cabinda (Eisenstein and Iley 2004).

75. I have slightly altered the translation for readability. Chicaia expressed this in Portuguese as, *"a ladainha 'independência não, autonomia sim, falta de interlocutor válido, FLEC dividida, vamos dialogar, a Constituição não prevê referendo', é um refrão que não rima com a realidade e por isso deixa de ser agradável ao ouvido. No fundo, maquiavelicamente a guerra continua"* (Ibinda 2004i).

76. Months later, Rocha's distaste for Mpalabanda's tactics became evident when he said he felt "disappointed with some civic associations that promote public disorder and agitation" (Ibinda 2004a).

77. Officials in Luanda estimated that 15,000 demonstrators participated in the July 2004 march, but Mpalabanda representatives claim twice as many, from all ages and backgrounds. The slogans in Portuguese were: *"O Povo Quer a Paz," "Parem com a Guerra,"* and *"Diálogo já!"* (Heitor 2004a).

78. Nzita Tiago occupied the role of president and Bento Bembe vice president of the united FLEC.

79. Luemba (2008) notes that FLEC founder Luís Ranque Franque had considered the path of non-violence espoused by Mahatma Ghandi, Martin Luther King Jr., and Hélder Câmara, but he ultimately assumed a more militant strategy to counter MPLA campaigns in the enclave. Offers of military assistance from the CIA, Zaire, and UNITA may have influenced this decision. Fr. Jorge Casimiro Congo alluded to another: during the socialist era Cabindans rarely received government scholarships to Europe, where liberation fronts blossomed from student movements. Thus, throwing its weight toward a military

solution and the hope of victory, FLEC "ended up losing the most propitious moment in our history", said Congo (Ibinda 2004j).

80. Historically, it was dangerous for Cabindans to discuss the treaty or commemorate its signature. In 1995 the Comité dos Nacionais de Cabinda, a nonviolent political organization founded by Pastor Afonso Justino Waco the previous year, convened a meeting to discuss the Treaty of Simulambuco. In accordance with the law, the group had announced their intent to hold the meeting to the government twenty-four hours in advance. Upon receiving no negative response, the committee proceeded with their planned discussion. Thirty PIR officers burst into the meeting wearing masks and wielding electric shock batons. They arrested twenty-seven committee members, including Pastor Afonso Justino Waco, handcuffed them and brought them to their provincial headquarters. Among those arrested were public functionaries and employees of Malongo: they were not even members of FLEC, just ordinary Cabindans. The police beat these citizens, walked on their backs, heads, and hands, and used electric batons to shock some of the detainees (AI 1998f). Amnesty International reported that the police commander in charge "reportedly told the victims that the police everywhere in the world were an 'instrument of repression'" and, likening the situation to a soccer game, he cautioned his victims "that they had been shown the yellow card, next time they would be shown the red" (AI 1999). Even local traffic police recruits who showed up late to a government parade on the Treaty of Simulambuco anniversary date in 1998 were subjected to beatings by PIR forces. Amnesty International reported that the beatings were so severe that Sergeant Nduli died, while Sergeant Selina Capita and others required hospitalization (AI 1998f).

81. The government employed creative techniques for discouraging protesters from joining the Mpalabanda march. Cabindans recalled how MPLA supporters lured excitable youths off the streets and into the stadium with free soccer tickets, contending that the government intentionally scheduled an exciting match between Primeiro de Maio and Petro Luanda on the same day as the Simulambuco march.

82. In Portuguese, the slogans were, *"Cabinda é nossa, Angola fora"* and *"Queremos o dinheiro do nosso petroleum e não as migalhas."*

83. The sign, in Portuguese, read: *"Com Espírito de Fevereiro, Angola Vencerá."* In 2004, the Angolan government denied Mpalabanda's request to organize a demonstration commemorating the Treaty of Simulamuco's 119th anniversary for fear that such an event would overshadow the February 4 holiday.

84. *Dia da Mulher Angolana* and *Organização da Mulher Angolana.*

85. When Bishop Madeca had reached retirement age he submitted his request for withdrawal, but stayed on a couple more years until the Church announced his replacement.

86. Many priests in the diocese went on strike in solidarity with Father Congo and Fr. Brito (a priest suspended for a homily Dal Corso disliked), closing several churches and suspending masses for over a month in the wake of the scandal.

87. Father Congo, unclear on what the accusations were to begin with, was cleared of all charges in September 2005.

88. To learn more about Swan, I contacted Patricia C. Behnke, author of popular fictional thrillers like *A Victorian Justice*, *Tortoise Stew* and *A Lethal Legacy*. She is collaborating with Brent Swan on a book about his kidnapping. (See Behnke 2005 for a preview.) Behnke said that Swan does not submit to interviews on the subject because of continued psychological trauma resulting from the event.

89. Some Cabindans suspect that the Angolan government tipped off U.S. officials about Bembe's presence in Holland and set a plan in motion to bring the FLEC leader under its control.

90. According to government reports, in January 2007 the FAA incorporated 615 of Bembe's FLEC militants into the Second Military Region in Cabinda (including 2 generals, 3 lieutenant-generals, 7 brigadiers, 9 colonels, 5 lieutenant colonels, 15 majors, 31 captains, 44 lieutenants, and 224 privates), added 113 of his fighters into the National Police, and celebrated the retirement of 53 others (including 2 generals, 4 lieutenant-generals, and 11 brigadiers) (UNPO 2007).

91. A few human rights activists continue to record confirmed violations of human rights abuses in Cabinda. One of them forwarded a document detailing several abuses occurring between June and August 2007. These included the kidnapping and presumed extrajudicial execution of Rafael Chidundo by FAA soldiers in Buco Zau, the kidnapping of four Cabindans by FAA troops during a cross-border raid on the Seke-Zole refugee camp in the Democratic Republic of Congo, the revocation of former Mpalabanda Vice President José Marcos Mavungo's passport by immigration officials, and a traffic cop denied a bribe fatally shot João Francisco Tati and shouted death threats at witnesses.

92. Sarah Wykes was arrested on February 18, 2007. Wykes spent three nights in a Cabindan jail cell, remained in Cabinda under police supervision until February 28, and was finally permitted to return to the United Kingdom on March 19, 2007.

93. Information from unpublished report authored by a former Mpalabanda leader, which covers human rights abuses in Cabinda from June to August 2007.

94. In the words of Mpalabanda's Agostinho Chicaia, "The war is gnawing away at the deep soul of this people, seeding death and hatred"(Ibinda 2004i).

95. This event occurred in February 2005, shortly after I left Cabinda.

CHAPTER 7

1. Michael Watts charts the rise of CSR in the oil industry from the Rio Earth Summit in 1992, emphasizing that the voluntary codes also emerged from negative factors like threatened mandatory regulations and imminent consumer boycotts on environmental and social grounds (2005).

2. Corporations can boost their reputation by pairing up with UN bodies

in "tricky cases" and "difficult areas" (Swanson 2002a; Christian Aid 2004). For example, Chevron is working with USAID on a micro-finance bank and collaborating with UNDP on the Angola Enterprise Fund to develop small and medium businesses. Chevron even tasked two staff members in the Luanda office, Dennis Flemming and Mamadou Beye, with developing these partnerships. For more information about the formation of these partnerships, see Chevron 2000 and Flemming 2004.

3. Each member of the block association pays for its part in the project, determined by its percentage stake in the concession. Joint project sponsors usually receive credit for contributions as a whole (e.g., Block 0 Association); but occasionally the operator—typically the largest shareholder (e.g., Chevron for Block 0)—is credited alone. Joint partnerships can "help dilute the patron-client relationships that permeate community development projects run by single donors such as corporations" (Barnes 2005:14).

4. The Cabindan case demonstrates the boundaries of political sensitivity. An organization like Mpalabanda would not receive consideration for CSR investments, but oil corporations have contributed to Catholic Church facilities. Chevron headed up Block 0 and 14 Association initiatives in Lândana, including the renovation of the Female Catholic Mission and the Diocesan Vocational School. The Catholic Church, an outspoken critic of Chevron and advocate for Cabindan civil society, runs these educational and vocational facilities. Chevron donated a truck to the Bishop of Cacongo and invested millions of dollars in the Dom Paulino Madeca School in Cabinda city.

5. Hydrogen sulfide gas cannot be used in elevation or reinjection because of its corrosive properties, so it is flared.

6. Original figure in imperial measurement: 350 million cubic feet. As of 2001, Cabinda produced 2 million barrels of LPG and condensate per year (Aguilar 2001:55). In 2005, the Sanha condensate complex began harvesting an additional 6,000 barrels of condensate per day (*Oil Voice* 2005).

7. Chevron is also pursuing gas reinjection activities in the Kuito field of deepwater Block 14.

8. Chevron was still Angola's largest foreign oil-industry employer in 2005 (Chevron 2006b).

9. Each year, Chevron also offers Cabinda's valedictorian a scholarship for university study in the United States and grants the province's salutatorian a full-ride to Agostinho Neto University in Luanda. Many of the scholars return to work for the corporation. Additionally, Chevron opened a training center in Malongo in the mid-1980s, but many of its employees received their training at the National Petroleum Institute in Sumbe.

10. His reference to "Congolese employees" is likely a prejudiced remark about the Bakongo in the human resource department or a reference to the fact that a fair number of *Malonguistas* did their schooling in Kinshasa. As such, he may be suggesting that poor education has compromised Cabindans' ability to gain employment in the oil sector.

11. In 2004, Chevron sourced 70,327 kg of local produce through the program at a cost of $102,006.

12. In 2004, Malongo's greenhouse was producing up to 1,000 kg of tomatoes, 350 kg of bell peppers, 300 kg of eggplant, 600 kg of lettuce, and smaller amounts of celery, parsley, mint, spring onion, and radishes each week. (Figures based on personal communication with greenhouse staff in July 2004.)

13. Tati financed six 900 m^2 greenhouses through the program and expected to construct four more 600 m^2 greenhouses through the program as of mid-2005.

14. Grémio ABC provided this information in 2005. IRIN (2008c) confirms that "in places patronized by businessmen and petroleum industry workers, sex professionals can charge as much as US$80 per client", whereas usually "sex with a condom costs one thousand kwanzas (US$13), and two thousand (US$26) without."

15. For the sake of clarity and emphasizing the transnational nature of CabGOC's operations, I will henceforth refer to them under the name of the parent company, Chevron.

16. Based in Lândana, the vocational school has the capacity to train sixty students over a period of one year in one of three fields: construction, business, and administration and agriculture.

17. Humana's German Web page on ADPP Angola (http://www.humana-de.org/05_ang/aointro.html) also omitted the EPF from its map of activities in Cabinda (as it had in Zaire province), listing only Child Aid (Kinderhilfe) and Vocational School (Berufsschule).

18. Teachers reside at the school for eighteen months of training and practice their skills for another year before graduating.

19. Humana probably supplies the remaining four percent from its own funds: representatives claim that the funds earned from selling donated clothes in the country cover ADPP's administrative costs.

20. I speculate that this training could encourage teachers to develop a favorable opinion of the MPLA ruling party and reject claims to Cabindan separatism. There was only one Cabindan in the first graduating class of teachers from the EPF, but now Cabindans make up half of the group.

21. By 1969, 25,000 Cabindan children attended primary school (Vicente 1995a:16). Cabinda had lost its primary center for higher education when, during the incorporation of the Cabinda under the Angolan diocese in 1942, the capacity of Lândana's mission schools were reduced from full philosophical and theological seminary courses to solely pre-seminary studies. Thereafter, students were required to proceed to higher institutions in Angola to complete their coursework.

22. The Portuguese once valued Nzita Tiago enough that they assigned PIDE agents to protect him (Luemba 2008).

23. *O Mais Importante é Resolver os Problemas do Povo*—this is a slogan attributed to Agostinho Neto.

24. The government also reiterated its promise to construct a deepwater

port for Cabinda (ANGOP 2004k). In addition, the government is planning to build a $2.55 million road from Luanda to Cabinda (*USA Today* 2009). Government officials engaged in talks with the China Road and Bridge Corporation about extending the road network from Luanda through Soyo, building a bridge over Congo River to Banana, and continuing the road from lower Congo up to Cabinda (Heitor 2007). A $37-million industrial park in Fútila is expected to create jobs and construction materials such as brick, plywood, tile, and cement (*USA Today* 2009). The Fútila Sea Breeze, a 10-hectare development offering 288 condominiums and 21 single-family residences, is also under consideration. The complex will feature amenities such as a swimming pool, business and community centers, a fitness trail and gym, a boat dock, basketball and tennis courts, and a site for picnics and barbecues.

25. Actual figure $7,309,441 based on 2003 expenditures (*Ngonje* 2004a). A government propaganda piece published in January 2009 claimed that Cabinda's annual budget had increased exponentially to $250 million but did not provide any details on how the figure was calculated (*USA Today* 2009).

26. With support from the World Bank, the Fundo Apoio Social announced concurrent investments in infrastructural repairs in Cabinda. In 2004, the fund pledged $1.6 million to 35 projects, including health posts and schools (ANGOP 2004a; WB 2004). The program funds are subject to World Bank oversight and projects are completed in a cost-effective manner. According to FAS staff, a typical FAS health post may be completed on one-half to two-thirds the budget of a CSR health post (Personal communication, 2005).

27. After losing two Angolan pilots in a hushed accident in July 2001, AirScan transitioned from manned 337 Cessnas fitted with sensors to drone planes, which Israeli AirScan pilots stationed in Cabinda described essentially as large remote-control toys (Campbell 2002; Isenberg 1997). After picking up contracts with the U.S. Department of Homeland Security, AirScan ordered thirty Adam A500 carbon fiber aircrafts valued at a base price of $895,000 apiece, but whether any of these planes are used in Angola is unclear (AFP 2002; EAA 2003).

28. Campbell reports, "Corporate records filed in Florida show that Holloway, the president, and John Mansur, the CEO, also started a second venture, Angola Africa International Inc., which Holloway also refused to comment on" (2002).

29. Dunning and Wirpsa, scholars of the Colombian oil complex, analyzed (2004) an incident in which AirScan monitors responsible for surveillance of Occidental Petroleum's Caño Limón pipeline supported the planning and execution of a Colombian military bombing of civilians in Santo Domingo and contended that AirScan's participation in bombing missions as the "eyes" of Colombian forces exemplified the regularized militarization of strategic upstream resources to secure the lifeblood of the petro-dependent U.S. economy.

30. I heard rumors of the United States' and Israel's involvement in the surveillance of Savimbi. Given that AirScan is an American company and that many of its pilot-operators are Israeli, I wondered whether these rumors could

be referencing AirScan. Not expecting to get a straight answer, I asked one of the AirScan operators about the corporation's "extra-curricular" surveillance activities. He neither confirmed nor denied involvement in tracking Savimbi and FLEC. Justin Pearce writes of aid workers confirming that during "January and February Luena had been full of Israelis operating electronic equipment that looked as though it might have had something to do with surveillance," and that the Israelis "had been busy right up until the day Savimbi died," when they packed up and bequeathed their falafel to a Middle Eastern humanitarian worker (Pearce 2005:62).

31. The Portuguese historian Joaquim Martíns wrote of two types of manioc common to Cabinda in 1968. He described *Manihot Mundele-Mpaku* as a sweet variety, commonly reaching fifty centimeters in diameter and sometimes growing up to six meters long, that may be eaten raw without soaking, and *Manihot esculenta*, which must be soaked in water for a few days or boiled to release the natural cyanide content (Martíns 1972:332). Although I question the validity of this rumor, I do not discount the fact that the type of cyanide intrinsic to the *Manihot esculenta* can decompose into prussic acid, a key component in chemical weapons such as Zyklon B, the insecticide infamously employed by Nazis during the Holocaust.

32. As of June 21, 2006, the photos of government officials remained on the Web site http://www.cabinda.net/WANTED.htm, but it appeared that FLEC had retracted the "warrants" for Chevron officials.

33. Assistant Secretary of State for the U.S. Bureau of Democracy, Human Rights, and Labor Lorne W. Craner declared, "If people are to understand the generosity, strength, and heart of the American people, our corporations can help shape this image" (2001). To many Cabindans, Chevron is tainted with memories of oil spills and collaboration with the government. Francisco Luemba sardonically wrote, "If Cabindan oil has a name, represents a model or lifestyle and is identified with a brand or symbol, these are the one of Chevron which is supposed to embody and promote American values in our hearts, democratic society par excellence" (2003).

34. Rice sat on Chevron's board of directors from 1991 to 2000 and also served as an adviser to the corporation on public policy. Chevron named a 138,000-ton tanker in her honor, but the Condoleezza Rice was renamed the Altair Voyager in 2001 when Rice joined the Bush administration as National Security Adviser (Ibinda 2004e).

35. In the wake of the terrorist attacks on September 11, 2001, the United States increasingly regarded FLEC as not just a nuisance, but a terrorist threat to U.S. national security (read: oil supply) and became determined to hunt down Tchibassa. It is conceivable that FAA operations in Cabinda henceforth became classified as part of an anti-terrorist mission and therefore eligible for special funding. Of course, Tchibassa himself characterized Swan's kidnapping as simply "the questioning of Brent Swan by the troops of our movement" and clarified that he had intended to commit "neither a terrorist act, nor a piracy

or kidnapping" (USCA 2006). According to the *Washington Post*, Tchibassa's arrest was designated as "non-terrorism related" (2005).

36. Some FLEC supporters claimed Tchibassa and his accomplices *had to* kidnap Swan to protect him from harm by the Angolan Armed Forces.

37. Bembe is now a minister without portfolio in the Angolan government.

38. Organizations like CARE and CRS support PWYP, petitioning oil corporations to publish their payments as a primary step toward improving accountability and governance in Angola. Chevron supports the EITI, placing the onus solely on the government to publish its earnings from the extractive sector.

39. At the time, Block 0 was the highest producing concession in Angolan history. In May 2004, the government renewed Chevron's concession contract through 2030.

40. Not long after accepting Chevron's support for the Planalto project, CARE signed on to PWYP and adopted a procedure for engaging with oil companies to support greater transparency that could preclude acceptance of further funds.

41. Data on Chevron's U.S. advertising from July 1 to November 30, 2004 from Ad*Views© 2004, a program of Nielsen Media Research.

42. Personal communication with a USAID official, November 2004.

43. The term "oiligarchy" used in the heading was coined by Global Witness (1999).

44. The Angolan government needed Chevron to spread development beyond the oil zones, where per capita social services expenditures are dramatically higher than in the Planalto. For example, expenditure on education in Kwanza Sul between 1997 and 2001 was $2.20 per capita, as compared to $24.50 in Cabinda (Vinyals 2002).

45. After the war, the government proposed elections in 2004 and 2005; Angolan leaders also advanced, and then delayed, the elections in 2006 and 2007 (Messiant 2008).

46. The MPLA steadily increased party membership from 544,639 in 1992 to 2 million in 2006 (Vidal 2008:144a). Human Rights Watch (2008a) noted how "government-sponsored events were used for party political purposes." Meanwhile, opposition candidates struggled to finance campaign events. They received state funds for their election campaign just one month before elections, whereas Angola's Electoral Law stipulates disbursements up to 90 days before voting day (HRW 2008a).

47. The government's failure to protect freedom of expression and assembly, provide equal access to the media, establish an impartial national electoral body, and ensure security and tolerance for all parties and citizens participating in the elections contravened several documents to which Angola is a signatory, including the International Covenant on Civil and Political Rights, the African Charter on Human and Peoples' Rights, and the Principles and Guidelines Governing Democratic Elections of the Southern Africa Development Community (SADC) (HRW 2008b).

48. Thousands of Cabindans signed a manifesto in January 2008 "calling

for dialogue on a political solution for self-determination," but Human Rights Watch explained such discussion was improbable given "that police and state security services regularly intimidate and harass journalists and individuals and groups from civil society who have publicly questioned the credibility of the peace agreement" (HRW 2008b). Many Cabindan voters proposed to boycott the 2008 elections in protest, as they had in 1992, but those who voted returned a higher proportion of votes for UNITA (31 percent) than the national average (CNE 2008).

49. An assortment of 22 political parties received less than 0.5 percent of the vote; they are now legally required to disband (Corkin 2009).

50. Angola's oil exports were valued at $29.9 billion in 2006 (Russell 2007).

51. Nevertheless, human rights advocates cautioned against assumptions that an elevated level of state social spending would automatically result in gains for the most vulnerable. They observed, "Despite high public expenditure, service delivery in the social sectors remains very poor, mainly owing to extra-budgetary spending, policies of under-allocation to social sectors, and corruption or mismanagement in the budgetary process" (Vines et al. 2005).

52. Violence, mainly perpetrated by the Movement for the Emancipation of the Niger Delta (MEND), "resulted in the shut-in of over 1.0 million barrels of crude oil per day" in Nigeria (Igbikiowubo 2008). In April 2008, Angola produced 1.81 million barrels per day and Nigeria produced 1.81 million barrels per day (Aimurie 2008). By May 2008, Angola was producing 1.9 million barrels per day and Nigeria was producing 1.86 million (Igbikiowubo 2008). At the time of elections in September 2008, Angola still retained this lead (IRIN 2008a).

53. Angola joined OPEC in 2007. Angolan leaders had hoped for a production quota of 2.5 million barrels per day to take advantage of the country's capability of production rates of up to 2.6 million barrels per day by 2014 (Russell 2007).

54. Vines et al. (2005) state that "at times of economic weakness, not only the value but also the share of social spending has fallen (and elite privileges such as foreign scholarships have risen)," thus suggesting "that vested interests are especially effective at capturing state spending when the state is weak." The 2009 budget apportioned 7.48 percent of spending for defense, 6.06 percent for security and public order, 7.9 percent for education, 8.38 percent for health, 10.69 percent for social protection, 23.01 percent for economic functions, 28.89 percent for transport, and 7.59 for other purposes (Sebastião and Londa 2009).

55. Corkin (2009) writes, "It appears that the World Bank has pursued a different approach in order to avoid marginalisation by other emerging financiers. The Bank has also been mollified by the Angolan Government's policy of debt normalisation in an attempt to move away from using oil as collateral for commercial loans."

56. Angola has 9–12 billion barrels of proven oil reserves and Sonangol estimates a total of 40 billion barrels of (as yet unproven) oil resources in Angola (EIA 2008; Lyle 2007). Sub-Saharan Africa's largest oil producer, Nigeria, has 35.3 billion barrels in proven oil reserves (EIA 2005).

CONCLUSION

1. According to Pastor et al. 2007, densely populated communities of color in the San Francisco Bay Area, which are characterized by relatively low wealth and a higher share of immigrants, disproportionately bear the hazard and risk burden of toxic industries. The study included Richmond in this category.

2. Original imperial figure: 2 million pounds.

3. According to Flournoy (2000), "One 1985 federal health research institute study cited 'a strong positive association between the degree of residential exposure and death rates from cardiovascular disease and cancer,' particularly in Richmond and Rodeo."

4. Of the twenty-two public housing projects in Contra Costa County, six are recognized as having high potential for toxic air pollution; but of all the county's predominantly white housing projects, none are sited within a mile of the county's refineries (Flournoy 2000).

5. Other environmental justice groups noted that proximity to "toxic hotspots" corresponds strongly with "breathing and eye irritation" (CBE 2004). The Refinery Reform Campaign (2008) cites similar problems near "toxic hotspots" in Texas and Louisiana, where 50 percent of U.S. refineries are located. More than 67 million Americans in 36 states and 125 cities breathe air polluted by refineries (RRC 2008).

6. Statistics from the U.S. Census Bureau (2000) reveal African Americans comprise 36 percent of Richmond's population and Latinos 26 percent; 31 percent of Richmond residents are white. On the other hand, San Ramon's population is nearly 77 percent white; African Americans and Latinos respectively make up around 2 percent and 7 percent of the population. More than 16 percent of Richmond's inhabitants live below the poverty line, compared with only 2 percent in San Ramon (ibid.).

Richmond's violent crime rate is more than ten times that of San Ramon. In 2006, authorities recorded 1,192 violent crimes per 100,000 persons in Richmond and 113 violent crimes per 100,000 persons in San Ramon (RAND California 2008). Richmond police requested assistance from the California Highway Patrol to help control the city's escalating homicide rate in 2008 (Johnson 2008).

7. Personal communication, May 8, 2009. Disparate levels of education may account for some of the gap in median household income. According to the 2000 U.S. census, 75 percent of Richmond's population over the age of 25 are high school graduates and 22 percent hold a bachelor's or higher degree. Of San Ramon's population over the age of 25, over 96 percent are high school graduates and more than 53 percent hold a bachelor's or higher degree.

8. Unfortunately, the number of toxic releases at Chevron's Richmond refinery is not uncommon in comparison with other refineries. As much as 80 percent of all U.S. refineries operate in violation of the Clean Air Act; twenty-nine states permit refineries "accidental" pollution releases to exceed limits set in the Clean Air Act through legal loopholes (Smith 2005).

9. For example, an instrument failure at the refinery caused a toxic gas release from a flaring unit in March 1994 (Tansey et al. 1999).

10. Original figure: 18,000 pounds (Smith 2005).

11. As of 2005, twenty-four community groups near refineries across the United States had joined the bucket brigades, including groups in California, Ohio, Pennsylvania, Texas, and Louisiana (Smith 2005). With the establishment of his Refinery Reform Campaign in 2001, Larson took the project beyond U.S. borders. For more information, see http://www.bucketbrigade.net.

12. A 2006 study questioned the "shelter in place" emergency response after finding that indoor levels of harmful pollutants associated with oil refining—like sulfates and vanadium—exceeded California's outdoor air quality standards in half of the homes tested in Richmond (BCN 2008).

13. Smith (2005) reports, "At one point, Chevron even argued that it should be exempt from monitoring because its emissions were 'trade secrets.'"

14. Sherman (1996) reports that Chevron "argued that the citizens were trying to 'extort $50 million' and denied that it had any responsibility to mitigate the problem."

15. Personal communication, May 8, 2009.

16. On the whole, the U.S. oil and gas industry gave nearly $35 million in political contributions (77% to Republicans and 23% to Democrats) during the 2008 election cycle (CRP 2009a). In 2000, George W. Bush, an industry darling, received $1.2 million from Exxon, $780,000 from Chevron, $800,000 from BPAmoco, and more from other energy sector donors, including $1.8 million from Enron (Palast 2001).

17. On November 10, 2007, hundreds of protesters decried proposed "upgrade" plans, which would enable Chevron to refine poorer quality crude. Community activists worried that Chevron would manipulate the upgrade to develop the capacity for refining oil produced from tar sands, resulting in five to fifty times more pollution in terms of mercury, sulfur, and greenhouse gas emissions (BADA 2008; *Oakland Tribune* 2008). Communities for a Better Environment cited a press release from Chevron citing new technological developments in processing of heavy and ultra-heavy oil at the Richmond refinery (see Chevron 2008).

18. Original figure from Amazon Watch: 18 billion gallons. Texaco incurred the damages before its merger with Chevron, but court proceedings continue in an effort to hold Chevron responsible for remediation activities.

19. Shareholder activists brought six resolutions to create corporate policies on human rights and environmental protection to Chevron's 2008 annual meeting in San Ramon, but all six failed.

20. On March 15, 2008, 1,000 demonstrators from Direct Action to Stop the War, Greenaction, West County Toxics Coalition, Amazon Watch, Richmond Progressive Alliance, Richmond Greens, Community Health Initiative, Communities for a Better Environment, Global Exchange, and Rainforest Action descended on the Richmond refinery in anticipation of the fifth anni-

versary of the Iraq war. A subset of seventy-five protesters blockaded the entrance to the refinery.

21. Still, the corporation notified Richmond city officials that it would pay $4 million less in taxes based upon a recalculation of its utility-user tax rate (Johnson 2008). Contra Costa County's tax assessor Gus Kramer bemoaned, "They do a $150 million addition and we run the numbers, calculate the added value and send them a bill—and in November they appeal." He acknowledged, "Heavy industry has the best lobbyists money can buy, and over the years they have changed the tax codes and made it harder to assess the value of a modernized plant" (ibid.).

22. Chevron spent $1.8 million on lobbying during the months lawmakers debated AB 32 and donated another $429,000 to business associations lobbying against the bill (Thompson and Hubbard 2007).

23. For a more complete look at the upstream and downstream impacts of oil, see O'Rourke and Connolly 2003.

24. According to Watts (2005), "Oil companies often operate in circumstances of (a) civil war and military insurgencies (Colombia, Sudan, Aceh), and occasionally (b) interstate conflicts (Iraq, Caspian basin, Afghanistan), and (c) military governments or undemocratic regimes in which the security and military apparatuses defend or secure oil operations (Nigeria, Kazakhstan, São Tomé)."

25. Swanson (2002b) suggests that CSR projects reflect corporate concern for consumer boycotts at the pump, but branding efforts mostly serve to help promote premium fuels.

26. Some Americans even suggested pawning off natural treasures as they let out cries of "Drill, baby drill!" Despite the provocative taunt, oil production from the U.S. outer continental shelf could supply only 1.2 percent of total U.S. annual oil consumption and would be sold on the market at international rates with no impact on gas prices (Wagner 2008). Senator Barbara Boxer rejected calls for offshore drilling and reminded the Department of the Interior that California's "coast is not only a God-given environmental treasure and our legacy to our children and grandchildren, it is also one of our greatest economic assets" (2009).

Bibliography

The following abbreviations are used throughout the text and notes to refer to frequently cited references:

ACD	Associação de Cooperação para o Desenvolvimento
AE	Africa Energy
AfDB/OECD	African Development Bank and Organisation for Economic Co-Operation and Development
AFP	Agence France-Presse
AI	Amnesty International
AIMES	Africa Initiative on Mining, Environment and Society
ANGOP	Angola Press Agency
AOJ	African Oil Journal
ARB	*Africa Research Bulletin*
BADA	Bay Area Direct Action
BBC	British Broadcasting Company
BCN	Bay City News
BDHRL	Bureau of Democracy, Human Rights and Labor
BP	British Petroleum
CADHC/CRTC	Comissão Ad-Hoc para os Direitos Humanos em Cabinda & Coligação pela Reconciliação, Transparência e Cidadania
CBE	Communities for a Better Environment
CCCHS	Contra Costa County Health Services
CIA	Central Intelligence Agency

CNE	Comissão Nacional Eleitoral
CPHA	Canadian Public Health Association
CPJ	Committee to Protect Journalists
CR	Conciliation Resources
CRP	Center for Responsive Politics
DW	Deutsche Welle
EAA	Experimental Aviation Association
EABW	East African Business Week
EIA	Energy Information Agency
EIU	Economist Intelligence Unit
EPA	Environmental Protection Agency
ERA	Environmental Rights Action
ESMAP	Energy Sector Management Assistance Programme
FAO	Food and Agriculture Organization
FESA	Fundação Eduardo dos Santos
GoA	Government of Angola
GPC	Governo Provincial de Cabinda
GPF	Global Policy Forum
GTD	Global Terrorism Database
GW	Global Witness
HRW	Human Rights Watch
IFAD	International Fund for Agricultural Development
IMF	International Monetary Fund
IRIN	Integrated Regional Information Networks
LUSA	Agência de Notícias de Portugal
MIPT	National Memorial Institute for the Prevention of Terrorism
MISA	Media Institute of Southern Africa
OECB	Oxford Economic Country Briefings
OFC	Oil Free Coast
OPHRD	The Observatory for the Protection of Human Rights Defenders
OSJI	Open Society Justice Initiative
PU	Project Underground
RFI	Radio France Internationale

RRC	Refinery Reform Campaign
SADOCC	Southern Africa Documentation and Cooperation Centre
TA	Tvind Alert
UN	United Nations
UNDP	United Nations Development Programme
UNDP-WB	UNDP-World Bank Joint Energy Sector Assessment Program
UNEP	United Nations Environmental Programme
UNHCHR	UN Office of the High Commissioner for HumanRights
UNPO	Unrepresented Nations and Peoples Organisation
USCA	United States Court of Appeals
VoA	Voice of America
WB	World Bank
WCTC	West County Toxics Coalition
WHO	World Health Organization
WIN	World Investment News
WRI	World Resources Institute

A Capital. 2004. Salários ou convite para corrupção? August 7.

Africa Confidential. 2006. Cabinda Dreaming. August 25. 47(17). http://www.blackwell-synergy.com/doi/pdf/10.1111/j.1467–6338.2006.00242.

Africa Energy. 2006. Congo-Brazzaville Profile. http://www.africa-energy.com/html/public/data/congo-b.html.

———. 2002. Angola Profile. http://www.africa-energy.com/html/public/data/angola.html.

Africa Initiative on Mining, Environment and Society. 2004. NEPAD—Can It Make a Difference in the Region or Is Angola Too Powerful? *AfricaFiles,* June 10. http://www.minesandcommunities.org/Charter/aimesdec.htm.

Africa Research Bulletin. 2008. Angola: Budget 2008.

African Development Bank and Organisation for Economic Co-Operation and Development. 2005. Angola: African Economic Outlook 2005–2006. http://www.oecd.org/dev/publications/africanoutlook.

Agence France-Presse. 2004. Oil Slick Brought under Control off Congo Republic Coast. *Independent Online,* June 25. http://www.int.iol.co.za.

———. 2002. AirScan Orders 30 Adam Aircraft A500s for Airborne Surveillance. December 20. Available at http://www.defense-aerospace.com.

Agência de Notícias de Portugal. 2002. Angola "Totally Available" to Aid in

Reconstruction—dos Santos ETAN, October 16. http://www.etan.org/et20 02c/october/13–19/16angola.htm.

Agora. 2004a. 2005 Será o ano de vacas gordas. December 18.

———. 2004b. Total-Fina-Elf contra formação de Angolanos. June 12.

———. 2004c. Sobe tudo depois dos combustiveis. May 22.

———. 2003. FLEC-FAC propôs tréguas, Presidência desconhece. May 31.

Agostinho, Duarte, Peter Fielding, Merle Sowman, and Mike Bergh 2005. *Overview and Analysis of Socio-Economic and Fisheries Information to Promote the Management of Artisanal Fisheries in the BCLME Region— Angola.* Luanda: BCLME.

Aguilar, Renato. 2003. "Angola's Private Sector: Rents Distribution and Oligarchy." Paper presented at conference "Lusophone Africa: Intersections between the Social Sciences," May 2–3. Cornell University, Ithaca, N.Y.

———. 2001. *Angola 2000: Coming Out of the Woods? Country Economic Report.* Stockholm: SIDA (Swedish International Development Cooperation Agency).

Aimurie, Isaac. 2008. Nigeria: Angola to Invest 100 Billion Dollars in Oil Production. *Leadership (Abuja),* July 5. http://allafrica.com/stories/200807 070683.html.

Alexander's Gas and Oil Connections. 2004. ChevronTexaco Confirms Sale of Congo Subsidiary to Perenco. August 4. http://www.gasandoil.com/goc/ company/cna43103.htm.

———. 2001. ROC Acquires Interest in Cabinda South Block Onshore Angola. 6(22). http://www.gasandoil.com/goc/company/cna14719.htm.

Alfredo, Augusto. 2004. Queima de gas em Cabinda vai ser reduzida em 2005. *Jornal de Angola,* August 24.

AllAfrica. 2004. Angola: Unlicensed Foreign Trawlers Deplete Fish Stocks. AllAfrica.com, April 26. http://www.flmnh.ufl.edu/fish/InNews/unlicensed 2004.html.

Amazon Watch. 2008. San Francisco Board of Supervisors to Vote on Resolution Condemning Chevron's Abuses Worldwide. June 3. http://amazon watch.org/newsroom/view_news.php?id=1594.

Amnesty International. 2008a: Angola: Unfair Trial of Fernando Lelo. September 22. http://www.amnesty.org/en/library/info/AFR12/008/2008/en.

———. 2008b. Angola: Intimidation. September 5. http://www.amnesty.org/ en/library/info/AFR12/007/2008/en.

———. 2006a. Angola: Further Information on Arbitrary Arrest/Possible Prisoner of Conscience: Raul Danda. October 31. http://www.amnesty.org/en/ library/info/AFR12/009/2006/en.

———. 2006b. Angola: Human Rights Organization Banned. http://web.am nesty.org/library/print/ENGAFR120062006.

———. 2004. Angola. http://www.amnestyusa.org/countries/angola/document .do?id=8D37DC316DD2B82C80256E9E005A905E.

———. 2003. Angola—Cabinda. http://www.amnestyusa.org/countries/angola/ document.do?id=B3ADE3AA5C6624C680256D24003790EB.

———. 2000. Angola: Freedom of Expression on Trial. http://www.amnesty usa.org/countries/angola/document.do?id=17AE2F65FE57CD8680256 912005576CC.

———. 1999. Angola: Freedom of Expression under Threat. November 1. http:// asiapacific.amnesty.org/library/Index/ENGAFR120161999?open&of= ENG-2F3.

———. 1998a. Angola. http://www.amnestyusa.org/countries/angola/document .do?id=767B38F9E939F61080256A0F005C025F.

———. 1998b. United States of America: Rights for All. October 1. http:// asiapacific.amnesty.org/library/Index/ENGAMR510351998?open&of= ENG-USA.

———. 1998c. Angola: Extrajudicial Executions and Torture in Cabinda. http:// www.amnestyusa.org/countries/angola/document.do?id=B23C99759AF 779518025690000692F1B.

———. 1998d. Africa Update: A Summary of Human Rights Concerns in Sub-Saharan Africa. March–September. http://www.amnestyusa.org/children/ document.do?id=FF7F5F01897EE702802569000068A254.

———. 1998e. Civilians Tortured and Killed in Cabinda's Forgotten War. April 29. http://www.amnestyusa.org/countries/angola/document.do?id=E2B19 CE77FAC61B98025690000692CAA.

———. 1998f. Extrajudicial Executions and Torture in Cabinda. March 31. http://www.amnestyusa.org/countries/angola/document.do?id=B23C99 759AF779518025690000692F1B.

———. 1997a. Amnesty International Annual Report 1997. http://www .amnestyusa.org/countries/angola/document.do?id=C2AFCFED94DF2 D7380256A0F005BEA9F.

———. 1997b. Angola—Reconciliation and Human Rights: Amnesty International's Appeal to the New Government. http://www.amnestyusa.org/ regions/africa/document.do?id=FC21229EEC627F03802569A500717E64.

———. 1996a. Amnesty International Annual Report 1996. http://www .amnestyusa.org/countries/angola/document.do?id=B08005 0DBD79FA428 0256A0F005BCC45.

———. 1996b. From War to . . . What? No Reconciliation without Accountability. October. http://www.amnestyusa.org/interfaith/document.do?id= B15B49D3822223BA8025690000692F66.

———. 1996c. Angola: Amnesty International Calls for Investigations at Mass Grave Site. July 26. http://www.amnestyusa.org/countries/angola/ document.do?id=050BC20D41B64E0C80256900006931E3.

———. 1992a. Angola: An Appeal for Prompt Action to Protect Human Rights. April 30. http://www.amnestyusa.org/interfaith/document.do?id=26A7DC F82219517A802569A600601B5C.

———. 1992b. Angola: Will the New Government Protect Human Rights? July 31. http://www.amnestyusa.org/countries/angola/document.do?id=99 66FC0411B82A79802569A6006024C9.

Angola Peace Monitor. 2004. October 12. 11(1).

Angola Press Agency. 2008a. Country Cuts Oil Output. November 5. http://allafrica.com/stories/200811060146.html.

———. 2008b. Revenues Remain Stable Despite Oil Production Cut. October 25. http://allafrica.com/stories/200810270024.html.

———. 2008c. Chevron Takes Full Responsibility for October 15 Oil Spill. October 22. http://www.portalangop.co.ao.

———. 2008d. Oil Experts Confirm Seven-Barrel Spill at Cabinda Coast. October 23. http://allafrica.com/stories/200810240127.html.

———. 2008e. Chevron Expects Daily Oil Production of 620,000 Barrels in 2009. October 8. http://allafrica.com/stories/200810080913.html.

———. 2008f. Oil Production Reaches 1.9 Million Barrels Per Day. February 26. http://allafrica.com/stories/200802260545.html.

———. 2008g. Total Grants USD 800,000 to Oil Institute. January 29. http://allafrica.com/stories/200801290608.html.

———. 2007. China, Country Increment Military Cooperation. March 30. http://www.angolapress-angop.ao.

———. 2006a. Cabinda: Chevron Oil Production to Rise by 40 Percent.May 25. http://allafrica.com/stories/200605250694.html.

———. 2006b. Zaire: Programa piscatório beneficia mais de 50 mil populares. March 17. http://www.angolapress-angop.ao/noticia.asp?ID=425396.

———. 2004a. Cabinda: Fundo de Apoio Social vai investir 1.600.000 USD em 35 projectos. June 14. http://www.angolapress-angop.ao.

———. 2004b. Hospital do Cabassango inicia funcionamento. June 11. http://www.angolapress-angop.ao.

———. 2004c. Aprovado plano de desenvolvimento económico e social para Cabinda. June 2. http://www.angolapress-angop.ao.

———. 2004d. Governo concede regime aduaneiro e portuário especial para Cabinda. May 29. http://www.angolapress-angop.ao.

———. 2004e. Oil Production to Rise to Two Million Barrels/Day by 2008. May 24.

———. 2004f. Esso doa em USD 102 mil à Cruz Vermelha para combater a malária. May 13. http://www.angolapress-angop.ao.

———. 2004g. Sonangol/Chevron-Texaco Sign Block Zero Concession Accord. May 13.

———. 2004h. Cabinda: Forças Armadas apoiam acções do Governo provincial. May 5. http://www.angolapress-angop.ao.

———. 2004i. Country Has 4,000 Landmine Fields. February 17. http://www.angola.org/news/NewsDetail.cfm?NID=16318.

———. 2004j. Comandante militar quer maior cooperação entre população e FAA. January 19. http://www.angolapress-angop.ao.

———. 2004k. Portos de Cabinda e Namibe serão reabilitados este ano. January 17. http://www.angolapress-angop.ao.

———. 2003. Cabinda: ChevronTexaco Will Operate beyond 2010. AllAfrica.com, October 6. http://allafrica.com/stories/200310070027.html.

———. 2001. Zaire: Diagnosticado mais de 200 casos de SIDA nos últimos

10 meses. December 12. http://www.angolapress-angop.ao/noticia.asp?ID
=301196.
AngoNotícias. 2003. Cabinda: FAA realizam operação de limpeza em Buco-
Zau. January 19. http://www.angonoticias.com.
African Oil Journal. 2007a. Angola to Create NOC and Taking Some Duty
Away from Sonangol. November 21. AfricanOilJournal.com. http://www
.africanoiljournal.com/11-21-2007_angola.htm.
———. 2007b. Total Finalizes the Agreements of its Entry into Two Blocks
in Angola. May 11. AfricanOilJournal.com. http://www.africanoiljournal
.com.
Apter, Andrew. 2005. *The Pan-African Nation: Oil and the Spectacle of Cul-
ture in Nigeria*. Chicago: University of Chicago Press.
Argíelles, Raúl Díaz. 1975. *Raúl Díaz Argíelles to the Armed Forces Minister
[Raúl Castro]*. Washington: Cold War International History Project—
Virtual Archive. Available at http://www.wilsoncenter.org.
Associação de Cooperação para o Desenvolvimento. 2003. Pena Pitra afirma
que "Ranque Franque é um independentista." November 23. http://www
sul-online.org/arquivo.asp?id=470.
Auty, Richard M. 2004. "Economic and Political Reform of Distorted Oil-
Exporting Economies." Paper presented at conference "Escaping the Re-
source Curse: Managing Natural Resource Revenues in Low-Income Coun-
tries," February 26. Center on Globalization and Sustainable Development,
The Earth Institute at Columbia University, New York.
———. 2001. The Political Economy of Resource-Driven Growth. *European
Economic Review*. 45:839–946.
———. 1998. *Resource Abundance and Economic Development*. Helsinki:
UNU World Institute for Development Economics Research.
———. 1993. *Sustaining Development in Mineral Economies: The Resource
Curse Thesis*. London: Routledge.
Azerbaijan International. 1996. Angolan President Graduated from Baku's
Oil Academy. 4(2). http://www.azer.com.
Banerjee, Neela. 2002. This Oil's Domestic, but It's Deep and It's Risky. *The
New York Times*, August 11.
Barnes, Sandra T. 2005. Global Flows: Terror, Oil and Strategic Philanthropy.
African Studies Review. 48(1). April 2005.
Bassey, Nnimmo. 2000. "Oil and Gas in Africa." Paper presented at "Globaliza-
tion, Ecological Debt, Climate Change and Sustainability: A South-South
Conference," November 27–30. Cotonou/Ouida, Benin.
Bay Area Direct Action. 2008. Chevron: War, Warming, Toxics and Human
Rights. bayareadirectaction.files.wordpress.com/2008/02/chevron-fact-sheet
.pdf.
Bay City News. 2008. Study: Refinery Pollution Trapped in Homes. April 9.
http://abclocal.go.com/kgo/story?section=news/local&id=6070514.
Beattie, Alan. 2004. The World Bank Digs a Hole for Itself. *Financial Times*,
February 25.

Behnke, Patricia C. 2005. Another New Moon in Africa. http://www.authors den.com/visit/viewShortStory.asp?AuthorID=189&id=17608.

Bender, Gerald I. 1980. *Angola under the Portuguese: The Myth and the Reality*. Berkeley and Los Angeles: University of California Press.

Benjamin, Walter. 1969. "The Storyteller: Reflections on the Works of Nikolai Leskov." In *Illuminations*, translated by Harry Zohn. New York: Harcourt, Brace and Jovanovich.

Berthelot, D. and H. Tonda. 2003. Safety in Deep Waters. *Technoscoop: Magazine of Exploration and Production Techniques*. (27).

Bhagavan, M. R. 1986. *Angola's Political Economy 1975–1985*. Motala: Scandinavian Institute of African Studies.

Bignell, Roger. 1977. Petroleum Developments in Central and Southern Africa in 1976. *American Association of Petroleum Geologists*. 3:1747.

Birmingham, David. 2004. "The Violence of Empire." Paper read at conference "Afrika im Kontext." University of Hannover, Germany.

———. 1998. Merchants and Missionaries in Angola. *Lusotopie*. 345–355.

Biro, Philippe. 1976. Petroleum Developments in Central and Southern Africa in 1975. *American Association of Petroleum Geologists*. 3:1814.

Blaikie, Piers. 1999. A Review of Political Ecology. *Zeitschrift für Wirtschaftsgeographie*. 43:131–147.

———. 1985. *The Political Economy of Soil Erosion in Developing Countries*. New York: Longman.

Blaikie, Piers, and Harold Brookfield. 1987. *Land Degradation and Society*. New York: Methuen.

Boavida, Américo. 1972. *Angola: Five Centuries of Portuguese Exploitation*. Richmond, British Columbia: LSM Information Center.

Boxer, Barbara. 2009. Statement by U.S. Senator Barbara Boxer. Department of the Interior Hearing. April 16. San Francisco.

Brashares, Justin S., et al. 2004. Bushmeat Hunting, Wildlife Declines and Fish Supply in West Africa. *Science*. 306(5699):1180–1183. November 12.

British Broadcasting Company. 2008. Observers Unsure on Angola Poll. September 8. http://news.bbc.co.uk/2/hi/africa/7603735.stm.

———. 2007. Angola "Clampdown" on Separatists. August 10. http://news .bbc.co.uk/2/hi/africa/6941185.stm.

———. 2004a. Exército Angolano acusado de abusos em Cabinda. December 4. http://www.bbc.co.uk/portugueseafrica/news/story/2004/12/print able/041223_angolacabindafil.shtml.

———. 2004b. Shell Admits Fueling Corruption. June 11. http://news.bbc.co .uk/2/hi/business/3796375.stm.

———. 2002. Angola Fines Chevron for Pollution. July 1. http://news.bbc.co .uk/2/hi/business/2077836.stm.

British Petroleum. 2007a. Angola LNG: A Lesson in How to Win Friends and Influence People. *BP Magazine*. Issue1.

———. 2007b. An Epic Tow from Korea to Angola in 71 Days. *BP Magazine*. Issue 1.

Bryant, Raymond L. 1999. A Political Ecology for Developing Countries. *Zeitschrift für Wirtschaftsgeographie.* 43:148–157.

Buela, Amélia. 2004. Governo de Cabinda financia a construção de 350 casas. *Ngonje.* 2 (6):18.

Buira, Ariel. 2005. The Bretton Woods Institutions: Governance without Legitimacy? In *Reforming the Governance of the IMF and the World Bank,* edited by Ariel Buira. London: Anthem Press.

Buffery, Vicky. 2007. Total Acquires Stakes in Two Angolan Exploration Blocks. Forbes.com. May 10. http://www.forbes.com/feeds/afx/2007/05/10/afx3706857.html.

Bullard, Robert D., ed. 1993. *Confronting Environmental Racism: Voices from the Grassroots.* Boston: South End Press.

Bunker, Robert J., and Steven F. Marin. 1999. Executive Outcomes: Mercenary Corporation OSINT Guide. July. Center for Army Lessons Learned. http://call.army.mil/fmso/fmsopubs/issues/merc.htm.

Bunker, Stephen G. 1985. *Underdeveloping the Amazon: Extraction, Unequal Exchange, and the Failure of the Modern State.* Urbana: University of Illinois Press.

Bureau of Democracy, Human Rights and Labor. 2005. Angola. U.S. Department of State, February 28, 2005. http://www.state.gov/g/drl/rls/hrrpt/2004/41587.htm.

Business for Social Responsibility. 2003. Overview of Corporate Social Responsibility. October. http://bsr.org/CSRResources/IssueBriefDetail.cfm?DocumentID=48809.

Cabinda.net. 2001. Chevron Denies Cabinda Oil Spill Responsibility. March 9. http://www.cabinda.net/Chevron.html.

Cafussa, Alberto. 2004a. Petrolíferas não observam Lei Geral do Trabalho. *Jornal de Angola,* June 22.

———. 2004b. Importação de combustíveis consome USD 100 milhões. *Jornal de Angola,* May 5.

Caley, Cornélio (a.k.a. Timóteo Ulika). 1996. *Os Petróleos e a Problemática do Desenvolvimento em Angola.* Lisbon: Centro de Estudos Africanos—ISCTE (Instituto Superior de Ciências do Trabalho e da Empresa).

Campbell, Duncan. 2002. War on Error: A Spy Inc. No Stranger to Controversy. June 12. Washington: Center for Public Integrity.

Campos, Indira, and Alex Vines. 2008. "Angola and China: A Pragmatic Partnership." Working Paper. March 2008. London: Chatham House. Paper originally presented at the conference "Prospects for Improving U.S.-China-Africa Cooperation." Center for Strategic and International Studies, December 5, 2007.

Canadian Public Health Association. 2000. Background to 2000—Resolution No. 3. http://www.cpha.ca/english/policy/resolu/2000s/2000/page5.htm.

Capita, Bernardo. 2003. Ex-Oficial da FLEC pede honestidade a antigos militares. *Jornal de Angola,* December 9.

Carneiro, Carlos. 1949. *O Mar de Angola.* Luanda: Emprêsa Gráfica de Angola.

Casimiro, Alex. 2004. Cabinda Agribusiness Development Project. *Jornal da Cabinda Gulf.* , January–March.

Castelo Branco, F., and D. A. Schaefer. 1969. Angola. *American Association of Petroleum Geologists.* 3:1731–1736.

Castro, Fidel. 2005. Castro Speech: 30th Anniversary of Angola Mission. December 2. Scoop Independent News. http://www.scoop.co.nz/stories/WO0512/S0 0184.htm.

———. 1985. Castro Visits Isle of Youth. May 29, 1985. http://lanic.utexas .edu/la/cb/cuba/castro/1985/19850530.

Cavumbo, Mateus. 2004. Subida brusca apanha consumidores desprevenidos. *Jornal de Angola,* May 5.

Center for Responsive Politics. 2009a. Oil & Gas: Long-Term Contribution Trends. OpenSecrets.org. May. http://www.opensecrets.org/industries/indus .php?ind=E01.

———. 2009b. Chevron: Summary. OpenSecrets.org. May. http://www.open secrets.org/orgs/summary.php?cycle=A&type=P&id=D000000015.

Central Intelligence Agency. 2007. *The World Factbook: Angola.* https://www .cia.gov/library/publications/the-world-factbook/geos/ao.html.

Chelapress. 2004a. Mpalabanda não nos tira o sono. July 30.

———. 2004b. Esta-se a pagar dividas do passado. July 30.

Chevron. 2008. Chevron Unveils New Refining Technology That Converts Ultra-Heavy Oil into Clean-Burning Fuel. March 6. San Ramon. http:// www.chevron.com/News/Press/release/?id=2008–03–06.

———. 2006a. *2005 Corporate Responsibility Report.* http://www.chevron .com/cr_report/2005/.

———. 2006b. Angola Factsheet. April. http://www.chevron.com/operations/ docs/angola.pdf.

———. 2003. *ChevronTexaco Corporate Responsibility Report 2002.* http:// chevron.com/cr_report/2002.

———. 2002. Angola Factsheet. http://www.angola.org.uk/pdf/angola_factsheet .pdf.

———. 2000. USAID and Texaco Announce Public-Private Sector Partnership to Advance Social Development Programs in Angola. August 23. http:// www.chevron.com/news/archive/Texaco_press/2000/pr8_23a.asp.

Chitata, Agostinho. 2003a. Vá, o Soyo espera-lhe! *Jornal de Angola,* June 14.

———. 2003b. Não é possível suportar um conflito com as FAA. *Jornal de Angola,* June 9.

Chivukuvuku, Abel. 2002. Paper presented at "Conferência sobre a Agenda da Paz e Reconciliação na República Visinha de Angola," September 18–19. Luanda.

Christian Aid. 2004. *Behind the Mask.* http://www.christian-aid.org.uk.

———, ed. 2003. *Fuelling Poverty: Oil, War and Corruption.* May. http:// www.christian-aid.org.uk/indepth/0305cawreport/fuellingpoverty.htm.

Coelho, Alberto. 2007. População enaltece empenho na conquista da paz. *Jornal de Angola,* August 13.

———. 2004. Agricultura ganha USD 20 milhões em Cabinda. *Jornal de Angola*, February 3.

Coelho, G. M., D. V. Aurand, and D. A. Wright. 1999. Biological Uptake Analysis of Organisms Exposed to Oil and Chemically Dispersed Oil. Proceedings of the Twenty-Second Arctic Marine Oilspill Program Technical Seminar. Ottawa: Environment Canada.

Coequyt, John, and Katie Albrecht. 2004. Liquid Natural Gas: A Roadblock to a Clean Energy Future. Clean Energy Now. Washington: Greenpeace. http://www.lngwatch.com/race/docs/GP%20LNG%20Report.pdf.

Colaço, Luís Filipe. 2004. Luanda: Perspectivas Demográficas Até o Ano 2025. *Agora*, December 18.

Collier, Paul. 2000. *Economic Causes of Civil Conflict*. Washington: World Bank.

Collier, Paul, and Anke Hoeffler. 2004. Greed and Grievance in Civil War. *Oxford Economic Papers*. 56(4):563–595. http://oep.oxfordjournals.org/cgi/reprint/56/4/563.

———. 2002. *The Political Economy of Secession*. Development Research Group. Washington: World Bank.

———. 1998. On Economic Causes of Civil War. *Oxford Economic Papers*. 50:563–573.

Comissão Ad-Hoc para os Direitos Humanos em Cabinda & Coligação pela Reconciliação, Transparência e Cidadania. 2002. Terror em Cabinda: Primeiro relatório sobre a situação dos direitos humanos em Cabinda. December 10.

Comissão Nacional Eleitoral. 2008. Cabinda. September 16. http://www.cne.ao/graficos_provinciais/mapa_cabinda.html.

Committee to Protect Journalists. 2000. Marques Gets Six Months for Defaming President. March 31. http://www.cpj.org.

Communities for a Better Environment. 2004. Refinery Flaring in the Neighborhood. Spring. Oakland, California.

Conciliation Resources. 2004. Chronology. From Military Peace to Social Justice? http://www.c-r.org/accord/ang/accord15/e.shtml.

Congo, Jorge, Manuel da Costa, Raúl Tati, Agostinho Chicaia, and Francisco Luemba. 2003. Um ano de dor: Relatório sobre direitos humanos.

Connolly, William E. 1995. *The Ethos of Pluralization*. Minneapolis: University of Minnesota Press.

Contra Costa County Health Services. 2007. Major Accidents at Chemical/Refinery Plants in Contra Costa County. Last updated January 15. http://www.cchealth.org/groups/hazmat/accident_history.php.

Cooper, Frederick. 2001. What Is the Concept of Globalization Good For? An African Historian's Perspective. *African Affairs*. 100:189-213.

Copin, D. 2003. 2002–2008 Growth of the Oil Majors. *Technoscoop: Magazine of Exploration and Production Techniques*. Issue 27.

Corkin, Lucy. 2009. Angola's Current Economic Prospects: Oil Curse or Blessing. ARI April–September 1, 2009. Real Instituto Elcano. http://www.realinstitutoelcano.org.

———. 2007. The China-Angola Oil Factor. May 31. http://www.business.iafri ca.com/features/924014.htm.

Coronil, Fernando. 1997. *The Magical State*. Chicago: University of Chicago Press.

Costa, Gustavo. 2004. Cabinda, Região Autónoma. *Expresso*, May 8.

Cramer, C. 2002. Homo Economicus Goes to War: Methodological Individual-ism, Rational Choice and the Political Economy of War. *World Develop-ment*. 30(11):1845–1864.

Craner, Lorne W. 2001. "Privatizing Human Rights: The Roles of Govern-ment, Civil Society, and Corporations." Paper read at conference "Business for Social Responsibility," November 8. Seattle.

Cristóvão, José. 2004. País perdeu este ano USD 2.8 milhões com exportação ilegal de combustivel. *Jornal de Angola*, October 19.

Cuteta, Augusto. 2003a. Defendida protecção dos interesses marítimos. *Jornal de Angola*, July 7.

———. 2003b. Repatriados pedem apoio ao Governo. *Jornal de Angola*, July 7.

da Assunção, Aldair. 2004. Cabinda está insuportavel. *Agora*, May 22.

da Costa, André. 2004. Taxistas querem cobrar mais de 30 kwanzas. *Jornal de Angola*, May 5.

Davidson, Terry R. 2003. Informed Questions on Angolan Political-Military Issues. National Defense University–National War College.

de Carvalho, Paulo. 2004. Subvenções devem beneficiar os mais necessitados. *Semanário Angolense*, May 29.

de Figueiredo, António. 1961. *Portugal and Its Empire: The Truth*. Letchworth: Garden City Press.

De Sousa, Paulo. 2008. "Current State and Future Prospect of Business and Reg-ulatory Environment—Angola." KPMG. Presented at the Gulf of Guinea Oil and Gas Conference. February 5–6, 2008. Abuja, Nigeria.

Denney, Dennis. 2005. Effects of Gas Flaring on Soil Fertility. *Journal of Petroleum Technology*. December.

Deutsche Welle. 2003. Managers Sentenced to Jail in Elf Corruption Trial. November 13. http://www.dw-world.de/dw/article/0,,1028135,00.html.

Duke, N.C., K. A. Burns, J. C. Ellison, R. J. Rupp, and O. Dalhaus. 1998. Effects of Oil and Dispersed-Oil on Mature Mangroves in Field Trials at Gladstone. *Australian Petroleum Production and Exploration Association (APPEA) Journal of International Development*. 38:637–645.

Dunning, Thad, and Leslie Wirpsa. 2004. Oil and the Political Economy of Conflict in Colombia and Beyond: A Linkages Approach. *Geopolitics*. 9(1): 81–108.

Durrenberger, E. Paul and Gísli Pálsson. 1987. Ownership at Sea: Fishing Ter-ritories and Access to Sea Resources. *American Ethnologist*. 14:508–522.

Dynes, Michael. 2003a. America Keen to Exploit Boom in Africa's Black Gold. *The Times*. http://www.timesonline.co.uk/.

———. 2003b. The Oil Flows But Angola's People Live on Handouts. *The Times*, February 24.

East African Business Week. 2008. Africa: Lessons from China's 20 Years of Reforms. AllAfrica.com, May 5. http://allafrica.com/stories/200805051734 .html.

Economist Intelligence Unit. 2008. Angola-gate. November 19. http://www .economist.com/daily/news/displaystory.cfm?story_id=12630028.

Edelhart, Courtenay. 2008. Soft Economy Pushes People to Pawn Shops. *The Bakersfield Californian.* March 27. http://www.bakersfield.com/102/story/ 400411.html.

Eggen, Dan, and Julie Tate. 2005. U.S. Campaign Produces Few Convictions on Terrorism Charges. *Washington Post,* June 12. http://www.washingtonpost .com.

Eisenman, Joshua. 2006. Sino-Japanese Oil Rivalry Spills into Africa. January 19. Institute for the Analysis of Global Security. http://www.iags.org/ no119062.htm.

Eisenstein, Zoe. 2005. Angolan Army "Abuses Cabindans." February 2. *BBC News.* http://news.bbc.co.uk/2/hi/africa/4228785.stm.

Eisenstein, Zoe, and Karen Iley. 2004. Oil Companies Relax as Cabinda Security Improves. *Reuters,* April 27.

Elkington, John. 1994. Towards the Sustainable Corporation: Win-Win-Win Business Strategies for Sustainable Development. *California Management Review.* 36(2):90-100.

Embassy of Angola. 2001. Oil Spill in Cabinda. *O Pensador.* 8(2). Washington, D.C.

Energy Information Agency. 2008. Angola Country Report. U.S. Department of Energy. http://www.eia.doe.gov/emeu/cabs/Angola/Oil.html.

———. 2006. Angola. Country Reports. U.S. Department of Energy, January. http://www.eia.doe.gov/emeu/cabs/Angola/Background.html.

———. 2005. Country Analysis Brief: Angola. U.S. Department of Energy. http://www.eia.doe.gov.

———. 2003. Sub-Saharan Africa: Environmental Issues. U.S. Department of Energy. http://www.eia.doe.gov/emeu/cabs/subafricaenv.html.

———. 1995. Country Analysis Briefs: 1994. U.S. Department of Energy. http:// tonto.eia.doe.gov/FTPROOT/international/059594.pdf.

Energy Sector Management Assistance Programme. 2001. Africa Gas Initiative— Angola, vol. 2. World Bank.

Environmental Protection Agency (United States). 2000. U.S. EPA Focusing Enforcement Efforts on Oil Spill Violations. *Enforcement Alert.* 3(8).

———. 1998. Chevron Richmond Refinery to Pay $540,000. October 15, 1998. http://yosemite.epa.gov/opa/admpress.nsf/34cef4854b892b8b8525645a004d e9a4/fb476240c30ba96b852570d8005e12e0!OpenDocument.

Environmental Rights Action. 2005. Gas Flaring in Nigeria: A Human Rights, Environmental and Economic Monstrosity. June. http://www.foe.co.uk/ resource/reports/gas_flaring_nigeria.pdf.

Epstein, N., R. P. M. Bak, and B. Rinkevich. 2000. Toxicity of Third Generation

Dispersants and Dispersed Egyptian Crude Oil on Red Sea Coral Larvae. *Marine Pollution Bulletin.* 40:497–503.

Eviatar, Daphne. 2004. Africa's Oil Tycoons. *The Nation.* April 12.

Experimental Aviation Association. 2003. Adam Customers Go Online for A500, A700 Update. March 7. http://www.eaa.org/communications/eaanews/030307_adam.html.

Fanon, Frantz. 1965. *The Wretched of the Earth.* New York: Grove Press.

Ferguson, James. 2006. *Global Shadows: Africa in the Neoliberal World Order.* Durham: Duke University Press.

———. 2005. Seeing Like an Oil Company: Space, Security and Global Capital in Neoliberal Africa. *American Anthropologist.* 107(3):377–382.

Food and Agriculture Organization. 2004. Fishery Country Profile: Angola. United Nations, December. http://www.fao.org/fi/fcp/en/AGO/profile.htm.

Fundação Eduardo dos Santos. 1999. Inside Cover. *FESA Magazine.* Edição Semestral (2).

Figueiredo, Jaquelino. 2004. Gas estranho intoxica habitantes do bairro Pângala. *Jornal de Angola,* January 10.

Financial Express of India. 2005. Angola's Luanda in World's Most Expensive Cities. October 26. http://www.financialexpress.com/latest_full_story.php?content_id=106842.

Financial Times. 2004a. Move That Could Weaken IMF Leverage. April 21.

———. 2004b. Angola's State Oil Group Seeks Dollars 2.5bn Syndicated Loan. April 21.

Flemming, Dennis. 2004. The Angola Partnership Initiative. *Jornal da Cabinda Gulf.* January-March.

Flournoy, Craig. 2000. Refinery Accidents, Anxiety Increase. Minorities Face "Ticking Time Bombs." *The Dallas Morning News.* October 1.

Folha 8. 2005a. Governo "deu" 80% da terra de petroleo aos australianos da Roc Oil. February 5.

———. 2005b. Má-fé do "comuna" Almeida gerou milhões de mortos. February 5.

———. 2005c. Milhares a favor da autonomia de Cabinda. February 5.

———. 2004a. Petrolíferos querem proteger ouro negro. July 17.

———. 2004b. Corrupção em Angola apoiada por interesses estrangeiros. July 10.

———. 2004c. Com a nossa pobreza e os nossos ricos—Vamos viver mesmo assim. June 5.

Fontoura, Manuel. 2004. Gasolina sobe para 100kz em Ndalatando. *Jornal de Angola,* January 23.

Fragoso, Garrido. 2004a. Cabinda recebe investimentos de USD 370 milhões. *Jornal de Angola,* June 3.

———. 2004b. Cabinda beneficia de regime aduaneiro especial. *Jornal de Angola,* May 29.

———. 2003. Pobreza em Angola regista niveis alarmantes. *Jornal de Angola,* December 18.

Frank, Andre Gunder. 1966. The Development of Underdevelopment. *Monthly Review*. 18(4).

Franque, D. Domingos José. 1940. *Nós, os Cabindas: História, leis, usos e costumes dos povos de N'Goio*. Lisbon: Argo.

French-McCay, D. P. 2001. Modelling Evaluation of Water Concentrations and Impacts Resulting from Oil Spills With and Without the Application of Dispersants. Proceedings of the Fifth International Marine Environmental Modelling Seminar. Trondheim, Norway: SINTEF Applied Chemistry.

Frynas, Jedrzej George. 1998. Political Instability and Business: Focus on Shell in Nigeria. *Third World Quarterly*. 19(3):457–478.

Ganaziol, D. 2003. Architecture for Deep Water Wells. *Technoscoop: Magazine of Exploration and Production Techniques*. (27).

Gary, Ian, and Terry Lynn Karl. 2003. Bottom of the Barrel: Africa's Oil Boom and the Poor. Catholic Relief Services. http://www.crs.org.

Gleijeses, Piero. 2002. *Conflicting Missions: Havana, Washington and Africa 1959–1976*. Chapel Hill: University of North Carolina Press.

Global Exchange. 1996. Human Rights and Environment in Tabasco. http://flag.blackened.net/revolt/mexico/reports/gxhrenv.html.

Global Policy Forum. 2001. Cornered Rebels May Lash Out in Cabinda. February 12. http://www.globalpolicy.org.

Global Terrorism Database. 2007. START/CETIS. http://www.start.umd.edu/data/gtd/ (accessed May 30, 2008).

Global Witness. 2004. Time for Transparency: Coming Clean on Oil, Mining and Gas Revenues. March. http://www.globalwitness.org/reports/show.php/en.00049.html.

———. 2002. All the President's Men: The Devastating Story of Oil and Banking in Angola's Privatised War. http://www.globalwitness.org.

———. 1999. A Crude Awakening. http://www.globalwitness.org/media_library_detail.php/93/en/a_crude_awakening.

Gomes Porto, João. 2003. Cabinda: Notes on a Soon-to-Be-Forgotten War. August. Pretoria: Institute for Security Studies.

Gonçalves, Gerónimo. 2004. FESA doa medicamentos ao hospital de Cabinda. *Jornal de Angola*, April 14.

Government of Angola. 2004. Relatório de fundamentação do orçamento geral do estado. Luanda: Government of Angola.

———. 2003a. Perfil sócio-económico do Zaire. April. Luanda: Government of Angola.

———. 2003b. Perfil sócio-económico de Cabinda. January. Luanda: Government of Angola. Re-evaluation prepared by KPMG.

———. 2002. Inquérito de indicadores múltiplos. Luanda: Instituto Nacional de Estatística.

———. 2001. Seminário sobre Legislação do Ambiente em Angola. Ministério das Pescas e Ambiente. Luanda: Imprensa Nacional.

Governo Provincial de Cabinda. 2004a. Ex-guerrilheiros da FLEC apresentam-se às autoridades. *Nsi Mbote*. http://www.gpcabinda.com/jornal/ed_06.htm.

———. 2004b. *Operacional província de Cabinda 2004–07.*

———. 1999. *Programa piloto de industrialização.*

Grundy, Trevor. 2004. African Oil Supply Boost "Ripe for Corruption." *Scotsman*, May 30.

Guardiola, Nicole. 2005. Os "novos ricos" apostam nos negócios. November 5. *Expresso África.* http://africa.expresso.clix.pt/dossiers/angola30anos/artigo .asp?id=ES197727.

Guimarães, Fernando Andresen. 2001. *The Origins of the Angolan Civil War: Foreign Intervention and Domestic Political Conflict.* New York: St. Martin's Press.

Gulf Restoration Network. 2002. The Threat of Mercury from Discharges from Oil and Gas Platforms. http://www.gulfrestorationnetwork.org/mercury/ issues.htm.

Gunn, Gillian. 1987. The Angolan Economy: A Status Report. In *Angola, Mozambique and the West,* edited by Helen Kitchen. New York: Praeger.

HalliburtonWatch. 2005. Bush Administration Distorts Science to Shield Halliburton from Pollution Laws. March 16. http://www.halliburtonwatch.org/ news/epa_whistleblower2.html.

Harsch, Ernest, and Tony Thomas. 1976. *Angola: The Hidden History of Washington's War.* New York: Pathfinder Press.

Hecht, Susanna. 1985. Environment, Development and Politics: Capital Accumulation and the Livestock Sector in Eastern Amazonia. *World Development.* 13(6):663–684.

Hecht, Susanna, and Alexander Cockburn. 1989. *The Fate of the Forest.* London: Verso.

Hedberg, Hollis D., John D. Moody, and Louis C. Sass. 1959. Petroleum Developments in Africa. *American Association of Petroleum Geologists.* 2:1640.

———. 1958. Developments in Africa in 1957. *American Association of Petroleum Geologists.* 2:1644.

Heitor, Jorge. 2007. Cabinda quer ter um porto de águas profundas. *Público.* August 12.

———. 2004a. FLEC Continua a defender separação. *Folha 8,* July 17.

———. 2004b. Poder em Angola é depravado. *Folha 8,* June 5.

Helvarg, David. 2009. Anatomy of an Oil Spill. *Sierra,* March/April:52-57,63.

———. 2006. A Real Energy Boom. *Sierra,* March/April:13.

Henderson, David. 2001. Misguided Virtue: False Notions of Corporate Social Responsibility. *New Zealand Business Roundtable.* http://www.nzbr.org .nz/documents/publications/publications-2001/misguided_virtue.pdf.

Heredia, Christopher, and Kevin Fagan. 2007. Some Say Richmond Beaches, Birds Were Overlooked after Oil Spill. November 16. *San Francisco Chronicle.* http://www.sfgate.com/cgi-bin/article.cgi?f=/c/a/2007/11/16/MNUBT DBMB.DTL.

Hodges, Tony. 2008. The Economic Foundations of the Patrimonial State. In *Angola: The Weight of History,* edited by Patrick Chabal and Nuno Vidal. New York: Columbia University Press.

———. 2003. *Angola: Anatomy of an Oil State.* Bloomington: Indiana University Press.

———. 2002. *Angola: Do Afro-Estalinismo ao capitalismo selvagem.* Lisbon: Principia.

———. 2001. *Angola: From Afro-Stalinism to Petro-Diamond Capitalism.* Bloomington: Indiana University Press.

Holing, Dwight. 1990. *Coastal Alert: Ecosystems, Energy and Offshore Oil Drilling.* Edited by Natural Resources Defense Council and the Central Coast Regional Studies Program. Washington D.C.: Island Press.

Human Rights Watch. 2008a. Angola: Irregularities Marred Historic Elections. September 14. http://www.hrw.org/en/news/2008/09/14/angola-irregularities-marred-historic-elections.

———. 2008b. Angola: Doubts Over Free and Fair Elections. August 12. http://www.hrw.org/en/news/2008/08/12/angola-doubts-over-free-and-fair-elections.

———. 2008c. Angola: Resume Negotiations with UN Rights Body. May 22. http://www.hrw.org/en/news/2008/05/22/angola-resume-negotiations-un-rights-body.

———. 2007. "They Pushed Down the Houses": Forced Evictions and Insecure Land Tenure for Luanda's Urban Poor. May 14. http://www.hrw.org/en/reports/2007/05/14/they-pushed-down-houses-0.

———. 2004a. Angola: In Oil-Rich Cabinda, Army Abuses Civilians. December 23. http://hrw.org/english/docs/2004/12/23/angola9922.htm.

———. 2004b. Angola: Between War and Peace in Cabinda. December. http://hrw.org/backgrounder/africa/angola/2004/1204/cabinda122104.pdf.

———. 2004c. Some Transparency, No Accountability: The Use of Oil Revenue in Angola and Its Impact on Human Rights. Human Rights Watch, January. http://www.hrw.org/reports/2004/angola0104.

———. 2003a. World Report 2003: Angola. http://www.hrw.org/wr2k3/africa1.html.

———. 2003b. Struggling through Peace: Return and Resettlement in Angola. August. http://www.hrw.org/reports/2003/angola0803/5.htm#_ftn8.

———. 2002. The War Is Over: The Crisis of Angola's Internally Displaced Continues. Human Rights Watch. http://hrw.org/backgrounder/africa/angola/2002/angola-idps.pdf.

———. 1999. Angola Unravels. http://www.hrw.org/reports/1999/angola/Angl998-05.htm.

———. 1998. World Report 1998: Angola. Human Rights Watch. http://www.hrw.org/worldreport/Africa-01.htm.

———. 1997a. World Report 1997: Angola. http://www.hrw.org/reports/1997/WR97/AFRICA-01.htm#P80_45186.

———. 1997b. Still Killing: Landmines in Southern Africa. May. http://www.hrw.org/reports/1997/lmsa/.———. 1996a. World Report 1996: Angola. http://www.hrw.org/reports/1996/WR96/Africa-01.htm.

———. 1996b. Between War and Peace: Arms Trade and Human Rights Abuses

since the Lusaka Protocol. February. http://www.hrw.org/reports/1996/An
gola.htm.

———. 1994. Angola: Arms Trade and Violations of the Laws of War since the
1992 Elections. Human Rights Watch, November 8. http://www.hrw.org/
reports/archives/africa/ANGOLA94N.htm.

Ibinda. 2006. Governo de Angola quer extinguir a Mpalabanda. June 19. http://
www.ibinda.com.

———. 2004a. Aníbal Rocha "satisfeito" com relacionamento—Governador de
Cabinda considera "excelentes" relações entre Governo e igrejas. December 30.

———. 2004b. Governador Aníbal Rocha Acusado de Privilegiar as suas Empresas em Cabinda. October 27. http://www.ibinda.com.

———. 2004c. Antigo governador de Cabinda responde a acusações de uso
indevido de fundos. October 11. http://ibinda.com/noticias.php?noticia=1170.

———. 2004d. ChevronTexaco ergue sede em Cabinda. September 24. http://
www.ibinda.com.

———. 2004e. Pedido de extradição de Bento Bembe foi assinado por Condoleeza Rice. September 14. http://www.ibinda.com.

———. 2004f. Ministro do interior de Angola afirma que repressão em
Cabinda é "ficção" e "fantasia." June 29. http://www.ibinda.com.

———. 2004g. Depois da malária e das anemias SIDA é a maior causa de mor-
talidade nos adultos em Cabinda. June 9. http://www.ibinda.com.

———. 2004h. Empresas estrangeiras operam ilegalmente na floresta do Maiombe. June 9. http://www.ibinda.com.

———. 2004i. Presidente da Mpalabanda sublinhou em Lisboa "resistência do
povo" Cabinda à opressão. May 28. http://www.ibinda.com.

———. 2004j. "Todo o Cabinda é Mpalabanda," afirma padre Jorge Congo.
May 17. http://www.ibinda.com.

———. 2004k. MPLA acusado de tentar provocar mal-estar entre Igrejas
Católica e Evangélica. May 17. http://www.ibinda.com.

Igbikiowubo, Hector. 2008. Angola: Oil Production—Country Beats Nigeria
Again. *Vanguard* (Lagos), June 16. http://allafrica.com/stories/printable/
200806161464.html.

Ignatyev, Oleg. 1977. *Secret Weapon in Africa.* Moscow: Progress Publishers.

Ikokwu, Constance. 2008. Nigeria: Country, Angola to Be Highest-Earning Oil
Producers by 2030. *This Day* (Lagos), November 26. http://allafrica.com/
stories/200811260009.html.

Iley, Karen, and Zoe Eisenstein. 2004. LNG Plants Seed of Hope in Soyo.
Upstream, December 10.

Independent Online. 2004a. Oil Slick Brought under Control off Congo
Republic Coast. June 25. http://www.int.iol.co.za.

———. 2004b. Heavy Oil Slick Oozes onto Congo's Beaches. June 25. http://
www.iol.co.za.

Integrated Regional Information Networks. 2008a. Angola: Government Pledges
to Provide Better Health Care. October 1. http://www.irinnews.org/Report
.aspx?ReportId=80693.

———. 2008b. Angola: Election Free and Fair, Sort of. September 9. http://www.irinnews.org/Report.aspx?ReportId=80253.

———. 2008c. Angola: Sex Work in Separatist Cabinda. April 11. http://www.plusnews.org/Report.aspx?ReportId=77724.

———. 2006a. Angola: Concern as Luanda Pushes through Cabinda Peace Deal. October 3. http://www.irinnews.org/report.aspx?reportid=61248.

———. 2006b. China Entrenches Position in Booming Economy. April 17. http://www.irinnews.org/report.aspx?reportid=58756.

———. 2006c. Chairs Stay Empty around the Cabindan Negotiating Table. March 14. http://www.alertnet.org.

———. 2006d. Cabindan Separatists Pin Their Hopes on International Law. March 6. http://www.irinnews.org/report.asp?ReportID=52038.

———. 2006e. Angola: Rebels Vow to Fight on Despite Peace Deal. August 1. http://www.irinnews.org/report.aspx?reportid=59812.

———. 2005a. Angola: Refugees Not Ready to Return to Cabinda. March 8. http://www.irinnews.org/report.asp?ReportID=45999.

———. 2005b. Angola: Oil-Backed Loan Will Finance Recovery Projects. February 21. http://www.irinnews.org/report.asp?ReportID=45688.

———. 2005c. Luanda Likely to Fare Badly at an African Peer Review, Says Analyst. February 2. http://www.irinnews.org/report.asp?ReportID=45356.

———. 2005d. Transparency on Oil Money Delaying Donor Conference. February 2.

———. 2005e. Angola: Appointment of New Justice Ombudsman Sparks Concern. January 26. http://www.irinnews.org/report.asp?ReportID=45244.

———. 2004a. Cabinda Separatists Merge to Negotiate with Government. September 8. http://www.irinnews.org/report.asp?ReportID=43085.

———. 2004b. Angola: Frustration as Oil Windfall Spending Neglects the Poor. September 3. http://www.irinnews.org/print.asp?ReportID=43013.

———. 2004c. Rights Groups Concerned over Rise in Political Violence. July 5. http://www.irinnews.org/report.asp?ReportID=41999.

———. 2004d. Angola: Survival Top Priority Rather Than Upcoming Elections. June 14. http://www.irinnews.org/report.asp?ReportID=41663.

———. 2004e. Economic Recovery Plan Fails to Appease Cabindans. June 3. http://www.unpo.org/article.php?id=738.

———. 2004f. Cabindans Claim Recovery Plan a Hoodwink. June 3. http://www.irinnews.org/report.asp?ReportID=41407&SelectRegion=Southern_Africa&SelectCountry=ANGOLA.

———. 2004g. President Denies Ongoing Unrest in Cabinda. May 17. http://www.irinnews.org/report.asp?ReportID=41087.

———. 2004h. Angola: Diamond Trade in Conflict with Human Rights. May 10. http://www.irinnews.org/report.asp?ReportID=40974.

———. 2004i. Angola: Urgent Work Needed to Improve Human Rights. August 23. http://www.irinnews.org/print.asp?ReportID=42803.

———. 2004j. Plan to Disarm Civilians. March 19. http://www.angolapost.com.

————. 2004k. Empowering Girls at Heart of AIDS Strategy. March 5. http://www.plusnews.org/webspecials/womensday/ang040305.asp.

————. 2003a. Web Special on Cabinda. October. http://www.irinnews.org/webspecials/cabinda/default.asp.

————. 2003b. Government Says Talks on Cabinda Close. August 6. http://www.irinnews.org/report.asp?ReportID=35825.

————. 2003c. Separatists and Government Urged to Resolve Cabinda Conflict. July 10. http://www.irinnews.org/report.asp?ReportID=35322.

————. 2003d. Separatists Stay Open to Talks over Cabinda. April 7. http://www.irinnews.org/report.asp?ReportID=33323.

————. 2003e. NGOs urge UN to Investigate Abuses in Cabinda. January 21. http://www.irinnews.org/report.asp?ReportID=31820.

International Crisis Group. 2003. *Angola's Choice: Reform or Regress.* April 7. Africa Report, No. 61.

International Fund for Agricultural Development. 2002a. *Angola: A Field Diagnostic Study. Gender Strengthening Program in East and Southern Africa.* March.

————. 2002b. Angola: *Northern Fisheries Communities Development Programme (PESNORTE).* November.

International Monetary Fund. 2009. IMF Concludes 2008 Article IV Consultation with Angola. April 30. Public Information Notice No. 09/51. Washington, D.C.: IMF.

————. 2007. Angola: Selected Issues and Statistical Appendix. October 26. Country Report No. 07/355. Washington, D.C.: IMF.

————. 2005. Angola: Selected Issues and Statistical Appendix. April 5. Country Report No. 05/125. Washington, D.C.: IMF.

Isenberg, David. 1997. Soldiers of Fortune Ltd.: A Profile of Today's Private Sector Corporate Mercenary Firms. Center for Defense Information. http://www.aloha.net/~stroble/mercs.html.

Jackson, Michael. 2002. *The Politics of Storytelling: Violence, Transgression and Intersubjectivity.* Copenhagen: Museum Tusculanum Press.

Jason. 2006. So I've Made It to Cabinda. Institute for International Cooperation and Development (Humana). http://www.iicd-volunteer.org/stories/angola/storie_006.html.

Johnson, Chip. 2008. Time for Richmond to Stand Up to Chevron. *San Francisco Chronicle.* February 8. http://sfgate.com/cgi-bin/article.cgi?f=/c/a/2008/02/08/BAQ9UUIGQ.DTL.

Johnston, Paul, Dave Santillo, Ruth Stringer, and Julie Ashton. 1998. Report on the World's Oceans. May. Washington D.C.: Greenpeace Research Laboratories.

Jornal de Angola. 2005a. Plataforma do Kizomba em Luanda. February 5.

————. 2005b. Petrolíferas com novo recurso. January 26.

————. 2005c. Presença das FAA em Cabinda evita acções desestabilizadoras. January 14.

————. 2004a. Alfándegas contra exportação illegal de combustíveis. September 20.

———. 2004b. Direitos humanos em Cabinda satisfazem representante da ONU. August 20.

———. 2004c. 75% das areas rurais terá agua potavel até 2016. August 4.

———. 2004d. Mais da metade de empresas está em Luanda. July 24.

———. 2004e. Angola e EUA discutem em pormenor cooperação militar. May 25.

———. 2004f. Taxistas especuladores serão punidos. May 5.

———. 2004g. UNTA-CS indignada com subida de combustíveis. May 5.

———. 2004h. Defendida actualização periódica de preços. May 5.

———. 2004i. Eliminação da queima de gas custa USD 1.5 bilião. April 3.

———. 2004j. Forças Armadas negam violações em Cabinda. March 15.

———. 2004k. Reservas da Bacia do Congo chegam a 10 biliões de barris. February 17.

———. 2004l. Fábrica de material de prospecção petrolífera arranca em fevereiro. January 28.

———. 2004m. Processo de paz para Cabinda tem 3 fases. January 24.

———. 2004n. Enchentes marcam postos de combustíveis. January 23.

———. 2004o. Fenómeno "criança feitiçeira" chega ao fim. January 14.

———. 2004p. Preço de combustível sobe no Zaire. January 12.

———. 2003a. Troço Soyo/Luanda clama por reparação. December 15.

———. 2003b. Sonamet arrecada 5 milhões de dolares este ano. December 9.

———. 2003c. Armadores industriais violam leis de pesca. November 20.

———. 2003d. Governo de Cabinda apoia desmobilização de ex-militares da FLEC. November 14.

———. 2003e. Ex-militares da Flec ingressam nas FAA. October 10.

———. 2003f. Governo busca vias para paz em Cabinda. August 15.

———. 2003g. Governo reitera disponibilidade para diálogo sobre Cabinda. August 13.

———. 2003h. Angola vai produzir 4 milhões de toneladas de gás. May 25.

———. 2003i. Punto d' ordem: Cabinda. May 14.

———. 2003j. Dirigente da Flec/Fac abandona organização. May 13.

Jornal Digital. 2005. 2004a. Angola inspira-se nas técnicas de propaganda das ex-tropas coloniais portuguesas. May 10. http://jornaldigital.com.

———. 2004b. Tropas angolanas presentes no Congo provocam regresso forçado de Cabindas. May 5. http://jornaldigital.com.

Juhasz, Antonia, et al. 2009. The True Cost of Chevron. http://truecostofchevron.com/report.

Kairos-Africa. 2003. Cabinda. http://www.africafiles.org/article.asp?ID=3332.

———. 2002. Update Angola. January 11. http://www.africafiles.org/article.asp?ID=38.

Kapuściński, Ryszard. 2001. *Another Day of Life*. New York: Vintage International.

Karl, Terry Lynn. 1997. *The Paradox of Plenty*. Berkeley and Los Angeles: University of California Press.

Kaure, Alexactus T. 1999. *Angola: From Socialism to Liberal Reforms*. Harare: Sapes Books.

Kharaka, Yousif K., and James K. Otton. 2003. *Environmental Impacts of Petroleum Production: Initial Results from the Osage-Skiatook Petroleum Environmental Research Sites, Osage County, Oklahoma*. Water-Resources Investigations Report 03-4260, United States Geological Survey. http://pubs.usgs.gov/wri/wri03-4260/.

Kilongo, Kumbi. 2004. Recursos marinhos na Província do Zaire no ámbito de monotorização e gestão da pesca artisanal. Luanda: Instituto de Investigação Marinha & Pesnorte.

———. 2003. Recursos marinhos na Província do Zaire no ámbito de monotorização e gestão da pesca artisanal. November. Luanda: Instituto de Investigação Marinha & Pesnorte.

Kirkland, Tracy. 2005. Nigeria: Grantees Campaign against Gas Flaring. October 6. Global GreenGrants Fund. http://www.greengrants.org/grantstories.php?news_id=85.

Kirsch, Stuart. 2002. Rumour and Other Narratives of Political Violence in West Papua. *Critique of Anthropology*. 22(1):53–79.

Klare, Michael. 2004. Bush-Cheney Energy Strategy: Procuring the Rest of the World's Oil. *Foreign Policy in Focus*. January. Posted to http://www.commondreams.org/views04/0113–01.htm.

———. 2001. *Resource Wars*. Boston: Beacon Press.

Klaus, Erich. 2003. Cuba: Air Force History. November 5. http://www.aeroflight.co.uk/waf/americas/cuba/Cuba-af-history.htm.

Koning, Tako. 2002. Oil and Diamonds: The Geology of Angola. In *Stories for Trees*. Luanda: Development Workshop.

Korten, David. 1995. *When Corporations Rule the World: Transformation and Resistance*. Hartford: Kumarian Press.

Kyle, Steven. 2005. Oil and Politics in Angola. Working Paper 2005-22. Ithaca: Cornell University. http://www.kyle.aem.cornell.edu.

Labov, William. 1997. Some Further Steps in Narrative Analysis. *The Journal of Narrative and Life History*. 7(1-4):395-415.

LaFraniere, Sharon. 2006. In Oil-Rich Angola, Cholera Preys Upon Poorest. *New York Times*, June 16.

Laidi, Zaki. 1990. *The Superpowers and Africa: The Constraints of a Rivalry 1960-1990*. Chicago: University of Chicago Press.

Lallemand, Alain. 2002. The Field Marshal. November 15. The Center for Public Integrity. http://www.publicintegrity.org.

Le Billon, Philippe. 2003. Buying Peace or Fuelling War: The Role of Corruption in Armed Conflicts. *Journal of International Development*. 15: 413–426.

———. 2001a. Angola's Political Economy of War: The Role of Oil and Diamonds, 1975–2000. *African Affairs*. 100:55–80.

———. 2001b. The Political Ecology of War: Natural Resources and Armed Conflicts. *Political Geography*. 20:561–584.

Lelo-Tubi, Barnabé. 1980. Alguns rasgos da problemática Cabindesa. In *Gri-

tos de Cabinda: Antologia de Poemas de Escritores Cabindeses, edited by Batuama. Lisbon: n.p.

Lindgren, Charlotte, Helene Lager, and Jonas Fejes. 2001. Oil Spill Dispersants: Risk Assessment for Swedish Waters. December. Swedish Environmental Protection Agency.

Los Angeles Times. 2004. Bush Sets the Right Course in Control of Land Mines. March 8.

Lovgren, Stefan. 1999. A Sorry Tale of Oil and Water. *U.S. News & World Report.* August 9.

Luemba, Francisco. 2008. *O problema de Cabinda exposto e assumido à luz do direito e da justiça.* Lisbon: PVP Bertrand.

———. 2005a. "Protectorado colonial ou direito internacional? Nem afirmação mas interrogação." Paper read at Simulambuco anniversary conference, February 1. Cabinda.

———. 2005b. "A responsabilidade social das multinacionais em Angola." Paper read at "Conferência sobre a Responsabilidade Social Empresarial," April 20–22. Cabinda.

———. 2003. "The Question of Oil and Gas, Its Impact on the Social and Economic Situation and the Role of the Multinationals." Paper read at conference "A Common Vision for Cabinda," July 8–9. Centro Cultural Chiloango, Cabinda.

———. 2002. "A Paz em Angola e a continuação da guerra em Cabinda: Causas profundas." Paper read at "Conferência sobre a Agenda de Paz e Reconciliação na República Visinha de Angola," September 18–19. Luanda.

Lujala, Päivi, Nils Petter Gleditsch, and Elisabeth Gilmore. 2005. A Diamond Curse? Civil War and a Lootable Resource. *Journal of Conflict Resolution.* 49(4):538–562.

Lyle, Don. 2007. Angola Launches 2007 Bid Round. *EP Magazine.* December 1. http://www.epmag.com/archives/specialReports/787.htm.

Mabeko-Tali, Jean-Michel. 2004. Cabinda: Between "No Peace" and "No War." Conciliation Resources. http://www.c-r.org/our-work/accord/angola/cabinda.php.

———. 2001a. *Dissidências e poder de estado: o MPLA perante si próprio (1962–1977): ensaio de história política.* Luanda: Editorial Nzila.

———. 2001b. La question de Cabinda. *Lusotopie.* http://www.lusotopie.sciencespobordeaux.fr/mabeko.pdf.

MacQueen, Norrie. 1997. *The Decolonization of Portuguese Africa: Metropolitan Revolution and the Dissolution of Empire.* New York: Longman.

Maier, Karl. 1996. *Angola: Promises and Lies.* London: Serif.

Malaquias, Assis. 2007. *Rebels and Robbers: Violence in Post-Colonial Angola.* Uppsala: Nordiska AfrikaInstitutet.

Manchon, X. 2003. Drilling Units: Moving from Third to Fifth Generation. *Technoscoop: Magazine of Exploration and Production Techniques.* (27).

Manje, Bernardino. 2003. Governador de Cabinda visita orgãos do Minint. *Jornal de Angola,* August 31.

Marcum, John A. 1986. Bipolar Dependency: Angola. In *Reassessing the Soviet Challenge in Africa,* edited by Michael Clough. Berkeley: Institute of International Studies, University of California.

———. 1978. The Angolan Revolution: Exile Politics and Guerrilla Warfare. Cambridge: MIT Press.

———. 1972. The Politics of Indifference: Portugal and Africa, a Case Study in American Foreign Policy. *Issue: A Journal of Opinion.* 2(3):9–17.

———. 1969. *The Angolan Revolution: Anatomy of an Explosion.* Cambridge: MIT Press.

Marques, Rafael. 2005a. O sacrifício do cabrito, diamantes e feitiçaria. September 5. http://macua.blogs.com/moambique_para_todos/2005/09/o_sacrificio_do_.html.

———. 2005b. Africans on Africa: Governance. July 6. http://news.bbc.co.uk/go/pr/fr/-/1/hi/world/africa/4655723.stm.

———. 2005c. Angola: A Lament of Hope. July 1. AfricaFiles. http://www.africafiles.org/article.asp?ID=9319.

———. 2004a. Angola: Farewell to a Victor. Luanda: Open Society Institute.

———. 2004b. "From Curse to Blessing for Developing Countries? Challenges to Governments, Companies and NGOs." Paper presented at Conference on Oil Revenues, December 9. Stavanger, Norway.

———. 2004c. "Global Information versus Local Information—The Angola Case." Paper presented at Fórum Barcelona 2004: "Information, Power and Ethics in the 21st Century," May 20. Barcelona.

———. 2004d. "Debate: Post-War Angola—Trends and Prospects." Paper presented at Woodrow Wilson International Center for Scholars—Africa Program Meeting, April 5. Washington.

———. 2004e. When the People's Silence Speaks. February 26. Pambazuka News. http://www.pambazuka.org/en/category/comment/20449.

———. 2003a. Angola: A Death for a Song and the Triumph of Impunity. December 4. AllAfrica.com. http://allafrica.com/stories/200312040283.html.

———. 2003b. "Cabinda: The Victims and the Perpetrators." Paper presented at conference "Listening to Cabinda," February 20. Lisbon.

———. 1999. The Lipstick of Dictatorship. *Agora;* reprinted by Afrol News/Misanet.com, July 3. http://www.afrol.com/features/10272.

Marques, Rafael, and Rui Falcão de Campos. 2004. *Lundas, The Stones of Death. Angola's Deadly Diamonds: Human Rights Abuses in the Lunda Provinces.* Luanda: Open Society Institute.

Martin, Phyllis M. 1977. The Cabinda Connection: An Historical Perspective. *African Affairs.* 76:47–59.

Martins, Manuel Alfredo de Morais. 1958. *Contacto de culturas no Congo Português.* Lisbon: Ministério do Ultramar.

Martíns, P. Joaquim. 1972. Cabindas: História, crença, usos e costumes. Comissao de Turismo da Câmara Municipal de Cabinda.

Mason, Barry. 2004. Documentary Focuses on Struggle to Control Angola's

Oil. November 3. World Socialist Website. http://www.wsws.org/arti
cles/2004/nov2004/ango-no3.shtml.

———. 1999. Angola: MPLA Inflicts New Defeats on UNITA. November 16.
World Socialist Website. http://www.wsws.org/articles/1999/nov1999/ango
-n16.shtml.

Mavinga, João. 2004. TOTAL perde 17 mil barris de petróleo em derrame.
Jornal de Angola, October 2.

———. 2003a. Consumo industrial de água afecta população no Soyo. *Jornal
de Angola*, October 28.

———. 2003b. Soyo terá instalações específicas da PIR. *Jornal de Angola*, June 27.

Mayer, Graciete. 2003. Petrobrás vai operar em águas profundas Angolanas.
Jornal de Angola, August 12.

McMillan, John. 2005. "'The Main Institution in the Country Is Corruption':
Creating Transparency in Angola." Working Papers. Stanford: Stanford Uni
versity Graduate School of Business.

McQuilling Services LLC. 2006. The Learning Curve: Major Oil Spills and
Their Impact on the Shipping Industry. http://www.mcquilling.com/pdf/
OilSpillImpact.pdf.

Media Institute of Southern Africa. 2004. Editor Faces Prison Term. March 30.
http://www.ifex.org/en/content/view/full/57803/.

Melby, Judith. 2003. Dirty Money, Dirty Water. In *Fuelling Poverty: Oil, War,
and Corruption*, edited by Christian Aid. London: Christian Aid. http://
www.christian-aid.org.uk/indepth/0305cawreport/fuellingpoverty.htm.

Mendes, Candido and Garth Theunissen. 2009. Angola Plans $9 Billion Bond
Sale to Fund Expenditure. April 15. Bloomberg.com. http://www.bloomberg
.com/apps/news?pid=20601116&sid=ag4000lLBLPI.

Messiant, Christine. 2008. The Mutation of Hegimonic Domination. In *Angola:
The Weight of History*, edited by Patrick Chabal and Nuno Vidal. New York:
Columbia University Press.

———. 2006. *1961: l'Angola colonial, et société: les premisses du mouvement
nationaliste*. Basel: P. Schlettwein.

———. 2003. Des alliances de la guerre froide à la justiciarisationdu conflit.
In *Guerres et sociétés: État et violence après la Guerre froide*, edited by
P. Hassner and R. Marchal. Paris: Karthala.

———. 1999. A Fundação Eduardo dos Santos (FESA): A propósito de "inves-
tida" do poder Angolano sobre a sociedade civil. *Politique Africaine*. 7(33):
82–102.

Milton, Cynthia E. 2005. Through the Grapevine. In *The Art of Truth-Telling
about Authoritarian Rule*, edited by Ksenija and Jo Ellen Fair Bilbija, Cynthia E. Milton, and Leigh A. Payne. Madison: University of Wisconsin Press.

Moeen, Muhammad. 2008. Oil Spill in Angola. April 11. See N Report. http://
www.seenreport.com/story/01-07-2008-oil-spill-in-angola/.

Moore, Solomon. 2003. Angola Hunts Rebels in Area Supplying Oil to U.S.
Chicago Tribune, March 17.

Morash, A. 2003. Discovering the Abysses of the River Zaire. *Technoscoop: Magazine of Exploration and Production Techniques.* (27).

Moritis, Guntis. 2003. Hubs, New Technologies Provide Access to More Deepwater Reserves. *Oil and Gas Journal.* 101(44):54. November 17.

Mouawad, Jad. 2005. A New Push to Mix Oil and Water. *New York Times,* October 14. http://travel2.nytimes.com/2005/10/14/business/14oil.html.

Mpalabanda. 2006. Cabinda, entre a verdade e a manipulação. 4° Relatório sobre a situação dos direitos humanos em Cabinda. April 4.

———. 2005. Cabinda, o reino da impunidade. 3° Relatório sobre a situação dos direitos humanos em Cabinda. January 30.

Munro, Thomas. 2006. Locals Riding Out Current Gas Storm. *The Durango Herald.* May 7. http://www.durangoherald.com/asp-bin/article_generation.asp?article_path=/news/06/news060507_4.htm&article_type=new.

Muttitt, Greg. 2005. Crude Designs: The Rip-Off of Iraq's Oil Wealth. http://www.globalpolicy.org/security/oil/2005/crudedesigns.htm.

Mvemba, Frederic. 2003. Ensuring an Effective Program on Disarmament, Demobilization and Reintegration. Luanda: Angolan Centre for Peace Education.

Namibian Online. 2001. Angolan enclave suffers oil spill. March 14. http://www.namibian.com.na/2001/March/marketplace/01DA7098C3.html.

———. 2000a. Mystery Slick Strikes Angola. February 17. http://www.namibian.com.na/Netstories/2000/February/Africa/oil.html.

———. 2000b. Slick hits Cabinda. February 14. http://www.namibian.com.na/Netstories/2000/February/Africa/slick.html.

National Memorial Institute for the Prevention of Terrorism. 2005. Group Profiles: Front for the Liberation of the Cabinda Enclave, Front for the Liberation of the Cabinda Enclave—Renewed, and Union for the Total Independence of Angola. Terrorism Knowledge Database. MIPT, National Memorial Institute for the Prevention of Terrorism.

Navarre, J. C., and S. Lheure. 2003. Deep Offshore Reservoirs: Characteristics and Challenges. *Technoscoop: Magazine of Exploration and Production Techniques.* 27.

Neto, Gilberto. 2005. O Poder do Crude. *Semanário Angolense,* January 22.

Neto, Sousa. 2004. Total pode perder mesmo concessões petrolíferas em Angola. *Semanário Angolense,* May 22.

———. 2003. Quão frias são as relações de Angola com o FMI. *Semanário Angolense,* April 12–19.

Neto, V. 1997. "Fisheries Resources of Angola." Paper presented at American Association for the Advancement of Science annual meeting, February 16. Seattle.

Ngonje. 2004a. Despesas correntes de 2003. January/August.

———. 2004b. Novo estabelecimento ao serviço das comunidades. 2(6).

Nijhuis, Michelle. 2006. How Halliburton's Technology Is Wrecking the Rockies. *On Earth.* Summer: 30–37.

Notícias Lusófonas. 2006. Angola contribui para viabilizar força de intervenção rápida africana. March 7. http://www.noticiaslusofonas.com.

O Apostolado. 2004a. Exploração petrolífera. November 3.

———. 2004b. Aldeias desapareceram em Cabinda. September 27.

———. 2004c. Igreja de Cabinda esclarece posição. June 14.

———. 2004d. Camas partilhadas no hospital de Cabinda. June 11.

———. 2004e. Plano de desenvolvimento de Cabinda. June 4.

———. 2004f. SIDA na Província do Zaire. May 31.

———. 2004g. Reacções ao aumento dos combustíveis. May 6.

———. 2004h. Not Diversions but Discrepancies in Accounts. January 15.

Oakland Tribune. 2008. Jerry Brown Calls Richmond Chevron's Report Inadequate. March 10. Bay City News Service.

O'Brien, Kevin A. 1998. Military-Advisory Groups and African Security: Privatised Peacekeeping? *International Peacekeeping.* Autumn: 78–105. http://www.kcl.ac.uk/orgs/icsa/Old/pmcsipk.html.

Observatory for the Protection of Human Rights Defenders. 2006. Closing Down of an NGO/Harassment/Defamation Campaign. November 15. http://www.fidh.org/article_print.php3id_article=3816.

Oil Free Coast. 2006a. Daily Pollution. http://www.oilfreecoast.org/threats.

———. 2006b. Seismic Testing. http://www.oilfreecoast.org/threats.

———. 2006c. Drilling Wastes. http://www.oilfreecoast.org/library/glossary.html#muds.

Oil Voice. 2005. ChevronTexaco Announces First Condensate from Angola's Sanha Field. March 2. http://www.oilvoice.com/ChevronTexaco_Announces_First_Condensate_From_Angolas_Sanha_/3349.htm.

Olomola, Ade S. 1998. Sources and Resolution of Conflicts in Nigerian Artisanal Fisheries. *Society and Natural Resources.* 11:121-135.

Ong, Aihwa. 1999. *Flexible Citizenship.* Durham: Duke University Press.

Open Society Justice Initiative. 2005. Angola Must Comply with UN Freedom of Expression Ruling. August 26. http://www.justiceinitiative.org/db/resource2?res_id=102944.

O'Reilly, David J. 2005. Statement before the Joint Hearing of the Senate Energy and Natural Resource Committee and the Senate Commerce, Science and Transportation Committee. November 9. http://energy.senate.gov/public/index.cfm?FuseAction=Hearings.Testimony&Hearing_ID=1517&Witness_ID=4307.

Orlitzky, Marc, Frank L. Schmidt and Sara L. Rynes. 2004. Corporate Social and Financial Performance: A Meta Analysis. December. Social Investment Forum Foundation.

O'Rourke, Dara, and Sarah Connolly. 2003. Just Oil? The Distribution of Environmental and Social Impacts of Oil Production and Consumption. *Annual Review Environmental Resources.* 28:587–617.

Ott, Riki. 2005. *Sound Truth and Corporate Myth: The Legacy of the Exxon Valdez Oil Spill.* Cordova, Ak.: Dragonfly Sisters Press.

Oxford Economic Country Briefings. 2007. Angola. *Oxford Economic Country Briefings.* December 18. Accessed at FindArticles.com on June 10, 2008. http://findarticles.com/p/articles/mi_qa5299/is_200712/ai_n21272969.

Paiva, Fernando. 1998/1999. *Legislação de Direito Financeiro e de Finanças Públicas*. I. Luanda: Universidade Agostinho Neto.

Palast, Greg. 2001. Bush Energy Plan: Policy or Payback? May 18. BBC News. http://news.bbc.co.uk/2/hi/americas/1336960.stm.

Parvin, Manoucher and Hashem Dezhbakhsh. 1988. Trade, Technology Transfer, and Hyper-Dutch Disease in OPEC: Theory and Evidence. *International Journal of Middle East Studies*. 20:469–477.

Pasipanodya, T. 2003. Report of the Conference "A Common Vision for Cabinda," July 8–9. Centro Cultural Chiloango, Cabinda.

Pastor, Manuel, James Sadd, and Rachel Morello-Frosch. 2007. Still Toxic after All These Years: Air Quality and Environmental Justice in the San Francisco Bay Area. Center for Justice, Tolerance and Community, University of California, Santa Cruz.

Patin, Stanislav. 1999. *Environmental Impact of the Offshore Oil and Gas Industry*. Translated by Elena Cascio. New York: Ecomonitor.

Paulo, João. 2004. O Belicismo Iluminado. *Folha 8*, June 5.

Pearce, Justin. 2005. *An Outbreak of Peace*. Claremont, South Africa: David Philip Publishers.

———. 2002a. Going to the Border. In *Stories for Trees*, edited by Margrit Coppé and Fergus Power. Luanda: Development Workshop.

———. 2002b. IMF: Angola's Missing Millions. BBC. October 18. http://news.bbc.co.uk/2/hi/africa/2338669.stm.

Peet, Richard, and Michael Watts. 1996. *Liberation Ecologies*. London: Routledge.

Pegg, Scott. 2003. Globalization and Natural-Resource Conflicts. *Naval War College Review*. LVI(4). Autumn.

Peluso, Nancy Lee. 1996. Fruit Trees and Family Trees in an Anthropogenic Forest: Ethics of Access, Property Zones and Environmental Change in Indonesia. *Comparative Studies in Society and History*. 38(3):510–48.

Peluso, Nancy, and Michael Watts. 2001. *Violent Environments*. Ithaca: Cornell University Press.

Pepetela. 1987. *Mayombe*. Portsmouth, N.H.: Heinemann.

Petroleum Economist. 2008. Deep-Water Start-Ups Accelerate. March. http://www.petroleum-economist.com/default.asp?page=14&PubID=46&ISS=24599&SID=702930.

Piçarra, António. 2005. Signs of Growth in Cabinda. *Austral: Inflight Magazine of TAAG*. January–March. Issue 51.

Pike, John. 2003. União Nacional pela Independência Total de Angola, UNITA. October 26, 2006. Intelligence Resource Program. http://www.fas.org/irp/world/para/unita.htm.

Pitcher, Anne, and Aubrey Graham. 2006. Cars Are Killing Luanda: Cronyism, Consumerism, and Other Assaults on Angola's Postwar Capital City. In *Cities in Contemporary Africa*, edited by Martin J. Murray and Garth A. Myers. New York: Palgrave Macmillan.

Pitsch, Anne, Silvia Milella, and Randi Mack. 2002. Minorities at Risk: Cabinda of Angola. January 2002. http://www.cidcm.umd.edu/inscr/mar/data/ang cabin.htm.

Planet Ark. 2000. Oil Spill Threatens Angolan Coast. January 4. http://www .planetark.org/avantgo/dailynewsstory.cfm?newsid=5262.

Polletta, Francesca. 2006. *It Was Like a Fever: Storytelling in Protest and Politics.* Chicago: University of Chicago Press.

Powell, Robert. 1993. Troops Guard U.S. Oil Installation after Recapture of Soyo. *Sapa-Reuters,* March 17.

Project Underground.1999. The Angolan Civil War Part 1: Oil. Drillbits and Tailings. October 8. http://www.moles.org/ProjectUnderground/drillbits/ 4_16/index.html.

———. 1998. Canadian Mercenary Miners Killed by Angolan Rebels. Drillbits and Tailings. November 21. http://www.moles.org/ProjectUnderground/drill bits/981121/98112102.html.

———. 1997. Militarization and Minerals Tour. http://www.moles.org/Project Underground/mil/milindex.html.

Proyart, Abbe. 1776. History of Loango, Kakongo and N'goyo. http://www .cabinda.net/1776.html.

Public Citizen. 2001. Record Oil Company Profits Underscore Market Consolidation. May 31. http://www.citizen.org/pressroom/release.cfm?ID=580.

Quinlan, Martin. 2009. Angola No Longer a Tiger. *Petroleum Economist.* March. http://www.petroleum-economist.com/default.asp?page=14&Pub ID=46&ISS=25318&SID=717620.

Rabanit, Paul M. 1963. Angola. *American Association of Petroleum Geologists.* 2:1358.

Rach, Nina M. 2003. Drilling Market Focus: Deepwater Drilling Remains Steady Worldwide. *Oil and Gas Journal.* 101(44):49. November 17.

Radio France Internationale. 2002. East Timorese Premier Urged to Intervene in Cabinda Conflict. ETAN, October 15. http://www.etan.org/et2002c/octo ber/13–19/16angola.htm.

Raines, Ben. 2003. Deep Trouble. *NRDC's On Earth.* Spring. Available at: http:// www.lawrencehallofscience.org/GSS/uptodate/articles-gss/5lbdeeptrouble .html.

———. 2001. Hair Tests Indicate High Mercury Levels. *Mobile Register.* September 20. http://www.al.com/specialreport/mobileregister/index.ssf?merc 10.html.

Raines, Ben, and Bill Finch. 2002. Mercury Speakers Seek Common Ground. *Mobile Register.* May 21. http://www.al.com/specialreport/mobileregister/ ?merc32.html.

RAND California. 2008. Community Crime Rate Statistics. http://ca.rand.org/ stats/community/crimerate.html.

Randerson, James. 2003. Marine Census Reveals Depth of Ignorance. *NewScientist.* November 1. http://www.newscientist.com/article/mg18024191.700 -marine-census-reveals-depth-of-ignorance.html.

Reed, Kristin. 2008. Waking from a Nightmare. In *Civil Society, Democracy and Human Rights* in Angola, edited by Nuno Vidal and Justino Pinto de Andrade. Lisbon: University of Coimbra.

Refinery Reform Campaign. 2008. Refinery Basics. http://www.refineryreform .org/refinery_basics.htm.

ReliefWeb. 2005. Angola: Fourth Phase of Repatriation from Congo-Brazzaville Postponed. September 26, 2006. http://www.reliefweb.int/rw/RWB .NSF/db900SID/HMYT-6GLRP4?OpenDocument.

Reuters. 2003. Exxon Mobil $3 Billion Angola Oil Project Under Way. February 19.

Risquet Valdés, Jorge. 2005. The Deep Roots of Cuba's Internationalism. Tricontinental. http://www.tricontinental.cubaweb.cu/REVISTA/texto22ingl .html.

Robinson, Deborah. 1998. *Ogoni: The Struggle Continues.* Geneva: World Council of Churches.

ROC Oil Company Ltd. 2005. *Typical Terrain in Locality of Planned 2005 3D Seismic Survey.* Cabinda South Block—Onshore Angola: Slide 32. Slideshow.

———. 2001. ROC Expands West African Portfolio. Press release. October.

———. 2000. ROC Sells Non-Core Onshore UK Assets for A$57 Million and Realises an Abnormal, Unaudited A$18 Million After Tax Profit from Seven Month Investment. January 5. http://www.rocoil.com.au/Pages/ASX _Releases/2000_Releases/May-2000.html.

Rodrigues, Agostinho. 2004. A pobreza mora aquí. *Semanário Angolense,* August 14.

Rose, Nikolas. 1999. *Powers of Freedom: Reframing Political Thought.* Cambridge: Cambridge University Press.

Rosenn, Keith S. 1997. Regulation of Foreign Investment in Angola. CAER II Discussion Paper No. 12, May.

Ross, Michael. 2006. A Closer Look at Oil, Diamonds and Civil War. *Annual Review of Political Science.* 9:265–300.

———. 2001. Does Oil Hinder Democracy? *World Politics.* 55:325–61.

———. 1999. The Political Economy of the Resource Curse. *World Politics.* 51:297–322.

Russell, Alec. 2007. Investors Sign Up to Angola's Miracle. *Financial Times.* http://us.ft.com/ftgateway/superpage.ft?news_id=ft008222007131949072.

Sachs, Jeffrey D., and Andrew M. Warner. 2001. The Curse of Natural Resources. *European Economic Review.* 45:827–838.

———. 1995. Natural Resource Abundance and Economic Growth. *Development Discussion Papers (Paper No. 517a).*October.

Saint, R., P. M. Rabanit, and Eugene A. Cordry. 1967. Developments in Central and Southern Africa in 1966. *American Association of Petroleum Geologists.* 3:1591–3.

Salopek, Paul. 2004. Fade to Blue: A Tribune Special Report. *Chicago Tribune,* August 15. http://www.chicagotribune.com.

———. 2000. CEOs of War Bleed Angola. *Chicago Tribune,* April 2. http://

www.pulitzer.org/year/2001/international-reporting/works/ceosofwar
.html.

Salvador, Raimundo. 2004. Finanças esclarece equívocos da Human Rights Watch. *Jornal de Angola,* January 15.

Santana, Mário. 2005. O nascimento dos primeiros magnatas angolanos. *Semanário Angolense,* February 12.

Sardinha, Maria de Lourdes. 2000. *The Marine Environment in Angola: Threats and Methods of Management.* 1: Benguela Environment Fisheries Interaction and Training Programme.

Sawyer, Suzana. 2004. *Crude Chronicles: Indigenous Politics, Multinational Oil and Neoliberalism in Ecuador.* Durham: Duke University Press.

Schreiber, Allan. 2008. After the Spill: In the Wake of the Cosco Busan. *Hydrosphere.* 23: Spring 2008. San Francisco: Farallones Marine Sanctuary Association.

Scott, James C. 1985. *Weapons of the Weak: Everyday Forms of Peasant Resistance.* New Haven: Yale University Press.

Sebastião, Armando and Emílio Londa. 2009. Anatomia da Crise Económica em Angola. April. Luanda.

Semanário Angolense. 2004a. Contabilidade questionável. June 12.

———. 2004b. Nzita Tiago deu com a língua nos dentes—Amigo de Samakuva ou da onça? June 5.

———. 2004c. Aldeias desaparecidas entre 2003 e 2004. January 10.

———. 2004d. Aldeias reduzidas a pó. January 10.

———. 2003a. Governo angolano instado a revelar quanto ganha com petróleo. July 5.

———. 2003b. Cidadãos viverão com mais dificuldades. June 21.

———. 2003c. Sonangol "desenrasca" USD 1 bilião. June 14.

———. 2003d. Questão de Cabinda: Um referendo? Por que não? June 14.

———. 2003e. Angola—São Tomé e Principe parcerias para enfrentar a glo-balização. June 14.

Serrano, Carlos M. H. 1983. *Os senhores da terra e os homens do mar: Antro-pologia política de um reino Africano.* São Paulo: FFLCH/USP.

Setas, Fernando, and Luís Baltazar da Rocha Jr. 1991. Projecção da população do país por províncias e grupos quinquenais de idade para o período 1985–2010. Boletim Demográfico. July 1991. Luanda: Instituto Nacional de Estatística.

Shankleman, Jill. 2006. *Oil, Profits and Peace: Does Business Have a Role in Peacemaking?* Washington: United States Institute of Peace.

Shaxson, Nicholas. 2007. *Poisoned Wells: The Dirty Politics of African Oil.* New York: Palgrave Macmillan.

Sherman, Scott. 1996. Environmental Justice Case Study: West County Toxics Coalition and the Chevron Refinery in Richmond, California. University of Michigan. http://www.umich.edu/~snre492/sherman.html.

Silverstein, Ken. 2004. Gusher to a Few, Trickle to the Rest. *Los Angeles Times,* May 13.

Smiley, Xan. 1983. Inside Angola. *The New York Review of Books.* http:// www.nybooks.com/articles/6321.

Smith, Gar. 2005. Toxic Tour: Driving through One of the West Coast's Deadliest Neighborhoods. *Earth Island Journal.* September 22.

Soares de Oliveira, Ricardo. 2007. *Oil and Politics in the Gulf of Guinea.* New York: Columbia University Press.

Sogge, David. 2006. Angola: Global "Good Governance" Also Needed. *FRIDE Working Paper.* June.

Sonangol. 2005. Covering the Risks. *Universo.* Winter(8):24.

———. 2004a. Roc's on a Roll in Cabinda. *Sonangol Universo.* Winter (4):6.

———. 2004b. Learning Curve. *Universo.* Summer(2):15.

———. 2004c. Liquid Assets. *Universo.* Summer(2):20.

Southern Africa Documentation and Cooperation Centre. 2003. Plan to Quell Cabinda Conflict. February 19. http://www.sadocc.at/news/2003–048.shtml.

State Department (U.S.). 2003. Patterns of Global Terrorism 2002. April 30. http://www.state.gov/s/ct/rls/pgtrpt/2002/html/19981.htm.

Stiglitz, Joseph. 2004. We Can Now Cure Dutch Disease. *The Guardian,* August 18.

Stockwell, John. 1978. *In Search of Enemies: A CIA Story.* New York: W. W. Norton & Company.

Stratfor. 2008. Angola: The Ongoing Threat in Cabinda. March 7. http://www .stratfor.com/analysis/angola_ongoing_threat_cabinda.

Suami, Joaquim. 2003. Batalhão de Caçadores das FAA Garante Tranquilidade em Cabinda. *Jornal de Angola,* September 19.

Swanson, Philip. 2002a. "Corporate Social Responsibility and the Oil Sector." Paper presented at "Energy: New Era, New Governance," March 18. London.

———. 2002b. Fuelling Conflict. Economies of Conflict: Private Sector Activity in Armed Conflict. Norway: Programme for International Co-Operation and Conflict Resolution, The Fafo Institute.

Swarns, Rachel L. 2000. In Big Offshore Oil Discoveries, Frail Visions of a Redeemed Angola. *New York Times,* September 24.

Tansey, Bernadette, Benjamin Pimentel, and Michael Taylor. 1999. Huge Explosion Rocks Richmond Oil Refinery. *San Francisco Chronicle.* March 26. http://sfgate.com/cgi-bin/article.cgi?f=/c/a/1999/03/26/MN78167.DTL.

Tati, Fr. Raúl. 2003. "Cabinda: A Civil Society Testimony." Paper presented at the conference "Listening to Cabinda," February 20. Lisbon.

———. 2002. Paper presented at "Conferência sobre a Agenda de Paz e Reconciliação na República Visinha de Angola," September 18–19. Luanda.

Taty, Abel, and Felipe Massanga. 2004. Uma grande conquista da Província de Cabinda foi a paz que se vive em toda a região. *Ngonje.* 2(6):14–17.

Thompson, A. C., and Sonya Hubbard. 2007. Oil Slick. Center for Investigative Reporting Web Exclusive Report. April 24. http://centerforinvestigativereporting.org/articles/oilslick.

Tomás, Manuel. 2003. Instituto de petróleos a formar quadros da SADC. *Jornal de Angola,* September 24.

Total. 2003a. Panorama and Global Challenges. *Technoscoop: Magazine of Exploration and Production Techniques*. (27):6.

———. 2003b. Zoom Out: The Deep Offshore. *Technoscoop: Magazine of Exploration and Production Techniques*. (27):38.

Tunga, Pemba. 2005. Populares garimpam gas. *Folha 8*, February 12.

Tvind Alert. 2006. Angola. http://www.tvindalert.com.

UN Office of the High Commissioner for Human Rights. 2005. Angola: Quarterly Report.

UNDP–World Bank Joint Energy Sector Assessment Program. 1989. Angola: Issues and Options in the Energy Sector. May.

UNICEF (United Nations Children's Fund). 2003. Angola at a Glance. http://www.unicef.org/infobycountry/angola_statistics.html.

United Nations. 2003. United Nations Operational Rates of Exchange. http://www.un.org/Depts/treasury/2003.htm.

———. 2002. Response to Angola's Serious Humanitarian Crisis Must Be Shared by International Community, Angolan Authorities, Under-Secretary-General Tells Council. Press Release SC/7455. July 17. http://www.un.org/News/Press/docs/2002/sc7455.doc.htm.

United Nations Development Programme. 2003. Human Development Report 2003.

United Nations Environmental Programme. 2002. Global Mercury Assessment—Draft. April 25.

United States Court of Appeals, District of Columbia Circuit. 2006. United States of America, Apellee, v. Artur Tchibassa, Appellant. July 7.

Unrepresented Nations and Peoples Organisation. 2007. Cabinda: Latest Developments. January 11. http://www.unpo.org/content/view/6178/236/.

UPASC. 1997a. Financial "Phantom" Scandal. Angola News Online. University of Pennsylvania African Studies Center, December 28. http://www.africa.upenn.edu/Newsletters/angno7.html.

———. 1997b. Angola News. University of Pennsylvania African Studies Center, December 18. http://www.africa.upenn.edu/Newsletters/angno7.html.

Upstream. 2009. Cobalt and Sonangol Take the Plunge. UpstreamOnline.com. April 23. http://www.upstreamonline.com/live/article176504.ece.

URS, Greiner Woodward Clyde. 2000. Block 14 Environmental Impact Assessment.

U. S. Census Bureau. 2000. U.S. Census data. www.census.gov.

———. 1999. U.S. Census data. www.census.gov.

USA Today. 2009. Angola. Special Section. January 20.

USAID. 2004a. Bureau for Democracy, Conflict and Humanitarian Assistance. http://www.usaid.gov/policy/budget/cbj2004/cent_prog/dcha.pdf.

———. 2004b. Situation Report: Angola—Complex Emergency. January 7. http://www.usaid.gov/our_work/humanitarian_assistance/disaster_assistance/countries/angola/fy2004/Angola_CE_SR01_01–07–2004.pdf.

Valdes Vivo, Raul. 1976. *Angola: Fin del mito de los mercenarios*. Havana: Imprenta Federico Engels de la Empresa de Medios de Propaganda.

Van Deste, Jorge. 2000. A actividade petrolífera em Angola: Situação actual e perspectivas. *Revista Energia*. December(58).

Van-Dunem, Sílvio. 2005. 5 + 3 = 3 biliões de dolares. *Folha 8*, January 8.

Vandergeest, Peter, and Nancy Lee Peluso. 1995. Territorialization and State Power in Thailand. *Theory and Society*. 24:385–426.

Vicente, Manuel. 2001. Manuel Vicente Chairman and CEO of Sonangol. Summit Communications. http://www.summitreports.com/angola/vicente .htm.

Vicente, São. 1995. *A gestão política da economia de Angola*. Luanda: INALD (Instituto Nacional do Livro e do Disco).

Vidal, Nuno. 2008a. The Angolan Regime and the Move to Multiparty Politics. In *Angola: The Weight of History*, edited by Patrick Chabal and Nuno Vidal. New York: Columbia University Press.

———. 2008b. Social Neglect and the Emergence of Civil Society. In *Angola: The Weight of History*, edited by Patrick Chabal and Nuno Vidal. New York: Columbia University Press.

Vines, Alex, Nicholas Shaxson, Lisa Rimli, and Chris Heymans. 2005. *Angola— Drivers of Change: An Overview*. London: Chatham House.

Vinyals, Lluis T. 2002. Financiamento público dos sectores sociais em Angola. Principia: Lisbon.

Voice of America. 2004a. Mpalabanda minimiza prémios oferecidos a quem matar dirigentes angolanos. AngoNotícias, May 31. http://www.angonoticias .com/full_headlines.php?id=1134%20.

———. 2004b. *Angola e EUA discutem cooperação militar*. May 21, 2004: Voice of America. Radio Program.

Wagner, Gernot. 2008. New Offshore Drilling in Perspective. Environmental Defense Climate 411. September 15. http://blogs.edf.org/climate411/ 2008/09/15/new_offshore_drilling/.

Washington Post. 2006. With Friends Like These . . . Condoleezza Rice's Inglorious Moment. April 18. http://www.washingtonpost.com/wp-dyn/content/ article/2006/04/17/AR2006041701368_pf.html.

———. 2005. 330 Suspects Charged. June 12. http://www.washingtonpost.com/ wp-srv/nation/dojstats/full330.html.

Watson, Thomas H. 1977. The Angolan Affair: 1974–1976. April. Maxwell Air Force Base, Alabama: Air War College.

Watts, Michael. 2005. Righteous Oil?: Human Rights, the Oil Complex and Corporate Social Responsibility. *Annual Review Environment and Resources*. 30:373-407.

———. 2004. Resource Curse? Governmentality, Oil and Power in the Niger Delta, Nigeria. *Geopolitics*. 9(1):50–80.

———. 2001. Petro-Violence: Community, Extraction, and Political Ecology of a Mythic Commodity. In *Violent Environments*, edited by Nancy Lee Peluso and Michael Watts. Ithaca: Cornell University Press.

———. 1999. Petro-Violence: Some Thoughts on Community, Extraction and Political Ecology. *Berkeley Workshop on Environmental Politics Working*

Papers. WP 99–1. http://globetrotter.berkeley.edu/EnvirPol/WP/01-Watts .pdf.

————. 1994. Oil as Money: The Devil's Excrement and the Spectacle of Black Gold. In *Money, Power and Space,* edited by S. Corbridge, N. Thrift and R. Martin. Oxford: Blackwell.

West County Toxics Coalition. 2005. Breathing Fire. Richmond, California.

Wheeler, Douglas L., and René Pélissier. 1971. *Angola*. New York: Praeger.

White, D., I. Ask, and C. Behr-Andres. 1999. Effectiveness Testing for Corexit 9500 on Alaska North Slope Crude Oil in Prince William Sound Seawater at 8 degrees Celsius. Anchorage, Ak.: Alaska Department of Environmental Conservation.

Wiig, Arne, and Madalena Ramalho. 2005. Corporate Social Responsibility in the Angolan Oil Industry. Bergen, Norway: Chr. Michelsen Institute.

Wiwa, Owens. 2005. Paper presented at "Ten Years Later: Remembering Ken Saro-Wiwa," October 6. University of California, Berkeley.

World Bank. 2005. *Private Solutions for Infrastructure in Angola, Country Framework Reports*. Washington: Public-Private Infrastructure Advisory Facility and the World Bank.

————. 2004. World Bank Approves Credit to Finance Social Services in Angola. http://www.worldbank.org.

————. 2002. Oil and Gas Industry Codes of Conduct and Angolan National Legislation. December. Washington.

World Health Organization. 2003. 100,000 Children and 1,500 Pregnant Women Killed Every Year by Malaria in Angola. Press release. April 25.

World Investment News. 2001. Teleservice—Interview with Mr. Henrique Morais, General Manager. March 30. http://www.winne.com/angola/t023 interview.html.

World Oil. 2002. Optimism Saturates the Continent. 223(8).

————. 1996. Angola. 217(8).

————. 1995. Angola. 216(8).

————. 1993. Angola. 214(8).

————. 1980a. Angola. 191(3).

————. 1980b. Offshore. July. 191(1).

World Resources Institute. 2003. Coastal and Marine Ecosystems—Angola. EarthTrends Country Profiles.

Yergin, Daniel, and Michael Stoppard. 2003. The Next Prize. *Foreign Affairs*. November/December.

Zalik, Anna. 2004. The Niger Delta: "Petro Violence" and "Partnership Development." *Review of African Political Economy*. 31(101):401–424.

Zinga Luemba, José Tibúrcio. 2003. "Contribuição da FLEC-Nova Visão no Forum para uma Visão Comúm sobre Cabinda." Paper presented at "A Common Vision for Cabinda," July 8–9. Centro Cultural Chiloango, Cabinda.

Index

Breinigsville, PA USA
19 January 2010
231005BV00006B/3/P